Production and Consump
English Households, 1600–1750

In pre-industrial England most production took place in the home. Some of this involved the production of goods for commercial sale, but items were also produced for use by the household itself. The household was also the focus for the consumption of goods that had been made elsewhere. This book uses evidence from households in the counties of Cornwall and Kent to explore changes in production and consumption and their interrelationships.

Evidence of production and consumption is taken from 8,000 inventories made at the death of the household head. Production activity is inferred from the presence of goods such as ploughs and looms. Consumption is inferred from the material environment of the household, including the number and use of rooms. This evidence significantly revises existing models of economic development in this period. The authors show that while Cornwall became impoverished by the development of the mining industry, Kent households increased the variety of their production activities. This resulted in the material culture of Cornwall becoming poorer, whereas in Kent the material culture was considerably enriched by many new goods and new social practices.

By considering the development of capitalism in early modern England from the perspective of the household, this book also contributes new evidence to the debate about a 'consumer revolution' in early modern England.

Mark Overton is Professor of Economic and Social History at the University of Exeter. He is author of *Agricultural Revolution in England* (1996) and many articles on the agrarian history of England. **Jane Whittle** is a senior lecturer in Economic and Social History at the University of Exeter. She has published *The Development of Agrarian Capitalism* (2000), as well as articles in 'Past and Present', 'Continuity and Change', and 'Agricultural History Review'. **Darron Dean**'s academic career developed from an interest in ceramics. From his Ph.D. on the development of the pottery industry 1650–1720, he became interested in the broader issues around household consumption. He is now writing a book on ICT in education. **Andrew Hann**'s research centres on trade, markets and consumption in early modern England, with particular emphasis on the geographies of retailing, moral and market economies, and kinship and social networks.

Routledge explorations in economic history

1 **Economic Ideas and Government Policy**
Contributions to contemporary economic history
Sir Alec Cairncross

2 **The Organization of Labour Markets**
Modernity, culture and governance in Germany, Sweden, Britain and Japan
Bo Stråth

3 **Currency Convertibility**
The gold standard and beyond
Edited by Jorge Braga de Macedo, Barry Eichengreen and Jaime Reis

4 **Britain's Place in the World**
A historical enquiry into import controls 1945–1960
Alan S. Milward and George Brennan

5 **France and the International Economy**
From Vichy to the Treaty of Rome
Frances M.B. Lynch

6 **Monetary Standards and Exchange Rates**
M.C. Marcuzzo, L. Officer and A. Rosselli

7 **Production Efficiency in Domesday England, 1086**
John McDonald

8 **Free Trade and its Reception 1815–1960**
Freedom and trade: volume I
Edited by Andrew Marrison

9 **Conceiving Companies**
Joint-stock politics in Victorian England
Timothy L. Alborn

10 **The British Industrial Decline Reconsidered**
Edited by Jean-Pierre Dormois and Michael Dintenfass

11 **The Conservatives and Industrial Efficiency, 1951–1964**
Thirteen wasted years?
Nick Tiratsoo and Jim Tomlinson

12 **Pacific Centuries**
Pacific and Pacific Rim economic history since the 16th century
Edited by Dennis O. Flynn, Lionel Frost and A.J.H. Latham

13 **The Premodern Chinese Economy**
Structural equilibrium and capitalist sterility
Gang Deng

14 **The Role of Banks in Monitoring Firms**
The case of the Crédit Mobilier
Elisabeth Paulet

15 **Management of the National Debt in the United Kingdom, 1900–1932**
Jeremy Wormell

16 **An Economic History of Sweden**
Lars Magnusson

17 **Freedom and Growth**
The rise of states and markets in Europe, 1300–1750
S.R. Epstein

18 **The Mediterranean Response to Globalization Before 1950**
Sevket Pamuk and Jeffrey G. Williamson

19 **Production and Consumption in English Households, 1600–1750**
Mark Overton, Jane Whittle, Darron Dean and Andrew Hann

20 **Governance, the State, Regulation and Industrial Relations**
Ian Clark

21 **Early Modern Capitalism**
Economic and social change in Europe 1400–1800
Edited by Maarten Prak

22 **An Economic History of London, 1800–1914**
Michael Ball and David Sunderland

23 The Origins of National Financial Systems
Alexander Gerschenkron reconsidered
Edited by Douglas J. Forsyth and Daniel Verdier

24 The Russian Revolutionary Economy, 1890–1940
Ideas, debates and alternatives
Vincent Barnett

25 Land Rights, Ethno Nationality and Sovereignty in History
Edited by Stanley L. Engerman and Jacob Metzer

Production and Consumption in English Households, 1600–1750

Mark Overton, Jane Whittle,
Darron Dean and Andrew Hann

Routledge
Taylor & Francis Group

LONDON AND NEW YORK

First published 2004
by Routledge
2 Park Square, Milton Park, Abingdon, Oxfordshire OX14 4RN

Simultaneously published in the USA and Canada
by Routledge
711 Third Avenue, New York, NY 10017
First issued in paperback 2012

Routledge is an imprint of the Taylor & Francis Group

Transferred to Digital Printing 2005

© 2004 Mark Overton, Jane Whittle, Darron Dean and Andrew Hann

Typeset in Baskerville by Wearset Ltd, Boldon, Tyne and Wear

British Library Cataloguing in Publication Data
A catalogue record for this book is available from the British Library

Library of Congress Cataloging in Publication Data
A catalog record for this book has been requested

ISBN 978-0-415-20803-1 (Hardback)
ISBN 978-0-415-65107-3 (Paperback)

Contents

List of illustrations   ix
Preface   xi

1   Household economies and economic development in
    early modern England   1

2   Probate inventories   13

3   Household production   33

4   By-employment, women's work and 'unproductive'
    households   65

5   The material culture of consumption   87

6   Rooms and room use   121

7   Wealth, occupation, status and location   137

8   Conclusions   170

    Appendix 1 The distribution of the inventory samples
                by parish   178

    Appendix 2 Production categories   181

    Appendix 3 Some characteristics of occupation and
                status groups   185

    Appendix 4 The ownership of material goods by status
                and occupation   190

Appendix 5 Logistic regression statistics   195

Notes   201
Bibliography   230
Index   247

Illustrations

Maps

2.1 The Cornwall sample parishes   30
2.2 The Kent sample parishes   31

Tables

2.1 Categorisation of inventories for analysis   18
2.2 Status groups represented by inventories (percentages)   22
2.3 The 1664 Hearth Tax for Cornwall compared with
     inventories (exempt households excluded)   24
2.4 Poll Tax, Hearth Tax and inventories in three Cornwall
     parishes   25
2.5 The 1664 Hearth Tax for Kent compared with inventories
     (exempt households included)   25
2.6 Life cycle stages of those leaving inventories in Milton,
     Kent, 1580–1711   27
3.1 Production activities 1600–1749 (percentages)   37
3.2 Inventories with evidence of production for exchange
     (percentages)   39
3.3 Percentages of inventories in four agricultural categories   40
3.4 Arable farming   43
3.5 Hops, hemp and flax in Kent   45
3.6 Percentages of inventories indicating textile production   47
3.7 Percentages of inventories with evidence of potential
     production for use   57
4.1 Inventories with evidence of commercial by-employment
     (percentages)   66
4.2 By-employment in Cornwall 1600–1749   67
4.3 By-employment in Kent 1600–1749   68
4.4 Craft workers also engaged in agricultural production
     1600–1749 (percentages)   74
4.5 Production activities per household   76
4.6 Women's work: percentages of activities by household
     categories 1600–1749   79
4.7 Percentages of households engaged in commercial
     activities headed by a woman   83

4.8	Inventories with no evidence of production 1600–1749	85
5.1	Furniture	91
5.2	Goods concerned with heating, cooking and eating	99
5.3	Linen	109
5.4	Miscellaneous goods (percentages)	111
5.5	Appraisers' descriptions (percentages)	114
5.6	Goods in retailers' inventories 1600–1749 (percentages)	117
6.1	The recording of rooms	122
6.2	The frequency of rooms recorded in Kent inventories (percentages)	124
6.3	Room types in Kent (percentages)	125
6.4	Activities and objects in Kent houses by room (percentages)	126–7
6.5	Activities and objects in five room types in Kent houses (percentages)	128–9
6.6	Great chambers in Kent inventories 1600–1749	132
7.1	Measures of wealth derived from inventories	140
7.2	Correlations between wealth and certain goods and activities	142
7.3	Ownership of certain items and production for use by quartiles of pooled material wealth (percentages)	144
7.4	*Exp(β)* values from logistic regression equations predicting ownership of certain goods from material wealth and county of residence	146–7
7.5	Wealth, status and occupational groups in Cornish parishes 1700–49 (percentages)	154
7.6	Wealth, status and occupational groups in Kent parishes 1700–49 (percentages)	156
7.7	Correlations between parish attributes 1700–49	157
7.8	Selected commodities and production activities for use in Cornish parishes 1700–49 (percentages)	158
7.9	Selected commodities and production activities for use in Kent parishes 1700–49 (percentages)	160
7.10	Correlations between parish attributes and new consumer goods	162
A1.1	The distribution of the Cornwall inventory sample	179
A1.2	The distribution of the Kent inventory sample	180
A3.1	Some characteristics of occupation and status groups	185–9
A4.1	Ownership of material goods by status and occupation (percentages)	190–4
A5.1	*Exp(β)* statistics for logistic regression equations predicting the ownership of goods in Cornwall	195–6
A5.2	*Exp(β)* statistics for logistic regression equations predicting the ownership of goods in Kent	197–8
A5.3	*Exp(β)* statistics for logistic regression equations predicting the presence of production for use in Cornwall	199
A5.4	*Exp(β)* statistics for logistic regression equations predicting the presence of production for use in Kent	200

Preface

This study has its origins in a research project funded by the Leverhulme Trust from 1996–8 on 'Household economies in southern England 1600–1750'. Mark Overton and Jane Whittle were the co-directors of the project and employed Darron Dean and Andrew Hann as Research Associates. We are extremely grateful to the Leverhulme Trust, and to the then Director, Professor Barry Supple, for help and support. Darron Dean collected the Kent inventories during the first year of the project and subsequently was responsible for the analysis of material culture and for drafting Chapters 5 and 6. Andrew Hann collected the Cornish inventories and went on to analyse production activity and draft Chapters 3 and 4. Mark Overton drafted Chapters 2, 7, 8, and part of Chapter 1, while Jane Whittle drafted the remainder of Chapter 1 and part of Chapter 4. The final version of the book was written by Mark Overton from 2001–3 and he bears responsibility for the analysis of the data presented. Nevertheless, the research activity was very much a team effort and all four authors contributed to the major arguments of the book.

We owe thanks to many people. Mark Allen was our Computer Development Officer from 1996–7, also funded by the Leverhulme Trust. Without his patience and skill in transforming and extending Mark Overton's ancient computer programs our analysis of inventories could not have been completed. The staff at the Cornwall County Record Office and the Centre for Kentish Studies were extremely helpful in facilitating our use of such a large number of documents. Helen Bailey gave us valuable help in transcribing some of the Kent inventories as deadlines drew close. We were fortunate to have the services of a number of consultants to the project who gave us their advice and support at a number of research workshops in Exeter: David Cullum, Pat Hudson, David Ormrod, Richard Smith and Jan de Vries. Many others have commented on our work, but we should especially like to thank Jonathan Barry, Roger Burt, Henry French, Paul Glennie, Christine North, Phillip Payton and Leigh Shaw-Taylor. We are also grateful for the comments of seminar and conference audiences in Exeter, Cambridge, Le Mans, London, Manchester, Oxford and Rotterdam. Henry French and Meemee Overton read the entire manuscript and the book is much improved as a consequence of their efforts.

Following on from the Leverhulme project the ESRC funded a study of wealth and consumption in Milton (R000222733) undertaken by Mark Overton and Darron Dean which we draw on for this book, and the AHRB funded Mark Overton for a period of study leave during 2002. Finally we should like to thank the University of Exeter for its support throughout the project and for granting Mark Overton a sabbatical year while the book was being written.

A note on monetary values

When specific sums are quoted in the text they are in the form £ s d, where £ represents a pound of 20 shillings (s) each comprising 12 pence (d). Decimal fractions of a pound are given in the tables.

1 Household economies and economic development in early modern England

In an urbanised, industrial economy few goods are produced in the home: households are dependent on the market. Members of the household earn money outside the home, and use this to purchase items the household needs and wants. Most of these items, whether they are basic foodstuffs or elaborately manufactured items, have been produced at some distance from the home, often wholly or partly in a foreign country. In a peasant economy without significant market development, the main aim of household production is to provide consumption needs directly: the household is largely self-sufficient, and exchange activities are minimal. Production is typically located in or near the home, which is a significant site of consumption. Because the household is self-provisioned, consumption goods are simple and lack variety.

By the sixteenth century very few English households were self-sufficient.[1] Yet many households had access to land and still produced much of their own food. Goods that were purchased had often been produced locally and were rarely from outside England. So how, and when, did the household economy move from self-sufficiency to complete market dependence? This study of production and consumption in the household is directed towards that question. It is a study of how the English economy changed during the early modern period, and how these changes affected people's everyday lives; and, inversely, a study of how normal people changed their everyday lives and how these changes affected the economy. In a nutshell, therefore, we are approaching an old problem, the development of capitalism, through the economic activities of the household.

'Household' and 'family' are sometimes used interchangeably by historians and there is an extensive literature on the family in early modern England, which includes the concept of the 'family economy'.[2] Our concern here is with the household, which is not the same as the family since it consisted of all those living together under the authority of a householder, linked not only by ties of blood and marriage, but also by contractual relationships of work and material benefits. Thus the household 'might include a spouse, children, other relations, servants and apprentices, boarders, sojourners, or only some of these'.[3] It is for this reason that some historians prefer to talk of the 'household economy' as opposed to the 'family economy'.[4]

The transition to capitalism in _____ is usually theorised from the point of v_____ ich define the field all empha_____ Adam Smith stressed t_____ of the means of produc_____ models also implies cha_____ *tions*, Smith described _____ activities necessarily l_____ s entering the market, _____ e. These trends resulte_____ range of goods and a _____ in turn specialisation w_____ Marx in *Capital* said a gr_____ under capitalism, but c_____ elopment. Neverthele_____ into his historical schem_____ expropriation of the mas_____ d, having lost their access to land, _____ pitalist owners of property to provide them _____ ation of small-scale agriculturalists became a nation _____ ourers. These proletarianised labourers were reliant on the market for their consumption needs, exchanging wages for goods and services. The loss of access to land meant losing the opportunity for self-sufficiency, or partial self-sufficiency.[6] In *The Protestant Ethic* Weber argued that modern capitalism was characterised by a distinctive work ethic, which caused people to work for the sake of work itself. In traditional societies work was orientated towards fulfilling the needs and wants of subsistence and leisure; thus work was driven by the desire for consumption. Methodical hard work for its own sake led to the generation of profits. The transformation of the work ethic has contradictory implications for consumption, which were not explored by Weber. On the one hand consumption ceases to be the main aim of work; on the other, extra work leads to increased wealth and thus the possibility of increased consumption.[7] The more profound implication of Weber's thesis is that cultural change can stimulate economic change, thus causes of and motivations for change should not be sought in the economy alone.

Yet the overarching models of Smith, Marx and Weber are far from perfect as a framework with which to investigate economic change in England between 1600 and 1750. They provide little detail, and are often inaccurate in describing the exact contours of change. They are not only biased towards production, but assume a workforce made up of adult men and neglect the dynamics within the household. Further, they are too dichotomous, contrasting a self-sufficient peasant or traditional society with a fully commercialised or capitalist economy. When applied to the reality of England's economic change these models leave a long interme-diate, transitional period stretching from at least the fourteenth century to the late eighteenth century. England's economy during the seventeenth and early eighteenth century was commercialised, with well-developed market structures: it was not a self-sufficient peasant economy, yet it displayed fundamental differences to the industrialised, urbanised economy of the nineteenth century. A number of alternative models suggest that there was an intermediate stage of economic development, one in which production was orientated towards sale in the market, but was small scale, located in the home, and more often rural than ur[...] We will discuss four of these models or approaches: 'peas[...]-industrialisa-tion, the history of women's work [...]ion'.

Although 'peasant st[udies...]le school of thought, it is u[...]small-scale agricultural[...]approach, insisted econ[...]d not be modelled in [...]ses. The primary intere[...]rvival of all its members[...]en sur-vival is precariou[...]select-ing the enterpr[...], the peasant farmer ai[...]t the household can sti[...]s to disease. Where lan[...]sify into craft productio[...]er strand in their prod[...]n Macfarlane, have insi[...] barely affected by ma[...]t studies has found that peasantries [...] the market are very rare: most peasants pr[...]portion of their goods for the market, and purchased [...] their household needs.[11] Yet their rela-tionship with the market is not the same as that of a capitalist farmer. Peasants diversify and retain an element of self-sufficiency not because markets are absent but because markets are unreliable. In addition, the production strategies of such households are influenced by the fact that they generally have more labour than wealth to invest. Risk-aversion leads to diversification of production, the opposite trend to Adam Smith's increased division of labour. If these two theories are correct, then there must be a point in economic development when markets become reliable enough for households to switch from diversifying to specialising, and it is possible that such a point was reached in southern England in the period 1600–1750.

Farming remained the dominant occupation in England from 1600 to 1750, yet in the same period England experienced both urbanisation and industrialisation. Wrigley has estimated that the proportion of the English population living in towns rose from 8 per cent to 21 per cent between 1600 and 1750, while the proportion [...]d in 'rural non-agricultural' occupations rose from 22 pe[...]nt.[12] The concept of proto-industrialisation atte[...]th of rural 'pre-industrial industry', o[...]ries producing goods for non-[...]ibes the development of [...]ocuses on how changes [...]rns and demographic [...]sation of production, w[...]ls were by-employed in[...]common with the aim[...]too narrow. Proto-indu[...]ntated industries. Thes[...]but the emphasis on th[...]icultural occupa-tions t[...]any served only local m[...]e production. For simi[...]proto-industry fails to c[...]which single house-holds mig[...]

Chayan[...]household should be regarded as a single, indi[...]oduction and consumption. However, more recent resea[...]many fields stress the division of tasks within the household, and unequal entitlements to aspects of consumption such as food and leisure between men, women and children.[15] With some notable exceptions, women have also often been absent as subjects of economic history, with the implicit assumption either that women had no role in the wider economy or that women were affected by economic and social change in the same way as men. This view was challenged nearly a century ago by Clark, whose study of women's work in the seventeenth century divided production into three co-existing types: 'domestic industry' solely for the use of the family, 'family industry' carried out at home but with the aim of selling or exchanging goods, and 'capitalist industry' undertaken for a wage payment. The work roles of men and women, and of unmar-ried and married women, differed according to the type of production, but were particularly strongly affected by the switch to capitalist industry, which removed work from the home.[16] Although Clark's labels for the dif-ferent types of production are rather confusing, the distinctions them-selves are crucial and have much in common with the peasant studies and proto-industrial approaches. While they represent a progression from sub-sistence economy to capitalism, Clark's recognition that they could and did co-exist in seventeenth-century England turns our attention to the balance between them. We might add that they could also co-exist in a single household, and thus the balance needs to be observed on that level

Proto-industrialisation – like
textiles suggests
a step away from home
Production but located
to a Commodity market
"Localised specilites"

as well as between households. Thus the notion of the 'family economy' as developed by Tilly and Scott is open to criticism because of its emphasis on subsistence and the absence of wage labour.[17]

Clark's survey of the range of occupations and productive activities undertaken by women warns against any simplistic assumption that women restricted themselves largely to household maintenance and child-care tasks.[18] In any case, to characterise women's work as 'domestic' in an era when most work by men and women was carried out within or near the home is largely meaningless. Instead men's work can be characterised as predominantly orientated towards producing goods (some for the market and some for home consumption, usually after processing), and only occasionally involving maintenance tasks such as house repair or collection of fuel. Women's work, on the other hand, typically combined tasks such as child-care, cooking and cleaning with tasks that produced and processed goods for sale or home consumption, such as gardening, spinning and dairying. Both men and women engaged in wage-earning activities, as servants living within their household of employment or as day labourers.[19]

The special position of women's work 'at the intersection of the household's functions: reproduction, production and consumption' prompted de Vries to stress its significance in his theorisation of an 'industrious revolution' in the early modern period.[20] He defines this as 'a household-based intensification of market-directed labour and/or production, related to an increased demand for market-supplied goods and services'.[21] It thus brings together an awareness of the market-orientated peasant economy, proto-industrialisation, and the changing nature of women's work, in an attempt to explain the increase in specialist market-orientated production and in the consumption of non-home-produced goods that preceded the Industrial Revolution. The industrious revolution occurred 'in those peasant households that could follow the course of specialisation by concentrating household labour in marketed food production'. Such a household reduces 'the amount of labour devoted to a wide variety of home handicrafts and services and replaces these activities with market supplied substitutes'.[22] Thus the switch of women's labour from producing everyday goods such as bread and beer in the home, to purchasing them, is an important indicator. This switch allowed women's labour to be turned to cash-earning activities instead. Due to women's position on the intersection of production and consumption, the different forms of women's work imply different modes of consumption as well as production, different patterns of earning and expenditure; in short, different household economies.

De Vries cites as evidence Thirsk's study of the proliferation of new industries and crops in seventeenth-century England. These new forms of production not only prompted changes in consumption patterns, but also had a particular demand for women's and children's labour, offering new

money-earning opportunities.[23] Rather than seeing peasants as conservative consumers, de Vries argues that changes in peasant household production strategies towards specialising in saleable goods were motivated by the desire to consume more market-distributed goods: 'the increased market orientation of such a household cannot be understood simply as a production response to market opportunities; it is also a response to the household's demand for marketed goods, revealed in a higher demand for the money income necessary to acquire such goods'.[24] Household members not only switched their labour increasingly to money-earning activities but, de Vries suggests, worked longer and more intensively.[25] Thus it appears as though Weber's work ethic was driven by consumption rather than by religious conviction.

The argument for changes in production and consumption occurring hand in hand is supported by de Vries's study of the early modern Dutch economy, as well as by other probate inventory based studies of England and America in the same period. Specialisation in Dutch agriculture occurred simultaneously with the emergence of new patterns of consumption: improved housing, increased domestic comfort, the appearance of cheaper and less durable household goods.[26] Similar trends seem to have been visible in England: increased regional specialisation in agriculture, the introduction of new crops often for industrial uses, and the spread of rural industries went side by side with the same consumption patterns observed in Dutch inventories.[27] Leaving aside the issue of the increased duration and intensity of productive labour, which is beyond the scope of the current study, a number of issues arise from the industrious revolution model. First, much of the argument remains to be verified in its historical detail. With regard to England, to what extent did household production actually become more specialised in this period? Did women switch from, say, food processing for their household to cash-earning activities? Although de Vries does pay attention to differences between the social strata, these distinctions become obscured in his argument. Existing evidence points to women of middling wealth moving directly from production of goods for home consumption to homemaking without showing a concern for generating cash income in the interim. The money-earning activities of such women were focused on the production of traditional farmhouse goods such as cheese, poultry, fruit, vegetables and honey, and not the new production activities stressed by Thirsk. On the other hand, in poorer families men, women and children switched from production for home consumption to wage earning and non-agricultural commodity production because they lost their access to land.[28] It was not a desire for market goods, but a lack of rights to land that pushed them into the commercial economy. Even if we except de Vries's scheme, it remains unclear which came first – changes in production or changes in consumption.

By this point in the discussion, it is evident that there are multiple links between production and consumption, both in the household and in the

wider economy. Within the household, decisions had to be made to use time either for production or leisure (which often involved consumption). The decision of whether to produce for direct use or for sale in the market (or to work outside the home for wages) was partly a consumption decision about the type of goods the household wished to consume. Goods owned by the household could embody both production and consumption: a butter churn is a 'production good' but the decision to acquire one is an issue of consumption. Production activities involve the consumption of goods and materials. In the wider economy, increased specialisation in production increases the consumption of purchased goods by reducing the range of home-produced goods. New types of production lead to the availability of new types of goods, stimulating consumer demand, which may cause households to turn away from home production for direct use. Similarly, the demands of consumers might stimulate new types of production.

Despite these links between consumption and production, consumption also has a dynamic of its own, quite separate from production activities. It is possible to study consumption independently from the availability of goods and services, or the means of acquiring them, by concentrating on the social and individual meanings attached to consumption activities and the motivation for desiring particular items or pastimes.[29] The meaning of consumption is slippery, implying different things in different contexts, with very different meanings for the different disciplines of the social sciences.[30] In western capitalism 'consumption has become linked with desires, through the use of signs and symbols in selling products to the majority of consumers'.[31] Such a definition is obviously problematic in the context of early modern England where much that was consumed was not sold. Indeed, we argue below that much of the production in early modern households was for home consumption.

The major historical debate over consumption in early modern England was launched by McKendrick when he argued that there was a consumer boom in the eighteenth century marked by an 'unprecedented propensity to consume' reaching 'revolutionary proportions' by the third quarter of that century. Thus there occurred a consumer revolution which 'was a necessary analogue to the industrial revolution'.[32] As Glennie points out, this is now only one of many claims for 'the birth of consumer society, emergent modern consumption, the rise of mass consumption and the rise of mass market culture' which have been applied to English history from 1500 onwards.[33] There is now general agreement among early modern historians of consumption that gradual but important changes in consumption patterns occurred between 1550 and 1750, deflating any suggestions of revolutionary change thereafter.[34] These changes included significant improvements in domestic comfort, changes in diet with the widespread adoption of imported goods such as sugar and tea, and changes in cooking and eating behaviour.[35] Even so, the value of non-production goods compared to production goods does not appear to have increased markedly, and in some studies shows a decline. This is because of another notable change in goods: they became both less durable (for instance pottery replacing pewter) and also cheaper due to reduced production costs.[36]

McKendrick's view was that his 'consumer revolution' was driven by emulation; as Langford puts it, 'Nothing unified the middling orders so much as their passion for aping the manners and morals of the gentry.'[37] More recent historical studies are questioning this view, arguing that particular social groups used consumption to fashion their own identities rather than to ape those of others.[38] This idea is also evident in work by sociologists which challenges Veblen's assumption that social competition produces imitation. It is now increasingly recognised that social groups can be seen as distinguishing themselves through consumption and material goods, appropriating the cultural traits of others and re-fashioning or appropriating them for their own ends.[39]

Closely related to historical studies of consumption have been historical studies of material culture. While the stock of material culture is not the same as consumption we can infer a great deal about consumption from material culture.[40] The emphasis in modern studies of material culture is on the meanings ascribed to material goods, although earlier studies of material goods in the English historiography were primarily in 'popular' histories, often written for children.[41] Thus the Quennells' multi-volume *History of everyday things in England* was written for 'boys and girls of public-school age'.[42] Although most has been written about what might be called high material culture, of the great houses in the early modern period, there are a number of books on the material goods of more humble households. Although at their worst these works degenerate into sentimental accounts of a lost rural idyll, many are still important because they describe the context of objects and how they were used, and there are also descriptions of production activities as well as consumption goods.[43] While much of this literature is not explicitly concerned with meanings, such descriptions help in the search for meaning. More mainstream historical interest in material culture has its origins with the French *Annales* school, and especially with the work of Fernand Braudel.[44] For England, one of the two major studies of consumption during the early modern period is explicitly concerned with material culture.[45]

These general considerations lead to a series of specific questions which this book attempts to answer. What production activities were carried out in early modern English households? Did production become more specialised over time? At the same time how did the balance change between production for use (or direct consumption) and production for exchange? What was the relationship between changes in household production and the gender division of labour? Was specialisation accompanied by increased consumption, or a richer and more varied material environment? What types of households were associated with new consumer goods and did these goods 'trickle down' the social hierarchy?

These are explicitly empirical questions and a major aim of this book is to provide a new body of evidence to answer them: for as is so often the case, theoretical speculation has run ahead of empirical research. It is no surprise that the new evidence is from probate inventories. Inventories have figured prominently in historical studies of consumption in the early modern world, and are particularly suited to the study of material culture, although historians using them have not always adopted that terminology. This study is based on a large number of inventories (8,103) and is an 'extensive' piece of research as opposed to an 'intensive' one, since it is mainly concerned with discovering some common properties and general patterns on a county scale.[46] As we shall see in the following chapter, inventories have their limitations since even within the sphere of material culture they say little about cheap items and the novelties that were the main focus of Thirsk's idea of 'the development of a consumer society'.[47] In addition, unlike the much rarer household accounts, inventories provide a snapshot in time of the goods owned at death, rather than a description of continuous consumption activities. Nevertheless, existing studies of consumption and material culture using inventories have not exploited their full potential, so a secondary aim of this study is to develop a methodology which does just that.

In addition to counting the frequency of new goods (for example, clocks, jacks and mirrors), or calculating the value of 'consumer goods', inventories can be used to study disappearing goods (for example, cauldrons and carpets), increased quantities of existing goods (for example, chairs and linen), an increase in the variety of goods, new assemblages of goods (used in cooking for example); and, finally, the linguistic analysis of inventories can reveal something of attitudes to change and novelty. While we cannot understand the meaning of goods by counting them we can infer meanings from the location of goods within the house and their relationships to other goods, and the adjectives used to qualify items can reveal changing attitudes to novelty. We can also infer origin and production techniques from materials, such as foreign woods or silk, revealing distances traded, and allowing some distinction between home-produced, locally produced and urban or foreign items. The inventories of merchants and shopkeepers reveal what goods were available, allowing comparison with goods other local households owned, and providing information about the small goods and foodstuffs that go unrecorded in most inventories.

Nevertheless, some aspects of the cultural context of consumption remain almost impossible to retrieve, such as the moral or ethical meaning of goods and activities, and their use in constructing identities. We can only attempt to infer these considerations from their presence or absence in certain contexts. Nonetheless it is important not to lose sight of these issues. Consumption studies are edging closer to a sophisticated explanation of the changes in consumption patterns over time.[48] Simpler explanations revolving around emulation and fashion are being rejected in favour of frameworks which explain changes in consumption patterns in terms of particular economic and cultural contexts. For instance, Campbell has argued, in a mode similar to Weber, that a new ethic of consumption arose in the eighteenth century. Once the provision of life's necessities (food, clothing, shelter, fuel) became secure, the middling classes had more time and attention to focus on obtaining new pleasures. Changes in religious thought and other cultural developments inadvertently compelled middle-class individuals towards increased consumption, particularly of new and fashionable items, just as Weber argued religious belief inadvertently encouraged hard work and the accumulation of extra wealth.[49] Similarly, studies of modern consumption increasingly stress the construction of social and individual identities, rather than the satisfying of need, as the key motivator behind consumption.[50] Clearly, probate inventories are not the best source from which to study such issues. Nevertheless they do occasionally provide hints of different 'cultures of consumption', particularly via the different collections of goods owned by people of varying occupations and status, and regional differences between people of the same status. How can differences in the ownership of goods be explained between groups with the same level of income and equal access to consumption goods? This is a reminder of the importance, not just of examining changes in patterns of production and consumption over time, as far as is possible, but of doing so with a careful awareness of differences between households in terms of wealth, status and locality.

Inventories have also been prominent in many studies of early modern industry, although rather surprisingly, since inventories refer to households, such studies have tended to focus on particular industries rather than household production in its entirety.[51] The emphasis on particular occupations has also meant that there are fewer studies of by-employment than one might expect.[52] This is particularly unfortunate given the importance of identifying specialisation in production as an element of economic development in early modern England. Many documents (including inventories) often provide occupational designations, although they sometimes only denote status (such as 'gentleman') and in the case of women only denote marital status. This type of data has been used to look at regional specialisation and the development of rural industry. When combined with evidence of landholding it can be used to show 'by-employment'. Yet, as is well known, this approach is flawed in two ways. First, it concentrates overwhelmingly on the occupation of adult males, while in the case of by-employment it remains unclear whether it is a male household head or the household as a whole that has two main occupations. Second, it precludes the possibility that households might have multiple occupations, or, given that defining what constitutes an occupation is somewhat problematic, that households might engage in multiple production activities. In this study, the whole range of household production activities are recorded, in so far as they can be detected from the goods in household. Moreover, this production combined the work activities of at least two adults, husband and wife, often supplemented by that of children and servants. In addition, this activity was not solely concerned with the production of goods for sale, whether in a local or distant market, but also with production for home use, work to maintain the family and household.[53] Unfortunately probate inventories do not allow us to identify with any certainty who did what work in any particular household. However, when wider knowledge of the gender division of labour in this period is combined with information from inventories, the range of male, female and non-gender-specific tasks within a household can be identified. The quantity of certain types of goods reveals the scale of production, suggesting the employment of servants in some cases, as well as indicating whether production was aimed at home provision or sale.

The choice of the counties of Cornwall and Kent as the locations for this study is in part pragmatic: both have large numbers of probate inventories, as opposed to, say, Devon or Essex. But they were also chosen because their economic histories differ from the conventional pathway of economic development associated with models of proto-industrialisation which are closely associated with the development of the textile industry. Although both counties had textile industries they were declining in economic importance, and the iron industry was also in decline in the Weald. By the eighteenth century Kent had a diversified economic base, whereas Cornwall was becoming increasingly dominated by mining.

Differences between the two counties far outweigh their similarities. Kent was highly commercialised; not only was it close to London but it lay between London and the Continent. The dramatic growth of London during the seventeenth century (its population doubled between 1600 and 1650 to 400,000 people and continued to rise to over 600,000 by 1750) stimulated the commercial production of corn, hops and fruit.[54] The traffic with London was, of course, two-way, and a wide variety of goods manufactured in and distributed from the capital were available in the county. Prominent among these return cargoes were luxury foodstuffs from overseas, dairy produce brought from East Anglia, the north-east and Cheshire, coal from Sunderland and Newcastle, and miscellaneous consumer goods.[55] The dockyards and ports of Chatham, Deptford, Deal, Dover, Sheerness and Woolwich owed a large part of their prosperity to the building of ships and fortifications. The rapid growth of many of these naval towns boosted Kent's economy by creating employment opportunities, both directly and indirectly, which, it has recently been argued, was an important element in restructuring Kent's economy during the seventeenth and eighteenth centuries as both the textile and iron industries went into relative decline.[56]

By contrast Cornwall was on the periphery of England, and its economic links with the capital were more limited. The dominant economic trend during the seventeenth century was the development of the mining industry, which is reflected in dramatic population growth from the mid-seventeenth century. Population levels remained virtually static in the largely agricultural east, whilst central and west Cornwall saw increases during the late seventeenth and early eighteenth centuries which were unprecedented within England at the time. The population of the hundred of Penwith grew by 89 per cent between 1660 and 1750 and Kerrier by 79 per cent, whereas the population of Stratton hundred (in the extreme north-east of the county) fell by 26 per cent.[57] Growth rates in some mining parishes could, indeed, be prodigious: the number of inhabitants in St Just-in-Penwith increased from 783 in 1600 to 1,540 in 1700, and 2,428 in 1740, and there were similar trends in Gwennap, St Austell, St Agnes, Redruth and Camborne.[58] Western ports such as Falmouth, Truro and Penzance also saw their populations rise substantially, as did the larger fishing villages such as Paul and Mevagissey.

Cornwall was also markedly less urbanised than Kent: by *c.*1670 Kent had seven towns with more than 2,500 inhabitants (Canterbury, Chatham, Deptford, Dover, Greenwich, Maidstone and Rochester), whereas Cornwall had none, although the county was covered by a network of relatively evenly distributed small market centres. Most were little more than villages, and even the larger boroughs such as Launceston, Liskeard and Bodmin had fewer than 1,500 inhabitants around 1660. The two main towns in Devon, Plymouth and Exeter, by comparison, had populations of 5,400 and 11,500 respectively.[59]

Different levels of urbanisation might be expected to have led to different cultures of consumption since towns are supposed to have had considerably higher levels of consumption than rural areas.[60] But a greater difference may have lain in the claims for a distinct Cornish cultural and ethnic identity in the early modern period. It has been argued that a distinctive Cornish identity exerted a powerful influence over 'politico-religious behaviour' in the early modern period, and we have the opportunity to explore its relation to consumption behaviour.[61] We return to this theme in the conclusion, but we start with the source material on which our arguments rest – probate inventories.

2 Probate inventories

Probate inventories are one of the most popular sources for the study of the economic, social and cultural history of the early modern world. They have an enduring fascination because of the unique window they open into the everyday-life of people and households; they abound with descriptions that can be comic, tragic, poignant, and perplexing. But they are also inherently quantitative documents. They count and value objects and so can provide statistics of economic and social activity. They are thus attractive to historians with very divergent interests; ranging from the representation of self through material objects, to the statistical analysis of price series.[1] Hitherto, aside from anecdotal usage, major studies of inventories have produced agricultural census-like data, frequency counts of household items and their locations, patterns of debt and credit, wealth statistics and price series.[2]

This study of production and consumption is based almost entirely on probate inventories, so it is essential to subject them to some scrutiny. While the use of a large number of inventories overcomes many of the limitations of individual documents, we need to be aware of how inventories may give a distorted picture of household production and consumption. This chapter outlines the role of inventories in the probate process, and discusses some of the issues concerned with their contents, consistency and representativeness, emphasising those characteristics that have been underplayed in the literature. The computer software developed for the analysis of inventories is outlined and the sampling procedure for selecting inventories from Cornwall and Kent is described.

An act of 1529 re-established the practice that executors or administrators of an estate were responsible for exhibiting an inventory at the time of probate to safeguard themselves against excessive claims on the estate; to assist in a just distribution of the deceased's assets and thus help prevent fraud; and to determine the fees that the probate court was to receive. They survive for many parts of the world, in England perhaps nearly two million were made between the mid-sixteenth and the mid-eighteenth centuries.[3] Inventories were drawn up (or 'appraised') by two or more people, in most cases shortly after the death of the deceased person, for the appraisers usually started with the money and clothes on the body. They then proceeded round the house, room by room, listing and valuing the goods and chattels before them.[4] When they were making the inventory of a farmer they would then move to the yards, barns and stables, and finally into the fields to record livestock and growing crops. At the head of the document they wrote the deceased's name and sometimes their status or occupation, the date the inventory was taken, and the name of the parish in which they lived. One copy of the indented inventory was presented to the appropriate ecclesiastical probate court and retained in the archives of that court.[5]

Contents and omissions

The Statute of 1529 called for a 'true and perfect inventory of all the goods, chattels, wares, merchandises..., of the person deceased'. Goods included, 'all the testator's cattle, as bulls, cows, oxen, sheep, horses, swine, and all poultry, household stuff, money, plate, jewels, corn, hay, wood severed from the ground and such like moveables'.[6] Contemporary legal texts were quite explicit as to what should, and what should not, be recorded in an inventory.[7] Anything that was not actually movable was to be omitted from the inventory, so ovens, furnaces, window-glass and wainscoting for example, which were integral parts of the fabric of a building, should be excluded. More significantly, inventories remain silent about real estate – that is land and buildings (although not about movable documents referring to real estate). Thus they cannot tell us directly about the extent of landownership, the size of houses, or the number of agricultural buildings. Nor can they tell us much about patterns of debt and credit since debts owed by the deceased to other people were also supposed to be omitted. Therefore inventories do not appear a very promising source with which to measure wealth.[8]

For other goods, legal commentators such as Burn make quite explicit distinctions as to what should and should not be included. Thus, 'fishes in the pond, conies in a warren, deer in a park, pigeons in a dove house ... are not chattels at all ... and are not to be put in the inventory', the rule being that only domesticated animals (but not pets) were included. For crops the principle was that products coming 'merely from the soil' should be excluded, whereas those grown with the 'industry and manurance of man' should be included. Thus inventories mention growing grain, but not standing timber, fruit, or grass growing in permanent pastures or meadows. Further, 'millstones, anvils, doors, keys, window shutters; none of these be chattels ... and therefore shall not go to the executors'.[9]

As far as omissions are concerned appraisers' behaviour seems in accord with Burn's statements. Inventories hardly ever mention permanent pasture or fruit for example. Some appraisers were less certain about what to do with items attached to the freehold such as anvils or furnaces, and occasionally included them. They were also inclined to include debts owed by the deceased to other people even though they were not supposed to. However categorical Burn and other commentators appear, there are considerable differences between the *de jure* ideal embodied in text books and the *de facto* reality of property transmission in early modern England. It is only by using inventories, particularly in conjunction with other probate documents, that their limitations begin to emerge more clearly.[10] Many of these limitations will be discussed in the context of particular issues throughout the remainder of this book, but some general problems can be mentioned here.[11]

Appraisers often listed rooms, presumably to assist in the identification of particular objects, but were not required to do so. It is impossible to know if all the rooms in a house are mentioned unless internal inconsistencies, for example the mention of a parlour chamber but no parlour, suggest it. Appraisers were unlikely to mention an empty room and may have simply forgotten to mention that they had entered another room. Thus counting rooms in inventories is problematic and may well underestimate the actual number of rooms.[12] Most inventories contain an entry along the lines of 'all goods unappraised', or some other equally unhelpful term, and it is clear that many goods with low values were not separately itemised but lumped together in one entry. This is also the case with clothing, which is usually described simply as 'apparel' although occasionally garments are individually itemised. Many ubiquitous items such as wooden candlesticks and trenchers, iron rushlight holders, and cups and spoons made of horn are only rarely separately itemised.[13] Most foodstuffs intended for consumption by the family are also excluded, with the exception of some preserved foods such as salted fish and smoked bacon, although others such as dried fruit are excluded. Food intended for sale is more likely to be included; so the inventories of tradesmen can provide some information on the variety of foods available for consumption and also the prevalence of small items of low value such as brushes and combs. While there is some consistency in these omissions, there are cases where practice seems to vary considerably between appraisers.

There are a number of reasons why items may still be omitted from an inventory even though we might expect them to be included. One of the purposes of the inventory was to help the executors wind up the estate, in particular by paying off creditors through the sale of the deceased's goods.[14] When a person died without making a will, administration was sometimes granted to the principal creditor of the estate. The inventory they produced may be incomplete because they only recorded the values of enough goods to pay off the debts owed by the deceased.[15] This probably explains why items bequeathed in a will are sometimes missing from the inventory, since they were not available to the executors to be sold along with other goods.[16] Occasionally appraisers imply that certain goods have been given away in the will; for example, the inventory of William Harris of Tregony lists only his 'unbequeathed apparrel'.[17] The inventory of Thomas Dixie of Lenham mentions tools in his shop that were 'not given away in his will', implying that others were and are therefore omitted.[18] On the other hand appraisers do occasionally itemise goods that have been bequeathed in a will, for example John Bateman's inventory lists and values 'feather beds, boulsters and pillows disposed of by the testators will'.[19] Missing items might have been taken away by the legatee before the inventory was made, or it is possible that the items were still present in the household of the deceased but were ignored by the appraisers.

According to the law the possessions of a married woman belonged to her husband. For this reason married women did not make wills or have inventories made for them if their husband was alive. Thus we should expect a man's inventory to include the possessions of his wife, and this is often the case – for example when women's clothing is listed. But there are exceptions. The inventory of Mary Harding of Biddenden in Kent mentions £3 worth of silver (a salt, toothpick, beaker and spoons) yet when her husband died seven months earlier no silver was recorded in his inventory, suggesting that the silver *de facto* belonged to his wife.[20] It is possible that goods owned by a wife before her marriage were excluded from her husband's inventory, as were her personal goods (clothes, jewels, bed linens and plate) termed 'bona paraphernalia'. There are many examples in the Kent and Cornish inventories that reinforce Erickson's discussion of the issue. In some cases it is clear that an inventory contains all the household goods, including those of the wife; in others there is either direct or indirect evidence to suggest that some or all of 'her' goods were excluded from her husband's inventory.[21]

One of the executors' tasks was the maintenance of minor children following the death of their father. Probate accounts often list these expenses, but the executors' responsibility began at the time of death, and if there was a delay in making an inventory goods could be removed to pay for the expenses involved in maintaining children before the inventory was made. As the appraisers of the goods of Richard Cunnack of Madron put it, 'as for his wearing apparell this was disposed of since his decease for the maintenance of his children'.[22]

Probably less common is the omission of heirlooms. These were usually personal goods which had been in a family for several generations and by will or custom were devolved to the heir as though they were part of the real estate. But new goods could also be designated as heirlooms by a testator and therefore be excluded from the inventory. While these were often small personal objects they could also include such items as beds, but according to Cox and Cox the practice of designating items as heirlooms was not widespread.[23]

It is quite clear therefore that there are many reasons why a given probate inventory might be an incomplete list of the movable goods of a deceased individual, and if the deceased was a married man why some or all of his wife's goods might be omitted. It is impossible to provide an independent check on the accuracy of the vast majority of inventories. Therefore the only way of identifying omissions, or rather suspected omissions, is through the internal logic of the document. For example, a farmer with a large acreage of growing crops but no farming equipment arouses suspicion: did he own such equipment but for some reason it is not appraised, or did he make use of equipment owned by someone else? Some inventories omit basic household necessities such as beds and cooking equipment. In these cases it is possible that the testator owned these goods but the appraisers failed to record them. On the other hand they may have been servants or lodgers in a household, so that they had the use of such objects even though they did not own them. Alternatively, they may have slept on the floor, or in a bed which was a fixture, and cooked with implements that had too small a value to be worth recording.

One other way in which possible omissions may be identified in any particular inventory is through regression analysis. The presence or absence of a particular item can be predicted through the technique of logistic regression, in which the dependent variable is categorical (for example the presence or absence of a clock) and the independent variables are both categorical and continuous (for example whether or not the deceased was a gentleman and the value of the inventoried estate).[24] As with the more familiar linear regression, logistic regression produces an equation which predicts the dependent variable on the basis of the independent variables. The residuals from this equation identify those inventories which might be expected to have a particular object (the dependent variable) but which in fact do not have it. For example, according to a residual from a logistic regression model predicting the ownership of clocks in Kent during the period 1700–49, the probability that one Thomas Longley, a butcher of Canterbury living in a house with at least 13 rooms and with an inventory made in 1735 and valued at over £1,400, has a clock is 0.998. No clock is recorded in his inventory, which either makes him an eccentric in that he is very different from his peers or that he did in fact possess a clock which for some reason is not recorded.[25]

The amount of detail that appraisers' put into their descriptions changes over time in both counties. Cornish inventories are at their most detailed at the start of the seventeenth century; they gradually become less detailed over the course of the seventeenth century, although they recover some of their detail into the eighteenth century. The Kentish inventories are much more detailed than those from Cornwall, and their level of detail increases considerably over our study period.

Given these many possible sources of error, it is obvious that inventories should not be used mechanistically, and that due account must be taken of an inventory that seems strange or unusual for any reason. In this present study inventories that aroused suspicion were categorised according to the guidelines in Table 2.1. As the table suggests, omissions from inventories vary in their significance depending on the type of analysis undertaken: the omission of household goods for example, renders the inventory a misleading source for consumption, but the remaining goods can still be used to calculate valuations or prices.[26]

The form of information

While inventories are broadly consistent in the kinds of information they contain, the manner in which that information is presented is not consistent and varies from inventory to inventory. Inconsistencies arise for two reasons.[27] First, from the structure of the entries: the most useful inventory is the one that lists items separately and gives each item both a quantity and a value; but inventories following this pattern are rare and the norm is for quantities (but rarely values) to be omitted, and for goods to be combined together and given a common value. Second, there is no consistency in the level of detail in descriptions of items, and general descriptions can conceal the presence of objects. For example, an entry for 'corn' could refer to any or all of the four major cereals; 'pots' could be of brass, copper, or iron; and a 'chair' could be a cane chair, an upholstered chair or a plain wooden chair.

Thus inventories should never be used in a negative way to claim that a particular item is not present because it is not recorded. In many cases a particular item may be present but concealed by a general description, and when this is the case the inventory cannot be used in calculating a statistic involving that item. These inconsistencies in the form of information mean that the investigation of a particular collection of inventories often involves using a different sub-set for each analysis. To calculate the proportion of inventories containing a particular item involves counting the inventories containing that item and expressing the number as a proportion of the total. However, the inventories that can be used to do this may

Table 2.1 Categorisation of inventories for analysis

Code	Meaning	Use
D	Damaged	Wealth total only
X	Must be partial record	Use only for prices
M	Trade goods present	Special use only
B	Household goods grouped together	Production only, not consumption
G	Household comprises an individual, some production evidence	Production only, not consumption
R	Cannot be used for room analysis	Exclude for room analysis
A	Inventory includes more than one property	Production, special use for consumption

differ in each case if appraisers use language that makes it impossible to determine whether the item is present or not. For example, to calculate the proportion of inventories with round tables involves counting up those with an explicit mention of round tables, and expressing that number as a percentage of the total number of inventories, excluding those that just mention 'tables'. Similarly, in calculating the proportion of inventories with upholstered chairs necessitates excluding those that just mention 'chairs'. The inventories excluded in each case are unlikely to be the same ones, so that the proportion of round tables and upholstered chairs are calculated from different sets of inventories within the collection as a whole. For the two proportions to be comparable it must be assumed that the different sets of inventories are random samples from the same population. This is indeed likely to be the case, since the distribution of inventories with items possibly concealed is likely to be random. For example, there is no reason to assume that the distribution of inventories using the word 'chair' instead of 'upholstered chair' is any different to those using the word 'table' instead of 'round table'.[28]

ITEM

Variations in the form of information are emphasised when it comes to analysing probate inventories by computer. Inventories were processed using a custom-written software package called ITEM.[29] The programs allow inventories to be virtually copy-typed into a portable computer in the archives, provide sophisticated checking facilities, and enable a wide range of quantitative analyses to be undertaken, producing output which can be further processed by a conventional spreadsheet or database program. Three specific principles underlie the programs: first, data from inventories should be entered into the computer in a form which is as close as possible to the original documents and no data should be discarded; second, the way in which the data is stored is best determined by the structure of the data itself; and third, there is no point in emulating existing software, so that output from the package should be capable of input into a range of commercial software packages.

Once the data has been typed into a computer in the archives, following some simple formatting rules, it is then checked and 'cleaned' using four programs. First, the syntax of the data is checked to make sure that the formatting rules have been followed and errors are flagged in the data file for subsequent editing. Second, once the syntax is correct, all unique words in a file of inventories can be examined to identify possible errors in transcription. Problematic words can be selected from an alphabetical list and are then flagged in the file of inventory data so they can be seen in context. This process speeds the identification of unusual words and is usually followed by the production of a concordance which gives the frequencies of all the words in a collection of inventories. Third, for the analyses in this book, a new file of data was created in which words are standardised. This is not essential but speeds up the analysis considerably since multiple spellings of words can be reduced to a single spelling and either the singular or plural forms of words can be eliminated. By so doing the inventory data is changed, but the original form is retained in a separate file and can be analysed if required. Fourth, the units of measurement attached to quantities are standardised for particular items, again to simplify the analysis by imposing a common set of units. For example, ounces can be converted to fractions of a pound for certain commodities such as pewter or plate.

In order to analyse the data it is necessary to define categories of objects for which information is required. This is necessary because appraisers had no standard vocabulary for defining objects. Thus in Kent for example, appraisers described 313 kinds of chair; for, say, a count of the number of chairs all these descriptions have to be assigned to the single category 'chair'. Items are assigned to categories using an interactive program. Thus if the category were 'horses', all the items referring to horses (colts, nags, jades, etc., but excluding wooden horses) could be tagged as belonging to that category. Any number of different categorisations can be produced and the process involves defining the categories in a file and then assigning items to them. At its most simple this categorisation can consist of only one category containing only one item, but up to 50 categories can be defined for any one analysis with an almost unlimited number of items for each category.[30]

It is also possible to define a hierarchy of categories to accommodate the variety of detail in the description of items and therefore use as many inventories as possible. In an agricultural classification, for example, the individual cereal crops could be assigned individual categories (wheat, rye, barley and oats) which, at the next level, could be grouped into winter corn (wheat and rye) and spring corn (barley and oats). At the top of the hierarchy all four crops could be lumped together as 'corn'.[31] Similarly, in classifying furniture the hierarchy of codes would range from the detailed (say feather bed) to the generic (bed). It is often desirable to use more than one set of hierarchical categories; animals for example can be categorised by age or type, and domestic goods can be described by their function (e.g. pot) or by the material from which they are made (e.g. iron or brass).

Using a hierarchy of categories is important in making full use of all the information in a particular inventory as well as guarding against misleading interpretations of the data. For example, in using the agricultural content of inventories to derive crop acreages, the software first checks for mentions of a particular crop (say wheat) in conjunction with an acreage figure. However, those acreage figures cannot be used if wheat is combined with some other crop (as in '2 acres of wheat and rye'), although the presence of wheat on the farm could be recorded. A check is also made for a generic term which could include wheat (say 'winter corn'), in which case it would be impossible to determine whether wheat was present on the farm or not, although the presence of winter corn could be recorded. Thus for each category the software determines whether items in that category are present or absent, or whether it is impossible to determine their presence, their quantity and value, or whether either or both are missing or combined with the quantity or value of some other item.

The software package provides five types of analyses of inventory data: the presence or absence of objects, the frequency count of mentions of individual objects, the quantities of objects, the values of objects, and the unit valuations (or prices) of objects. The first of these, presence or absence, simply indicates whether a categorised object is recorded in the inventory, not recorded, or whether its presence might be concealed by a generic description. Frequency counts are similar, except that the number of separate entries for categorised objects is counted: for example, the number of times the word 'chamber' is mentioned. The quantities of objects are calculated by adding up the numbers of particular objects where it is possible to do so: for example, the total number of chairs recorded in an inventory, or the total acreage of wheat. The values of categorised objects are the sums of the values given to them: for example, the value of bedsteads, or debts, or the total value of all the items recorded. Finally, unit valuations are the valuations per unit for a particular object (or its 'price') and are calculated by dividing the value of an object by its quantity if both are present.

The inventories used for each of these five types of analysis can be filtered in a number of ways so that only certain data or inventories are included in or excluded from the analysis. This is necessary to put the principles of Table 2.1 into practice and exclude problematic documents, but is also used to restrict results to inventories representing particular status or occupation groups, parishes, or wealth groups for example, and can also be used to confine the analysis to goods in particular rooms within an inventory. Output from all analyses comes in the form of tab-delimited tables which can be read directly into a spreadsheet program or database. The output can be in summary form where results are summarised by periods, or as a list of data with the information retrieved from each inventory. The latter form is useful for combining results from several analyses into a new spreadsheet; it can also be used to extract non-quantitative data such as the names of appraisers.

The principal merits of the programs are their flexibility and speed. They can accommodate any inventory, and can also be used for documents with a broadly similar structure such as accounts and wills. In this present study it took about a year for one person to enter 4,000 inventories into a portable computer in the archives. It took about two months to 'clean' these data (that is, to check and correct the syntax, identify difficult words, and standardise spellings and units), but only another two months to produce the initial quantitative findings of the project.

Representativeness

One of the most important questions for any study using inventories is how representative they are of the population as a whole. Clearly a collection of inventories for a particular place is most unlikely to constitute a random sample of the individuals living there, but it is difficult to determine exactly what kind of sample they represent. The two most important concerns in this study are, first, the degree to which inventories reflect the social status and wealth of the population as a whole, and, second, whether inventories of individuals give us a complete picture of the household in which they lived.

Common sense tells us that there would be no point in making an inventory when a deceased person left nothing of value or of little value in relation to the costs of obtaining probate. At the other end of the scale, those with property in more than one diocese had their probate proved in one of the two Prerogative Courts of Canterbury and York, where few inventories survive before 1660. Local studies estimating inventoried testators as a proportion of all deaths in an area suggest wide variations from place to place, reflecting the contrasting levels of wealth between different areas, but also variations in the customs of probate courts.[32]

When appraisers described the deceased they did so in one of two ways, by status or by occupation. Occupation is treated in detail in Chapter 3, but the frequency of status descriptions gives an indication of the social bias of inventories. Table 2.2 shows the proportion of inventories in various status groups expressed as a percentage of all inventories mentioning a status or occupational label.[33] It is clear that the status of those leaving inventories was higher than average for the two counties as a whole. The proportion of gentry inventories, for example, averages 7 per cent in Cornwall and 6 per cent in Kent. Although counting gentry is difficult, in the mid-seventeenth century perhaps 2 per cent of Kent families were gentry and some 1.5 per cent of those in Cornwall.[34] The clergy are

Table 2.2 Status groups represented by inventories (percentages)

	Cornwall			Kent		
	1600–49	*1650–99*	*1700–49*	*1600–49*	*1650–99*	*1700–49*
Esquire	0.8	1.0	0.1	0.5	0.5	0.2
Gentleman	8.6	8.2	5.3	4.7	7.7	3.0
Yeoman	24.5	30.4	31.9	23.8	25.2	23.8
Husbandman	19.8	8.7	5.3	12.1	9.2	7.8
Labourer	1.8	0.5	1.4	2.8	1.5	0.9
Servant	0.0	0.0	0.0	0.0	0.1	0.2
Single woman	2.1	4.6	2.9	2.3	2.1	1.3
Widow	19.6	20.2	13.9	23.5	17.6	15.2
Clergyman	0.8	0.3	0.0	1.8	1.1	0.2

very under-represented in the inventories used in this study because their probate was usually dealt with by a Bishop's or Consistory Court, rather than by the Archdeaconry courts used here.[35] At the other end of the scale, we show in Chapter 3 that wage earners are almost entirely absent from our sample of inventories.[36]

It has already been pointed out that in law the goods of a wife belonged to her husband, thus the surviving inventories for women refer to those who were unmarried or widowed; a wife who pre-deceased her husband did not have an inventory made. Thus the proportion of the Cornish and Kentish inventories referring to women is only 17 per cent and 15 per cent respectively. Except for very rare occasions probate inventories were not made for minor children, and children's possessions (toys for example) are not included.[37]

Another way to check the relationship between those leaving inventories and the total population is by matching inventories with taxation records listing names in particular parishes. This is most easily done with the Hearth Tax of 1664, since the records of those paying the tax have been published.[38] Tables 2.3–2.5 were compiled by identifying those people listed in the Hearth Tax for whom an inventory survives before 1699. This is a problematic procedure, since it cannot capture those who left the parish between their listing in the Hearth Tax and their death, and the evidence on which to make a positive identification is not as strong as we would like.[39] In the first place, we took a sample of inventories for some parishes rather than recording all those available.[40] The proportion of the population of a parish who were present in 1664 and remained until the end of the century would also vary by wealth and social group. The poor were more mobile than the 'chief inhabitants', who tended to remain in their parish for a longer period.[41] Thus matching an inventory to a name in the Hearth Tax is more likely for the 'chief inhabitants' of the parish than it is for poorer people, and so gives an upward bias to the matches that can be made. Moreover, while the 1664 assessment usually lists occupiers of property, owners were responsible for the tax. Thus a house with many chimneys owned by a man of some status may in fact be a tenement let to poor people. Most serious of all, the Hearth Tax listings for most of Cornwall omit those exempt from the tax because they were poor.[42]

Despite the omission of the poor, Table 2.3 shows that whereas 48 per cent of the households taxed in the Cornish parishes had only one hearth, they produced only 36 per cent of the extant inventories. At the other end of the scale, 7.8 per cent of households had five or more hearths, but this group represented 13.7 per cent of those leaving inventories. For two Cornish parishes (Altarnun and St Gennys) those households exempt from the Hearth Tax payment on grounds of poverty are also listed. Over 80 households (33 per cent) were listed as too poor to pay the Hearth Tax, and only one of these had a surviving inventory. The upward social

Table 2.3 The 1664 Hearth Tax for Cornwall compared with inventories (exempt households excluded)

No. of hearths	No. of households	% of all hearths	No. with inventories	% of all inventories
1	823	47.5	234	35.6
2	421	24.3	177	26.9
3	249	14.4	102	15.5
4	105	6.1	54	8.2
5	45	2.6	25	3.8
6	36	2.1	15	2.3
7	13	0.8	15	2.3
8	12	0.7	13	2.0
9	7	0.4	14	2.1
10 and over	20	1.2	8	1.2
Totals	1,731	100.0	657	100.0

Note
The Cornish parishes listed in Appendix 1 are used, with the exception of Cuby, Roche and Temple.

and economic bias in inventories is reinforced by the evidence from three Cornish parishes for which we have evidence from the 1661 Poll Tax shown in Table 2.4. This tax assessed all those with an income of over £5 a year (described as 'yearly income or rank' in the table), all married couples, and single people over the age of 16 provided they were not 'receiving alms'. The table shows the number and proportion of people in these various Poll Tax categories, and the number and proportion of those people in each category who are mentioned in the Hearth Tax and who have an extant inventory. In Gwennap 14 per cent of those in the Poll Tax were in the highest category, being taxed on the basis of their yearly income or rank. Over 90 per cent of these were recorded in the Hearth Tax, and over half have an extant inventory. Only 8 per cent of the majority of Poll Tax payers in the poorest category have an extant inventory. These proportions are very similar for the other two parishes and demonstrate that inventories are more likely to have been made for those of higher status in these communities.

Because the lists of those exempt due to poverty survive for the Kent Hearth Tax, the upward bias in inventories appears greater. Matching the names of householders listed in the tax record to surviving inventories is more difficult in Kent because the Hearth Tax was not collected by parishes but by the lathes which were divided into hundreds and boroughs. Some parts of the county lay in separate jurisdictions and were not assessed, including the Cinque Ports and the liberty of Romney Marsh. While Hearth Tax returns survive for the City and County of Canterbury, they omit those exempt through poverty and are therefore out of line with the other returns and have not been used. Table 2.5 shows very clearly

Table 2.4 Poll Tax, Hearth Tax and inventories in three Cornwall parishes

Tax category	Poll Tax (1661)		Hearth Tax (1664)		Inventories (1661–1700)	
	Number	%	Number	% in Poll Tax	Number	% in Poll Tax
Gwennap						
Yearly income or rank	54	14	49	91	30	56
Husband and wife	119	31	40	34	20	17
Others (single people?)	217	56	10	5	17	8
Not found in Hearth Tax			11			
Total	390	100	110	28	67	17
Luxulyan						
Yearly income or rank	55	29	46	84	20	36
Others (single and married?)	136	71	11	8	17	13
Not found in Hearth Tax			14			
Total	191	100	71	37	37	19
Roche						
Yearly income or rank	28	16	25	89	16	57
Husband and wife	49	27	18	37	8	16
Others (single people?)	103	57	9	9	14	14
Not found in Hearth Tax			8			
Total	180	100	60	33	38	21

Table 2.5 The 1664 Hearth Tax for Kent compared with inventories (exempt households included)

No. of hearths	No. of households	% of all hearths	No. with inventories	% of all inventories
1	1,215	44.8	70	20.5
2	641	23.6	81	23.8
3	335	12.3	76	22.3
4	237	8.7	50	14.7
5	100	3.7	30	8.8
6	81	3.0	15	4.4
7	33	1.2	8	2.3
8	22	0.8	4	1.2
9	13	0.5	2	0.6
10	14	0.5	3	0.9
Over 10	23	0.8	2	0.6
Totals	2,714	100.0	341	100.0

Note
The Kent parishes listed in Appendix 1 are used, with the exception of Burmarsh, Canterbury, Ebony, Folkestone, Headcorn, Iwade, Orlestone, River, Ruckinge, Stelling, Walmer, Waltham, and Westbere.

that the distribution of surviving inventories is biased towards those with an above average number of hearths.[43] For example, whereas 45 per cent of the households assessed in the Kent parishes had only one hearth, they produced only 21 per cent of the extant inventories. At the other end of the scale, 10.5 per cent of households had five or more hearths, but this group represented 18.8 per cent of those leaving inventories. Only 2.6 per cent of Kent inventories that can be matched to the Hearth Tax are for those exempt from the tax. Overall, for the Hearth Tax in Kent, as for England as a whole, the proportion exempt on grounds of poverty was about 30 per cent.[44] Households taxed on one hearth are also under-represented by inventories; so, as a very rough estimate, perhaps the poorest 40 per cent of the population are not represented by inventories. This figure must be used with caution, since there was great regional variation in levels of poverty and in the coverage of inventories, but it suggests that the inventories used in this study exclude the richest 10 per cent and the poorest 40 per cent of the population, and therefore cover 50 per cent of the population as a whole.[45]

This covers a wider range of people than those now considered to belong to the 'middling sort' in early modern England. There is a growing literature on this group, but they are not easily captured by a simple definition. According to Kent, 'In rural areas lesser gentlemen, yeomen, and the better-off craftsmen and tradesmen can, in socio-economic terms, be lumped together and labelled "the middling sort".'[46] They have been defined more specifically in terms of their wealth, or as the 'chief inhabitants' of a provincial community.[47] Wrightson summarises the general consensus as follows:

> Unlike the gentry they had to work for a living, but unlike labouring people they did so independently. They frequently employed others, but were rarely themselves employees. In addition, most of them were able to generate a significant income by the standards of the day (at least forty pounds a year).[48]

Thus the 'middling sort' are captured by the sample of inventories for both Kent and Cornwall; but the inventories include more than just the middling sort. At one extreme they include some gentry and esquires, at the other some employees and those on the margins of poverty. It would be difficult, if not impossible, to equate the samples with some definition of the 'middling sort'. Not only do definitions vary but the most useful conceptualisations are impossible to measure within the terms of our analysis.

Households

Direct evidence is lacking about household structures in the parishes under study. For Kent, details of some 456 households are available for

1705 in listings produced under the terms of the Marriage Duty Act of 1695, but unfortunately not for the parishes in our sample.[49] Although there was variation between parishes, some 80 per cent of these households were headed by a married couple, 10 per cent by a lone male and 10 per cent by a lone female. Some 74 per cent contained children and only 5.5 per cent included resident kin (other than children). Although these households were nuclear families in terms of kin, in another sense they were 'extended' because a quarter contained servants.

To what extent do the households represented by inventories accord with this picture? It is impossible to identify inventoried households headed by a single man, but some 17 per cent of Cornish inventories are headed by a women as are some 15 per cent of those from Kent (with 15 and 10 per cent respectively of these described as single women, with the remainder widows). Thus the proportion of households headed by a women is slightly higher than for the Marriage Act listings, but this is to be expected given that inventories were made following the death of the householder. Given the social bias in inventories discussed above it is likely that the proportion of inventoried households with servants was much higher. By the early eighteenth century over 20 per cent of the Kent inventories explicitly mention the presence of servants, usually when describing chambers, but given that many appraisers did not use such specific descriptions the actual proportions of households with servants must have been much higher.[50]

Inventories were produced at death, so inventoried household heads must have been older than heads of the average household. They do not, however, give the age of the deceased, so it is impossible to relate the ages of inventoried individuals to the overall age distribution of the population. However, a study of one Kent parish, Milton, has related inventoried individuals to their stage in the life cycle as shown in Table 2.6.[51] It is remarkable that the pattern of survival of inventories accords so closely with the age distribution of the population when we should expect their distribution to be closer to the distribution of male deaths across the life-cycle stages. Thus 46 per cent of the Milton inventories referred to

Table 2.6 Life cycle stages of those leaving inventories in Milton, Kent, 1580–1711

Milton		England	
Age	*% of inventories*	*Age*	*% of population >15*
Unmarried, under 26	14.5	15–24	26.1
Married with minors, 27–47	46.2	25–44	40.3
Married with minor and adult children, 48–59	24.8	45–59	20.7
All children adult, over 60	14.5	Over 60	12.8
Total	100.0		100.0

household heads who were married with minor children, whereas nationally some 40 per cent of the population were in the age range 25–44. If Milton is in any sense representative of other communities then this finding is extremely important, for it suggests that inventories may be more representative of the population in terms of age and household structure than would be expected. For example, over 70 per cent of the Milton inventories refer to households with resident children whereas 74 per cent of the Kent households listed in the Marriage Act returns contained children.

In the majority of cases it is likely that inventories do in fact refer to households, although it has already been shown that most are not necessarily a complete record of the movable goods and chattels in the household. However, there are cases where inventories were made for individuals living in a household who enjoyed the use of household goods but did not own them. For example, John Sanders of Elmham had his inventory made in May 1681. All that was recorded were his money, apparel and three silver spoons. Henry Sanders's inventory was made in January 1685/6. A substantial yeoman, his house had at least 18 rooms and the value of his goods came to over £73.[52] The Hearth Tax record for Elmham shows that John and Henry Sanders were jointly liable for a house with five hearths in 1664.[53] If these are the same people then John was enjoying the household goods owned by Henry as his father or brother.

To take another Kentish example, Edward Stringer, gentleman of Goudhurst, had his inventory made in 1680. The value of the inventory was £2,475 15s 6d, yet most of this was accounted for by mortgages, leases, debts and hops. His personal possessions only consisted of girdles, purses and money; wearing apparel; three joined chests, some books and two holland sheets. All these were located in the 'lodging chamber'.[54] Perhaps he was a lodger in his own house, being looked after by kin, or conceivably a lodger in someone else's house. In any event his household possessions must have consisted of much more than the goods listed in his inventory. Most of these partial or incomplete households are fairly easy to identify and the strategies for using them are shown in Table 2.1.[55]

Inventories in Cornwall and Kent

During the period covered by this study Cornwall was in the Diocese of Exeter, which had nine ecclesiastical courts dealing with probate. Those having jurisdiction in Cornwall included the Principal Registry of the Bishop of Exeter, the Consistory Court of the Bishop, and the Archdeaconry Court of Cornwall. Probate records for the first two courts were destroyed in 1942, so the main source of inventories for Cornwall is that for the Archdeaconry Court housed at the Cornwall Record Office in Truro.[56] Most parishes are covered, with the exception of 30 that were peculiars of other courts. Indexes were produced of the Consistory Court wills and inventories before they were destroyed, and although the Court's jurisdiction covered most of Cornwall, very few of the remaining parishes appear in the indexes, suggesting that most Cornish people had their probate dealt with by the Archdeaconry Court.[57] The exceptions are those who owned land in more than one Archdeaconry, in this case land inside and outside the county whose probate was administered by the Consistory Court, as was that of most clergy. Those of the highest social status, or with property in more than one Consistory Court, had their probate granted by the Prerogative Court of Canterbury; no Cornish inventories survive for this court before 1660 and only three for our sample parishes thereafter.[58]

There were five ecclesiastical jurisdictions in Kent administering probate: the Archdeaconry and Consistory courts of Rochester; the exempt Deanery of Shoreham, the Consistory and Archdeaconry Courts of Canterbury, and the peculiar of Cliffe. Inventories from the Archdeaconry Court of Canterbury only have been used, because they are the only series to survive in consistent numbers for the entire period 1600–1750. The Archdeaconry courts covered well over half of the county's parishes in mid and east Kent. The surviving inventories consist of two series: Registers and Papers. The Registers, which are copies of the original inventories made at the time of probate, cover the period 1564–1638, and the Papers, which are the original inventories, cover the period after 1639, with few inventories surviving after 1750.[59] Some 47 inventories for our sample of parishes survive in the Prerogative Court of Canterbury, with 22 for the parish of Goudhurst, although they have not been used in this study.[60]

Sampling

Given the above discussion of the representativeness of inventories it is clear that a sample of inventories is not a random sample of the households in a county. It follows therefore that we cannot use inventories to make statements about production and consumption in Kent and Cornwall as a whole; rather, we are restricted to making statements about households represented by the inventories we use. To put it in more technical terms, we cannot identify a statistical population (all households in Kent and Cornwall) and then devise a sampling strategy to represent that population, but are forced to define the statistical population that we study from the sample that we have.[61] Thus, unlike a modern survey, we cannot identify the households we would like to find information about and then design a sampling strategy to obtain that information: rather, we treat the extant evidence as a sample which we then use to define the households for which we can obtain information.

Nevertheless, given the number of extant inventories in Kent and Cornwall it is still necessary to select a sample for study. Roughly four thousand were chosen for each county. The choice of this number was partly pragmatic since this is the number that one researcher can enter into a computer in the archives in one year, and the project funding provided for two person-years of data collection. Rather than take a random sample of all available inventories in the counties of Kent and Cornwall, inventories were taken from a selection of parishes chosen randomly. The advantage of this strategy is that we have a sizeable number of inventories for each parish and so have sufficient data for comparing parishes of various types.

Twenty parishes were initially selected at random, from each of which approximately 200 inventories were required. However, the small number of inventories surviving in some of these parishes meant that more were needed to create a sample of 4,000 inventories. For those parishes with fewer than 200 inventories, all the surviving inventories were used. For those that had many more than 200 inventories, it was necessary to take a random sample of the extant inventories. The sample parishes are shown in Maps 2.1 and 2.2, and the numbers of inventories for each decade in each parish in our sample are shown in Appendix 1.

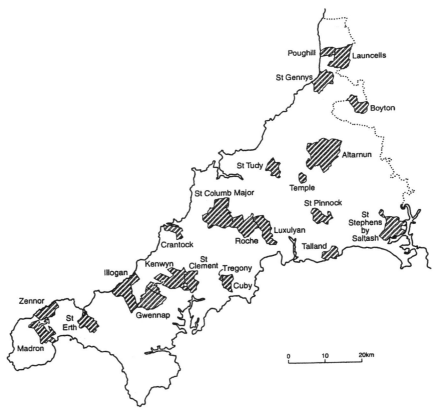

Map 2.1 The Cornwall sample parishes

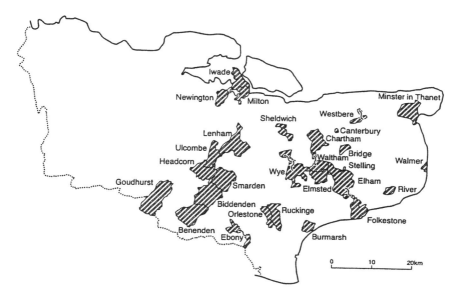

Map 2.2 The Kent sample parishes

Conclusion

It should be evident from this discussion that the sample of inventories we have from Cornwall and Kent are not in any sense fully representative of the households in the two counties. They exclude the very rich, those of very high status, most clergy, and those with property in more than one ecclesiastical court. At the other end of the scale they exclude almost all of those contemporaries regarded as 'poor' in that they were exempt from local taxes. Rather surprisingly perhaps, inventories may not be biased towards the households of the elderly, reflecting the pattern of households in society, although this conclusion is based on the findings from the inventories of a single parish and needs to be corroborated.

The discussion of the content and form of inventories reveals a depressingly long list of possible reasons why any single inventory may be misleading. We need to be aware of what, in theory, they should include, and the reasons why in practice they might not contain the goods we should expect them to. Generally speaking we do not expect to find details of clothing, 'natural produce', 'wild' animals, pets, fresh food, debts owed by the deceased and everyday objects of little value. Aside from actual fraud, appraisers might omit heirlooms, goods bequeathed in a will, goods given by a husband to his wife before his death and goods 'belonging' to his wife. Thus it would be unwise to put too much weight on any single document. How serious the problem might be depends on how an inventory is being used. The omission of some goods from an inventory has no effect on the accuracy of unit valuations (prices) for example, but would lead to an undervaluing of the movable goods of the deceased.

However, individual errors have less influence when statistics are derived from a large number of inventories; indeed, some kinds of error may cancel themselves out. This is the case in calculating unit valuations of commodities for example, since, for a collection of inventories, there is no reason to assume systematic bias either towards low valuations or to high valuations.[62] Nor is there any reason to assume systematic biases will result from transcription errors by appraisers or historians.

Generally speaking, however, there must be a tendency for statistics to be underestimates. Things might have been present but explicitly omitted by the appraisers' use of language, in which case we can at least say that although a particular item is not necessarily present it might nevertheless be present. In other cases we might be oblivious to the omission. If the inventory arouses suspicion then tagging it as such, using the categories in Table 2.1, can prevent erroneous inferences being drawn. Above all, we can only use inventories in a positive way. If an item is mentioned we can be almost certain that it was there; if an item is not mentioned it may still have been present in the household.

3   Household production

For the majority of the population in early modern England the household was the locus of production: 'going to work' meant staying at home. The majority of households were engaged in farming activity of some sort, which took place around the home, and most manufacturing and craft activities also took place in the home or in workshops attached to the home. There were exceptions, such as building, ship construction, mining and quarrying, for example, when labourers would leave their homes to work. But even in these cases the house was still the site of production of commodities for use within the household. This chapter investigates household production from the perspective of the material goods recorded in inventories. It identifies the main production activities in the two counties, their development over time, and scale of operation. We shall be making a distinction between commercial production activity for exchange, and production activity that is for the use of the household and not for exchange. If the model of an 'industrious revolution' is applicable to Cornwall and Kent, then we expect to see a fall in production for use as households increasingly purchase goods from the market and an increase in the specialisation of production for exchange.

Household form and structure varied considerably over the life cycle, with work requirements, and with levels of wealth, reflecting amongst other things the circulation of servant labour and the propensity of kin to rely upon family networks of support. For the purpose of this study all inventoried individuals are regarded as being head of a household production unit regardless of their status. Thus, where a separate inventory exists, lodgers, servants and the elderly living in with their adult children are considered as households in their own right for the analysis of production, although in reality they were components of the wider household within which they resided and are viewed as such when looking at consumption. There is some difficulty involved in such a definition in that all those residing in a particular dwelling have contributed materially to the production and consumption of that household unit, and therefore the production profile drawn from the inventory would reflect the presence of servant labour or an extended family structure. However, so long as a distinction is made between these different forms of household in recognition of the fact that one is a component of the other, then significant information about the specialisation of production within the household can be drawn from these part-households.

Identifying production activity

A variety of sources are available to identify occupations in early modern England.[1] Most are lists of some sort, such as the militia lists or indexes to wills, which describe the occupation or status of named individuals. There are three serious problems with using such sources to describe occupations. The first is that status descriptions, such as 'esquire', 'gentleman', and 'yeoman' cannot be mapped onto occupations. Roughly 90 per cent of our sample of yeomen in Cornwall and Kent had evidence of agricultural activity, but only 74 per cent of gentlemen in Cornwall and 63 per cent in Kent.[2] The second is the prevalence of by-employment. The majority of individuals in early modern England had more than one occupation, yet in the vast majority of cases they are assigned a single occupation or title in the listings.[3] Thus, for example, in his study using occupational designations in wills, Patten is able to show the spread of industries in the countryside in Norfolk and Suffolk, but not their association with farming, or indeed their association with each other.[4] The third problem is that most sources only give a description of the male head of household's status or occupation, hiding the work activities of women, children and servants.

The appraisers gave the deceased's occupation or status in the heading in just over half the inventories used in this study. The occupation recorded was the one that they considered to be the most important if the individual was engaged in more than one activity, and consequently often differed from that stated by the decedent in his or her will. Although they are subject to the three problems mentioned in the previous paragraph, these occupational designations prove useful in revealing production activities such as butchering and tailoring which are otherwise hard to identify due to their lack of specialised tools and equipment.

The more important means of identifying production activities is from goods listed in the inventories. Most of the documents record production goods in significant detail, including crops, livestock, tools and equipment. Production information can also be drawn from room descriptions, particularly in Kent where houses were generally larger and described in greater detail. For instance, many had rooms described as dairies, brewhouses or malt houses. Using information from the body of the inventory in this way has the advantage of capturing the diversity of production within the household. In particular, it picks up evidence of female employment such as dairying and spinning in men's inventories.

However, the utility of inventory data for the identification of production activities is dependent on a good level of description within the document and the existence of relatively valuable specialist production equipment. Some occupations may be under-recorded as they require few specialist tools. For instance, a tailor needed only a pair of shears or scissors, a smoothing iron, cloth, needle and thread. Richard Gewen of Boyton, for example, was described in his inventory as a bachelor, yet it is likely that he was a tailor for he had a piece of new cloth valued at ten shillings although his scissors were only worth twopence.[5] Most of these goods are, however, not specific to tailoring and thus difficult to use as identifiers of the activity. In such cases combinations of items can often be used to determine the type of production taking place. For instance, the presence of both wool and yarn is indicative of spinning, and both shears and a smoothing iron of tailoring.

The scale of production is of central importance as it can often be indicative of fundamentally different enterprises and is one factor in determining whether production was for use or for exchange. However, the relationship between scale and specialisation is not a simple one. Not all large-scale operations need necessarily have been commercial, and it was possible to specialise in a particular production activity yet work on a small scale. For example, a tippler or alehouse keeper could make a living from brewing using only the most basic equipment due to the high turnover of stock. Many gentry families, on the other hand, kept a well-equipped brew-house and produced large quantities of beer, yet served only their own household and estate employees.

The scale of production can be deduced from examination of the specialist production equipment listed in the inventory. A combination of the type of goods, their quantity and value is usually sufficient to determine the level of production. For example, the scale of agricultural activity can be ascertained from the acreage of crops, volume of stored grain or fodder and quantity of livestock. Other activities where scale can readily be identified include milling, malting, tanning and fish processing. Where the scale of operation alone is not sufficient to determine whether production was commercially orientated a more complex procedure is used to distinguish between producers. In the case of brewing, certain common characteristics of commercial brewers have been identified which are applicable both to Kent and Cornwall. Analysis of the inventories showed that commercial brewers tended to be based in urban centres and to have some specialist brewing vessels or equipment. Beer stocks made up a significant element of their inventoried value, and generally they had few agricultural goods. Such checklists are open to interpretation, but they allow more accurate categorisation of some production activities than can be achieved by a simple measure of scale.

A major problem in identifying production activities from the contents of inventories is the tendency for the level of detail recorded in the documents to decline over time. This is of particular concern in Cornwall where inventories become noticeably briefer after 1660. Thus we adopt the strategy of identifying potential production activities, which may be inferred in the absence of detailed descriptions, as well as production based on specific positive evidence. For example, Cornish households frequently had vessels such as vats, tubs and keeves which could be put to a number of uses in dairying, brewing and food preservation. While we cannot use them to make a positive identification, we can say that potentially these households had the physical capacity to undertake these activities. Their counterparts in Kent, on the other hand, often had an adjective attached to the noun, so brewing keeves, butter churns and powdering tubs are recorded, enabling the positive identification of the production activity. The differences between the two counties indicate a contrast in the level of technology and extent of functional specialisation, but do not necessarily suggest that these activities were less prevalent in Cornwall.

Each inventory can show that a production activity is present (or rather that the material objects needed for that activity were present), apparently absent, or possibly present. The positive figures measure the number of inventories where an activity can definitely be identified, whereas the potential ones indicate where it might possibly be taking place. Such dual indices have been applied to those production activities particularly prone to under-recording – namely brewing, malting, baking, cider making, food preservation and spinning. These all involved the use of common or low-valued goods, which were the most likely to be hidden where there was insufficient detail in the inventory. Spinning is included because of the tendency for wool and yarn to appear in inventories where there was no spinning wheel. Spinning could have been carried out with a distaff, since these were of negligible value and therefore unlikely to be documented, or it is possible that a wheel used by the household was in fact owned by a clothier. This last example illustrates the difficulties that arise when the producer is separated from the means of production. This is particularly significant when analysing waged work, which cannot be positively identified unless wages owing are recorded or the decedent is described as a wage earner in the document. Labourers are thus likely to be under-recorded, and some of those seemingly without any production activities were perhaps in reality wage labourers.

Production activities

Table 3.1 shows production activity identified in Cornwall and Kent for the whole period 1600–1749 using categories of activity defined in Appendix 2, indicating both the variety of activities and the relative importance of each in the two counties. Farming was the most common activity, with evidence in over 65 per cent of households. Textile production, especially spinning, was the second most common, followed by mining, which was

Table 3.1 Production activities 1600–1749 (percentages)

	Cornwall		Kent	
	Positive	*Potential*	*Positive*	*Potential*
Farming	68.9	68.9	65.3	65.3
Textiles	21.4	21.4	44.0	44.0
Preparation	4.2	4.2	13.1	13.1
Spinning	12.1	19.1	36.8	39.7
Weaving	2.3	2.3	3.7	3.7
Dyeing	0.8	0.8	1.8	1.8
Finishing	0.9	0.9	1.3	1.3
Leather production	1.4	1.4	1.4	1.4
Metalworking	2.4	2.4	2.2	2.2
Woodworking	4.2	4.2	4.7	4.7
Carpentry	3.4	3.4	3.5	3.5
Coopers' work	0.6	0.6	0.7	0.7
Wheelwrights' work	0.3	0.3	0.5	0.5
Building	0.9	0.9	1.5	1.5
Glazing	0.2	0.2	0.2	0.2
Tile and brick making	0.6	0.6	0.6	0.6
Thatching	0.1	0.1	0.2	0.2
Clothing	3.0	3.0	3.1	3.1
Tailoring	1.4	1.4	1.0	1.0
Shoemaking	1.5	1.5	1.6	1.6
Glove making	0.1	0.1	0.4	0.4
Miscellaneous crafts	2.1	2.1	0.9	0.9
Luxury crafts	0.1	0.1	0.2	0.2
Butchering	1.0	1.0	1.5	1.5
Maritime	3.7	3.7	4.3	4.3
Fishing	2.1	2.1	2.9	2.9
Tin mining	9.5	9.5	0.0	0.0
Retailing	3.3	3.3	4.5	4.5
Personal services	1.4	1.4	2.0	2.0
Waged work	1.4	1.4	2.0	2.0
Labourers/servants	1.0	1.0	1.2	1.2
Naval/military	0.4	0.4	0.2	0.2
Dairying	48.4	48.4	59.2	59.2
Butter making	11.6	47.5	41.3	49.2
Cheese making	16.4	48.0	32.1	42.1
Milling	3.2	3.2	17.1	17.1
Large-scale milling	1.3	1.3	1.8	1.8
Small-scale milling	2.3	2.3	15.9	15.9
Malt milling	0.3	0.3	5.0	5.4
Baking	1.8	2.2	37.5	37.5
Malting	1.2	1.7	10.7	14.0
Brewing	11.9	39.6	43.8	56.4
Distilling	1.5	1.5	7.5	7.5
Cider making	1.8	4.0	0.9	4.6
Food preservation	17.0	43.3	47.5	64.2
Fish preservation	2.5	2.5	0.8	3.0

evident in 9.5 per cent of Cornish households. A somewhat larger proportion of the inventoried population in Kent were engaged in maritime occupations compared with Cornwall: 4.3 per cent compared with 3.7 per cent. This is perhaps associated with the expansion of coasting traffic along the Thames estuary.[6] However, it is also likely that the Cornish figures significantly underestimate the true level of maritime activity in the county, since the selected parishes do not include any of the major emerging fishing centres such as Paul and Mevagissey, and also miss most of the thriving ports, which were concentrated in the south-east of the county in the early seventeenth century and around Falmouth Haven during the latter part of the study period.[7] Retailing and service provision were also more common in Kent, reflecting higher levels of consumption. For example, imported groceries such as tea, sugar and tobacco were more widely consumed than in Cornwall, and provision of these commodities would have supported an extensive network of retail outlets.[8] Kent also had more builders, reflecting the growing fashion for brick-built houses. Additionally there were more Kentish households engaged in woodworking, indicative of the shortage of timber in Cornwall and the higher level of construction in Kent.[9] Amongst the remaining commercial production activities there is a remarkable similarity between the figures for the two counties.

Most forms of production for use can be identified within a far greater proportion of inventories in Kent than they can in Cornwall. Brewing, cheese and butter making and food preservation were all potentially present in over 40 per cent of Kentish inventoried households. In Cornwall the figures were lower, and considerably lower when comparing the positive production percentages. For instance, while there was clear evidence of butter making in 41 per cent of Kent inventories, this was the case for only 12 per cent in Cornwall, although the potential figure was higher at 48 per cent. Nevertheless, brewing, dairying and food preservation were, after farming, the most commonly found activities in both counties, suggesting that they were essential elements of the domestic economy within most seventeenth- and early eighteenth-century households.

Specialist craft and industrial activities were usually undertaken by men and did not involve production for household use. With the exception of mining in Cornwall, none of these involved more than 5 per cent of the inventoried population. All those activities found in more than 15 per cent of households, with the exception of spinning, involved the production and processing of food and drink, and could be either for home use or for sale. These were seen as female tasks in early modern England. However, when undertaken on a large scale for commercial purposes, food and drink processing became a male or mixed occupation. Similarly, farming, although perceived in early modern England as a male responsibility, in fact involved the labour of men and women. This indicates some of the difficulties in summarising and classifying household production

Table 3.2 Inventories with evidence of production for exchange (percentages)

		1600–29	1630–59	1660–89	1690–1719	1720–49
Total inventories (n)	Cornwall	837	517	1,122	964	635
	Kent	1,142	739	1,131	664	250
All commercial	Cornwall	78	75	68	70	75
	Kent	64	66	74	81	85
Commercial agriculture	Cornwall	64	63	50	48	49
	Kent	47	47	54	55	49
Textiles	Cornwall	45	33	15	9	10
	Kent	51	50	37	41	33
Crafts	Cornwall	19	15	14	14	17
	Kent	17	18	18	22	19
Commercial food	Cornwall	21	17	12	12	17
	Kent	29	30	30	39	34
Maritime	Cornwall	5	3	4	3	4
	Kent	3	3	3	6	12
Mining	Cornwall	6	5	9	12	14
Retail/provisioning	Cornwall	1	3	4	4	4
	Kent	2	2	6	7	10
Services	Cornwall	1	0	1	1	1
	Kent	2	2	2	2	2

activities. The gender division of labour and the commercial orientation of production are of central importance. The typical household had a diversified production profile, not necessarily because the male household head was engaged in more than one commercial activity but, to a large extent, because households normally contained at least two active workers: a man and a woman. These ideas about by-employment and the gender division of labour will be examined further in the next chapter.

The major categories of commercial production, or production for exchange, are defined in Appendix 2 and are shown in Table 3.2 for five 30-year periods.[10] The contrast between the two counties is quite clear. In Cornwall the only activity to show a substantial increase is mining; both agriculture and textiles appear to be in decline. In Kent all commercial activities, with the exception of textiles, increase, and there are significant increases in both commercial food processing, retailing and maritime. These activities are discussed in the following sections.

Agriculture

Farming in Kent has always been extremely varied in character, primarily because of the very wide range of soils and variations in situation, but also on account of the multifarious demands of the London market. The extensive areas of poor soils in the Weald, and also on the dip slope of the North Downs, made the county one of the most heavily wooded in England. Other tracts of infertile soils created heaths and commons. As Mingay has pointed out, such a large proportion of the county was taken up by hilly woodland, windswept commons, bleak downland and desolate marshes that Kent, taken as a whole, hardly merited its celebrated description as 'the garden of England'.[11] The Kent parishes used in this study cover all the major farming regions of the county.[12] By contrast there is less variation in the farming regions of Cornwall, and the land was generally of poorer quality; as a contemporary put it, 'more inclined to sterility than fertility'.[13] Once again our sample of parishes provides an adequate representation of the major farming regions.

Inventories have long been used to study agriculture in early modern England, providing census-like data on the frequencies, quantities and values of both livestock and crops.[14] We start our analysis, however, by using inventories in a rather different way to give an indication of the scale of agricultural activity and the likely amount of land that a household had available. Table 3.3 divides agricultural activity into four categories in terms of access to land and likely degree of commercialisation, rather than by the characteristics of different agrarian regimes. The evidence suggests that overall involvement in agriculture remained fairly stable in Kent with agricultural activity present in around 65 per cent of inventories. In Cornwall there was a steady decline in the proportion of

Table 3.3 Percentages of inventories in four agricultural categories

		1600–29	1630–59	1660–89	1690–1719	1720–49
Group 1 Poultry, and/or bees, and/or 1–2 pigs	Cornwall	6	3	5	2	2
	Kent	5	4	3	4	3
Group 2 3–10 pigs, and/or 1–10 sheep, and/or 1–2 cattle, but no arable crops	Cornwall	10	11	10	13	14
	Kent	14	10	9	11	5
Group 3 >10 pigs, and/or >10 sheep, and/or >2 cattle, but no arable crops	Cornwall	10	9	7	8	10
	Kent	6	7	8	7	5
Group 4 Arable crops, and/or arable farming equipment	Cornwall	54	54	42	40	39
	Kent	40	40	46	48	44
All groups	Cornwall	80	77	64	63	65
	Kent	65	61	66	70	57

the inventoried population in farming: from some 80 per cent in the early seventeenth century to 63 per cent in the early eighteenth century.

Those allocated to the first category in Table 3.3 (Group 1) could be classed as cottagers. The main criteria used was that they should have no access to land other than a garden, and no common grazing rights. Thus their inventories must contain no evidence of arable production, and the livestock they possessed was restricted to bees, poultry and one or two pigs. Less than 6 per cent of inventories fell into this category in either county, and in both cases the trend was for the number of cottagers to decline over time. Group 2 consists of smallholders with access to grazing, perhaps on common land, but again no involvement in arable farming. Households fell into this category if they had between three and ten pigs, a small flock of sheep, or one or two cattle. In this case the trends for the two counties contrast sharply. In Kent the proportion in this category falls from 14 per cent in the first three decades of the seventeenth century to 5 per cent in the three decades 1720–49. On the other hand, the number of Cornish households covered by the smallholding category increased steadily from around 10 per cent in the early seventeenth century to more than 14 per cent at the close of the period.

The third category is large-scale pastoral farming. Unlike the previous two groups the scale of activity suggests farming on a commercial scale but without any evidence of arable farming. Commercial pastoral farming was not common in either county, although it appears to have been more prevalent in Cornwall. Here around 10 per cent of inventoried households were involved in the early seventeenth century; the figures then dip to fewer than 7 per cent during the 1660–89 period and only recover to their former level in the 1720s. In contrast, pastoral farming in Kent seems to have peaked in the latter part of the seventeenth century at around 7 per cent before falling back to 4–5 per cent by the end of the period. The final category, arable farming, is the most broad-ranging and, as a consequence, the most common in both counties. It includes all those households where there is evidence of some arable production, meaning that the household owned or rented land for cultivation. Overall evidence of arable farming was found in a slightly larger proportion of inventories in Kent, and here there was a gentle upward trend in the level of involvement from 40 per cent in 1600–29 to 44 per cent by 1720–49. Conversely, in Cornwall the trend was downwards from 54 per cent to only 39 per cent by the close of the period.

This decline in agricultural activity in Cornwall contradicts Whetter's characterisation of the Cornish agrarian economy during the seventeenth century as 'stable and regular'.[15] However, the geography of decline was not uniform. There was little or no change in the extent of commercial agriculture in the eastern parishes of Poughill, Launcells, St Gennys and Boyton for example, whereas there was significant decline in most western parishes. In the mining parish of Gwennap the proportion of inventories in the commercial farming groups fell from 74 per cent in 1600–49 to 36 per cent in 1700–49, and in neighbouring Kenwyn from 55 per cent to 34 per cent, although the greatest fall was in Madron (67 per cent to 25 per cent). There is supporting evidence for a decline in arable husbandry from other studies, which have identified a gradual withdrawal from the cultivation of crops on small and middling farms during the late seventeenth century and the early eighteenth in west Cornwall.[16] Husbandmen in the west of the county came increasingly to focus upon the raising of cattle or extended their interests in the non-agrarian sector. Where the household's livestock holdings were small such an abandonment of arable farming might lead to reclassification into the smallholding category. This partially explains the growth of smallholding, which runs parallel with the decline in arable agriculture. In Gwennap the proportion of inventories in Group 2 rose from 13 to 25 per cent and in Kenwyn from 13 to 26 per cent. These trends can be explained in terms of the major changes taking place in the economy of Cornwall as a whole. The 1660–1750 period was one of considerable population growth, mostly in west Cornwall, associated with the expansion of tin mining, which led to a reduction in the average size of holdings, while at the same time providing new opportunities outside agriculture.[17] There was also a growth of corn imports to the county during the early eighteenth century, although the volume varied considerably from year to year depending on the size of the harvest.[18] In such circumstances switching to pastoral farming or non-agrarian activities had significant implications for the wealth and prosperity of the farming sector.

In contrast to the declining involvement in commercial agricultural activity in Cornwall, in Kent the aggregate picture shows a rise in commercial mixed agriculture at the expense of small-scale livestock farming in Groups 1 and 2. In 1818 William Marshall declared that 'Kent, more than any other county, I think, of equal extent, naturally separates into well-defined districts', and indeed in Kent there was a good deal of regional specialisation.[19] Thus examining the economic groups involved in agriculture on a parish by parish basis reveals sharper trends. Although a few parishes show little change in the proportion of inventories with commercial mixed farming, in some the rise is quite dramatic. In the majority of cases this rise was associated with a decline in the proportion of inventories in Group 2, suggesting perhaps that access to land for grazing livestock was being restricted. This could be because common rights were removed or smallholders were losing grazing land, but this is impossible to tell from the inventories alone. The population of Kent ceased to rise markedly after 1620 and competition for tenancies remained minimal in the 1680s, indicating an absence of pressure on land which could have encouraged engrossment associated with the continuing commercialisation of agriculture.[20] The most dramatic change in the balance of the various agricultural groups came in the parish of Burmarsh in Romney

Marsh. Here, the proportion of farmers in Group 4 rose from zero to 22 per cent of inventories between 1600–49 and 1700–49. In contrast, commercial farmers without arable crops declined from 66 to 22 per cent, so that overall the proportion of commercial farmers declined from 61 to 44 per cent. Those in Group 2, with access to land to keep stock on a small scale but with no evidence of growing crops, decline from 33 per cent of inventories to zero, while those in group one, cottagers with no access to land, increase from zero to 33 per cent. The sample of 46 inventories for this parish is rather small, but the pattern of development suggests the growth of larger farms, involving some arable, and a reduction in access to land by others: a pattern confirmed in a recent analysis of landholding change in Romney Marsh.[21]

Apart from this analysis of access to land, our examination of farming in Kent and Cornwall largely confirms the broad conclusions of other studies, particularly the descriptions of agricultural practice in the *Cambridge Agrarian Histories*.[22] Table 3.4 shows the changes in arable husbandry in the two counties. Hemp and flax have been excluded from the analysis of crops, and this has a significant impact upon the Kent figures, accentuating the impression of an expansion of arable farming. Only inventories made in the summer months of June and July are used for the analysis of cropping so the available number is rather small.[23] The different scale of farming in the two counties (at least as represented by inventories) is evidenced by the difference in the mean cropped acreage per farm. In Kent the cropped acreage rose from 27 in 1600–29 to 52 in 1720–49, but in Cornwall only from 6 to 13 acres.[24] The main feature of arable development in Kent was

Table 3.4 Arable farming

		1600–29	1630–59	1660–89	1690–1719	1720–49
Adjusted cropped acreage (mean per farm)	Cornwall	6	9	7	7	13
	Kent	27	23	35	35	52
Cereals as % of cereals and fodder	Cornwall	100	85	79	100	54
	Kent	66	68	69	74	53
Commercial farmers with clover (%)	Cornwall	0	0	0	0	0
	Kent	0	0	4	11	24
Wheat as % of cereals	Cornwall	35	36	48	41	43
	Kent	45	50	35	32	60
Rye as % of cereals	Cornwall	3	1	3	0	0
	Kent	1	0	0	0	0
Barley as % of cereals	Cornwall	15	14	32	26	42
	Kent	37	35	46	44	33
Oats as % of cereals	Cornwall	46	50	16	34	15
	Kent	18	15	18	24	7

the extension of barley cultivation at the expense of wheat in the period 1660–1719, especially on the downlands and Chartlands. The widespread growth of barley in the north was associated with the expansion of brewing and the huge demand for malt in London: 19,090 quarters were exported to the capital in 1638.[25] However, by the mid-seventeenth century there is some evidence of a reversal of this trend; wheat was replacing barley as the principal crop, associated with the cultivation of clover. There was also a considerable increase in the proportion of the cereal acreage under barley in Cornwall, although here at the expense of oats.

Increased specialisation is one indicator of increased commercialisation in farming activity.[26] It is also evident in Kent from the incorporation of grass substitutes such as clover and sainfoin into arable rotations.[27] In 1723 Lewis noted that on the Isle of Thanet sainfoin had first been grown about fifty years before and was now widespread on the poorer chalk soils, while clover and trefoil were used on the better croplands.[28] Sainfoin is first mentioned in our sample of inventories at Bridge in 1662, and clover at Goudhurst in the same year. By the period 1720–49 almost a quarter of commercial farmers were growing clover.[29] In Cornwall, clover and sainfoin do not appear in our sample of inventories, although Colepress spoke of their use, and there is evidence that clover seed was being imported into a number of Cornish ports as early as 1687–8.[30] Even so, the milder climate and extended grass-growing season of Cornwall meant that there was less incentive to cultivate grass substitutes than in the colder east. The only innovation to feature in Cornish inventories is indicative of the differing status of agriculture in the two counties: potatoes first appear in 1727 although there are only five mentions of the crop before 1749, suggesting the main period of their introduction lay in the second half of the eighteenth century since they were very prevalent in the west of Cornwall by 1801.[31] Unlike clover, which is indicative of an improved commercialised agriculture, potatoes suggest the necessity to find new types of food because of a shortage of conventional supplies.

Changes in the scale of farming activity are also indicated through herd sizes. The average size of Cornish cattle herds fell from 11 in 1600–49 to nine in 1700–49, while those in Kent grew from seven to ten animals. This reflected an increase in the number of dairy cattle on our Kentish farms and a decline in Cornwall, while the proportion of inventoried households with store cattle also rose in Kent from 13 per cent before the Civil War to 21 per cent in the latter half of the seventeenth century. At the same time the mean number of steers and bullocks found in herds increased from 5.5 to 8.7. There was also a somewhat smaller increase in the size of Cornish beef herds, but the number of households keeping beef cattle here actually fell. It appears that the beef industry in the county was held back by continued shortage of winter feed, and the area increasingly specialised in rearing young animals which were then fattened in Somerset and East Devon.[32]

Sheep were an important element of Kentish agriculture. Flocks were folded on fallow land and grazed the downland and Wealden pastures considered unsuitable for cattle. Over the course of the period 1600 to 1750 the proportion of households with sheep remained relatively stable at around 40 per cent, but the mean size of flocks increased from 43 to 50. Most of this growth was in the marshland region, which was the chief sheep-grazing area of the county. Between 1600 and 1620 flocks here were treble the size of those elsewhere in the county, and by the last two decades of the century they were five times bigger, containing on average 376 animals.[33] In Cornwall flocks were generally small, and seem to have declined over the course of the seventeenth century to a mean of only 25, before recovering to 37 in the period after 1700. Additionally, fewer farmers were keeping sheep: 53 per cent of inventoried households did so at the beginning of the period, but only 35 per cent in the early eighteenth century. It seems that, over the period, smaller farmers were tending to abandon sheep raising, which increasingly became the preserve of larger farm enterprises.[34]

The trends for the keeping of pigs show the familiar pattern of decline in Cornwall and expansion in Kent. Pigs appear to have been more numerous in Kent from an early period, with the Weald providing particularly good swine pasture from Saxon times.[35] In the north, the increasing supplies of brewers' grains also helped sustain a relatively high level of urban pig-keeping by the early eighteenth century. During the period 1600–49 over 57 per cent of Cornish farmers raised swine, but a hundred years later this had fallen to only 38 per cent. Pigs appear to have been kept more for home consumption here since few households had more than half a dozen.

A conspicuous innovation in Kent was hop cultivation. As Table 3.5 shows, hops were mentioned in under 5 per cent of inventories in the first half of the seventeenth century, but were found in 19 per cent of households a century later.[36] Hop cultivation required considerable investment and was to be found in both large- and small-scale enterprises. By 1700 some 3,000 acres of hops were cultivated in the county, many of which were part-time projects of farmers and others. Indeed 30 per cent of those growing hops had no other growing crops in their inventory.[37] Hop

Table 3.5 Hops, hemp and flax in Kent

	% inventories growing (May–July)			% inventories mentioning (all months)		
	Hops	*Hemp*	*Flax*	*Hops*	*Hemp*	*Flax*
1600–49	0.9	11.1	0.2	4.7	21.9	1.8
1650–99	6.1	2.4	1.1	9.1	12.8	4.3
1700–49	15.0	5.0	2.1	18.6	8.3	5.1

cultivation represents a diversification of production rather than special-isation, since it was often added to an existing enterprise, and most of this 30 per cent had another commercial activity or were described as 'gentle-men', corroborating Baker's view that 'townsmen and tradesmen' also became hop growers.[38] Thus while Kent became an area specialising in hop production (with a third of the English acreage for 1723–31), growers were not specialising in hops to the exclusion of other agricultural or commercial activities. Hops were found in parishes throughout the county, but there were particular concentrations in the high weald parishes of Goudhurst and Benenden, and also in the chalkland parishes of Newington, Bridge and Lenham. Hop cultivation was not particularly related to the natural environment, and the distinctive nineteenth-century pattern of production had not yet emerged.[39]

While hop growing increased, the cultivation of hemp declined in the county as a whole. This was another example of a commercial, small-scale production activity, since one-third of inventories mentioning growing hemp during the months of May, June and July had no other growing crops. Hemp was an ideal crop for the poor because its cultivation was labour intensive, it brought a cash income and could be grown 'in small crofts on peasant holdings.'[40] In the early decades of the seventeenth century over 20 per cent of inventoried households in Kent listed hemp amongst their possessions, although only 8 per cent did so by the 1700s. Decline was not uniform throughout the county: in the first half of the eighteenth century over 50 per cent of inventories in the parish of Elmsted mention the crop, and hemp was still being grown in some quan-tity in the adjacent parishes of Stelling and Waltham. The other industrial crop found in Kent inventories is flax. Although there was an increase in cultivation it was still uncommon, with only 5 per cent of inventories including it in the early eighteenth century. But again there were signific-ant regional variations, with two parishes, Biddenden and Smarden, having the crop mentioned in 20 per cent of inventories.

Hops appear in Cornish inventories and may possibly have been grown in the county, but we have no conclusive evidence that they were, since there are no instances in our sample of them being recorded as growing. About 5 per cent of inventories mention hemp in the first half of the sev-enteenth century but this figure declines to under 1 per cent a century later, and under 1 per cent of inventories mention flax throughout the period under study.

The general picture of agricultural development in Kent and Cornwall that emerges is quite clear. In Kent farm sizes were increasing, farms were becoming more specialised, new crops were being grown and agriculture was becoming more commercialised. Farmers were becoming more wealthy, innovative and market orientated. In Cornwall, from all the per-spectives offered by inventories, agriculture appears to decline in import-ance and the majority of farmers remained subsistence producers with small mixed farms. By the 1760s Borlase was noting that whereas corn had been exported periodically from west Cornwall during the seventeenth century, the area could now no longer supply its own needs.[41] The contrasting fortunes of agriculture in the two counties is reflected in the trend of cereal yields. In Kent wheat yields showed steady, but unspectacular growth from around 14 bushels per acre in the early seventeenth century to around 18 bushels per acre in the early eighteenth century. Barley yields also rose, but to a lesser extent, from around 18 to 20 bushels over the same period. In Cornwall there are too few inventories to have much confidence in yield estimates, but it is likely that average wheat yields in the first half of the seventeenth century were roughly the same as the average yield in Kent. Thereafter, however, wheat yields in Cornwall overall may have fallen.[42]

Textiles

Although the Cornish textile industry has never been considered to be of much importance (especially in comparison with Devon), over 45 per cent of our Cornish inventories for the 1600–29 period contain evidence of textile production of some sort; while the majority of the activity was spinning, the proportion of weavers was only slightly below that of Kent as Table 3.6 shows. Traditionally Cornwall produced coarse kersey cloth for local markets. Carding and spinning were extensively practised, especially in the centre and east, with most of the yarn being bought up by Devon clothiers. This relatively even distribution of textile activity across the county ended with the replacement of woollen cloth by worsted cloth production during the latter part of the seventeenth century. Worsted cloths such as serge required a different organisation of the production process, leading to the emergence of a number of clothiers whose activities encouraged a concentration of the trade in a central band from Truro to Liskeard.[43] Production, however, remained on a small scale, with many of

Table 3.6 Percentages of inventories indicating textile production

		1600–29	1630–59	1660–89	1690–1719	1720–49
Textiles	Cornwall	45	33	15	9	10
	Kent	51	50	37	41	33
Weaving	Cornwall	4	2	2	2	1
	Kent	5	4	4	3	1
Spinning	Cornwall	34	21	6	3	4
	Kent	43	44	30	33	27
Potential spinning	Cornwall	42	31	12	7	9
	Kent	46	47	33	37	30

the clothiers also being involved in weaving, dyeing or fulling. East Cornwall turned to yarn manufacture, supplying the expanding Devon serge industry, and over time spinning became more concentrated into certain, mainly urban parishes such as Liskeard, Callington and Bodmin.[44] At the beginning of the eighteenth century these yarn-producing areas suffered as a result of competition from cheap Irish imports, but there continued to be a sizeable spinning industry in east Cornwall in 1750.[45] Even so, the proportion of inventories indicating textile production fell to some 10 per cent by the mid-eighteenth century.

In the sixteenth century the Kent cloth industry was concentrated in the Weald and adjacent areas: this includes our sample parishes of Biddenden, Benenden and Goudhurst making broadcloths; Lenham and Ulcombe making kerseys; and Headcorn and Smarden making both broadcloths and kerseys.[46] The Wealden cloth industry was organised on an elaborate putting-out system, employing many thousands of spinners and hundreds of specialist craftsmen at the start of our period.[47] During the first half of the seventeenth century the Weald was affected by a series of depressions which hit the English woollen cloth industry, mainly brought about by the disruption of foreign markets, government policy, foreign competition and the English Civil War. Although its cloth manufacture survived until the early eighteenth century, output gradually fell. The decline of the textile industry in the Weald is well known, although the rate of decline in Cornwall is greater than for Kent according to our samples of inventories.[48]

The reduction in activity is most evident in spinning; in Cornwall the proportion of inventories with specific equipment for spinning fell from a third in the early seventeenth century to 4 per cent by 1720–49. There is no obvious pattern to the decline, and from the inventories at least no obvious reason why some parishes continued to have households where spinning took place while others did not. During the first half of the seventeenth century, for example, the neighbouring eastern parishes of Poughill and Launcells had about 20 per cent of their households with spinning wheels or turns; a century later there were none in Poughill but 11 per cent in Launcells. There were significant decreases in the number of looms in St Stephens, Launcells and Cuby, and also in the west in the parish of Zennor, presumably reflecting the disappearance of the local 'penwit' cloth.[49] Despite the general picture of decline, some parishes, such as St Pinnock and St Columb Major actually saw an increase in the proportion of inventories mentioning looms. In Kent, despite the well-documented collapse of the textile industry, some parishes, including Goudhurst, Stelling and Waltham, showed an increase in the proportion of inventories with looms, although the number of inventories involved is small. The decline in spinning also showed no obvious pattern: the most dramatic change was in the parish of Burmarsh where spinning disappeared completely.

In Cornwall there was an increase in the number of weaver-clothiers; that is, men who played an organisational role in the textile industry as well as weaving. For example, William Bone, who died in 1684, had a pair of looms, plus cloth, wool and yarn valued at £20 out of a total inventoried wealth of only £31. Some 40 per cent of weavers fell into this category by the first half of the seventeenth century. In Kent, on the other hand, less than 20 per cent of clothiers were involved in weaving, and these were mainly kersey makers working in parishes such as Smarden which were peripheral to the main textile-producing belt. Most weavers in Cornwall appear to have owned only one loom, with only 25 per cent having two and 3.3 per cent more than this, whereas in Kent individuals with two or more looms were relatively commonplace.[50] Moreover, the types of looms used in the two counties differed significantly. Cornwall produced mainly kerseys during the early seventeenth century and these required only a narrow loom. From around 1670 production shifted in favour of serge, a woollen and worsted cloth of better quality than kersey; its similar width meant that it could also be produced on a narrow loom.[51] The staple product of the Weald, however, was high-quality broadcloth, woven on a broad loom, although kersey making was common in a band of parishes such as Smarden and Egerton to the north of the main broadcloth area.[52] Whereas a narrow loom could be operated by a single man, the broad loom weaver had to employ an assistant to catch the shuttle at the end of a line and return it to him.[53] Thus a Kentish weaver with two looms probably employed three apprentices or journeymen, indicating a scale of operation which differed significantly from the independent craftsman working alone. Indeed the proportion of weavers with three or more looms appears to have increased over time, particularly in Kent, where 37 per cent fall into this category by the beginning of the eighteenth century.

These changes reflected the diversification of the textile sector in Kent which was taking place over the course of the seventeenth century. Depression in the broadcloth industry encouraged a switch to new drapery, worsted and linen manufacture, aided by the massive influx of Protestant refugees to the county.[54] These new industries lacked the complex organisational structure which had evolved in the woollen trade, and were no longer restricted to the narrow geographical confines of the central Weald but could be found spread throughout Kent. Silk weaving was concentrated in Canterbury, while worsted and linen production was notable in the area around Sandwich. In the period after 1660 the number of linen and silk weavers appearing in the inventories increases substantially, before falling off again after around 1720.

The increase in the proportion of weavers with three or more looms, particularly in Kent, indicates perhaps that weavers were becoming more independent as the role of the large clothier declined. Certainly the Canterbury silk industry was 'dominated by prosperous master weavers' who were supplied with imported silk yarn directly by London merchants.

Linen weavers, too, appear to have had some measure of independence since many were smallholders and hence able to cultivate their own flax.[55] Only three flaxmen appear amongst the inventories and they seem to have been involved merely in the preparation and supply of flax rather than acting as clothiers in the wider sense. This greater control over the organisation of the industry may well have encouraged weavers to invest in additional looms and expand their level of production.

Mining

The most important element of the Cornish economy throughout the period 1600–1750 was tin mining. After remaining stable during the first half of the seventeenth century, output had more than doubled by the end of the century.[56] Such dramatic growth was made possible by significant changes to the organisation of the industry and the marketing of its product during the latter part of the seventeenth century. Since medieval times miners had been organised by the Duchy of Cornwall into four Stannaries, which policed the industry in a manner not dissimilar to an urban guild, ensuring standards of the refined tin, limiting membership and adjudicating on disputes between tinners. Under the laws of the Stannaries tinners had the freedom to search for tin on any waste ground and establish 'bounds', for which privilege they had to pay coinage duty of 4 shillings per hundredweight at four designated coinage towns, Liskeard, Lostwithiel, Truro and Helston.[57] Tin was also subject to 'pre-emption', the right of the Crown to purchase all that was produced, although this right was usually farmed out to London merchants and pewterers, who consequently had a monopoly over the trade. During the first half of the seventeenth century pre-emption gave the tinners guaranteed prices, but often kept them artificially low. Thus its abandonment in the 1660s can be seen as a significant factor in the rapid expansion of production that subsequently took place. At the same time, locally based merchants and adventurers were able to gain control of the export trade in tin.

From 1600 to 1750 mining became concentrated in certain areas of west Cornwall associated with the switch from tin streaming to lode mining. Streaming, the exploitation of secondary ore deposits found in river valleys, was common throughout the county from medieval times, although many of the best deposits had been exhausted by the mid-seventeenth century. The best tin lodes, on the other hand, were found in specific locations, notably west of Truro and in the area immediately north of St Austell. By 1700 mining was concentrated into around a dozen parishes, including St Agnes, Gwennap, Redruth, Camborne, St Just, Breage and Illogan. Moreover, copper ores were found in the same areas, and thus the rapid expansion of copper mining from the 1690s with the ending of the Royal Monopoly tended to accentuate this pattern.[58]

The growth in mining activity shown in Table 3.2 cannot be taken as an indicator of growth in the mining industry of Cornwall as a whole because of our partial coverage of mining parishes. Almost all references to mining concern tin, although there are six references to copper mines in Gwennap and Kenwyn between 1696 and 1743.[59] Nevertheless, our sample includes inventories from parishes in the stannaries of Penwith (Zennor and Madron), of Tywarnhayle (Illogan, Gwennap and Kenwyn) and of Blackmoor (Roche and Luxulyan), though not of the stannary of Foweymoor in the East.[60] The greatest increase in the proportion of mining inventories is in Luxulyan, where the rise is from 4 to 26 per cent between 1600–49 and 1700–49, although the highest proportion of mining inventories is in the parish of Gwennap where over half of all inventories had evidence of mining in the century after 1650.

The major change in the organisation of the industry was the transition from independent miners and tin streamers to piece-workers and wage labourers. Such changes were associated with the move from small-scale tin-streaming operations to larger mines which required higher levels of capital investment. This was often provided by outside interests, such as merchants and gentlemen known as tin adventurers.[61] The various groups involved in the industry were described by Dodridge in 1630:

> As touching the persons that deale or entermeddle with Tynne, and therefore carry the name of Tynners, they are of foure kindes. First, the owners of the soile where Mynes are found. Secondly, the aduen-turer for Tynne, which may haue by the law of Tynners, power and disposition of a Myne or Tyn-worke, although he be not owner of the soile. Thirdly, the merchant, Broker or Regrator of Tynne, which either buyeth to transport out of the Realme, or else to regrate and sell againe within the realme. And fourthly, the Spadiard or Spaliard so called, because he liueth by his Spade, and is the Myne-worker and labourer for Tynne, who commonly in respect of his poore estate, is eaten out by the hard and vsurious contracts for Tynne, which he is driuen to make with the merchant or regrator. For those poore labourers hauing no wages certaine, but onely shares in the mynes, as the quantity thereof shall arise; and being not able to sustaine them-selues and their family, vntill the Tynne of coinage, and Marts for Tynne shall come, which are halfe yeerely; hee is by necessity com-pelled for a small summe of money aforehand, to enter into bond vnto the Merchant or Regrator of Tynne, to deliuer him at the time of the next ensuing coinage, Tynne, in value much more than the money he had formerly receiued.[62]

It is possible to look for evidence of transition to wage labour by sepa-rating out leases for tin works and rights to tin from goods which indicate active participation in mining. Those who have both shares in tin works and are actively engaged in mining can be considered to fall within the traditional category of the independent tinner since they have ownership of their means of production. However, those noted as tinners who have no recorded stake in tin bounds or tin works are regarded as being proletarian miners, while those with tin leases alone have been grouped together as tin adventurers or entrepreneurs. Over the course of the period 1600 to 1749 there is a small decline in the proportion of independent tinners from 34 per cent to 27 per cent, although this process does appear to be gathering pace in the opening decades of the eighteenth century. The numbers of entrepreneurs involved in tinning appears to increase significantly between the first and second halves of the seventeenth century before falling off again in the early eighteenth century, the complete opposite of the trend in proletarian miners who seem to decline in importance from 41 per cent between 1600–49 to 26 per cent in 1650–99 before recovering to 53 per cent in the early eighteenth century.

These fluctuations can be explained by the changing fortunes of the mining industry. The post-Restoration period was one of rapid expansion prompted by the ending of pre-emption and the pent-up demand for tin on the Continent which had built up while supplies were curtailed during the Civil War.[63] This encouraged local men to invest in mines, and to stake claims to tin bounds in hope of their future exploitation. By the closing decade of the seventeenth century, however, the boom was over, and ownership of mines and bounds became increasingly concentrated in the hands of the small number of wealthy merchants who dominated the smelting and export of tin. This explains the decline in the proportion of individuals regarded as having an entrepreneurial role. Men such as William Angove Junior of Illogan had considerable interests in the various stages of the tinning. He held adventures and a stamping mill at Carnkey valued at £920, plus a 75 per cent share in a new blowing house worth £350, along with blowing house gear, tin ore and mining equipment in a total inventoried value of £2,588. The seeming decline in the proportion of proletarian miners in the later seventeenth century can be explained in terms of the small scale of many of the new enterprises established when the industry expanded after the Civil War. Many of the new operations were established by co-operatives of working miners and yeomen investors. It was only at the onset of the eighteenth century that larger-scale mines employing significant numbers of wage labourers began to emerge.[64]

Other commercial production

While the textile and mining industries feature prominently in economic histories of early modern England, commercial food processing has largely been ignored, even though, as Table 3.2 shows, it was practised in around a third of inventoried Kent households and up to a fifth of Cornish ones. In both counties the most important activity was commercial dairying. This is particularly difficult to identify since most households engaged in butter and cheese making would have been selling some of their produce in the marketplace. It is, therefore, necessary to determine a scale of production which could be considered to be commercial by reference to the number of cows owned and the quantity of butter and cheese produced. Markham, writing in the 1650s, reckoned that a cow grazing on fertile pastures such as those in the Wiltshire Vales could produce 300–400 pounds of cheese per season, with the price fluctuating around 3 to 4 pence per pound, giving a total value of around £4 5s.[65] Given that pastures were poorer in Kent and Cornwall, and neither were specialist dairying areas, output per cow of 200–300 pounds of cheese would seem more plausible. Bearing this in mind the criteria for commercial dairying was set at ownership of four milk cows or butter and cheese valued at more than one pound.[66] Such a scale of operation would have produced a small but consistent surplus. The figures for Kent are remarkably stable, showing that around 18 to 19 per cent of the inventoried population were engaged in dairying at this level throughout the period 1600–1750.[67] In Cornwall, however, the picture is rather different: 14 per cent were involved in dairying on a commercial basis in the early seventeenth century, but this rapidly fell to under 6 per cent after the Civil War, and the decline continued into the eighteenth century. This can perhaps be linked to the general trend towards the rearing of beef cattle in the county.

Commercial baking too, was an activity found fairly widely in Kent, but was virtually absent in Cornwall.[68] Cornwall did, however, have a greater involvement in commercial food preservation than Kent. This was entirely due to the presence of fish processing operations in a number of coastal parishes such as Madron and Talland. The fish, mostly pilchards, were pressed in hogsheads or pickled before export to continental markets.[69] Commercial brewing was identified within the inventories primarily by the quantity of beer and ale found and the value of the brewing equipment recorded. Over the course of the study period brewing appears to have become more commercialised in both Kent and Cornwall. In Kent the level of commercial brewing rose from 1.5 per cent of the inventoried population in 1600–49 to 4.2 per cent in 1700–50, whereas in Cornwall it increased from 1.3 to 3.4 per cent. Most of these brewers in both counties were urban, particularly in the ports where they supplied passing ships as well as the local population. Throughout the period brewing was conducted on a far larger scale in Kent, probably as a result of the greater local urban population in the county rather than demand from the capital. For example, Edward Smith of Milton near Sittingbourne had a stock of 5,760 gallons of beer and brewing equipment valued at over £50, whereas the largest brewer found in the Cornish inventories had only 621 gallons.[70] Moreover, in Kent there appears to have been an increase in the scale of production over time, especially after 1700, indicated by the increasing proportion of brewers whose inventories contained 400 or more gallons of beer. In Cornwall change was less noticeable and mostly restricted to the 100–399 gallon category, although this may, to some extent, be explained by the parallel expansion of cider making. By the first half of the eighteenth century over 7 per cent of Cornish inventories revealed evidence of cider making, and 13 per cent of these contained stocks of 400 gallons of cider or more. Many of those brewing on a large scale in the later periods were innholders, victuallers or alehouse keepers. These groups expanded in numbers nationally as excise statistics show that there were 39,469 brewer victuallers in 1700, rising to 48,370 by 1749.[71]

The number of inventories showing evidence of milling doubled in both counties over the period, reaching 2.6 per cent in Kent by the early eighteenth century. This trend is supported by a growth in the number of windmills in the county from 23 in 1695 to 51 in 1736.[72] Malting was also an important commercial activity in Kent, being found in over 10 per cent of inventories throughout the 1600–1750 period. Malt was produced in large quantities both to supply local brewers and for export to London: the coastwise trade from the ports of Sandwich amounted to 12,677 quarters in 1628 and 27,368 quarters in 1684.[73] In Cornwall malting remained an activity of only local importance, occupying only around 2 per cent of the inventoried households. Maltsters such as Agnes Hunking of St Stephens by Saltash, who had 295 bushels of 'ready for sale malt' valued at £82 when she died in 1672, were the exception rather than the rule.[74]

The inventories suggest an expansion of large-scale commercial malting at the expense of smaller-scale production. In Kent the proportion of maltsters with stocks of over 100 bushels rose from 5 per cent to 16 per cent over the study period, while those with less than 20 bushels fell from 38 to 18 per cent. Much of this malt supplied the dockyard towns or was shipped to London. A similar though less dramatic trend can be seen in Cornwall, since the absence of a large urban population here limited the demand for beer and hence malt. Malting had always been a relatively capital intensive enterprise and hence been conducted on a fairly large scale in both counties throughout the 1600–1750 period. For instance, the inventory of William Brissenden of Smarden shows that in 1606 he was storing 560 bushels of malt valued at £52.[75] However, men such as Brissenden were yeomen farmers, whereas, certainly in Kent, those malting commercially at the turn of the seventeenth century were often professional maltsters and grain dealers with few farming interests, indicative of the increasing specialisation within the food processing sector. Their stocks of malt frequently exceeded 1,000 bushels, an example being William Grant of Milton whose goods were appraised in 1703. He had 1,020 bushels of 'dried malt', 232 bushels of 'green malt' and 74 bushels of 'malt in the cistern', clearly illustrating the various stages of the malting process.[76]

The maritime category in table 3.2 encompasses both fishing and water transport since in many cases they cannot be distinguished from one another. In Cornwall there was little change over time in the proportion of the inventoried population engaged in such activities, and the figures for Kent were very similar throughout the seventeenth century. From the 1690s, however, there appears to have been a dramatic increase in the level of Kentish maritime activity caused primarily by an expansion of fishing. This growth in fishing may be somewhat overstated, since Folkestone, noted by Defoe as 'eminent chiefly for a multitude of fishing boats ... employ'd in catching mackerel for the city of London', is included amongst the list of study parishes.[77] Conversely the failure to include Margate, Ramsgate, Sandwich, Faversham or Whitstable almost certainly leads to an under-recording of the growth in maritime transport, since most ships were owned by men from these centres.[78] In reality there was a genuine expansion of both industries, which gathered pace in the early eighteenth century. Fishing was locally important in Folkestone and Broadstairs, but it was the growth of coastal trade that accounted for most of the expansion in the maritime sector. In Cornwall, too, the apparent stagnation of maritime activities may be more the consequence of the choice of parishes. Fishing here became increasingly concentrated into a small number of centres such as Mevagissey and St Ives during the seventeenth century, and none of these large fishing villages are in our sample. Sea trade expanded too, especially coastal traffic to South Wales, Hampshire and London, with the number of local boats rising from 67 in the period 1635–41 to 169 in 1687/8, something which is not reflected in the inventory figures.[79]

The retail and service sectors seem also to have been subject to growth during the seventeenth and early eighteenth centuries. In both cases the expansion was more pronounced in Kent and started from a higher base, indicating the more developed nature of the consumer economy here. This might reflect the greater incidence of wage labour in the county (which inventories cannot reveal) since shops were particularly numerous in the Wealden textile areas. By the close of the period over 10 per cent of the Kent inventory sample was involved in retailing, while the figure for Cornwall was closer to 5 per cent. Indeed, even the figure of 10 per cent may be an underestimate since many country shopkeepers operated on a very small scale without specialist equipment or much in the way of stock, and some would have been too poor to have appeared within the inventoried population. This growth in retailing confirms the argument of Cox that historians have underestimated the extent of retailing activity before the Industrial Revolution.[80] Some retailers in both counties were increasing the scale of their activities during the seventeenth century. Whereas in the 1600–49 period the median value of mercers' trade goods amounted to only £8 10s, by the end of the century it had almost quadrupled in Cornwall and increased tenfold in Kent. At the same time the proportion of mercers' shops containing stock valued at less than £20 almost halved, suggesting that demand for groceries and manufactured goods was growing, and shopkeepers were responding by expanding the size of their businesses. On the other hand many of the emerging shopkeepers were operating on a relatively small scale. Such shops supplied a wide range of goods in small quantities to the poor, who were rarely catered for by the larger urban-based retail establishments. For instance, the 1741 inventory of Elizabeth Kennett of Folkestone lists spices, soap, raisins, sugar, glass bottles, tumblers, snuff and rice amongst her wares, but their overall value amounted to little over £5.[81] The proliferation of such petty shopkeepers is a noted feature of the early eighteenth century. They formed part of an increasingly complex network of retail outlets which supplied the growing demands of the population for consumer goods.[82]

For commercial production as a whole we can identify distinctive trends for three groups of activities. First, the most consistent expansion was of those production activities associated with provisioning and the supply of consumption goods. Clear support for this hypothesis comes from the growth of retailing, and commercial brewing and baking. Second, activities more often linked to the servicing of the agricultural sector remain relatively static. The third group show more diverse trends. Some activities, such as textile production, appear to decline, while others like mining and fishing show evidence of rapid expansion. These trends should be treated with a degree of caution, however, since the locational specificity of activities such as mining and maritime means that the sample parishes may not be representative of the industries as a whole.[83]

The overall trends do, however, disguise some significant differences in the fortunes of individual craft activities in the two counties. For example, those crafts associated with textile production (that is, weaving, dyeing and finishing) were more important in Kent, and showed a significant decline over the course of the study period in both counties. Building, on the other hand, was an expanding industry, particularly in Kent, involving only 0.7 per cent of the inventoried population in the 1600–49 period but 2.6 per cent in the period after 1700. This growth resulted from the spread of brick-built houses with tiled roofs, especially in the north of the county, which provided plentiful work for the growing number of bricklayers and tilers. Bricks and tiles were also manufactured throughout the county – mostly to meet these local demands but also to supply builders in the capital.[84] Cornish houses were made primarily of stone, and thus it is unsurprising to find that there were more masons here. Cornwall also suffered from a severe shortage of timber, which may go some way to explaining the relatively small numbers involved in woodworking. The county had to import large quantities of deal boards from London, the Low Countries and direct from Scandinavia for boat building and the tin mines, as well as for domestic use.[85] Kent, on the other hand, had rich timber supplies in the Weald and elsewhere, and thus developed a substantial shipbuilding industry associated with the naval dockyards.[86] Carpenters were also numerous, sharing the benefits arising from the expansion of house building, and there was a small but developing vernacular furniture industry in the county. As a consequence the proportion of the inventoried population involved in woodworking increased from 3.8 per cent in the early seventeenth century to 6.9 per cent in the early 1700s. Other crafts, mostly activities such as smithing and leather working, which were closely allied to agriculture, were found at similar levels in the two counties.

Production for use in the household

Table 3.7 shows the change over time in the proportion of inventories indicating production for use within the household. In some cases surplus produce may occasionally have been sold, but the underlying motivation must have been the provision of goods and services to meet household needs. Thus small-scale agriculture and dairying is included within this category despite the fact that the household may have sold small quantities of poultry, eggs, milk, butter and cheese. In both these cases it is the scale of market involvement that is central to the definition. Where the sale of goods provided a significant element of overall household income the activity has been designated as commercial, where it did not the activity was regarded as for household use.

Table 3.7 Percentages of inventories with evidence of potential production for use

		1600–29	1630–59	1660–89	1690–1719	1720–49
All production for use	Cornwall	81	73	56	52	58
	Kent	80	81	84	92	89
Subsistence farming	Cornwall	16	13	15	15	16
	Kent	19	14	12	15	8
Baking	Cornwall	6	2	1	0	1
	Kent	34	34	39	46	36
Alcohol	Cornwall	50	45	28	24	31
	Kent	33	48	61	74	79
All dairying	Cornwall	60	59	41	42	47
	Kent	55	56	62	67	54
Dairying for use only	Cornwall	43	48	35	37	42
	Kent	38	38	43	47	36
Food preservation	Cornwall	66	52	34	25	24
	Kent	65	70	76	83	81
Milling	Cornwall	5	3	1	1	1
	Kent	27	19	8	7	10

Evidence of baking was found in 34 per cent of inventoried households in Kent in the first half of the seventeenth century, rising to 46 per cent for the period 1690–1719. Ovens were not recorded in inventories since they were not movable. Thus baking was identified by moulding boards, kneading troughs and various other articles of specialist baking equipment, often situated in a room specifically described as a bakehouse. This sort of equipment suggests the baking of wheaten bread.[87] In Cornwall, on the other hand, very few households were identified as being involved in baking. In the 1600–29 period some 6 per cent of the inventory sample had baking equipment, but the figure soon falls off to less than 1 per cent by the 1660s. To an extent this lack of evidence can be explained in terms of the generally poor level of detail in which household goods are described in the Cornish documents; however, the large contrast between the two trends does seem to indicate that home baking was much less common in Cornwall. It is possible that there was a greater reliance upon communal ovens, although it is also likely that many Cornish households baked their loaves in a more rudimentary fashion, using an iron pan covered with a lid and hanging over the open fire or standing in the hot ashes of the hearth.[88] Moreover, much of the bread in Cornwall was made from barley or oats and did not require such thorough kneading or moulding into shape as wheaten manchet loaves.[89] The barley was mixed with scalded skim milk and extra yeast, producing loaves which were 'little inferior to the second sort of white bread', but which could be baked over the fire rather than in an oven.[90] Pococke does, however, describe the manufacture of earthenware ovens in Calstock in 1750, suggesting that wheaten bread was being produced in the wealthier households by this period, something which is supported by the appearance of oven peels in several of the later inventories.[91]

The inventories suggest that the production of alcohol for domestic use was more prevalent in Cornwall in the early eighteenth century, with evidence found in 50 per cent of households for the period 1600–29. There then seems to be a significant decline in the proportion of households involved, followed by stabilisation at the lower level of around 28 per cent after 1660. The trend is in the opposite direction in Kent, with a steady rise in the proportion of households making alcohol, to 79 per cent by the 1720–49 period. Most of this alcohol was in the form of beer or ale, followed by cider, and, more rarely, spirits. These figures must, however, be treated with caution, since the criteria used to determine whether a household was involved in brewing were significantly different for the two counties. In Cornwall possible brewers were identified by the possession of various pieces of basic equipment which might potentially have been used for brewing, including keeves and tubs. It was necessary to include these items in the categorisation, because Cornish brewers appear to have used quite basic equipment which was often poorly recorded in the documents. This may, however, lead to some households being incorrectly identified as being involved in brewing, since such vessels could have been used for other purposes like washing or storage. Under these circumstances the high level of brewing identified for the early seventeenth century is perhaps an overestimate, which can be explained partly by the greater level of detail within the Cornish inventories in this period. Subsequently household goods are often grouped together so that keeves and tubs are not separately identified.

The trend in Kent is more certain since brewing here was usually identified by ownership of specific brewing equipment or the presence of a brew-house or brewing kitchen. Regardless of methodological problems, both trends seem to run contrary to Mathias's view that there was a movement away from home brewing towards increasingly large-scale commercial production, beginning in London but spreading over most of the country by the close of the seventeenth century. Indeed, they appear to confirm Clark's tentative view that there was an 'apparent revival' of private brewing in the late seventeenth century.[92] This is also borne out by Shammas's findings from inventories in Gloucestershire, Staffordshire, Shropshire and Essex, where the proportion showing evidence of brewing and cider making rises from the late seventeenth century to the early eighteenth.[93] It also raises questions about the gender division of labour. Bennett and Mate have stressed the transition from small-scale commercial ale production by women in the medieval period, to the large-scale production of beer by men in early modern England, excluding women from an important area of employment.[94] The inventory evidence demonstrates that ale production persisted in Cornwall until the late seventeenth century, while in Kent increasing numbers of households produced beer on a small scale at home. Both these activities are likely to have been dominated by women.

Ale was replaced by beer from the fifteenth century onwards. Ale was an unhopped malt liquor which could be made easily using basic equipment: a copper vessel to heat the water, and wooden casks or tuns for cooling and fermentation. Ale could not be produced in large quantities because it deteriorated rapidly and hence was largely domestically produced.[95] It would appear to be ale brewing that is being picked up in the majority of the Cornish inventories, and a few of the earlier Kentish ones. By the late sixteenth century beer was commonly available – not only in the cities and small towns of south-east England but in rural Sussex as well.[96] Brewing beer involved the use of more sophisticated equipment such as enclosed furnaces, but could be carried out on a far larger scale since the hops acted as a preservative.[97] The spread of beer brewing can be traced in the inventories through the possession of furnaces and the establishment of specialised brew-houses.[98] In the early seventeenth century, furnaces were present in only around 10 per cent of the inventoried households in Kent, whereas by the 1700s they could be found in over 40 per cent, while 35–40 per cent of houses contained a brew-house by this period. In Cornwall only a handful of the more wealthy inventories contained either a furnace or brew-house. Another indicator of the expansion of beer brewing is the increasing cultivation of hops. As we have seen in Table 3.5, 19 per cent of Kentish inventories were mentioning hops by the first half of the eighteenth century. These indicators confirm that Kent was one of the earliest areas to adopt beer, while Cornwall was one of the latest.

However, this alone does not explain why domestic brewing seems to have declined in Cornwall but expanded in Kent. Beer was less suited to home production than ale, and this may explain the decline in domestic brewing in Cornwall, particularly since Cornish ale was notoriously bad.[99] Perhaps here households switched to purchasing supplies from the growing number of brewer-victuallers and alehouse keepers. In Kent, on the other hand, the inventory evidence suggests that households preferred to continue domestic brewing despite the expansion of the commercial industry in the county. The greater levels of wealth here enabled them to upgrade their brewing facilities and build separate brew-houses so that they could produce beer in the home. Despite the capital cost of such ventures there was an incentive for home production or private brewing because it was not subject to the excise. This tax was introduced in 1643 and at first both home-brewed and commercial beer were liable; however, the levy on domestic brewing was abandoned in 1651.[100] Only in urban areas did domestic brewing decline due to the economies of scale offered by the large common brewers in Canterbury, Maidstone and Faversham.

Domestic dairying in Cornwall occupied 43 per cent of the inventoried population during the early seventeenth century, falling to 36 per cent after 1660, before recovering to 42 per cent by the close of the study period. In Kent the proportion involved was also around 40 per cent, with a slightly rising trend over time. The similarity of these figures is not surprising since the main indicator used for dairying in each case was the presence of milk cows, and these were consistently found in more than a third of inventories in both Kent and Cornwall.[101] However, there were significant differences in dairy production between the two counties. A large number of the inventories in Kent had dairy rooms, churns, cheese vats and other dairy equipment, suggesting that production here was relatively sophisticated. Nevertheless, almost all the butter and cheese produced was for domestic or at least local consumption, as the Kentish diet was rich in dairy produce. Bread with butter and skimmed milk cheese were staple products for the labouring population, and butter was added to most dishes during the seventeenth century.[102] Commercial dairying in the county appears to have remained on a small scale, with only occasional mentions of the sale of butter and cheese in local markets. Indeed, Kent was a major importer of dairy produce throughout the period: butter came from the north-east ports, cheese from London and East Anglia.[103] There are frequent references to large quantities of Essex, Suffolk and

Cheshire cheeses in mercers' inventories attesting to the scale of the trade. The first two were skim-milk cheeses, which were badly regarded but imported by cheesemongers in large quantities to feed the county's poor, a clear indicator that they could not sufficiently be supplied by local dairying.[104]

The inventories have much less material evidence of butter and cheese production in Cornwall, particularly in the late seventeenth and early eighteenth centuries: no households had churns, and only 10 per cent could be identified as making butter, almost all of these in the period before 1660. There was evidence of cheese making in 34 per cent of inventories in the early seventeenth century, but less than 5 per cent subsequently. The contrast between the numbers designated as dairying on account of possessing a cow, and those who can be positively identified as producing dairy products, can be explained by the unique characteristics of production in the south-west. Robert Fraser, writing in 1794, noted that butter

> is made in a way intirely peculiar to the people in the counties of Devon and Cornwall, and no where else practised, I believe in England. The use of the churn is not known. They put the milk in pans, either made of copper tinned, or brass, or in brown earthen vessels, glazed, which they place on a stove gently heated with charcoal, and scald it until the cream is raised to the surface of the milk, by the operation of the heat ... The cream is then taken off, and it is worked by the hand, without any churn, into butter.[105]

This explains the absence of churns and the frequent appearance of large brass or earthenware pans in the inventories. Cheese production, on the other hand, may indeed have declined over the course of the seventeenth century, since Risdon, writing about dairying in Devon during the 1630s, described the cheese made there as inferior and produced 'not so much for the market, as for the use of the farmers servants and labourers'.[106]

According to Shammas, 'almost no family did its own milling of grain for bread' in the early modern period, yet the proportion of inventories with milling equipment in Table 3.7 is of some significance in Kent.[107] In both counties the proportion with such equipment declines, but from a much higher level in Kent than in Cornwall. This contrasting picture may partly be a consequence of the differing levels of manorial control. The use of hand querns was usually prohibited where the lord of the manor retained control of milling, as was the case in Cornwall.[108] The manorial system in Kent, however, had always been much weaker due to the large number of freeholders, and large-scale milling was dominated by entrepreneurs. Thus the decline in home production here was probably the result of competition from these commercial millers, who were growing in number at the close of the seventeenth century.[109] They purchased corn direct from farmers or middlemen and supplied flour in bulk to bakers and shopkeepers, allowing most Kentish households to abandon the chore of milling at home. The Kentish preference for wheaten bread may also have contributed to the greater use of hand querns here. These may not have been able to produce the finest flour, but could supply that required for inferior brown bread eaten by labourers and servants.[110] Malt milling was part of the preparation for brewing and was more important in Kent where home brewing was much more extensive. The milling of mustard, on the other hand, was associated with more refined forms of cooking using sauces and a wider range of herbs which had been introduced from the Continent and became popular in the Home Counties after the Restoration. Both these forms of milling declined over time in Kent, but at a slower pace than domestic milling overall.

Facilities for food preservation must have been present in most households in both Kent and Cornwall throughout the study period, although they may have varied considerably in their level of sophistication. Stone larders, designed to keep food cool in hot weather can be found in both counties, while some Kent inventories reveal the existence of more specialised storage rooms such as apple lofts and granaries. Equipment used specifically in the salting and pickling of meat and fish was found in 65 per cent of Kentish inventories in the early seventeenth century, rising to 83 per cent by the turn of the eighteenth century. The prevalence of salting troughs and brine tubs indicates that both dry and brine salting were widely practised in the county. The most common method of preservation in Kent appears to have been to rub the meat with a pickling salt made up from saltpetre, bay salt and sugar before packing it tightly into a barrel containing a further layer of salt at the bottom.[111]

Although food preservation equipment was found in over 66 per cent of Cornish households in the early seventeenth century, this figure had fallen to around 24 per cent by the close of the period. This apparent downward trend is partly a consequence of the declining level of detail in the Cornish inventories, since it matches that found for small-scale brewing. Both these activities have, in Cornwall, largely been identified by the presence of keeves and tubs, items which regularly appear in the early inventories but less often in those after 1660. It would also seem to indicate the less sophisticated nature of preservation techniques used in the home here, suggesting that the Cornish figures represent not necessarily a reduction in the incidence of preservation but perhaps merely a decline in the ability to identify the process from the inventories. In Cornwall, bacon and beef were frequently smoked in the chimney before being left hanging from the rafters.[112] This form of preservation can sometimes be clearly identified by the presence of meat described as 'at the roof', as it is for around 10 per cent of Cornish households during the early seventeenth century, but would not be visible in summer inventories when fresh meat was available. Moreover, the generally lower level of preservation found in the county could reflect the relatively greater importance of fish in the Cornish diet. This was often eaten fresh, and if it was to be preserved was usually pickled in barrels or smoked over the fire without the need for specialised equipment. Nevertheless there may have been a genuine fall in the amount of salting and smoking taking place, reflecting the impoverishment of the Cornish diet. Certainly Richard Baxter, writing at the beginning of the eighteenth century, noted that 'he is a rich man that can afford a joint of fresh meat (bief, mutton or veale) once a month or fortnight. If their sow piggs or their hens breed chickens, they cannot afford to eate them, but must sell them to make their rent'.[113]

Overall the trends in production for use show a mixture of expansion and decline reflecting the conflicting impulses impacting upon the household. In general the Cornish inventories appear to indicate a gradual disengagement from such activities, while those for Kent suggest a rise in home production for use. Some activities, notably milling, declined in both counties as home production was replaced by purchase in the marketplace. In other sectors, however, the preference for home-produced goods appears to have increased or at least held its own against purchased alternatives.

Greater production for use was associated with an expansion in the range and complexity of household tasks and an increase in the sophistication of these activities so that they become more visible within the inventories. Indeed, there appears to have been a significant investment in the facilities for domestic production during the late seventeenth century in the Home Counties, revealed in the spread of service buildings such as brew-houses and bakehouses.[114] In 1600 brew-houses were found in only 6 per cent of Kentish inventories, yet by 1700 this figure had risen to 40 per cent. This seeming preference for home production can be viewed as a consumption choice associated with the growing affluence of the county, since the diffusion of domesticity brought with it an increase in the demand for household servants.[115] Households were choosing to make use of servant labour in order to produce foodstuffs at home rather than relying upon purchase for their supplies. Home-produced food and drink was generally considered to be superior by this period: home-brewed beer and ale were stronger than their commercially produced counterparts, while baking bread oneself removed the fear of adulteration which was a common practice amongst commercial bakers.[116] Home-based milling did not produce better-quality flour than that milled commercially, and it is surely significant that milling for use declined in Kent whereas those home-based production activities that could improve on the quality of purchased foodstuffs became more prevalent.

In Cornwall the inventoried households appear to have got relatively poorer over the course of the study period, and this to some extent may explain why there was not a corresponding expansion of domestic production. Indeed, there seems to have been a decline in home brewing, baking and preservation, which cannot entirely be put down to deficiencies in the source material. It is not being suggested that these activities disappeared, but merely that they failed to develop in the same manner as they did in Kent. The employment of servant labour seems not to have been as commonplace, perhaps due to the relative poverty of the county. This can be seen in the less frequent mention of servants quarters or beds, and the lower level of investment in domestic production goods. Less than 5 per cent of inventoried households in the county had specialised service rooms in the early eighteenth century, compared with more than 70 per cent in Kent.

Conclusion

This survey of inventoried households shows that in Kent production on a commercial scale was becoming more common, with some 85 per cent of inventories indicating commercial production activity by 1720–49. A decline in the textile industry was matched by increased activity in a variety of other fields, leading towards a more diversified economy. In Cornwall there was a slight fall in commercial production activity, although this might to some extent reflect a deterioration in the quality of the inventories. What is clear, however, is the development of the mining industry and the relative decline of both agriculture and textiles. And in both counties there is considerable growth in the retail and provisioning sectors, reflecting an increase in commercialisation, which is also evidenced by the growth of maritime activity in Kent. Increased commercial activity is consistent with the models of economic development discussed in Chapter 1, but by itself does not provide the empirical support for any particular model. Of more importance in this respect is the finding that in the more commercialised of the two counties, Kent, there was an increase in the proportion of households engaged in production for use. More engagement with the market went hand in hand with more home production, which runs counter to de Vries's arguments for an 'industrious revolution', where more market activity is associated with less production for use and an increase in purchased commodities.[117] In Cornwall, however, there does seem to be a fall in production for use related to a fall in the relative importance of agriculture and a rise in mining activity.

However, the discussion of production activity in this chapter ignores a particularly distinctive feature of production in early modern England. By-employment was commonplace and we need to factor this into our discussion of production activity. Further, both the nature and change in production activity have important implications for the gender division of labour in the household. Both these issues are considered in the following chapter, together with those part-households that appear from an inventory to be unproductive.

4   By-employment, women's work and 'unproductive' households

Household by-employment

It is well-known that by-employment, or the practice of more than one occupation, was common in early modern England. The association between pasture farming and rural industry has been pointed out by Thirsk, and many other studies have shown how farming was combined with other trades.[1] Subsequently, by-employment has become an essential ingredient of models of proto-industrialisation.[2] By identifying production activity from goods in inventories rather than by occupational designations alone, we are able to explore the combinations of occupational or productive activities in some detail. Indeed most studies of by-employment in early modern England have used inventories, although not on the scale that we are able to here. Thus the picture of by-employment that emerges in the literature is based on a number of small-scale studies of inventories usually focusing on a particular industry. Perhaps the classic image of by-employment in pre-industrial England is of the combination of weaving and pastoral farming, with the 'farmer' milking his cows in the morning and evening and weaving in between.[3] In fact his wife would have probably done the milking so we need to emphasise the distinction between household by-employment and individual by-employment. Moreover, the combination of different activities on a daily basis implied by this image is not the only possibility. Different production activities could be combined on a seasonal basis as well. This was the case with activities combined with arable farming, or at least certain types of arable farming, which required little labour at certain times of the year.[4] Available labour time is thus seen as one of the reasons for by-employment to exist. It is also seen as a typical form of risk aversion: offering some security and protection against both the uncertainties of farming and of working in textiles for uncertain foreign markets. However, as we shall see, by-employment was associated with other economic strategies and was by no means confined to risk-averse peasants.

The extent of by-employment involving production for exchange is shown in Table 4.1, both including and excluding spinning as a commercial activity. Since spinning was carried out by women the difference

Table 4.1 Inventories with evidence of commercial by-employment (percentages)

		1600–29	1630–59	1660–89	1690–1719	1720–49
Excluding spinning	Cornwall	42	33	31	32	38
	Kent	51	48	47	53	44
Including spinning	Cornwall	65	57	41	37	43
	Kent	75	73	65	70	58

between the two halves of the table might reflect the distinction between household by-employment and individual by-employment. When spinning is included we are clearly looking at men's and women's work; when it is excluded the majority of production activity would be carried out by men, and probably by the same man, although without details of household compositions this must be a rather speculative assumption. While certain activities were done by women alone, part of the nature of women's work was to help men in their tasks; fewer tasks were solely male than solely female. Overall, there was a slight fall in the extent of by-employment in the two counties, although the degree of decline is steeper in Cornwall than it is in Kent. Indeed, in Kent a fall in the level of by-employment is only evident from the 1720s onwards: for the preceding hundred years around half the inventories indicating commercial production show evidence of two or more production activities, or around 70 per cent if we include spinning. When spinning is included the decline in by-employment is greater, suggesting a reduction in the amount of commercial production activity undertaken by women. But apart from this there is no clear trend of increased specialisation in commercial production within the household.

Tables 4.2 and 4.3 show the interrelationships between the main production categories, for both use and exchange, for Kent and Cornwall over the whole period 1600 to 1749. Each production category is shown both as a row and a column, and at the intersection of the two for a particular category is the number of inventories in that category. Thus in Cornwall, for example, there are 625 inventories with evidence of commercial food production. There are two numbers at the intersection of rows and columns for different categories. The top left number is the percentage of those inventories in the column category that are also in the row category. For example, in Table 4.2, at the intersection of the row for retailing and the column for crafts we see that 4 per cent of those inventories with craft activity also have evidence of retailing. The number at the bottom right is the percentage of those inventories in the row category that are also in the column category. Thus, using the same example, 20 per cent of those involved in retailing in Cornwall also have some craft activity.

Table 4.2 By-employment in Cornwall 1600–1749

	Arable	Pasture	Farming 1&2	Farming 3&4	Crafts	Commercial food	Maritime	Mining	Retailing	Spinning	All commercial	Dairying for use	Food processing for use	Brewing for use	All production for use
Arable	**627**														
Pasture	0	**628**													
Farming 1&2	0	0	**616**												
Farming 3&4	100	100	0	**2,190**											
Crafts	15 / 16	50 / 20	0 / 13	47 / 77	**632**										
Commercial food	23 / 43	12 / 21	19 / 22	13 / 29	16 / 8	**625**									
Maritime	2 / 18	18 / 34	13 / 2	2 / 16	7 / 4	5 / 22	**148**								
Mining	7 / 19	1 / 13	20 / 11	2 / 31	4 / 34	6 / 29	3 / 16	**382**							
Retailing	1 / 18	17 / 46	14 / 2	11 / 65	4 / 44	6 / 54	3 / 49	2 / 34	**133**						
Spinning	16 / 39	1 / 14	23 / 27	32 / 75	20 / 27	29 / 54	16 / 49	19 / 65	11 / 67	**793**					
All commercial	100 / 37	14 / 36	12 / 74	75 / 74	100 / 44	100 / 22	100 / 31	100 / 48	100 / 41	86 / 74	**2,947**				
Dairying for use	58 / 39	100 / 37	9 / 62	62 / 73	39 / 46	22 / 9	31 / 46	48 / 11	32 / 3	54 / 26	91 / 51	**1,634**			
Food processing for use	58 / 43	65 / 44	15 / 53	53 / 63	46 / 18	64 / 25	46 / 4	31 / 7	45 / 4	57 / 28	86 / 47	51 / 52	**1,602**		
Brewing for use	51 / 43	40 / 30	14 / 46	46 / 71	44 / 19	54 / 24	49 / 5	34 / 9	41 / 4	58 / 32	85 / 41	52 / 45	72 / 81	**1,426**	
All production for use	82 / 36	81 / 36	17 / 84	84 / 72	67 / 17	79 / 19	65 / 4	65 / 10	67 / 3	74 / 23	85 / 85	64 / 52	100 / 63	100 / 56	**2,558**

Note

The categories are defined in Appendix 2; farming categories are defined in Table 3.3.

Table 4.3 By-employment in Kent 1600–1749

	Arable	Pasture	Farming 1&2	Farming 3&4	Crafts	Commercial food	Maritime	Mining	Retailing	Spinning	All commercial	Dairying for use	Food processing for use	Brewing for use	All production for use
Arable	**349**														
Pasture	0 / 0	**349**													
Farming 1&2	0 / 0	0 / 0	**575**												
Farming 3&4	100 / 18	100 / 18	0 / 0	**1,988**											
Crafts	12 / 19	50 / 18	19 / 15	82 / 47	**735**										
Commercial food	45 / 42	40 / 43	9 / 20	24 / 82	16 / 27	**1,236**									
Maritime	2 / 13	11 / 2	9 / 3	2 / 0	3 / 11	4 / 32	**169**								
Mining	0 / 0	0 / 0	0 / 0	0 / 0	0 / 0	0 / 0	0 / 0	**0**							
Retailing	2 / 13	18 / 2	7 / 23	31 / 62	4 / 18	6 / 41	4 / 4	0 / 0	**177**						
Spinning	41 / 29	32 / 45	23 / 15	51 / 67	23 / 25	53 / 40	47 / 5	0 / 0	33 / 4	**1,643**					
All commercial	100 / 33	100 / 32	42 / 44	100 / 70	44 / 20	100 / 42	100 / 19	0 / 0	100 / 31	82 / 49	**2,975**				
Dairying for use	53 / 34	56 / 33	55 / 8	56 / 90	51 / 21	28 / 21	19 / 6	0 / 0	31 / 5	49 / 50	45 / 50	**1,599**			
Food processing for use	87 / 30	84 / 36	78 / 20	90 / 72	85 / 22	94 / 38	79 / 2	0 / 0	88 / 3	93 / 51	83 / 63	69 / 82	**3,007**		
Brewing for use	70 / 34	65 / 29	49 / 13	72 / 65	66 / 22	75 / 42	69 / 4	0 / 0	49 / 4	67 / 50	85 / 50	47 / 47	94 / 96	**2,199**	
All production for use	94 / 29	93 / 31	100 / 17	96 / 58	91 / 20	97 / 36	86 / 4	0 / 0	94 / 5	96 / 48	89 / 80	100 / 48	91 / 91	96 / 64	**3,306**

Note
The categories are defined in Appendix 2; farming categories are defined in Table 3.3.

Given our methods for identifying production activity it follows that Tables 4.2 and 4.3 can only be used to derive positive evidence; for example, it cannot be assumed that 96 per cent of craft inventories are not engaged in retailing, or, to take another example from Table 4.2, that 87 per cent of those in commercial agriculture were not engaged in craft production. Nor is it possible to measure the relative contributions of different activities to household income and therefore rate their relative importance. It is also likely that our methods introduce some distortions. For example, the extent of by-employment among farmers is probably exaggerated. Dairying and food processing for use are regarded as two separate activities, whereas they might be regarded as part of farming as a whole. Farmers were often involved in a number of activities that were necessary to maintain their farming operations yet could also be associated with other occupations. Some farmers appear by-employed as carpenters or workers in wood as well, yet it may well be that the woodworking tools on their farm were not for commercial production but for maintenance on the farm. On the other hand the extent of by-employment with service occupations is probably understated because of the absence of material goods involved in such activities.

Thus the extent of by-employment as we have measured it partly depends on the categories we have used to define particular occupations. In most instances this is not a problem since the categories themselves are relatively discrete. However, where a number of different activities have been grouped together into one category, such as crafts and commercial food processing for example, there may be by-employment within the sector. For instance, baking and milling were often combined together as were brewing and malting. The problem should not, however, be overstated. Examination of the Cornish inventories reveals that just 3.3 per cent of those involved in craft production had within-sector by-employment alone, with a further 5.9 per cent having within- as well as between-sector by-employment. Moreover, this type of by-employment seems to have declined over time from around 12 per cent to only 6 per cent of those in craft production activities. Indeed many of these individuals were engaged in closely related activities such as weaving, dyeing and finishing, and were in all probability clothiers. Few craftsmen appear to have engaged in two unrelated occupations such as smithing and carpentry.

Tables 4.2 and 4.3 demonstrate the complexities of the structure of by-employment in the two counties. As is to be expected, commercial agriculture was commonly combined with other production activities. In both Cornwall and Kent almost half of those inventories with evidence of craft activity also had evidence commercial farming and, as we might expect, around 80 per cent of those engaged in food processing on a commercial scale were also farming commercially. Almost a third of those with evidence of retailing were also farming. On the other hand, the proportion of farmers involved in other activities was lower. Thus under 20 per cent of farmers in both counties had evidence of craft activity; in Kent just half were also processing food on a commercial scale, while in Cornwall only 22 per cent of farmers were engaged in this activity. In Cornwall, 65 per cent of miners were also farming but only 11 per cent of farmers were miners. Thus farming was the activity most likely to be combined with something else, but at the same time was the activity that was most likely to be carried out alone. There were also combinations of other production activities. In Cornwall, for example, some 20 per cent of those households with maritime activities were also involved in craft production, and in Kent 27 per cent of those with evidence of craft production were also producing food on a commercial scale.

The differences in the apparent extent of production for use between Cornwall and Kent is also evident in Tables 4.2 and 4.3. In Kent, for example, all those involved in non-commercial farming had some evidence of production for household use, whereas in Cornwall only 69 per cent had such evidence. The question as to whether this is simply a consequence of poor recording in Cornwall has already been discussed.[5] Nevertheless, almost all those producing dairy products for their own use were engaged in farming (98 per cent in Cornwall and 90 per cent in Kent). Production for use by the household was combined with all commercial activities, so that beer brewing for example, was a feature of 50 per cent or more of all commercial production categories in Kent and 30 per cent or more in Cornwall.

The data in Tables 4.2 and 4.3 conceal the varying nature of by-employment. Far from being typical, the conventional, risk-minimising, farmer-craftsman represents one end of a spectrum. At the other end are the aggressively entrepreneurial risk-takers who diversify their production portfolio in an attempt to make more money rather than to avoid losing it. Examples of the conventional farmer-weaver include John Cheeseman of Smarden, who had a small farm in 1642 growing wheat and oats, with both cattle and sheep, together with kersey cloth, a loom and equipment worth £2. John Groombridge of Goudhurst had a similar sized farm in 1629 with 13.5 acres of growing crops, cattle and sheep, and two looms.[6] Farming was combined with many other crafts. For example, William Dunning of Bridge had cordwainers tools, nine pairs of ready-made shoes, with cows, young cattle and sheep in his meadow.[7] Thomas Gouldsmith of Ulcombe was a farmer with some 20 acres of growing grain in March 1600, but his inventory also included 'coopers timber' and timber, boards and laths to the value of £5.[8] Sometimes this small-scale production diversification was extended to three occupations: Francis Keast of Crantock, for instance, had cattle, sheep and 8 acres of corn, together with two looms and the fourth part of a fishing boat.[9] Mining was particularly prone to reversals of fortune brought on by price fluctuations, and the very high proportion of miners with some kind of agricultural enterprise – although usually on a fairly small scale – suggests by-employment was primarily motivated by considerations of security and risk-aversion.

It is impossible to tell from the inventories alone whether the various production activities were carried out concurrently, as in the farmer-weaver model, or whether there was a strong seasonal component. Thus it is difficult to know how Robert Dabson, a husbandman of Iwade, combined his fishing and farming, since he had 13 cattle and 69 sheep with a boat and three fishing nets.[10] In Cornwall, however, we do know that fishing for pilchards was a seasonal activity, so it had to be conducted in conjunction with some other occupation, usually farming.[11] Thus William Mellow of Talland had cows, bullocks, sheep, oxen and wheat, along with pilchard nets, although Thomas Paynter was both a fisherman and carpenter.[12] During most of the seventeenth century the fishery was conducted in late summer, although from about 1670 onwards there was a switch in favour of winter drift netting which proved more productive due to the later arrival of the pilchards off the Cornish coast. The replacement of seines by drift nets did, to an extent, increase the number of full-time fishermen since the latter were more versatile: they could be used for catching a variety of fish, allowed the fisherman to operate further from the shore, and could be used throughout the year.[13] Indeed, drift nets were widely used in Kent where herring was the main catch.[14]

We have already noted that retailing was an activity that could be carried out on a small scale, and was often taken up by women.[15] But retailing is also a good example of an occupation that was combined with other activities in an increasingly entrepreneurial way. In Cornwall, for example, retailers were often merchant traders involved in maritime transport, and retailing was a natural extension of their activities. In Kent, on the other hand, high levels of multiple occupation amongst retailers were largely a consequence of their diversification into other aspects of service provision: some worked as barbers or apothecaries, others were tallow chandlers. George Brown of Smarden was a 'Doctor of Physic' with over £80 worth of goods for retail sale and a farm with 15 acres of growing crops, while Thomas Addey of Biddenden was a retailer, farmer and glazier. His inventory of 1722 includes tools and glass in his glazing shop, 272 sheep, and grocery goods and mercery goods to the value of nearly £120.[16] Moreover, victuallers and innholders, increasingly common in Kent, also fell within the retailing category and were often engaged in brewing, baking, distilling or other forms of food processing. This helps partially to explain the particularly high levels of by-employment found within the commercial food processing category. Additionally those working in this field were frequently also farmers, since the income derived from farm produce could be increased considerably if it was processed before leaving the farm gate. Thus almost all dairying was carried out on farms, as was much malting and milling. Agriculture and malting were readily combined and complementary, since one provided the raw material for the other. In this case the farmer was seeking not to limit risk but to earn extra profits from processing the barley he had grown. Diversification might vary in scale and complexity: from the farmer who had a sideline in malting to the merchant with interests in a wide range of different activities, but their motivations were essentially the same. Only the more specialised activities such as large-scale baking, butchering and brewing tended consistently to be carried out by independent tradesmen away from the farm, often in an urban setting.

'Entrepreneurial' as opposed to 'risk-averse' by-employment becomes increasingly common into the eighteenth century, especially in Kent. By combining an agricultural interest with involvement in other forms of production such as textiles, leather working or malting, households sought to maximise their income and ensure best possible use of family labour resources. An early example is John Hilles of Goudhurst, a scythesmith with 528 scythes on his premises in the early seventeenth century, wheat growing, and 72 pounds of butter.[17] Francis Perkins, a blacksmith of Milton who died in 1719, had a shop selling ready made tools, nails, locks and other iron goods in addition to his workshop, and the total value of his inventory came to £613 10s, far higher than one would normally associate with a craftsman.[18] In this case the combination of production activities was undertaken in order to maximise the income Perkins derived from his trade. Craftsmen in Kent were generally wealthier than their counterparts in Cornwall, so it would seem reasonable to assume that the growth of by-employment in the former county was a consequence largely of households seeking to maximise their returns, whereas in the latter the need to supplement income was more important. Clothiers were particularly likely to extend their operations: Robert Tate of Goudhurst, for example, also had 72 pounds of butter in his household in addition to his £40 worth of wool, and John Birch had 5,600 hop poles as well as unsold broadcloths worth £73 in 1712.[19] Indeed, one of the highest concentrations of hop growing was in the clothing parish of Goudhurst. Those described by their status rather than their occupation could also exhibit this entrepreneurial by-employment, such as Thomas Henman, Esquire of Lenham, a large farmer with crops in his barns worth £178, 56 cattle and 297 sheep, but in addition 55,000 bricks.[20]

In Cornwall there were fewer opportunities outside agriculture, despite the fact that farming was not the most important commercial activity in the county. Mining and fishing were the source of much of Cornwall's wealth, but the local economy lacked the diversity found in Kent and this limited the extent of by-employment. Dual occupations were generally most prevalent amongst those categories of production associated with provisioning the consumer, which were some of the least-developed sectors within the Cornish economy. There were some entrepreneurs in Cornwall, notably amongst the merchant class and those involved in food processing activities, but they formed a much smaller group than their counterparts in Kent and were largely urban based. One example is Robert Goulston, a gentleman of St Stephens by Saltash who had a medium-sized farm with 16 acres of growing corn and 114 sheep, but three boats worth £95.[21] Boats and fishing equipment were becoming increasingly expensive, leading to a growing role for entrepreneurs in the industry, and much of the maritime by-employment in the later part of our period resulted from merchants, landowners and large yeoman farmers owning shares in nets and boats which they then leased out to working fishermen.

Arable and pasture

The examples of by-employment including agricultural activity already given demonstrate a mixture of both pasture farming and arable farming. In view of the significance historians have attached to the relationship between the type of farming and by-employment, Tables 4.2 and 4.3 include categories for pasture farming and arable farming. These categories have been applied to commercial farmers (that is those farmers in the categories 3 and 4 from Table 3.3), and the distinction between pasture and arable is calculated using the values of livestock and cereals.[22] Livestock is expressed as a percentage of the value of livestock and cereals, and those farms above the median for a particular period are categorised as livestock and those below the median as arable. Thus in Tables 4.2 and 4.3, 100 per cent of arable and pasture farmers are in the commercial farming category, and 50 per cent of commercial farmers are in each of the arable and pasture categories. The advantage of using values as opposed to acreages and quantities is that inventories can be used for all seasons of the year if we make the assumption that cereals not in the ground after the harvest would be in the barn.[23] Only a minority of inventories can be used to calculate the arable to pasture ratio in this way because crop and livestock values can be combined together or omitted. Furthermore, the distinction between pasture and arable is crude and has to be based on the values of animals and crops rather than acreages of land since inventories do not record pasture or meadow.

There is no universal distinction between by-employments associated with pasture farming as opposed to arable farming. In Kent 29 per cent of craftsmen can be identified as pasture farmers on the definition given above, (Table 4.3) and 19 per cent as arable farmers. In Cornwall, on the other hand, a higher proportion of craftsmen were identified as arable farmers (Table 4.2). In both counties there is little difference between the proportion of farmers classified as arable or pasture who were also engaged in retailing or maritime activity. Only with mining in Cornwall is there a clear association with pasture farming: 46 per cent of those involved in mining were pasture farmers and 19 per cent arable farmers.

However, the picture changes if we include those in categories one and two of the agricultural classification in Table 3.3. These are not commercial farmers, but all are rearing animals on a small scale and therefore can be classed as pastoral farmers. So if those in this category are added to the commercial pastoral farmers the proportion of craft workers in pasture farming in Kent rises to 44 per cent (as opposed to 19 per cent arable) and in Cornwall to 40 per cent (as opposed to 26 per cent arable).

Thus far, craft activities have been lumped together in a single category; Table 4.4 separates out 13 activities and looks at their combination with both commercial and non-commercial agriculture, and their association with pasture and arable farming. Because of the relatively small numbers of inventories involved for some activities the data refer to the entire study period 1600–1749. Overall, the proportion of craftsmen who were farming commercially was just under 50 per cent for the two counties, while the proportions engaged in non-commercial farming were between 15 and 20 per cent. However, there were considerable variations between crafts. In both Cornwall and Kent tailors and shoemakers were the least likely to be farming commercially, while in both counties over 50 per cent of weavers, millers, bakers, brewers, builders and woodworkers were also commercial farmers. Given the considerable differences between Cornwall and Kent it is notable that there is a degree of similarity between the figures for the two counties. This may be coincidence, but it prompts speculation that some occupations offered more security than others. For example, there was probably more continuity of employment for shoemakers and tailors (with the lowest proportions engaged in farming), because demand for their products was less cyclical and the producer was also the retailer and in closer touch with consumers than, say, a weaver.

Table 4.4 Craft workers also engaged in agricultural production 1600–1749 (percentages)

	Cornwall				Kent			
	1&2	*3&4*	*Pasture*	*Arable*	*1&2*	*3&4*	*Pasture*	*Arable*
Weaving	18	52	18	34	14	53	43	10
Milling	11	54	14	41	15	72	31	41
Leather production	25	47	27	20	13	39	16	23
Shoemaking	25	25	17	8	14	19	10	10
Butchering	33	48	8	40	19	60	39	21
Baking	18	70	21	49	14	64	30	34
Brewing	15	69	27	42	14	64	31	33
Building	6	61	6	55	14	56	25	31
Metalworking	23	46	17	29	21	40	9	31
Grocery	18	36	14	22	14	33	17	17
Tailoring	19	25	19	6	12	19	13	6
Woodworking	17	57	20	37	18	52	30	22
Carpentry	15	62	25	37	19	50	25	25

While Tables 4.2 and 4.3 show that in Cornwall there was a tendency for craft activity to be combined with arable farming and in Kent with pasture farming, Table 4.4 reveals how this could vary considerably between crafts. Weavers in Kent conform to the traditional pattern, with pasture farming outnumbering arable by 4:1, or 5:1 if non-commercial farmers are included. But the reverse is the case in Cornwall, where arable farmers predominate. The patterns for the two counties are quite different, reflecting their different agricultural systems and making it impossible to make any simple generalisations about the relationships between by-employment and farming type on the bases of these data.

In view of the relatively small number of usable inventories it is difficult to determine whether the balance between pasture and arable farming by-employment changed over time. However, it is clear that the proportion of pasture farmers involved in mining rises over the course of the period 1600 to 1749, and the proportions of miners involved with non-commercial farming rise from 5 per cent in 1600–49 to 19 per cent in 1700–49. This reflects the growing proletarianisation of mining, as miners withdraw from commercial farming (from 84 per cent to 56 per cent).[24]

Overall, as we have seen in Table 4.1, the extent of by-employment declined over the course of the study period in Cornwall indicating some increase in production specialisation, especially when spinning is included in commercial by-employment. Thus those with evidence of craft activity who were also engaged in commercial farming fell from 58 per cent in the first half of the seventeenth century to 37 per cent in the first half of the eighteenth, and retailers too were also less likely to have another production activity. These figures reflect the decline in importance of commercial farming in Cornwall (Table 3.3 shows a fall from 64 per cent during 1600–29 to 49 per cent during 1720–49), especially in the west of the county during the late seventeenth century and the early eighteenth, as a response to the difficult conditions for cultivation, the growth of corn imports and the availability of alternative employment in the mines and fisheries. However, in Kent there is virtually no change in the proportion of craft workers also engaged in commercial farming (a slight fall from 46 per cent during 1600–49 to 42 per cent during 1700–49) and no change in the proportion involved in non-commercial agriculture (about 16 per cent). Certain production activities, however, do show increases in the extent of by-employment. In Kent, for example, the expansion of the retailing sector (Table 3.2) was through individuals adding retailing to their existing production activities rather than by starting a specialist enterprise. Thus the proportion of retailers also involved in craft activity rose from 14 per cent to 23 per cent between 1600–49 and 1700–49.

In Kent the extent of by-employment changed little between the early seventeenth century and the early eighteenth. Spinning declined, though there was no change to the distribution of spinning amongst the major production activities. Home brewing for domestic consumption increased, though again the increase was spread throughout all commercial activities. However, the most striking change in the pattern of by-employment concerns those in small-scale agriculture (Groups 1 and 2 in Table 3.3). In 1600–49 only 35 per cent of these farmers were involved with commercial production in another field, by 1700–49 this figure had risen to 71 per cent.

The broad trend in by-employment in the two counties is summarised in Table 4.5, which shows the mean and median numbers of production activities per household. While the number of commercial production activities was the same in both counties at the start of the seventeenth century, it fell in Cornish households during the next century and a half but remained roughly constant in Kent. The number of production activities for use was higher in Kent than in Cornwall at the start of the seventeenth century and once again fell in Cornwall while remaining constant in Kent.

In general our findings do not sit easily with the models of pre-industrial economic development discussed in Chapter 1. By-employment was the norm amongst those households described by an inventory, and, while there was some decline in its extent in Cornwall, it was still evident in nearly 60 per cent of households in Kent during 1720–49. Here, there is no evidence of household specialisation in commercial production activity that both the models of proto-industrialisation and the 'industrious revolution' would lead us to expect. In Cornwall there is a tendency for production to become more specialised, but it is not associated with economic development or growth; rather, it is the consequence of a

Table 4.5 Production activities per household

		1600–29	1630–59	1660–89	1690–1719	1720–49
Mean commercial	Cornwall	2.0	1.8	1.5	1.4	1.5
	Kent	1.8	1.9	1.7	1.9	1.7
Mean for use	Cornwall	2.0	1.8	1.3	1.2	1.3
	Kent	2.5	2.6	2.6	2.9	2.6
Overall mean	Cornwall	4.0	3.6	2.8	2.7	2.9
	Kent	4.3	4.4	4.4	4.8	4.4
Median commercial	Cornwall	2.0	2.0	1.0	1.0	1.0
	Kent	2.0	2.0	2.0	2.0	2.0
Median for use	Cornwall	2.0	2.0	1.0	1.0	1.0
	Kent	3.0	3.0	3.0	3.0	3.0
Overall median	Cornwall	4.0	4.0	3.0	2.0	3.0
	Kent	4.0	5.0	5.0	5.0	4.0
% no production	Cornwall	6.0	10.0	16.0	17.0	14.0
	Kent	12.0	13.0	9.0	5.0	5.0

declining agricultural sector and the economic development of the mining industry.

Moreover, the nature of by-employment does not conform to the stereotype of the models in Chapter 1. We can identify the classic weaver-farmer in Kent, diversifying his production activities as a form of security and concentrating on pastoral farming, but he was not typical. Food processing and spinning, rather than craft activities, were the two forms of commercial production most likely to be combined with commercial farming; shoemaking and tailoring were the least likely to be combined. Nor was there any clear link between the type of farming (admittedly in terms of a crude arable/pasture distinction) and by-employment. While 43 per cent of Kent weavers were also pasture farmers (or 57 per cent if we include non-commercial farming), many craft occupations were combined in roughly similar proportions with arable and pasture farming. This is not surprising, since there are many possible forms of connection between farming practice and other production activities. The combination of livestock husbandry with weaving on a daily basis is one form, but there are many others, including the seasonal combination of arable farming with fishing for pilchards for example. Arable farming is also most likely to be associated with commercial food processing, including milling, malting, baking and brewing. Nor should it be assumed that by-employment involved different production activities carried out by the same individual. By-employment in household production usually involved division of labour within the household: spinning or dairying, for instance, was carried out by women. Moreover, while nuclear, conjugal households are widely believed to have been universal throughout England during the early modern period much of the labour for household production would have been carried out by servants or apprentices.

Finally, the idea that by-employment is indicative of a risk-averse peasant mentality, undertaken because of chronic insecurities in pre-industrial occupations, needs dramatic modification. It is true that crop and livestock disease and the vagaries of the weather made early modern farming a precarious business, and it was especially risky for small farmers.[25] Other occupations too carried uncertainties, mainly because continuity of employment depended on an even demand for the finished product, which was particularly difficult for export industries, which were subject to considerable logistical difficulties in transporting goods abroad and severe fluctuations in demand.[26] Yet, once again, this is particularly true of the small-scale weaver-farmer, who was not typical. Many occupations that were combined together did not carry such risk. Larger farmers had more resources to weather a storm; in fact, they would make more money when yields fell.[27] Production activities supplying local needs were more secure than those destined for export, especially in the food processing industries. Thus in some cases by-employment was a means of maximising household income rather than avoiding risk. Taken further, 'by-employment' becomes the means by which capitalist entrepreneurs can make the most money. In Kent, but to a far lesser degree in Cornwall, we see wealthy entrepreneurs undertaking a number of large-scale economic enterprises to make money. This type of by-employment is indicative of capitalist production rather than peasant subsistence. These households were also undertaking considerable production for use in the household, but again it is not indicative of a subsistence economy: indeed, it represents an important form of consumption to which we will return in Chapter 7.

Division of labour within the household

Certain types of work in early modern England were done almost exclusively by women:

> Countrey women look unto the things necessary and requisite about Kine, Calves, Hogs, Pigs, Pigeons, Geese, Ducks, Peacocks, Hens, Feasants, and other sorts of Beasts and Fowls, as well for the feeding of them, as for the milking and making of Butter and Cheese, and keeping of all things neat and clean about the house, getting and providing the labouring men their Victuals in due season; and furthermore they have the charge of the Oven and Cellar, and the handling and ordering of Hemp and Flax, &c, as also the care of looking to the clipping of Sheep, of keeping their Fleeces, of Spining and Combing of Wooll...[28]

All forms of spinning, as well as small-scale dairying, brewing, baking and food preservation lay within the woman's sphere.[29] Table 4.6 examines these five forms of production, looking at the proportion of male- and female-headed households engaged in each of the activities, and breaking the figures down according to status group and commercial production category. The percentages for dairying include both production for use and for exchange, since dairying was exclusively a female activity, whereas the figures for brewing, baking and food preservation refer only to production for use since men often undertook these activities on a commercial scale.[30]

Table 4.6 indicates that male-headed households were more likely than their female counterparts to be engaged in all five production activities. In Kent, for example, 41 per cent of men's inventories show evidence of spinning but only 34 per cent of those for women, while the figures for dairying, brewing and baking show an even greater contrast. This does not, however, suggest that men were more heavily involved in what have traditionally been considered female occupations. On the contrary, it indicates that such activities were most often carried out within the households of married couples, and these of course consisted of a man and a

Table 4.6 Women's work: percentages of activities by household categories 1600–1749

Category	No. inventories		Spinning		Dairying		Brewing		Baking		Preservation	
	Cornwall	Kent	Cornwall	Kent	Cornwall	Kent	Cornwall	Kent	Cornwall	Kent	Cornwall	Kent
Esquire	17	10	7	30	71	40	65	60	18	40	53	60
Gentleman	190	127	7	33	63	62	46	66	4	42	41	74
Yeoman	762	548	12	49	69	87	43	77	2	49	48	85
Husbandman	276	225	19	45	59	80	43	57	3	37	53	82
Bachelor	17	25	0	4	21	16	5	4	0	16	5	12
Spinster	88	50	6	32	13	16	6	16	0	14	9	26
Widow	470	429	9	36	32	43	26	38	2	27	30	62
Farming 3&4	2,190	1,988	17	48	78	92	46	70	3	47	53	88
Farming 1&2	616	575	11	40	41	57	30	46	2	36	36	74
Crafts	632	735	19	48	46	59	42	64	5	45	45	83
Com. food	625	1,236	16	51	77	86	52	72	6	52	62	92
Maritime	148	169	12	46	36	28	49	67	7	37	43	75
Mining	382	–	12	–	59	–	34	–	2	–	30	–
Retail	133	177	6	32	35	40	38	45	1	43	44	84
Services	27	80	11	40	33	39	33	60	4	39	37	73
Waged	57	77	9	32	26	57	12	35	0	34	18	66
Female	688	589	10	34	28	38	21	34	1	24	26	57
Male	3,387	3,337	13	41	53	63	37	57	2	40	41	76
All	4,075	3,926	12	38	49	60	34	54	2	37	39	73

Note
The occupational categories are defined in Appendix 2.

woman. Many women's inventories, on the other hand, relate to part households: either widows who might have been living with their children or spinsters employed outside the family in service. Both of these groups would have been heavily involved in these five production activities but did not own the production goods used, and consequently these do not often appear in their inventories.

In Kent, evidence of women's work was found most frequently in yeomen's inventories: 87 per cent of them were involved in dairying, 77 per cent in brewing and 49 per cent in baking. A large proportion of husbandmen's households were also involved in spinning, dairying and preservation, but in the case of brewing and baking gentry households had greater involvement. This suggests that the latter activities were more dependent on wealth, requiring more specialist equipment.[31] Both activities remained relatively rare amongst the waged population, reflecting the fact that home production of bread and drink was a relative luxury. Dairying and spinning, on the other hand, were widespread across the status divide. In Cornwall the level of involvement in all five activities was considerably lower, but here too was concentrated within the higher status groups. Households headed by an esquire showed the most frequent evidence of baking, brewing and dairying, but spinning and preservation were found almost as regularly amongst the households of yeomen and husbandmen. Again the contrast between higher and lower status categories was most pronounced for baking and brewing, and least significant in the case of spinning. This ties in with the notion of a distinction between work for use within the household and for sale or exchange.[32] Spinning was primarily a commercial activity, which provided a source of income for the household, whereas small-scale brewing and baking was largely for home consumption.

It has been argued that from the late seventeenth century there was a growing separation of gender roles, particularly in the south-east of England, associated with the gradual withdrawal of some women from income-generating work as levels of wealth increased and bourgeois values were more widely assimilated.[33] This can be seen in the increased emphasis on domesticity and the adoption of more genteel lifestyles by the middling sort, which increased the number of household tasks.[34] The expansion of home baking and brewing in Kent, and the prevalence of domestic outbuildings here by the close of the study period, provides clear evidence of this development. The main role of the wife frequently became more that of supervision, with much of the actual work being done by servant labour. The prevalence, and even increase of some small-scale food and drink processing activities must be seen as an indirect indicator of the employment of female servants in large numbers. Given the increase in wealth in Kent it is likely that both the proportion of households containing servants and the overall number of servants was increasing.[35]

Inventories do not record the presence of servants directly, but their presence is referred to indirectly by the use of the word 'servant' in descriptions of rooms and as an adjective to qualify things such as beds. Counting the frequency of the word 'servant' in these contexts in Kent is revealing, since the percentage of inventories including the word rises steadily from some 6 per cent in the 1600–29 period to 21 per cent in the period 1720–49.[36] Obviously this grossly underestimates the proportion of households with servants because appraisers were not obliged to use the word 'servant' as an adjective, but it does suggest that a household was more likely to have servants in the early eighteenth century than it was in the early seventeenth. However, the increase in frequency may not have been as great as the rise from 6 per cent to 21 per cent suggests, since room descriptions in Kent inventories were becoming more detailed as the number of rooms in the household grew.[37]

Another indication of the likely increase in the numbers of servants is the fact that the average number of beds in Kent households rose over the course of the seventeenth century from a mean of 3.67 per inventory during 1600–29 to 4.28 by 1690–1729, while the corresponding median number rose from 3 to 4. This increase is unlikely to reflect a rise in the number of children in the household, given falling fertility rates, and therefore suggests an increase in the number of servants, albeit not of the same magnitude as the frequency count of the previous paragraph suggests.[38] On the other hand a decline of the incidence of bed-sharing could have the same result, although we have no evidence for this.

A similar analysis cannot be undertaken with the Cornish inventories: indeed, only six inventories mention the word 'servant' in the entire sample of 4,119. This, to some extent, explains why the same processing activities were less often found in Cornwall, since the inventoried population here was much less wealthy than in Kent and was getting poorer over time.[39] Moreover, there was a greater bias in favour of higher status groups here, suggesting that the new more comfortable lifestyles were being adopted by the wealthy but had not percolated down the social spectrum to the same extent as in Kent. In both counties levels of food and drink-processing activities amongst the labouring population remained relatively low suggesting that housework here was simpler and more functional, and consequently less visible in the documents.

The gender division of labour in income-generating work has been associated with by-employment. Within farming and textile-producing households men usually wove and performed agricultural tasks such as ploughing and caring for cattle, while their wives and daughters attended to dairying and spinning yarn as well as housework.[40] The figures in Table 4.6 show that households involved in large-scale agriculture, craft activities and commercial food processing were the most likely to show evidence of income-generating female work in spinning or dairying. Smallholders and labourers had much lower levels of engagement in either activity, suggesting that women from these households were more likely to earn money by working for wages.[41] Whereas 78 per cent of Cornish commercial farmers were involved in dairying, only 26 per cent of wage-earning households were thus employed. Clearly, fewer smallholders had sufficient pasture resources to keep a cow, and thus were excluded from dairy production. Spinning was also less commonly found amongst the wage earners, although this could simply reflect the fact that fewer of them owned their own spinning wheels. Over the course of the study period, however, there was a noticeable decline in the proportion of households involved in spinning. In this case changes in the nature of female employment were largely a response to processes taking place in the wider economy.

It has been argued by some that the gender division of labour within the household became more distinct, especially in the south and east, as the relative equality of the family economy was undermined by this economic change at a national level.[42] Others, however, have suggested that women were always firmly subordinated to men within the economy of the household: their work was clearly divided, less specialised and generally less respected.[43] Nevertheless, the increasing regional specialisation of agriculture and textile production, and the consolidation of farm holdings, did lead to a fall in demand for women's labour in some localities, which accelerated from the early eighteenth century.[44] The impact of these changes would have been felt in the corn lands of northern Kent where arable production expanded considerably at the expense of dairying, and in the Weald where the woollen cloth industry was declining. In the west, holdings remained relatively small and pastoral farming predominated, so that although textile production declined here too, opportunities remained for women to participate in income generation for the household. This possibly explains why evidence of dairying is spread more evenly across the various production sectors in Cornwall, whereas in Kent it appears to have remained important only for higher status groups. Additionally those households engaged in urban-focused activities such as retailing and professional services show the lowest level of involvement in production for use, again suggesting specialisation and a movement away from agricultural by-employment.

Table 4.7 shows the proportions of households with evidence of various commercial activities headed by women, who were of course single or widowed. Taking all commercial activities there is very little change over 150 years, suggesting that there were no major developments in the involvement of single women and widows in commercial activities. However, the figures in Table 4.7 hide some more specific changes since women tended to become excluded from the management of commercial production activities when these became more specialised and capital intensive. Thus there were large numbers of female brewers in the medieval period when this was a localised, small-scale industry using only basic equipment and yielding small profits.[45] By the early eighteenth century, however, commercial brewing was no longer considered as potentially women's work; it was a highly capitalised industry serving large regional markets.[46] In our sample of inventories no women headed households involved in large-scale brewing, although a significant proportion of women were brewing on a scale that left them a surplus to sell. Some 20 per cent of commercial brewers were women in Cornwall and 10 per cent in Kent. Similarly, malting went from being considered women's work in the early seventeenth century to an increasingly specialised and exclusively male occupation over the course of the study period: under 5 per cent of inventories with evidence of malting were headed by a woman in Kent and 10 per cent in Cornwall.[47] On the other hand, retailing offered new opportunities for women as the widening demand for groceries and cheap consumer goods encouraged the proliferation of petty shopkeepers during the early eighteenth century.[48] This is shown quite dramatically in Table 4.7, especially for Kent, where the proportion of retailing households headed by a woman rose from 5 per cent in the first half of the seventeenth century to 17 per cent during the first half of the eighteenth. This retailing activity involved little capital investment and offered only low returns, the classic features of women's work throughout the early modern period. This suggests that although the low status and restrictions on women's income-generating work did not change significantly over the early modern period, the range of occupations open to women did, as a result of structural changes in the economy as a whole.[49]

Table 4.7 Percentages of households engaged in commercial activities headed by a woman

	Cornwall			Kent		
	1600–49	1650–99	1700–49	1600–49	1650–99	1700–49
Service	0	0	8	0	0	8
Retail	0	9	9	5	8	17
Maritime	0	6	4	5	8	7
Waged	0	5	0	7	0	0
Food processing	5	11	8	5	6	7
Crafts	4	5	3	3	2	5
Commercial agriculture	10	9	6	5	6	7
Spinning	13	18	12	14	11	14
Mining	0	3	3			
Subsistence agriculture	22	24	13	18	15	14
All commercial	8	9	6	6	6	8

'Unproductive' households

Given our methodology of identifying commercial production through the evidence of material goods it is obvious that some apparently unproductive households were in fact engaged in some form of production that left no obvious material evidence. People 'producing' services are particularly difficult to identify. For example, we know that Richard Ellis of Kenwyn was a musician because he describes himself as such in his will, even though there are no musical instruments in his inventory. We can therefore classify him as belonging to the category of personal services, but he would have appeared as 'unproductive' if his will had not been consulted and we went on the evidence of the inventory alone.[50]

Roughly 20 per cent of inventories in both counties for the whole period 1600–1749 have no evidence of commercial production, although the proportion rises over the study period in Cornwall and falls in Kent. These inventories have been categorised in Table 4.8 according to status designations, where they are available, with the intention of identifying particular types of household. There can be no doubt that some of these 'non-productive' inventories are simply the result of omissions by appraisers, or more commonly by their lumping items together under general headings. While we have tried to exclude inventories from the analysis where this is obviously the case, some must be included in our calculations.[51]

Nevertheless there is some pattern to the characteristics of these 'non-productive' inventories, and we may divide them roughly into four groups. The first consists of those elderly people who had 'retired' and disposed of most of their material goods before their death, probably to their children, with whom they continued to live. Thus their inventory records their personal possessions but no household goods and usually refers only to one room. This type of inventory can be found across the social spectrum: for example, the inventories of gentlemen such as Humphrey Mayer of Canterbury recording his apparel and wig, personal possessions including his sword and prayer book, and a considerable sum of money, or James Daye of St Columb Major whose possessions were his clothes, money and three leases. At the other end of the scale the inventory of the husbandman Thomas Fox of Chartham records his few personal possessions and his fowling piece.[52]

These inventories refer to 'part households' since they list only a part of the material goods in the household where the individual died, and their proportions are shown in Table 4.8.[53] Taking Kent and Cornwall together, 35 per cent of the yeomen classed as unproductive have inventories describing part households, although for yeoman as a whole only 8 per cent in Cornwall and 6 per cent in Kent had probably retired and handed on their property. About a third of the 'non-productive' gentry inventories describe 'part-households', and a higher proportion (18 per cent in

Table 4.8 Inventories with no evidence of production 1600–1749

Status	Cornwall				Kent			
	Number of inventories	No commercial production (%)	No production for use (%)	Part households (%)	Number of inventories	No commercial production (%)	No production for use (%)	Part households (%)
Bachelor	19	42	53	47	25	72	56	84
Esquire	17	18	24	18	8	50	25	0
Gentleman	190	27	29	18	126	31	15	11
Husbandman	276	25	22	11	225	15	6	9
Virgin or maiden	0	–	–	–	14	86	71	79
Singlewoman	11	64	91	55	7	57	43	71
Spinster	76	78	67	45	29	59	59	62
Widow	467	48	44	15	427	43	26	13
Yeoman	761	14	22	8	548	9	9	6
Unspecified	1,493	27	33	14	1,699	25	17	13
Female	688	53	50	23	589	46	32	21
Male	3,387	17	29	11	3,337	16	13	10
Total	4,075	23	33	13	3,926	20	16	12

Cornwall and 11 per cent in Kent) had retired. The second type of 'part household' is referred to in inventories for single men and women (bachelors, virgins, maidens, singlewomen and spinsters). In Kent *all* those so described with no commercial production activity were living in 'part households'; in Cornwall, only about 50 per cent of corresponding inventories were part households, possibly suggesting a different usage of the terms for single people. Those described as single people in part households were clearly living in other people's houses as children, servants, apprentices, or lodgers, but in the absence of other information it is impossible to ascribe them to one of those four categories. Some of those described as 'virgin' in Kent were quite rich young women who had recently inherited money from their fathers. Examples include Sarah Terry of Minster in Thanet whose inventory records her wearing apparel worth a mark and a legacy given to her by her father of £50 and Joanne White of Canterbury who had a legacy of £500 from her father, and, appropriately enough, a pair of virginals.[54]

The third group with a higher than average prevalence of non-productive inventories are widows. While many widows took over their husband's enterprise, over 40 per cent had no obvious means of material support. As with the other groups some of these may have been making a living in ways not revealed by material goods. But the majority were probably surviving from legacies left by their husbands, or were being supported by their children or even by the parish; but we cannot determine this from their inventories.

The majority of 'unproductive households' fall into the fourth category and were probably not unproductive at all, but earning their living through activities that left no material evidence. In some cases the appraisers of an inventory indicated an individual's occupation, but in others they did not. Although about 30 per cent of gentlemen had no material evidence of production, many were probably living off the income from real estate, but in most cases we have no evidence as to the source of their wealth.[55] For example, Mr Hills of Canterbury who died in 1683 was owed £2,355 in bills, bonds, and debts for 'goods', and John Moyle of Wye died in 1677 with bills, bonds and mortgages to the value of £1,424. William Dray, though, died in 1691 leaving a prosperous household in Canterbury with goods worth over £300, but no debts owed to him and no inkling in his inventory as to the source of his wealth.[56]

5   The material culture of consumption

Consumption is a dynamic process involving decisions by individuals as to how to spend time and money. The thing being consumed may be a durable material object, a relatively short-lived commodity such as fresh food, or something that is intangible such as music and dance. The study of consumption therefore, as de Vries has pointed out, should be dealing with flows: flows of consumption goods and services through the household, which can be related to the flows of income into the household.[1] If we had this sort of information on household income and consumption it would be possible to calculate the economists' measures of the propensity to consume which could be one quantitative indicator of a 'consumer revolution'.

Given the sources we are using such an approach is impossible. Inventories measure stocks and not flows.[2] They show the stock of goods in the household at the death of their owner, not consumption activity, and they tell us little about the frequency or the number of purchases made during an individual's lifetime. As we have seen, inventories omit a number of items and are inconsistent in their recording of certain items, especially clothing.[3] Moreover, inventories only list durable goods. They do not record expenditure on services (including education), entertainment, transitory items such as newspapers, and petty purchases like trinkets and children's toys. At the other end of the spectrum, they do record goods that are so durable that they function as a store of value, such as silver or even pewter, which can be seen both as evidence of consumption and investment. For most households in early modern England the greatest expenditure was on food, yet inventories record few foodstuffs, so they cannot be said to represent the majority of consumption activity.[4]

Furthermore, we cannot even be sure that the goods recorded in inventories are the result of a deliberate act of consumption, since they could have been inherited rather than purchased. Goods that were acquired through inheritance say little about current demand, or current fashions and tastes. Moreover, inherited items will form a greater proportion of a household's stock of goods in a period of population stability or decline than in a period of growth. In a period with a declining population (such as England from 1680–1720), even growing stocks of highly durable goods may represent no net additions, and hence no increased demand or consumption.[5]

Nor can the wealth of an individual, or rather the value of the movable goods in their inventory, be taken as an accurate reflection of their income. The value of movable goods in an inventory varies by occupation, so that, for example, the inventory of a farmer includes much of his working capital (livestock and farm implements) and if the inventory were made in the summer, the revenue from his crops for an entire year. On the other hand, the inventory of a clothier will contain some stocks but is unlikely to include a year's worth of working capital. Thus in terms of movable goods, the farmer might appear wealthier than the clothier, whereas in terms of income flows the reverse may well be the case.[6]

Given the relationship of evidence in inventories to the consumption process we are on much safer ground in using inventories to talk about the material culture of households rather than consumption itself. Material culture is used here to refer to the world of goods as it exists and given meaning by the inhabitants of that world.[7] While the stock of material culture is not the same as consumption, we can infer a great deal about consumption from it. The stock of material goods present in the household implies consumption choices, either in purchasing the goods, or keeping them when they are inherited. An increase in the range and variety of material goods implies acquisition through consumption rather than inheritance. Above all, the goods in early modern houses give us clues, albeit ones that are tantalising and oblique, to help us understand the cultural meanings of material objects.

Historians of consumption tend to concentrate on the meanings ascribed to goods, and on leisure and comfort, but, as we have seen in the previous two chapters, a household also invested in goods in order to enable or ease production processes: it is important to remember that consumption and work are not separate in these households as they are in modern industrialised society. For example, a clock can be seen as a status symbol or conspicuous piece of decoration, but clocks also had a utilitarian function. Their presence and location in the household can suggest a significance for production as well as consumption. Furthermore, 'production for use' identified in the previous chapters can also be seen as a form of consumption, albeit routine and mundane.

A great many studies have used inventories to examine the material culture of early modern England, but fewer have employed them to quantify the characteristics of early modern households. Inventories enable material culture to be measured in a number of ways. The most straightforward, and in many ways the safest method, is simply to count the frequency of objects. This is one of the methods adopted by de Vries in his pathbreaking study, and the principal method adopted by Weatherill in the first major quantitative study of material culture from English inventories.[8] This can be strikingly effective in showing the spread of conspicuously new goods such as clocks and mirrors. But it can also exaggerate novelty if goods that decline in number are not considered. To some extent consumption is a cyclical process, and as new goods spread others start to disappear. Court cupboards, for example, are replaced by new forms of storage, benches by chairs, and cauldrons by new kinds of cooking equipment. Thus the frequency counts in this study, based on the presence or absence of goods in inventories, look at new goods, disappearing goods, and indeed at goods whose presence remains constant.

Historians have also looked at the values in inventories; inferring expenditure patterns from the value of goods listed, and relating the value of consumer goods to the total value of movable wealth.[9] There are dangers in attempting to measure consumption in this way, not least because of the uncertain relationship between expenditure on consumption and the value of material goods in the inventory. We consider the issue further in Chapter 7, but this approach does not form a key element of our analysis.

Inventories can reveal more than the values and the presence or (apparent) absence of objects in households. Increased levels of consumption did not necessarily mean the acquisition of new types of goods, but often involved the acquisition of more of the same type of good. Thus Muldrew adopts the strategy of counting the number of goods in inventories 'to measure consumption' in the sixteenth century.[10] This is a fairly crude technique since it is rarely possible to count all the goods in an inventoried household, because even the most detailed inventories contain general descriptions, such as 'all the lumber', to describe a miscellany of small items. Therefore, rather than attempt to count all items as Muldrew does, we ignore those inventories where items are lumped together and count only those goods, such as linen or chairs, that were commonly enumerated by appraisers. Nevertheless, we can identify important changes taking place in households because of increased quantities of particular goods. It is also possible to demonstrate changes in the variety of goods in the household, for example the number of different types of eating and drinking utensils. This is not the same as the quantity of particular items but indicates the richness (or poverty) of the domestic environment in terms of the variety of objects in the home.

We consider material culture to be concerned with the meanings ascribed to material goods by people.[11] While inventories record the goods they say nothing directly about meanings and thus some historians have been quite critical of the use of inventories for the study of material culture. Vickery considers, 'social meaning cannot be read off the bare fact of ownership', while Breen thinks inventories 'show us decontextualised things that have lost their meanings, that no longer tell us stories about the creative possibilities of possession, about the process of self-fashioning, or about the personal joys and disappointments that we sense must also have been a product of that eighteenth-century commercial world'.[12]

There is some obvious truth in these comments, but we can tease some meanings from the changing patterns of objects in the household. As we shall see, changes in the material world revealed by inventories imply profound changes in household activities and practices, and in the relationships between individuals in the household. Aside from looking at the rates of adoption of new commodities, and the quantity and variety of goods, this chapter also looks at the language of inventories to see if it can suggest changing attitudes to consumption and the acquisition of goods. The search for meaning continues in the two subsequent chapters through the examination of where objects were located in the household and how rooms were used, and by relating patterns of ownership to wealth, status, location and production activities. The remainder of this chapter will describe the changes in the material culture of households in Kent and Cornwall.

Furniture and furnishings

Before the seventeenth century the furniture of most English households consisted of beds, a table, a few benches, forms and stools for sitting, and a number of chests for storing linen and other valuables. During the seventeenth and eighteenth centuries English households acquired many new types of furniture. These added to the comfort and convenience of the domestic environment and were also associated with new social rituals, such as new dining practices and the consumption of new drinks such as tea, coffee and chocolate. At the same time, some other types of furniture became much less common as they were superseded by newer types. As Table 5.1 shows, the ownership of new types of furniture (court and press cupboards, chests of drawers, cabinets, and new types of tables and chairs) increased in Kent from around 30 per cent of households in the early seventeenth century to nearly 80 per cent by the middle of the eighteenth.

The chest was the most common type of furniture for storage, used primarily for clothing and household linen such as tablecloths, napkins, sheets and towels. Over 90 per cent of Kent inventories mention chests throughout the period, as do some 50 per cent of Cornish ones. The chest provided only limited access from the top, and its contents, particularly those items at the bottom of the chest, could only be reached with difficulty. When personal possessions were few in number this was not such a problem, but as they multiplied more practical storage furniture became necessary and desirable. The limitations of chest storage was overcome by providing one or more unlidded boxes, or drawers, which could be withdrawn from the front. Chests fitted with one or two drawers in the base were made from the sixteenth century onward; the chest of drawers completely composed of drawers and without a lidded compartment on top,

Table 5.1 Furniture

		1600–29	1630–59	1660–89	1690–1719	1720–49
New furniture (%)	Cornwall	15	19	25	26	38
	Kent	29	36	55	64	77
Chest of drawers (%)	Cornwall	0	0	4	6	14
	Kent	0	2	19	39	59
Court cupboards (%)	Cornwall	1	2	4	2	1
	Kent	12	20	26	12	2
Press cupboards (%)	Cornwall	11	15	18	18	25
	Kent	15	21	30	33	34
Chairs (median number)	Cornwall	1	1	2	4	6
	Kent	3	4	6	10	13
Benches (%)	Cornwall	59	56	48	39	43
	Kent	76	75	73	65	47
Stools (%)	Cornwall	32	27	27	19	9
	Kent	59	65	72	70	62
New tables (%)	Cornwall	5	5	6	6	14
	Kent	9	9	12	13	25
Tables (median number)	Cornwall	1	2	2	2	2
	Kent	2	2	3	3	5
Carpets (%)	Cornwall	21	22	13	6	1
	Kent	18	20	26	10	3
Upholstered furniture (%)	Cornwall	1	1	5	6	8
	Kent	16	32	69	79	74
Feather beds (%)	Cornwall	33	32	29	28	26
	Kent	44	48	55	62	51
Cushions (%)	Cornwall	12	9	6	2	1
	Kent	37	40	38	15	9
Decorative woods (%)	Cornwall	0	0	1	1	3
	Kent	0	0	1	8	18
All furniture (median number of items)	Cornwall	5	6	5	5	6
	Kent	12	13	20	23	24
Variety of furniture (median no. of types)	Cornwall	4	4	4	3	3
	Kent	7	9	11	12	12

appeared around the middle of the seventeenth century.[13] Since access to a chest of drawers did not depend upon a hinged lid, there was no reason to limit its height, and drawers could be stacked up, greatly increasing storage capacity without taking up any further floor space. The need to save space became an increasingly prominent issue in many households as the number of domestic goods multiplied. This helps to explain the popularity of some of the new furniture that appeared at this time, including chests of drawers and also gateleg tables.[14] The chest of drawers was an eminently practical innovation, and they were the most popular new item of furniture in Kent households. Less than 1 per cent of Kent households had chests with drawers in the first three decades of the seventeenth century, but by 1720–49 almost 60 per cent of households in the Kent sample contained at least one example of this item of furniture. In Cornwall the chest with drawers steadily increased in popularity, but at a much slower rate. Only 14 per cent of households here had chests with drawers during the 1720–49 period, a figure reached some 70 years earlier in Kent.

One type of cupboard that increased in popularity during the early seventeenth century was the 'court cupboard'. This large and decorative piece of furniture consisted of two open shelves, usually finely made and often with carved ornament. Court cupboards were used for displaying plate and as a side table on which food was placed during meal times.[15] As Randle Holme put it:

> This [dish] is a vessell … much in use in all houses, and fameleys; both for necessary use (as, putting of meate into them) to serue vp to tables; as also to adorne their countrey houses, and court cuberts: for they are not looked vpon to be of any great worth in personalls, that haue not many dishes and much pewter, Brasse, copper, and tyn ware; set round about a Hall, Parlar, and Kitchen.[16]

In Kent, court cupboards rose in popularity from around 12 per cent at the start of the seventeenth century, reaching a peak of just over 26 per cent during the 1660–89 period. Thereafter they steadily declined to less than 2 per cent by the final period. In Cornwall, court cupboards declined in similar fashion, but were apparently very rare.[17] The court cupboard was an elaboration of the 'dresser board' of the Middle Ages, a basic surface or shelf on which food was prepared. In Cornwall this type of furniture probably remained common. There are many references to boards and shelves amongst the furniture of Cornish households on which food could either be served or utensils stored and displayed: Richard Addam of Crantock, for example, was typical in possessing '1 old cage and 1 little board 4d'.[18] This style of furniture echoes the medieval tradition of furniture in its simplicity.

By the end of the seventeenth century the court cupboard had become unfashionable over much of England, and specialised dressers, press cupboards and sideboards were taking its place.[19] In Kent, press cupboards steadily rose in popularity from around 15 per cent in the early decades of the seventeenth century to around 30 per cent in latter decades. Press cupboards in Cornwall were only slightly less popular, and they follow a similar pattern of development, from around 11 per cent to just over 25 per cent by our final period. Press cupboards were large and important pieces of furniture. Like court cupboards, they were used for serving food and were usually given pride of place in a hall, parlour or best chamber. Although occasionally boarded, most press cupboards were of joined and panelled construction, which is further evidence of their importance.[20] Press cupboards combined the display function of court cupboards with a more practical storage space. They usually had a recessed upper section where plate could be displayed and food served, below which shelves were concealed by two doors. The linen stored in these cupboards, such as napkins and tablecloths, was used at the table for meals. Press cupboards became increasingly specialised in their function during the seventeenth and eighteenth centuries. Besides those described specifically as storing linen, such as 'linen presses', new types, such as the 'hanging press' appeared, which were for hanging clothes and are the antecedents of modern-day wardrobes.

Cabinets, like court cupboards, were essentially decorative items, used for storing curiosities that were shown to friends and guests, and displaying plate or other decorative items, particularly oriental porcelain. They were decorative, luxury items of furniture. While there is a slight increase in their number from the late seventeenth century in Kent (from less than 1 per cent in 1670 to 13 per cent in the 1740s), they were the least popular item of new furniture amongst those households in our sample. In Cornwall, cabinets were extremely rare, and were found in only 2 per cent of households as late as the 1740s. On the other hand, press cupboards with specialised storage functions steadily increased in popularity, and chests of drawers, the most practical innovation in storage furniture introduced during this period, increased much more rapidly by comparison. The new types of furniture, which became popular in Kent and, to a lesser extent, in Cornwall, therefore, suggest a greater concern with convenience and practicality than with display.

Aside from storage and display, there were also changes in furniture used for seating and eating. Chairs were already common in Kent in the early seventeenth century, when nearly 79 per cent of households recorded their presence, increasing to over 90 per cent by the 1740s. Chairs were far less common in Cornwall, being found in about a third of households in the early seventeenth century and just over half by the 1740s. New types of upholstered furniture, however, were acquired in addition to, or as replacements for these chairs as Table 5.1 indicates. The number of chairs in both counties dramatically increased between 1600 and 1750. In the first three decades of the seventeenth century, Kentish households possessed an average of three chairs, but by 1720–49 this number had increased to 13. The rate of increase was similar in Cornwall, with numbers increasing from a median of one at the start of the seventeenth century to six by the 1740s.[21]

The corollary to the rise of the chair is the decline of the bench.

Consequently, in Cornwall where the adoption of chairs was slower, the decline of benches was less dramatic. Stools also declined in Cornwall from around 30 per cent in the first decades of the seventeenth century to under 10 per cent by the mid-eighteenth century. In Kent, however, stools increased in popularity even though most households acquired increasing numbers of chairs. The continued high level of stool ownership in Kent was due to the increasing acquisition of new upholstered stools, whereas upholstered furniture was comparatively rare in Cornwall.

The increase in the numbers of chairs and decline in the numbers of benches is partly explained by the appearance of new types of table, since a bench is impracticable for seating at a round or oval table. New types of table included gateleg tables, and numerous types of occasional table. Gateleg tables (usually described by appraisers as an 'oval table', and occasionally as a 'folding table' or 'leaf table') first appeared in the sixteenth century but were rare before the mid-seventeenth.[22] The gateleg technique was used for tables in a wide range of sizes. Varieties include those with swivel tops that folded completely flat, small tables for occasional use, some with only a single leaf, and very large dining tables with four gates, capable of accommodating sixteen or more people. The gateleg table had the advantage of saving space but it also indicated the trend towards a new informality of dining, since it could be brought out when required. These tables are usually found in great chambers and parlours and were used for a more private and intimate mode of dining than the communal meals served at long tables with the complete household (including servants) present. These new types of furniture formed part of the changing use of domestic space taking place in many households during the seventeenth and eighteenth centuries, in which divisions between living and service areas within the house became more clearly demarcated, reflecting growing distinctions between family and servants.

Smaller occasional tables also appeared at this time. They are frequently described as 'side' or 'corner' tables, indicating where they were kept when not in use. In Kent, descriptions such as 'chamber tables' also suggest how they had miscellaneous occasional uses. Occasional tables were an essential prop for the genteel practice of taking hot drinks such as tea, coffee and chocolate.[23] In Kent, occasional tables became increasingly common during the 1740s, matching the growth in tea-drinking with which it was closely related, many of these small tables are indeed described as 'tea-tables'. In Cornwall the acquisition of these new types of table was much slower, with evidence of their presence in less than half the number of households as in Kent. These new tables were comparatively specialised in their function, and were not capable of carrying heavy wear, as was required of a conventional kitchen table, and they were therefore acquired in addition to more solidly constructed furniture.

'Carpets' were used from medieval times to cover crudely constructed furniture, and were usually more valuable than the piece over which they were laid.[24] As furniture became more decorative with improvements in construction and the treatment of woods, the practice of covering furniture declined. In Kent the popularity of carpets parallels that of court cupboards, which were often covered with decorative textiles, both reaching a peak in the 1650s. Carpets steadily declined after this date and disappeared by 1740. A similar pattern of decline is found in Cornwall where carpets were slightly more common at the start of the seventeenth century. The smaller numbers of carpets in Cornwall after the second half of the seventeenth century, as with the decline in cushions, is more likely to be due to a general decline in the quality of furniture and furnishings than an improvement. This is suggested by the relatively small numbers of new types of furniture found here, in contrast to the widespread use of furniture made with decorative woods in Kent by the early eighteenth century.

In Cornwall 'tableboards' were very common, found in 70–80 per cent of inventories for most of the period 1600–1750. Tableboards were also found in Devon, where they were often polished on one side and left rough on the other, and rotated for different uses. Some were used as a cover to protect the surface of a table.[25] There is evidence for this for Cornwall where tableboards sometimes occur with complete tables. More commonly, however, they are listed with frames, from which they appear to have been detachable, since the tableboard and frame are usually itemised individually. Tableboards also sometimes occur without a frame, which suggests they might have been placed on another piece of furniture when used. Although more permanent, this type of table, with its detachable board and frame, echoes medieval styles of furniture. The popularity of the Cornish tableboard indicates the persistence of a local tradition of furniture which, when compared with the furniture in contemporary Kentish households, appears to have been little affected by new fashions.

The acquisition of better-quality furniture can also help explain the decline of cushions and carpets. Upholstered furniture, most commonly 'turkey work' chairs, steadily increased in Kentish households as Table 5.1 indicates, being present in over three-quarters of the sample of inventories by the eighteenth century.[26] In Cornwall upholstered furniture was much rarer, with under 10 per cent of inventories mentioning it in our last period. Before seating furniture was upholstered, cushions were used to make it more comfortable; the decline of cushions, therefore, corresponds closely with the rise in popularity of upholstered furniture in Kent. In Cornwall, cushions were much less common than in Kent, found in only 12 per cent of households at the start of the seventeenth century. Although the proportion of Cornish households with cushions declined to less than 1 per cent after 1720, upholstered furniture did not become popular, once again suggesting a decline in standards of comfort.

The upholstered furniture found in Kentish homes during the seventeenth and eighteenth centuries would have been made by London craftsmen. The production and distribution of furniture gradually changed during the seventeenth and eighteenth centuries from a position in which local craftsmen made and sold the majority of domestic furniture for all social levels to one in which production was increasingly subdivided into specialist crafts that were concentrated in a few towns and cities.[27] Defoe comments on the geographical separation of production from consumption in the furniture trade, suggesting that by the middle of the eighteenth century even ordinary sorts of furniture were no longer usually supplied by local craftsmen:

> Come next to the furniture of [a country grocer's] house; it is scarce credible, to how many counties of England, and how remote, the furniture of but a mean house must send them; and how many people are everywhere employ'd about it; nay, and the meaner the furniture, the more people and places employ'd.[28]

Many local craftsmen continued to make a variety of simple furniture throughout the seventeenth and eighteenth centuries, but in urban locations the craft became subdivided into a number of specialist trades related to the supply of parts as furniture design and construction became more complex. Turned parts were the prerogative of the turners, chair carvers supplied the carved decoration, while the textile components were fitted by upholsterers.[29] The chair frame was put together by a specialist craftsman, and chair stuffing was yet another specialist craft. Upholsterers would usually co-ordinate all these different activities, the manufacturing process varying according to the size of the upholsterer's business and the complexity of the furniture.[30] These new types of furnishings thus imply not only new levels of comfort and display or changing fashions, but a significant alteration in the nature of production. Defoe described the complexity of the trade, highlighting the dominance of London as the principal centre for furniture manufacture:

> The Hangings, suppose them to be ordinary Linsey-Woolsey, are made at Kidderminster, dy'd in the country, and painted or water'd at London. The Chairs, if of Cane, are made at London; the ordinary Matted Chairs, perhaps made in the place where they live. Tables, Chest of Drawers etc. made at London; also the looking glass.[31]

Before *c.* 1660 furniture was decorated by carving, painting and a small amount of rough inlay in materials of contrasting colours. During the second half of the seventeenth century some furniture makers began using the wood itself in a decorative manner, exploiting its natural features and distinctive markings to pattern the furniture's surface. Techniques such as veneering, and the use of 'exotic' woods such as walnut from North America and France, and mahogany from Jamaica, became popular as a result of this fashion.[32] The manufacture of furniture using these imported woods was a specialist craft, and nearly all such craftsmen were based in London. Thus furnishings not only provide evidence of altered production processes, but also changing patterns of national and international trade.

Mahogany was the most popular of the new woods. It was used for making furniture from the early sixteenth century, but was very rare in England until the late seventeenth century. A clear indication of its growing economic importance was the instigation of the collection of mahogany import statistics in 1699. Production of mahogany furniture expanded, particularly after 1722 when import duties were abolished. In 1720 the value of imported mahogany was £42 13s 0d, by 1724 it had increased to £1,220 5s 6d, and by the 1750s almost £30,000 worth of mahogany was being imported annually.[33] Amongst the decorative woods available mahogany was by far the cheapest. In the early eighteenth century it cost around £8 per ton compared to £40 to £50 per ton for walnut. It was also strong, easily worked and suitable for all sizes of furniture.

Until the 1690s furniture made from imported woods was entirely absent from Kentish households, thereafter it slowly increased in popularity, although by the period 1720–49 only 18 per cent of households possessed furniture of this kind. Ownership was restricted to a relatively small group, possibly due to its expense, and possibly because of a lack of interest in this type of fashionable commodity.[34] The almost complete absence of cane furniture in Kent is surprising, as this was fashionable from around the 1660s until the early eighteenth century, and specialist cane chairmakers set up in London to cope with demand.[35] Either the majority of Kentish households could not afford these items, which seems unlikely, or they were not interested in acquiring these essentially decorative types of furniture. In Cornwall, ownership of mahogany and other similar types of new furniture was even more restricted, rarely rising above 4 per cent of households for most of the seventeenth and early eighteenth centuries, and mostly confined to the households of esquires, gentry and merchants.

Overall, more types of furniture were gained than were lost and so the median number of pieces of furniture, excluding beds, in Kentish households doubled from 1600–29 to 1720–49 as Table 5.1 shows. Cornish households contained a median of only five pieces in the early seventeenth century, which increased slightly to six pieces by the 1740s. If chairs and beds are excluded, the median number of pieces of furniture in Kent increased during the period 1600–1750 from 9 to 13. Comparable figures for Cornwall show a slight fall from a median of five to only four pieces in the 1740s, suggesting a decline in the standard of domestic comfort for about half of the households sampled, and reflecting the growth in house size in Kent as compared to Cornwall.[36]

As might be expected, the introduction of new types of furniture in

Kent led not only to more pieces but also to greater variety in the types of furniture present. The variety of furniture in the Kentish households sampled steadily increased from a median of seven distinct types in the first quarter of the seventeenth century, to around 12 in the second quarter of the eighteenth century, an increase of some 70 per cent. This is consistent with the increasing ownership of the new types of furniture discussed earlier, and demonstrates that they did not always replace older types but were often acquired in addition to existing furniture. In Cornwall the range of types remained more or less unchanged during this period with a median of around four different types. As already discussed, new types of furniture, such as chests of drawers, were being acquired by some Cornish households, but the majority showed no net addition.

The hearth and cooking

In the early seventeenth century the open hearth was the centre of all cooking in the home. An open hearth burning wood consisted simply of iron bars supported by andirons. As the century progressed the use of coal, initially at least for cooking, can be identified by the presence of grates, ranges and coal in inventories.[37] The frequency of occurrence of these items is shown in the row headed 'coal' in Table 5.2. In Kent less than 5 per cent of households were cooking in this way in the first three decades of the seventeenth century, but by 1720–49 nearly 30 per cent had at least one of these three items listed in their inventories and the proportion was continuing to rise. In Cornwall, by contrast, the domestic use of coal was virtually non-existent, confined to a very small number of gentry households. There is no obvious explanation for this. No coal was mined in either county and was therefore imported by sea to both. According to Houghton, the price of coal was higher in coastal Kent than it was in coastal Cornwall.[38] Coal was imported into Cornwall in increasing amounts during the seventeenth century, but apparently for industrial rather than domestic use.[39] The presence of coal-grates implies changes must also have taken place in the design and construction of flues and chimneys, and perhaps also in the ventilation of houses. Fireplaces designed for burning wood were not suitable for burning coal, which must be kept in a compact mass with a strong draft in order to burn efficiently. Furthermore, smoke from coal is heavier than wood smoke, and so needs a more efficient flue to draw it upwards.[40] Perhaps, in comparison with Kent, the Cornish were unwilling to make these structural changes to accommodate domestic coal and may have also been averse to the sulphurous smell of burning coal. But it still remains a puzzle as to why coal was not adopted for domestic cooking and heating, especially since wood was scarce.[41]

The traditional method of cooking in the early seventeenth century was boiling. Cauldrons were used at every social level, but especially amongst

Table 5.2 Goods concerned with heating, cooking and eating

		1600–29	1630–59	1660–89	1690–1719	1720–49
Coal (%)	Cornwall	2	1	3	2	3
	Kent	4	8	13	17	27
Cauldrons (%)	Cornwall	24	21	10	4	1
	Kent	22	11	4	0	0
Skillet (%)	Cornwall	35	32	33	29	32
	Kent	5	11	54	69	65
Saucepans (%)	Cornwall	0	0	0	1	5
	Kent	0	0	2	11	33
Jacks (%)	Cornwall	0	0	2	2	6
	Kent	4	13	33	45	49
Cooking and hearth (median variety)	Cornwall	6	6	5	5	6
	Kent	10	10	12	13	14
Pewter (%)	Cornwall	46	71	87	90	95
	Kent	94	93	94	95	90
New pottery (%)	Cornwall	13	6	2	1	6
	Kent	9	11	11	22	49
Plates (%)	Cornwall	4	3	17	49	85
	Kent	14	24	37	72	85
Plates (median number)	Cornwall	1	2	7	9	12
	Kent	2	2	3	13	19
Platters (%)	Cornwall	74	49	22	22	32
	Kent	85	74	53	50	33
Glass bottles (%)	Cornwall	6	3	3	3	10
	Kent	1	1	4	24	30
Knives and forks (%)	Cornwall	0	0	0	0	3
	Kent	0	0	1	5	13
Hot drinks (%)	Cornwall	0	0	0	0	6
	Kent	0	0	0	4	27
Tableware (median number)	Cornwall	16	12	10	12	18
	Kent	13	8	10	13	28
Eating and drinking (median variety)	Cornwall	5	3	2	2	3
	Kent	5	4	4	5	8

the poor who regularly used them to prepare an entire meal.[42] These were large round pots with three legs, which provided stability and enabled them to stand in the fire. They also had two ears close to the rim from which the pot could be suspended over the hearth. As Table 5.2 shows, cauldrons were recorded in over 20 per cent of households sampled in Kent and Cornwall in the first three decades of the seventeenth century.

Thereafter they steadily declined and had virtually disappeared in Kent by 1690. In Cornwall they were slightly more common and declined at a slower rate. In addition to cauldrons, many Cornish households also possessed another large cooking pot known as a 'crock' which was peculiar to the south-west of England. This type of pot was found in just under 82 per cent of Cornish households in the first decade of the seventeenth century, declining slowly to around 54 per cent by the 1740s. The difference between 'cauldrons' and 'crocks' is not clear. Their similar high valuations indicate that both were large metal pots used for cooking, and they probably shared a similar function. They often appear in the same inventory, and may simply have had different shapes. Boiling as a method of cooking undoubtedly remained important in Cornwall, but the decline of cauldrons suggests the disappearance of cooking with one large pot in Kent.[43]

Skillets came to be increasingly used for cooking smaller quantities of food. They had three short legs to enable them to stand directly amongst the embers of a fire, and a long straight handle so the cook did not have to stand too close to the hearth. In the eighteenth century skillets gave way to flat-bottomed saucepans, made of iron, bronze or tinned copper, which were placed on circular trivets or the hobs of a range.[44] The adoption of the skillet in Kent was very rapid, with the proportion of households possessing one rising fivefold between 1630–59 and 1660–89. The rise in ownership of saucepans was equally spectacular. Saucepans are not found in our Kentish sample before the 1640s, and by 1700 only about 4 per cent of households possessed a saucepan. After this date their ownership quickly increased, reaching 33 per cent of households in the three decades after 1720. In Cornwall, skillets were fairly popular throughout the seventeenth and early eighteenth centuries, present in around 30 per cent of households for most of the period; saucepans were much less popular, and did not appear until the 1680s, some 40 years later than in Kent. Saucepans spread rapidly thereafter, although by the 1740s still less than 9 per cent of Cornish households possessed one. The consistent numbers of skillets, and the slower growth of saucepans in Cornwall, suggests less change in cooking methods and a smaller demand for new types of cooking utensils.

As the eighteenth century progressed, the kitchen range transformed the process of cooking. There was no longer any need for three-legged utensils like the cauldron and skillet, and flat-bottomed pots and pans took their place.[45] The use of saucepans enabled a greater level of control than previous types of cooking pots, since they were smaller and lighter and could be picked up from the fire comparatively easily. *The art of cookery made plain and easy*, a well-known cookery book written by Hannah Glasse, first published in 1747, lists only two recipes which required a skillet.[46] Elsewhere she recommends saucepans. The saucepan, which was usually made out of sheet metal, provided a quite different kind of heat to the skillet, which was nearly always made from cast iron. The skillet heated up slowly, and therefore cooked like the cauldron; the saucepan heated up quickly, and was associated with the new style of cookery popularised by contemporary cookery books. This new cookery involved sauces (obviously enough), but also shorter cooking times compared with the broths usually boiled for several hours over a fire. It was therefore a more intensive and skilful type of cookery, which helps explain the need for cookery books. The growth in popularity of skillets, and especially saucepans, in Kent suggests the county to have been in the vanguard of new cookery methods.

Another new piece of cooking equipment, which became popular during the seventeenth century, was the 'jack' for turning spits used for roasting joints of meat over the fire. Spits had to be rotated for anything up to five hours for large joints.[47] This was a laborious and uncomfortable job. It is perhaps not surprising, therefore, that it was one of the first domestic processes to be fully mechanised. 'Spit-jacks' were introduced in about 1600; the most popular type had a weight on the end of a line, which was wound up around a barrel. As the weight descended the barrel rotated, and a chain transferred the motion to the spit. To ensure the spit turned evenly the barrel was geared to a flywheel. This gear arrangement was simple enough to be copied by local smiths, and production increased rapidly throughout the country after 1660.[48] In Kent the ownership of jacks increased from around 4 per cent in the first three decades of the seventeenth century to nearly 50 per cent by 1720–49. In Cornwall only 6 per cent of households possessed jacks during the latter period.

The differential pattern of the ownership of jacks between the two counties is partly a reflection of the ownership of spits. In Kent more than 75 per cent of households possessed spits for roasting throughout the seventeenth and eighteenth centuries, whereas in Cornwall only 24 per cent of the households sampled owned one at the start of the seventeenth century, and this number declined to just under 15 per cent by 1750. The low proportion of spits in Cornwall may be explained by Celia Fiennes's comment in 1695:

> I was surprised to find my supper boyling on a fire allwayes supply'd with a bush of furse and that to be the only fewell to dress a joynt of meat and broth, and told them they could not roast me anything, but they have a little wood for such occasions but its scarce and dear.[49]

In Kent the variety of cooking and hearth equipment increased from a median of 10 to 14 items from 1600–29 to 1720–49. The increase took place steadily over the seventeenth century, and may have accelerated during the 1740s. Most of this new equipment could be described as 'accessories'; that is, items acquired in addition to the basic hearth and cooking equipment present in the majority of Kentish homes by the start of the seventeenth century. This extra equipment enabled new and varied types of cookery, and more convenient cooking. Typical examples found in Kent include wafering irons, spice boxes, cranes, irons to put before the fire to heat flagons of drink, and multitudinous types of pans. In Cornwall the variety of cooking and hearth equipment showed little change throughout the period. The much smaller variety of equipment in Cornish households suggests very different cooking practices, and this became more marked during the seventeenth century and the first half of the eighteenth. Variation in house sizes probably account for many of these differences, but the degree of variety in Cornwall is also considerably smaller than in Kent, suggesting wider cultural differences, since even the wealthiest households did not have such a wide range of cooking and hearth equipment as in Kent. This lack of variety suggests the continuation of very simple methods of cooking in the majority of Cornish households, as already suggested by the types of cooking pots they possessed.

Tableware

Changes in the way food was cooked were accompanied by changes in modes of eating and drinking. An early change was the introduction of pewter – one of three changes in domestic furnishings William Harrison noted had recently been 'marvellously altered' in his *Description of England* published in 1587:

> The third thing they tell of is the exchange of vessel, as of treen platters into pewter, and wooden spoons into silver or tin. For so common were all sorts of treen stuff in old time that a man should hardly find four pieces of pewter (of which one was peradventure a salt) in a good farmer's house.[50]

In Kent almost all our inventories in the period 1600–29 mention pewter, and ownership of pewter remained at a high level (above 90 per cent) for the entire period. Cornish households lagged behind. In the first three decades of the seventeenth century 46 per cent of them possessed it; thereafter, the figure steadily rose, although ownership of pewter did not reach the same level as Kent until the 1680s. New forms of pewter vessel were acquired in both counties, the most notable example being dinner plates which replaced or supplemented wooden trenchers.[51] The ownership of plates steadily increased in Kent from around 14 per cent in the first three decades of the seventeenth century to over 85 per cent by 1720–49. The adoption of plates was initially slower in Cornwall, with less than 10 per cent of households possessing plates before 1670, but ownership increased rapidly thereafter to reach the same levels as in Kent by the 1740s. This rise in Cornwall coincides with the growth in the number of pewterers in the county following the Mining Act of 1669. Before this time Cornish tin had been bought by London merchants, who sold it on to pewterers in and around the capital. This monopoly broke down during the Civil War, and led to a growth in the number of pewterers in Cornwall, which no doubt made pewter goods cheaper and more widely available in the county.[52]

Increasingly, pottery began to supplement pewter.[53] During the late sixteenth century, and first half of the seventeenth, large quantities of pottery were imported into England. It has been estimated that between 1600 and 1640 about 10 million German stoneware vessels entered British ports, in addition to large quantities of earthenware from many European countries.[54] Imports of pottery steadily declined after this date as the English earthenware industry expanded. Between 1680 and 1710 the number of potteries increased by 47 per cent, while employment went up by 70 per cent.[55] Tin-glazed pottery had been made in England since the late sixteenth century, but the growth in production was slow until the late seventeenth century when the output of tin-glazed, lead-glazed and stoneware pottery rapidly expanded. Between c.1670 and 1705 employment in the London tin-glaze potteries increased threefold, making it the fastest growing sector.[56] The pottery industry as a whole expanded a further 25 per cent between 1710 and 1750, largely due to the growth in stoneware production in Nottingham, Bristol and Staffordshire. Technical innovations in the 1720s and 1730s improved the efficiency of production processes, including the introduction of plaster of Paris moulds, which enabled large numbers of high-quality products to be produced. From the late seventeenth century, and probably earlier, London dominated the wholesale trade in pottery. Specialist pottery dealers bought large stocks from manufacturers around the country, which they then re-distributed to provincial merchants and shopkeepers.[57]

It is not always possible to distinguish imported pottery from English products in inventories. In the seventeenth century 'china' may have been used to describe imported or English tin-glazed earthenware, much of which imitated Chinese porcelain; the various descriptions used for tin-glazed pottery, such as 'white' and 'painted', do not distinguish between imported or native products. However, the new pottery found in over 13 per cent of Cornish households in the first three decades of the seventeenth century was probably imported. This pottery consisted largely of German stoneware drinking jugs often mounted with silver. A small number of other types of imported pottery occur, such as the 'painted dishes' in the possession of Christopher Bligh, a gentleman in St Gennys whose inventory was appraised in 1605.[58] Between 1640 and 1740 less than 4 per cent of households possessed any imported or new English pottery. Ownership of the new pottery products did not start to expand in Cornwall until the 1740s: during that decade around 11 per cent of households included this type of pottery.

Kentish households show a different pattern. Ownership of imported pottery was actually lower in Kent in the early seventeenth century than it was in Cornwall. It showed a gradual rise until the end of the century, and thereafter new items of pottery increased rapidly. From the 1720s increasing amounts of stoneware appear, much of which was probably used for drinking tea, coffee and chocolate. English stoneware production began in London in 1671, but was being manufactured in Staffordshire and Nottingham from the 1690s, after which production rapidly expanded.[59] Stoneware is a much harder type of ceramic material, and it could be potted much more finely than other types of pottery made in England before this time. Stoneware, therefore, quickly came to dominate the market for ceramic drinking vessels during the first two decades in the eighteenth century.[60] The fact that a greater proportion of Cornish households possessed imported pottery in the early seventeenth century than new English pottery in the eighteenth century, suggests a poorer quality of material culture and a reduced level of market participation at the end of the period.

Whether of pewter or earthenware, the ownership of plates in both Cornwall and Kent increased rapidly. The majority of these plates were of pewter, but from the early eighteenth century earthenware plates became increasingly popular. These were found in less than 1 per cent of Kentish households before the 1690s, but by the 1740s just under 35 per cent of households possessed them and the extent of their acquisition more than doubled during the decade.[61] Virtually all the plates found in Cornish households were of pewter. Less than 1 per cent of the households sampled possessed earthenware plates before 1740; thereafter the figure rose slightly to 4 per cent in the 1740s, suggesting the acquisition of earthenware plates probably continued to accelerate from this time.[62]

In Kent, earthenware plates were nearly always acquired in addition to pewter plates, since pewter plates are usually found in the households that acquired these new items of pottery. Therefore earthenware plates did not necessarily replace pewter at the table, but provided a second service. Earthenware plates had a number of practical advantages over pewter. They were cheaper, could carry colourful decoration and did not scratch as easily. Pottery could also be fashioned into more varied designs, and could be decorated in more varied ways, enabling continual changes of style. The development of new ceramic bodies from the late seventeenth century onwards introduced a greater variety of pottery to suit different markets. Since earthenware was cheaper, larger sets could be bought for less money than equivalent pewter services, although earthenware plates needed to be replaced more often than metal goods such as pewter.[63] Since earthenware was so much cheaper, the replacement of pewter by earthenware would have led both to a reduction in expenditure and more frequent purchases.[64] The increasingly wide variety of pottery available from the late seventeenth century onwards meant that consumers could exercise greater individual choice, and producers increasingly used the vagaries of fashion to manipulate these choices.[65]

Changes in the way food was served led to the decline of certain types of tableware, thus the ownership of platters in both Kent and Cornwall halved in the period between 1600 and 1750. Platters were large dishes (of wood or pewter) from which food was taken and transferred to individual plates, and these were replaced by a greater number of smaller dishes.[66] The number of dishes and courses served at a meal could vary considerably. Contemporary descriptions of yeomen's meals of the seventeenth century suggest that three 'dishes' were common, but varied according to circumstances and occasion.[67] The substantial drop in the ownership of platters in Kent during the 1740s corresponds to the rapid growth of earthenware dinner services taking place at this time. Platters were not simply replaced by dinner plates, but the changes in ownership of these items are indicative of changing fashions in tableware and dining practices.

Glass drinking vessels and bottles were not common until the last quarter of the seventeenth century and, compared with other materials, were relatively expensive. Most drinking glasses were made in Venice. In 1606, for example, a merchant in Tregony had 22 'Venice glasses' for sale at 12d each.[68] Subsequently, technical innovations in the English glass industry enabled glass drinking vessels and bottles to be produced at a lower cost. From 1685 George Ravenscroft manufactured a new flint glass, which reduced the price of glass to 1s 6d per pound during the last decade of the seventeenth century, by which time glass imports had virtually ceased, except for the finest types. Glass production started in the 1640s in Greenwich, and developed on the London fringe of Kent in the late seventeenth century.[69] Two glasshouses are known have been working in Woolwich in the 1690s, making ordinary, flint, crown and plate glass, in addition to various consumer goods. Drinking glasses were most commonly used for wine, and bottles almost exclusively so in this period. The growth in production and consumption of these glass products can, therefore, be largely attributed to the popularity of wine, imports of which greatly expanded during the late seventeenth century and the eighteenth.[70]

Drinking glasses are found in less than 2 per cent of our Kentish inventories before the 1720s; ownership accelerated from this date, doubling each decade, so that just over 20 per cent of Kentish households had acquired them by the 1740s. Glass bottles were found in increasing numbers from the 1680s and by 1720–49 30 per cent of households sampled had glass bottles amongst their possessions as shown in Table 5.2. Drinking glasses were more common in Cornwall at the start of the seventeenth century, when just under 9 per cent of households possessed them, but they had virtually disappeared by 1650. The appraisers' descriptions tell us that most of these glasses were imported, usually from Venice. Glass bottles were also more common in Cornwall than in Kent at the start of the seventeenth century, and their ownership declined during the seventeenth century. This trend reflects the decline of imported glass, and, until the English glass industry expanded, glass was rare in Cornwall during the second half of the seventeenth century and the early eighteenth. Perhaps due to the greater distances involved, the English glass industry did not have an impact on the material culture of Cornish households until much later in the eighteenth century. Pottery, leather, wood and pewter vessels remained in common use in Cornwall throughout the period 1600–1750, whereas new glass products from the London glasshouses began to supplement and supplant many of these traditional products in Kent.

Before the eighteenth century most people ate with a knife and spoon. These implements were usually owned by individuals, and were not provided by hosts.[71] The adoption of the fork was associated with changes in the way food was prepared and served, and was part of a more elaborate range of tableware and table settings which many households acquired during this period.[72] The use of knives and forks to eat with was associated with the introduction of plates to replace trenchers.[73] Forks for eating at the table are known in England amongst the aristocracy by the sixteenth century. Peter Erondell, writing towards the end of the reign of Elizabeth I, described 'little forks to go beside each plate', although others thought it a custom only practised in Italy in the early seventeenth century.[74] Knives and forks, however, did not begin to be used by people of more humble status until much later. By 1720–49 knives and forks were only being used in just over 13 per cent of households sampled in Kent (although this reached 25 per cent in the decade of the 1740s), and by only 3 per cent in Cornwall. The very early examples found in the first half of the seventeenth century in a small number of wealthy households in Cornwall suggest the social exclusivity of this way of dining.

While the use of forks spread slowly, the adoption of new social practices associated with hot drinks spread rapidly. The East India Company began importing Chinese tea in the 1660s, but shipments were sporadic and often of relatively small amounts because the Company had no direct access to China. Then in 1713 they established trade with Canton, and imports became more regular and voluminous.[75] There were substantial numbers of Londoners consuming tea by 1700, but, given the uncertainties of supply prior to 1713, the 1720s was probably the first decade in which mass consumption could have taken place nation-wide, with a doubling in per capita consumption occurring between the 1730s and 1740s as prices fell.[76] The equipment used for making and drinking both tea and coffee – tea kettles, teapots, teaspoons, and such like – first appear in Kentish households in the 1680s, but they are not found in more than 10 per cent of inventories until after 1720. James Leeds, a brewer of Milton, had two coffee pots in 1681, and the first mention of tea is in the inventory of Richard Godfrey, a gentleman of Chartham, in 1697. Thereafter tea and coffee diffuse very rapidly, being found in nearly 74 per cent of Kentish households sampled by the 1740s.[77] Tea and coffee equipment was not found in Cornish households before 1720. It first appears in four merchants' inventories, and the first non-merchant with tea equipment was a gentleman in Penzance with five teaspoons, a pair of tongs, and a tea strainer in 1727. Domestic consumption of tea and coffee increased rapidly in popularity after 1740, but during this decade only about 12 per cent of Cornish households possessed equipment associated with hot drinks.

As a result of these new introductions the number of pieces of table-ware doubled in Kent from a median of 13 in the first three decades of the seventeenth century, to 28 in the period 1720–49. Tableware is difficult to count because appraisers did not always itemise each object separately. However, plates, platters, dishes, saucers, porringers and condi-ment pots were consistently counted, and their numbers have been analysed. In Kent, platters and porringers declined in number from 1600–70, which accounts for the decline in the overall number of pieces of tableware during the seventeenth century. Growth in the quantity of tableware in both counties was largely due to the increased number of plates, which grew rapidly from the late seventeenth century. Before 1680 Kentish households possessed on average two plates; during the 1680s the number more than doubled to five, and in the 1690s this more than doubled again to 12; the number of plates continued to increase more slowly after this date, reaching 21 in the 1740s. This was sufficient for more than one set of dinner plates; not all of these would have been used at most meal times, so some of these must have been spare and possibly reserved as 'best'. The number of dishes in Kentish households also increased during this period, from between eight and nine in the first decade of the seventeenth century to 12 in the 1740s, contributing to the increase in tableware in Kent. The numbers of condiment pots, such as salts, mustard pots, cruets and sauce pots, did not change, with an average of between one and two per household.

In Cornwall as in Kent, the number of pieces of tableware declined for much of the seventeenth century, and then increased from around 1680. In the first three decades of the seventeenth century Cornish households possessed a median of 16 pieces of tableware, which increased to 18 pieces by 1720–49. For much of the seventeenth century Cornish households possessed greater quantities of tableware than their Kentish counterparts, but were overtaken during the 1690s when the latter started to acquire large numbers of plates. The number of saucers, platters and porringers declined in Cornwall, but at a slower rate than in Kent. As in Kent, the overall increase in tableware in Cornwall was due to the acquisition of plates in greater numbers.[78] Plates were acquired at a somewhat later date than in Kent; whereas Kentish households began acquiring greater numbers of plates from the 1680s, significant increases in the number of plates possessed by Cornish households did not take place until the 1730s, when numbers increased by half to 12. By the 1740s, Cornish households possessed a median of 14 plates, a smaller number than in Kent, but plentiful in a household of less than six people.

The variety of eating and drinking utensils in Kent increased from a median of five different types to eight. The majority of this growth in variety took place in the period after 1720 reflecting an increase in the number of different types of drinking vessel, which more than doubled in the 1740s. New types of drinking vessel were acquired as a wider range of drinks became available to more people, such as tea, coffee, chocolate, wine, brandy and posset.[79] These functionally specialised drinking vessels were owned in addition to tankards, mugs and other functionally nondescript vessels that were present in virtually every household throughout the seventeenth and eighteenth centuries. Although tableware changed in material and quantity, there was little change in the variety of types used, which remained around a median of four. These consisted usually of plates, platters, dishes and a salt.

In Cornwall, a similar range of eating and drinking utensils can be found, but they are much less common.[80] The median variety of eating and drinking utensils declined by 40 per cent between the first decade of the seventeenth century and the 1740s. Many Cornish inventories do not list drinking vessels, and when they do they rarely describe their shape, material or function, suggesting inexpensive drinking pots made out of earthenware, wood and leather were probably common. There was probably little variety in the drinks consumed by most Cornish people. New drinks, such as wine, tea and coffee were rare in most households before 1750, and thus there was no need for the more specialised types of drinking vessel that appear in many Kentish households at this time. The median variety of tableware also declined from three in the first quarter of the seventeenth century to two in the second quarter of the eighteenth century. Again, the small variety of tableware suggests very simple place settings, and the decline in variety points to a declining sophistication of dining from platters, porringers and saucers to plates and dishes.

Overall the increased number of objects associated with cooking and dining are evidence not only of changes in eating habits but also of an alteration of the nature of work within the household. Using saucepans, frying pans and jacks to produce a number of dishes was a great deal more time-consuming than preparing pottage in a cauldron; likewise increased tableware implies an increased amount of washing up. Together with a wider variety of furniture, especially soft furnishings, and the increased ownership of linen discussed below, this suggests that time spent on housework (cooking and cleaning) increased over the period.

Linen

Household linen, consisting of towels, tablecloths, napkins, sheets and pillowcases, was one of the most important categories of domestic goods.

The acquisition of greater quantities of linen, and better-quality linen, by many households appears to have begun in the late sixteenth century. Richard Carew wrote in his survey of Cornwall (first published 1602) that within living memory husbandmen had for their beds only 'straw and a blanket; as for sheets, so much linen cloth had not yet stepped over the narrow channel between them and Brittany'.[81] Similarly, William Harrison wrote of the 'great amendment of lodging' in the previous two generations, describing the lack of mattresses, pillows and sheets for servants during the youth of the people now grown old in his Essex parish. He noted the great improvements in comfort that had taken place in living memory, and singled out for comment the introduction of feather beds, and coverlets, and carpets made of tapestry, in addition to chimneys and pewter.[82]

The proportion of inventories mentioning linen, shown in Table 5.3, fell slightly in Kent, from around 90 per cent in the early seventeenth century to around 80 per cent in the period 1720–49. In Cornwall the proportion fell quite dramatically over the same period from 59 per cent to 18 per cent. Table 5.3 also shows the frequencies with which the main items of linen are mentioned. Sheets were the most common, followed by

Table 5.3 Linen

		1600–29	1630–59	1660–89	1690–1719	1720–49
Linen (%)	Cornwall	59	54	31	23	18
	Kent	92	89	87	86	80
Sheets (%)	Cornwall	52	47	24	15	13
	Kent	92	88	86	86	80
Tablecloths (%)	Cornwall	32	31	17	13	10
	Kent	69	66	66	68	61
Napkins (%)	Cornwall	15	20	8	5	3
	Kent	61	63	65	70	58
Towels (%)	Cornwall	8	5	1	0	1
	Kent	41	46	56	64	53
Linen (median number)	Cornwall	3	4	4	4	2
	Kent	28	28	41	51	50
Sheets (median number)	Cornwall	2	3	3	2	2
	Kent	14	14	16	20	20
Towels (median number)	Cornwall	2	2	3	0	0
	Kent	5	6	8	12	12
Tablecloths (median number)	Cornwall	2	2	2	1	2
	Kent	4	3	6	6	8
Napkins (median number)	Cornwall	6	6	12	10	10
	Kent	12	12	18	18	18

tablecloths, napkins and towels. Although the slight fall in the presence of linen in Kent suggests a decline in consumption, this is not the case, as the remaining rows in Table 5.3 demonstrate, since the number of pieces of linen per household rises considerably.

The situation was very different in Cornwall. Not only did the proportion of inventories mentioning linen decline, but those households with linen had slightly fewer pieces at the end of the study period than at the beginning.[83] Large Cornish households appear similar to those in Kent with great quantities of linen, but these are a minority. Thomas Clyes, a gentleman in Madron, for example, possessed 322 pieces of linen (sheets, tablecloths, napkins and towels), when his inventory was taken in June 1644.[84] It was not uncommon in Cornwall, however, for each bed to have only one sheet, and pillowcases were extremely rare. Thus, although some sections of Cornish society were acquiring more linen, the majority of Cornish households used in this analysis appear to have continued the earlier sixteenth-century practice, described by Carew, of sleeping on very simple beds and using only very small quantities of linen. Again, very little change appears to have taken place in the style of living and standards of comfort in many Cornish households when compared to contemporary households sampled in Kent.

Since the size of households in Kent increased only slightly during this period, the increase in the amount of linen represents a considerable accumulation of extra linen. In the early seventeenth century, when there was a median of three beds per household, an average of 14 sheets provided a spare set for each bed, and an additional spare set. By the 1740s, with over 25 sheets and only four beds, there were more than three sets for each bed. The number of pillowcases increased in a similar pattern, resulting in many spare items of linen. It is not certain why these extra sets of sheets, pillowcases, and table linen were present or how they were used: perhaps sheets were changed more frequently, but we cannot be certain. The higher numbers of tablecloths was perhaps the result of a continuation of the medieval practice of putting more than one cloth on the table, with subsequent 'layers' being removed after each course. This would correspond with the elaborate tableware and dining practices discussed above, but again we cannot be at all certain.[85] The quality of linen was also increasingly mentioned by appraisers. 'Fine' and 'coarse' linen was often distinguished, and higher quality types, such as damask, are increasingly found. The acquisition of different qualities of linen appears to correspond to the accumulation of other household items, such as tableware, where multiple sets of dinner plates, for example, were acquired, suggesting a hierarchy of use distinguished by quality. Since the price of many sorts of textiles were declining, the increased quantity of linen in Kentish households did not necessarily entail a greater expenditure, but it does imply more frequent purchasing.[86]

An accumulation of linen in this period has been found in other countries, where it often acquired considerable cultural significance. There is, however, no evidence to suggest that linen was used in England at this time specifically in this way. 'Marriage goods' – that is, items given by parents to their children to help them set up a home upon marriage – may have included linen and a linen cupboard, but these were amongst a variety of other types of goods.[87]

Miscellaneous goods

Thus far we have dealt with those material goods concerned with the essentials of living in the seventeenth century: furniture, cooking equipment and linen. Many of the objects discussed were novel in the sense that they provided new ways of doing things (for example, saucepans for cooking and upholstered chairs for sitting on), but there were also new goods that involved completely new behaviour. These were clocks and mirrors.

Less than 1 per cent of the households sampled in Kent had a clock in the first three decades of the seventeenth century, but by the period 1720–49 over half of them contained a clock. Table 5.4 shows that the rate of acquisition was rising rapidly, so that by the 1740s over 78 per cent of the Kent households owned a clock. Only one sampled Cornish household possessed a clock before 1660, and by the 1740s only about 12 per cent of households in Cornwall possessed a clock, about six or seven times fewer than in Kent.[88] The majority of clocks found in both counties would have been manufactured in London and it was not until after the 1650s, when the pendulum clock was invented, that domestic clocks were manufactured on a wider scale and became much more popular.[89] The

Table 5.4 Miscellaneous goods (percentages)

		1600–29	1630–59	1660–89	1690–1719	1720–49
Clocks	Cornwall	0	0	1	2	9
	Kent	1	1	18	41	54
Mirrors	Cornwall	1	1	4	4	8
	Kent	3	10	18	36	52
Pictures	Cornwall	0	0	0	1	4
	Kent	2	6	5	6	25
Window curtains	Cornwall	0	0	0	1	1
	Kent	6	8	11	16	22
Books	Cornwall	9	10	8	6	8
	Kent	19	31	25	25	20
Weapons	Cornwall	37	26	4	2	2
	Kent	38	35	23	17	21

pendulum clock was quickly improved to produce much more accurate timepieces after about 1670, and the growth in ownership of clocks in Kent, which quickly accelerated from around 1660, coincides with these technological innovations. Clocks remained fairly expensive. In the first half of the eighteenth century the median value of a clock in Cornwall was £1 10s, with the minimum at 10s and the maximum value at £4: the figures were the same in Kent except that the maximum was £5. The comparative rarity of clocks amongst the Cornish households sampled is striking, espe- cially since clocks were made in the county.[90] Some growth in ownership of clocks in Cornwall took place in the second quarter of the eighteenth century, but they remained largely a luxury item here before 1750.

The growth in the number of households containing mirrors or looking glasses was more steady, but reached similar proportions as clocks in both counties by the middle of the eighteenth century, as Table 5.4 shows.[91] Mirrors ranged a great deal in size and quality, from small hand- held looking glasses to large wall-mounted types, and were therefore more affordable than clocks.[92] Mirrors had two distinct functions within the household. The first was to enhance the power of artificial lighting; the second was to view the self within the surroundings of the home. Randle Holme considered that looking glasses 'are most used by Lady's to look their faces in, and to see how to dress their heads, and set their top knots on their fore heads vpright'.[93]

It is not possible to establish what proportion of these mirrors were of English manufacture, but it is likely that a significant proportion were imported since the production of English mirrors was probably small until the late seventeenth century. Despite attempts to prohibit the importation of mirrors, large numbers were imported. In one summer alone during the 1660s, for example, 4,000 gilt looking glasses were imported from France.[94] Increased ownership of mirrors in Kent during the second quarter of the eighteenth century, however, is likely to be due to the expansion of English mirror-glass production. Competition between man- ufacturers kept the prices of mirrors down, and technical innovations, such as the process of casting which was introduced in London glasshouses from the late seventeenth century, enabled larger and higher- quality glasses to be made, as well as cheaper products. In Cornwall, the English glass industry made little impact, the ownership of mirrors increasing from around 4 per cent in the late seventeenth century to just under 11 per cent by the decade of the 1740s. The rapid spread of mirrors in Kent parallels a 'mirror craze' in urban France at the same time, while the relative absence of mirrors in Cornwall compares to their absence in rural France.[95]

Pictures and window curtains were two decorative types of goods that increased in popularity during the seventeenth and eighteenth centuries. Pictures, consisting of paintings of portraits and landscapes, and prints of various subjects, grew more popular in Kent from around the second decade of the eighteenth century. Before 1700 around 5 per cent of the Kentish households sampled possessed pictures, but by 1720–49 over a quarter of inventories contained them. Paintings remained rare; the increase was entirely due to 'prints' that were produced in large quantities and became more widely available from the second half of the seventeenth century.[96] Very few pictures are recorded in the Cornish sample. A small growth in ownership took place during the 1740s, when the households with pictures increased threefold, but only 7 per cent of Cornish households possessed pictures in this decade.

Window curtains were decorative, as pictures were, but they were also a means of displaying taste to the outside world, and, more functionally, a way of preventing drafts from windows. In Kent more than 10 per cent of households had window curtains by the end of the 1650s, but the pattern of growth was uneven, suggesting they were probably confined to particular social groups. For the period as a whole some 10 per cent of inventories contained window curtains, but they were mentioned in over 50 per cent of gentlemen's inventories.[97] In Cornwall window curtains were extremely rare, found in less than 1 per cent of households.

The ownership of both pictures and window curtains is related to the size and quality of housing. The average size of a house grew substantially in Kent, with the number of rooms doubling during the period 1600–1750.[98] The simple style of housing in Cornwall during this period helps to account for the lack of pictures, window curtains, and other types of decorative furnishings. The majority of Cornish houses probably remained small, dark and smoky places, in which pictures would not have been easily seen; nor would there have been much space in a small dwelling to hang them. New lighter houses were built, but these were confined to the comparatively wealthy strata of society.[99]

Table 5.4 shows that the ownership of books changed little between the early sixteenth century and the early eighteenth century, although the peak period for ownership, in both Cornwall and Kent was 1630–59. Clark has shown how the incidence of book ownership amongst males in Canterbury inventories rose from 8 per cent in the 1560s to 46 per cent in the 1630s, and our figures match his since the proportion for our Canterbury inventories during 1600–29 is 47 per cent.[100] However, thereafter the percentage mentioning books in Canterbury falls: to 40 per cent during 1660–89 and to some 35 per cent thereafter. It is possible that appraisers became less conscientious in recording books, although in general the Kent inventories contain more detail over time rather than less. While there seems to have been a rise in literacy from the mid-sixteenth to the mid-seventeenth century, for the next century the trend appears irregular, possibly suggesting the proportion of those able to read books did not rise very much.[101] In Cornwall, levels of ownership were a half to a third of those in Kent and there was a slight fall over the course of the period, but in neither county was there a conspicuous change in the consumption of books.

The decline of military weaponry (such as body armour, pikes, and muskets) does show a conspicuous change, especially in Cornwall where weapons declined rapidly between 1640 and 1660, from being present in nearly 39 per cent of inventories in the 1630s to less than 5 per cent in the 1660s. Such a dramatic fall presents something of a puzzle. It is possible that appraisers deliberately omitted weapons or that they were concealed. On the other hand, perhaps their absence is associated with the restoration of the Monarchy in a county that had fought for the Royalist cause during the Civil Wars.[102] Sporting weapons (such as 'birding guns') account for a much higher proportion (up to 13 per cent in the 1740s) of weaponry found in Kent compared to that in Cornwall (typically around 1 or 2 per cent). In both counties, sporting weapons do not show any consistent pattern of development in ownership. The higher proportion in Kent was probably due to wealth, since this was a form of leisure the poor could not afford.

Linguistic analysis

It has been claimed that the linguistic analysis of probate inventories can reveal certain aspects of 'past systems of meaning' of relevance to material culture.[103] The idea is that 'modifiers' of objects (usually adjectives) provide clues to the ways in which contemporaries regarded their material world. The adjectives used in probate inventories can be categorised into four groups. The first contains references to material and construction (such as a 'joined' table); the second aesthetic attributes, including decoration, colour, and shape; the third group consists of qualitative judgements, concerning the age, condition and quality of goods; and the last group describes the function of an object (such as a 'tea' table). As Table 5.5 shows, in Kentish inventories the number of times each of these

Table 5.5 Appraisers' descriptions (percentages)

		1600–29	1630–59	1660–89	1690–1719	1720–49
'New' as an adjective	Cornwall	6.1	4.0	2.1	0.8	2.4
	Kent	7.0	8.5	11.4	17.3	16.5
Material description	Cornwall	5.9	4.8	4.4	4.1	5.3
	Kent	8.6	11.3	12.1	12.1	14.5
Aesthetic description	Cornwall	0.3	0.1	0.2	0.1	0.3
	Kent	1.8	2.2	2.1	1.6	2.8
Qualitative description	Cornwall	5.6	4.4	4.0	4.4	3.9
	Kent	7.2	10.6	9.9	10.7	9.5
Functional description	Cornwall	3.4	2.4	2.2	1.6	2.5
	Kent	10.0	12.9	13.3	15.4	18.6

descriptions occurred per inventory increased, with quite dramatic rises for the use of 'new' as an adjective and for functional descriptions. Aesthetic descriptions changed the least, while the use of functional and material descriptions increased considerably in Kent, indicating greater functional specialisation and the presence of goods made in a wider variety of materials and a greater variety of construction techniques. The decline in these descriptions in Cornish inventories suggests the variety of goods declined in most Cornish households during the same period.

Adjectives referring to the age of goods can tell us something about the frequency of consumption. It is not possible to quantify 'old' goods since these are described in a multitude of ways, such as 'broken', 'decayed', 'much-worn', as well as 'old'. It is reasonable to assume, however, that the term 'new' was only applied to those goods recently acquired, which would be in new condition and therefore valued at a greater price than a good of the same type in poorer condition. Changes in the occurrence of 'new', therefore, can be related to the frequency of purchase of domestic goods. In Kent usage of the term 'new' roughly doubled between the early seventeenth and the early eighteenth centuries; in Cornwall it declined by two-thirds over the same period. These figures cannot be used quantitatively to calculate levels of consumption, but they strongly suggest more frequent purchasing of domestic goods in Kent, confirming our earlier suggestions about the pattern of purchase for tableware and linen.[104] In Cornwall, frequency of purchasing declined, since the proportion of households with 'new' goods fell considerably during the seventeenth century, and continued to fall slightly in the first half of the eighteenth century.

Simple linguistic analysis of this kind is dependent on the level of detail given in an inventory, which in turn is dependent on the thoroughness of appraisers, this latter varying considerably between individual appraisers and different locations. The adjectives we are discussing were applied by the appraisers of the goods and not the owners, which affects how we interpret them. But in any case the level of description was a practical matter, and it is difficult to read into this great cultural significance as some historians have attempted. Thus the level of detail, and the quality of description, was related to the variety of the goods to be appraised. The smaller number and range of goods found in most Cornish households undoubtedly accounts for much of the difference in the level of detail used by appraisers. The level of descriptive detail increased as the variety of domestic goods increased because it was necessary for appraisers to distinguish between goods of the same or similar type. Hence, textiles are usually described in considerable detail, and appraisers usually specified colour, quality, condition, and size or weight, because most households possessed a wide variety of these goods. Clocks, on the other hand, are rarely given any description because there was usually only one in each household, so it could not be confused with other domestic goods.

Although the use of adjectives was a practical way of differentiating between objects, appraisers had a choice as to what type of adjectives they used. In Kent, they preferred adjectives that referred to the function of items and differentiated between what was new and what was not. On the other hand, their use of aesthetic descriptions changed little. Did the fact that they were much less likely to differentiate on aesthetic grounds mean that novelty was of more significance than aesthetics, or was it just easier to describe objects in terms of their age rather than their colour, texture or shape?

Conclusion

Perhaps the most striking finding from the results presented in this chapter is the contrast between Kent and Cornwall. In Kent more and more varied material goods reveal higher standards of comfort, new methods of heating and cooking, and new ways of eating and drinking associated with new social rituals. In Cornwall, by contrast, the domestic environment became more impoverished. Whereas the variety of domestic goods increased by 44 per cent between the first half of the seventeenth century and the first half of the eighteenth century in Kent, in Cornwall it declined by about 43 per cent in the same period from a median of 23 to just over 13.[105] This is around 50 per cent less than in contemporary Kent, and this gap widened during the seventeenth century and the first half of the eighteenth, so that by 1750 Cornish households contained only around 10 or 15 per cent of the variety of goods found in contemporary Kentish households. Weatherill's figures for the ownership of goods in eight regions of England can be compared with those in this present study, which places Kent as one of the more 'progressive' regions of the country in terms of the adoption of novelty, following closely behind London, and Cornwall as one of the most 'backward', on a par with rural Cumbria.[106]

It is unlikely that the difference between the two counties is solely the result of Cornish appraisers systematically omitting large numbers of items. Cornish inventories are usually less detailed than those from Kent, but this is because there were fewer items in Cornish inventories and so less description was necessary to distinguish between items. For the Cornish inventories to be seriously misleading there must have been systematic widespread fraud in the process of probate in Cornwall, and there is no evidence of this. Almost all the commodities found in Kent inventories were also found in at least a few Cornish ones, so the new domestic objects that became common in Kent inventories were known in Cornwall. Cornwall was remote from London, yet there is plenty of evidence from the inventories of retailers and merchants that goods were imported into the county.[107]

The figures in Table 5.6 shows some of the goods in retailers' inventories in Cornwall and Kent. They should be treated with some caution since the sample sizes in both cases are small, and they must be influenced by the structure of the retailing trade in the two counties. Yet these figures reveal that imported goods such as spices, raisins and tobacco were available in Cornwall for those who wished to purchase them. By 1700 most Cornish towns had several mercers, grocers, haberdashers, and the like. At the beginning of the seventeenth century many of these shopkeepers were merchants in their own right, selling goods they had imported themselves, an example here being John Rashleigh of Fowey, who had regular trade links with Europe and the Mediterranean in the 1600s.[108] Quite a number, however, got their stocks from larger merchants in Plymouth or Exeter with international trade linkages. For instance, John Gandy of Exeter supplied cloth to Philippa Randle of Bodinnick near Fowey during the 1680s, sending consignments both by barge along the coast and overland by pack horse.[109] Robert Bennett of Tregony was also the client of an Exeter merchant, William Tottell, and was listed as one of his debtors in his inventory of 1609.[110] Clearly there were extensive networks of trade within Cornwall whereby imported goods could be filtered down the urban hierarchy so as to appear amongst the stock of the most lowly retailer or chapman.

In both Kent and Cornwall consumption was a cyclical process: goods left households as well as coming into them. Carpets came off furniture, court cupboards came then went, and cauldrons all but disappeared.

Table 5.6 Goods in retailers' inventories 1600–1749 (percentages)

	1600–49		1650–99		1700–49	
	Cornwall	*Kent*	*Cornwall*	*Kent*	*Cornwall*	*Kent*
Groceries	71	60	90	77	64	80
Cloth	86	40	55	62	55	50
Clothing	71	0	30	60	50	48
Haberdashery	71	67	75	73	77	76
Hardware	71	44	75	40	57	40
Earthenware	29	40	30	46	50	38
Spices	57	33	29	45	39	41
Raisins	29	33	14	39	28	23
Soap	63	25	63	36	32	52
Candles	43	55	43	53	37	69
Cheese/butter	0	25	0	47	0	61
Paper	43	11	13	21	42	29
Sugar	29	0	89	55	53	59
Tobacco	14	0	29	38	55	58
Pipes	29	0	13	19	5	21
Rice	14	0	14	12	11	18
Gingerbread	0	0	0	3	0	18
Tea/coffee	0	0	0	0	0	18

Things went out of fashion as well as coming into fashion. The replacement of goods also suggests that the accumulation of goods in households
was not primarily a consequence of inheritance from one generation to
the next.[111] The cyclical nature of consumption patterns makes it difficult
to identify a particular period during which changes in consumption were
particularly rapid, or indeed 'revolutionary'. Chronologies varied for different commodities. Thus in Kent there was a dramatic acceleration in the
consumption of tea and coffee from the third decade of the eighteenth
century, and this was the period which also saw the comparatively rapid
adoption of plates, new pottery and saucepans. On the other hand the
ownership of upholstered furniture grew steadily from the early seventeenth century and the rate of adoption began to level out by the start of
the eighteenth. In some cases the acquisition of certain goods was closely
related to technological developments, for example with glass, clocks and
ceramics, and in others price reductions and enhanced distribution and
retail networks made certain goods more freely and cheaply available.[112]
However, as we shall see in Chapter 7, the ownership of commodities was
by no means a simple function of their availability.

Changes in the material culture of the majority of Kent households and
a small minority of Cornish households, revealed through the particular
objects discussed in this chapter, show that the domestic environment
became richer, more comfortable and more specialised. Not only did the
number and variety of goods increase but the value of material goods in
inventories rose, despite generally falling prices for most domestic
items.[113] Moreover, the type of goods acquired, such as earthenware
plates, suggests more frequent purchases – in other words a change in
consumer behaviour. This is also suggested by the description 'new' being
applied with greater frequency in Kent. In Cornwall, the opposite appears
to have taken place for the majority of households sampled, where a
reduction in the frequency of the term 'new' occurred.

The majority of new goods that appeared in the households sampled in
Kent and Cornwall, such as jacks, chests of drawers, and the use of coal for
cooking and heating, were practical additions or modifications which
improved the quality of the domestic environment. On the other hand,
certain fashionable goods, such as cane chairs, are virtually absent from
our sample. Additional expenditure on familiar items, such as linen,
further warns against explanations that use fashion and emulation as the
primary motive behind consumption. Linen was a 'traditional' item of
consumption in the sense that it reflected status through its quality. In
Kent many of the households sampled appear to have spent considerably
greater sums on acquiring higher-quality linen. Tablecloths and napkins,
when used for entertaining, could be used to display status. However, new,
higher-quality bedding, and towels, which were considerably more valuable than table linen because of the quantity of material involved, was for
personal and private use. Of the different types of household linen exam-

ined here, napkins increased in number the least, which is perhaps the opposite to what might be expected if the motive for increased consumption was for 'public' display. Again, increasing personal comfort appears to have been the primary reason for acquiring new and better-quality linen. The difference in ownership of linen provides the greatest single contrast between Kent and Cornwall. If differences of wealth account for this contrasting pattern of ownership it suggests that Kentish householders spent a significant part of their disposable income on linen, a 'traditional' and familiar commodity.

The relatively late adoption of knives and forks in both Kent and Cornwall by the majority of households also warns against explanations of increased consumption in the early modern period that emphasise emulation of elite social groups. There appears to have been little effort to adopt this style for dining for many years by most households. On the other hand, other types of new goods, such as tea and coffee, became popular within a very short space of time. The precise form in which meals are taken, like dress, provides one of the most direct expressions of culture. The adoption of knives and forks for the majority of early modern households required a cultural change more fundamental than simply copying the aristocracy.

More significant than fashion is the arrival of new household goods that suggest changes in behaviour implying quite fundamental alterations in social customs and traditional culture.[114] Changes in kitchen equipment in Kent indicate developments in cooking methods, suggesting both changes in diet and in the forms in which food was eaten. Food was cooked in more complicated and sophisticated ways. The social context of eating also changed so that households ate their new meals at round rather than rectangular tables. In many households hierarchical seating arrangements were no longer so important and it was less common for the whole household – including servants and probably children – to eat together: in other words, hierarchy was expressed by eating in different rooms rather than in sitting in different places around one table. And, as we shall see in Chapter 6, eating took place more in private spaces within the home as the use of space within the household became more specialised.[115] Furthermore, by the close of our period the majority of households in Kent were consuming tea and engaging in new social rituals associated with its consumption.

Although similar developments can be found in some Cornish households, changes in consumption in the majority of households sampled were much more subdued. Overall Cornish households had a much simpler material culture, indicated by smaller varieties and quantities of domestic goods. Similar new types of goods, such as dinner plates, appear in Kent and Cornwall, but generally these emerge earlier and are more widespread in Kent than in Cornwall. Cornish houses were much smaller and their plans simpler than those in Kent. Whereas substantial increases took place in the size of houses in Kent (indicated by the number of rooms) there appears to have been very little change in the size or arrangement of Cornish houses (indicated by a consistent lack of detail concerning the number and type of rooms). Moreover, whereas in Kent the variety and quantity of domestic goods steadily increased during the seventeenth and eighteenth centuries, in many Cornish households it declined, suggesting a reduction in the standard of their domestic environment.

The new goods Cornish households acquired, such as greater quantities of pewter plates, were practical and traditional in the sense that pewter was an investment since it could be sold or re-fashioned. Although Cornish households had smaller quantities of tableware, tableware is one of the few types of domestic goods that increased in quantity and value. It suggests a pragmatic type of consumption. Compared to Kent, Cornish consumers were much less adventurous, and bought far fewer decorative and novel goods, but these changes show that Cornwall was not entirely immune from changing fashions but highly selective in its consumption behaviour.

Moreover, when seen within the domestic environment as a whole, it can be shown that considerably greater expenditure went on more mundane (and inconspicuous) goods, such as new cooking equipment, linen, pewter and earthenware plates, and furniture, than on goods designed to display one's fashionableness or to copy the nobility. All domestic goods reflect taste and status, but there is little evidence in the changes that took place in the domestic environment as a whole – in either Kent or Cornwall – to suggest most consumers were preoccupied with keeping up with fashion or copying their social superiors. Rather, the motive for the majority of these purchases appears to have been primarily improving personal comfort and convenience, as and when the goods became available, and when they could afford them.

6   Rooms and room use

The previous chapter looked at the material culture of the household as a whole, in so far as it was revealed by an inventory. This chapter looks at the rooms in the house and the objects that were in them. Rooms themselves are part of the material culture of the household, and the number of rooms and their descriptions provide indications of the use of space and can suggest both changes in behaviour and in the social relationships within the household. The location of objects within houses can provide insights into the meanings ascribed to them; for example, whether they are on display in 'public' rooms or hidden away in more 'private' spaces. Many studies have illustrated the physical development of vernacular houses in England from the Middle Ages onwards, but comparatively few have looked at the location of objects within the house.[1]

The information on rooms in inventories has to be treated with some caution since appraisers were not obliged to record them. Orlin lists ten reasons why a given room may not be listed in an inventory, even when the appraisers were recording rooms, although we have no way of knowing how frequently this happened.[2] Rooms would be omitted if, for whatever reason, the appraisers did not record any goods in the room. This could be because there were none; the goods belonged to someone else, such as a servant, child, apprentice, or lodger; had been moved to another room; or were excluded for one of the many reasons given in Chapter 2. Other household spaces, such as passages or galleries, are also likely to have been ignored by the appraisers if they had no items in them.[3] Sometimes it is obvious that the appraisers simply forgot to mention that they had entered a new room, or moved outside – for example, when farm animals seemingly appear in chambers. As with other evidence from inventories we can only draw positive conclusions about the presence of rooms: because a room was not recorded it does not mean it did not exist, and generally speaking we might expect the number of rooms recorded in inventories to be underestimates.[4] On the other hand it is more likely that appraisers would record rooms in larger houses than in smaller ones, producing an upward bias in the number of rooms counted in a collection of inventories. Although we can only guess at why appraisers recorded rooms, the most likely explanation is that associating an item with a room assisted its identification by differentiating it from goods of the same type in other rooms. When the number of goods in the household was small, or the house had very few rooms, there was less need for the appraisers to differentiate in this way. Although appraisers recorded rooms inventories do not enable us to reconstruct house plans, merely the number of rooms. This is important for it prevents the more sophisticated analysis of domestic space, developed by Hillier and Hanson for example, which depends on knowing how rooms are connected, and therefore how movement and interaction in the house was channelled and constrained.[5]

Inferences about the uses of rooms are based on the objects within them. There are more potential problems here since we have no way of knowing whether objects in the household were moved after the death of their owner. It is possible, for example, that goods would be grouped together in a room for sale or disposal, although it seems unlikely that this was a common occurrence. Nevertheless we must be aware of the possibility that the disposition of objects when the inventory was taken may not have been as it was before the death of their owner.

Table 6.1 shows that under 20 per cent of Cornish inventories mention room names, and in the first three decades of the seventeenth century less than 7 per cent do so. This suggests that the majority of houses appraised remained small and that their interiors were not subdivided into functionally specialised rooms. Architectural studies of surviving buildings suggest that small houses with simple plans were very common in Cornwall throughout the seventeenth and eighteenth centuries.[6] These small houses had a general living area, supplemented by a separate room for domestic purposes. Subdivisions of interior space were achieved in the simplest possible way by partitioning off one end of the ground floor room with a post and panel screen. The front door opened directly into the hall against this screen, with a rear door slightly offset on the back wall. These 'rooms' were not, therefore, entirely separate, which may help to explain why appraisers did not always describe them separately; sim-

Table 6.1 The recording of rooms

		1600– 29	1630– 59	1660– 89	1690– 1719	1720– 49
Inventories recording	Cornwall	7	12	13	12	19
rooms (%)	Kent	63	68	75	85	87
Median number of recorded	Cornwall	6	6	6	6	6
rooms	Kent	6	6	7	8	7
Median number of rooms for all inventories	Kent	3	5	6	7	7

ilarly simple rooms above the hall may have been constructed from post and lintels, which were not entirely enclosed or separate from the main living area. The evidence of surviving houses shows that the idea of using a corner of a room to provide a partitioned service area was adopted in many parts of the county.

Carew wrote in 1602 that until recently husbandmen had lived in 'very mean' dwellings, with walls of earth, a low, thatched roof, little in the way of partitions, no glass at the windows and only a hole in the wall to serve as a chimney. Now, however, 'most of these fashions are universally banished, and the Cornish husbandman conformeth himself with a better supplied civility to the eastern pattern'. As for yeomen of the region, their circumstances, he claimed, were indistinguishable from those of their counterparts elsewhere.[7] Our work shows that this is an exaggeration, although there are some examples of quite large houses. The appraisers of the inventory of Edward Herle, Esquire, mentioned 16 rooms in his house in Luxulyan in 1620, including a dining room complete with a pair of virginals.[8] Carew thought that Cornish gentlemen, 'keep liberal, but not costly builded or furnished houses', and the Cornish gentry represented in the inventory sample had an average of nine rooms recorded in their houses compared with 11 for their Kentish counterparts, while the yeomen had six rooms compared with nine in Kent.[9]

The median numbers of rooms per household in Cornwall shown in Table 6.1 are calculated from those inventories recording rooms and are therefore inflated, given that so small a proportion of inventories fall into this category. The room count includes domestic living rooms and rooms used for storage in the house. Outbuildings, such as barns and workshops, are not counted. The distinction between outbuildings and domestic rooms is not always clear, but is usually suggested by the order in which the inventory was taken, the appraisers walking from one room to another. In most Kent inventories domestic rooms were appraised first, followed by outbuildings and farm stock. Closets and cupboards built into interior walls are not included, but storage spaces such as butteries and garrets are.

The figures for Kent, calculated in the same way, show a small rise in the median number of rooms from six to seven between 1600–29 and 1720–49. However, the proportion of inventories mentioning rooms rises from 63 per cent to 87 per cent, which might suggest houses had more rooms. If we assume that those inventories not mentioning rooms refer to houses with three rooms or fewer, then the median number of rooms would be as shown in the final row of the table which includes all inventories, whether they record rooms or not in the calculation. In reality, of course, not all those inventories that fail to mention rooms refer to houses of three rooms or fewer, but the great majority do. Thus it is likely that the median number of rooms in our samples of Kent inventories roughly doubled from the early seventeenth to the mid-eighteenth century.

This possibility is reinforced by the data in Table 6.2 showing the frequency distribution of inventories by number of rooms mentioned, excluding those inventories not mentioning rooms. Small houses, with three rooms or fewer, decline from over 22 per cent in 1600–29 to 5 per cent in 1720–49, while the modal category rises from 4 to 6 rooms to 7 to 9 rooms.[10] This increase reflects both the subdivision of existing space, for example by flooring over an open hall or putting a sleeping chamber in the roof, and the physical extension of houses. Kent appears to have been in the forefront of the so-called 'great rebuilding' in England and was far in advance of the rest of the country.[11] Most yeomen's houses were probably extended at some time between 1560 and the mid-seventeenth century by the addition of service rooms such as a brew-house. Unique to Kent among the south-eastern counties was the wash-house, distinguished from other rooms by having a water supply, which began to appear in the 1630s. Houses were also extended upwards, by the addition of a first floor, as nearly all yeomen had chambered over their hall, formerly open to the roof, by 1600. The greatest innovation in the south-east, bringing greater comfort to many farmhouses, was the introduction of a brick fireplace at one end of the hall with a brick stack also serving another fireplace at its back in a service room such as the kitchen. Beside the stack a newel staircase was inserted in the place of a ladder.[12] This led to a chamber, which by the end of the century often also contained a hearth.

Many types of room are mentioned by the Kent appraisers, and these are distinguished in a variety of ways. Chambers, for example, were identified by their location ('over the kitchen'), their colour ('red chamber'), their function ('bed chamber'), the goods that were stored in them ('apple chamber'), and by the individual or individuals that used them ('Mr Culpeppers chamber', 'the maids chamber'). The word 'shop' was applied to rooms in which some activity took place that nearly always involved production for sale; for example, the 'barbers shop', the 'leather shop' and the 'weaving shop'. On the other hand, the word 'house' was applied to rooms in which activities involved production for use ('wash-house' and 'bakehouse'), or to rooms used for storage ('apple house' and 'coal house'). Since most houses had only one parlour and hall they did

Table 6.2 The frequency of rooms recorded in Kent inventories (percentages)

Rooms	1600–29	1630–59	1660–89	1690–1719	1720–49
1–3	22	14	8	4	5
4–6	33	36	30	24	28
7–9	23	25	26	32	33
10–14	13	14	20	23	19
15 or more	9	10	15	16	16

not need qualification. The word 'room' was not commonly used, and was qualified by the name of an individual, location, appearance, or function. The most exotic was the 'billiatt room' in the house of Sir Arnold Braems of Bridge whose inventory was made in 1681. In addition to the billiard table the room contained a side table, eight chairs, a squab and hearth equipment.[13]

Six categories of room are used to illustrate changes in room frequencies and room use in Tables 6.3–6.5: halls, parlours, kitchens, chambers, great chambers and service rooms. Table 6.3 shows the frequencies with which specific rooms are mentioned: for each of the six categories the proportion not mentioning the room, with one room in the category, and with more than one room in the category, are shown. Additionally Table 6.3 shows the frequency with which certain specialist rooms are recorded.

Room use is shown in two ways. Table 6.4 takes the six major categories

Table 6.3 Room types in Kent (percentages)

	1600–29	*1630–59*	*1660–89*	*1690–1719*	*1720–49*
Number of inventories	727	511	846	537	207
No hall	6	7	17	43	59
1 hall	49	39	32	27	33
>1 hall	45	54	51	30	9
No parlour	53	53	48	46	52
1 parlour	18	20	20	26	25
>1 parlour	29	27	32	28	22
No kitchen	52	48	37	29	29
1 kitchen	33	33	35	34	40
>1 kitchen	15	19	29	36	31
No chamber	14	13	5	4	4
1 chamber	27	27	23	25	35
2 chambers	26	28	30	33	33
>2 chambers	32	32	42	38	28
No great chamber	97	93	80	59	49
1 great chamber	3	6	18	38	50
>1 great chamber	0	1	2	2	1
No service room	54	46	31	17	27
1 service room	30	33	34	31	34
>1 service room	17	21	36	52	39
Milk-house	35	43	51	54	39
Bakehouse	2	3	3	4	2
Boulting house	6	5	3	4	1
Wash-house	5	7	16	28	34
Brew-house	10	16	34	46	35
Drink buttery	9	17	21	19	10
Loft	21	16	2	0	0
Servants' rooms	6	9	13	16	21
Fire room	0	0	0	7	10

Table 6.4 Activities and objects in Kent houses by room (percentages)

	1600–29	1630–59	1660–89	1690–1719	1720–49
Hall					
Cooking	64	68	63	54	58
Sleeping	4	3	3	4	4
Eating	32	34	36	42	52
Work	16	12	13	17	19
New chair	2	2	5	7	5
Clocks	0	1	12	28	40
Pictures	2	2	3	2	19
Mirrors	0	4	4	9	24
Hot drinks	0	0	0	0	11
Pewter	38	44	44	48	46
Parlour					
Cooking	6	8	5	5	7
Sleeping	61	50	37	27	16
Eating	5	8	7	8	13
Work	3	5	6	8	10
New chair	2	4	18	20	16
Clocks	0	0	4	6	11
Pictures	3	3	5	4	20
Mirrors	2	3	4	14	29
Hot drinks	0	0	0	1	13
Pewter	10	10	7	6	6
Kitchen					
Cooking	76	76	82	88	82
Sleeping	1	2	1	2	2
Eating	32	28	38	52	59
Work	46	49	42	31	31
New chair	0	0	2	2	2
Clocks	1	0	3	24	27
Pictures	0	0	0	1	6
Mirrors	0	1	2	6	16
Hot drinks	0	0	0	2	17
Pewter	33	37	47	62	62
Chamber					
Cooking	15	8	8	3	4
Sleeping	94	95	98	98	98
Eating	20	14	16	13	26
Work	27	20	13	15	16
New chair	2	3	8	14	17
Clocks	0	0	3	4	5
Pictures	3	1	4	4	15
Mirrors	3	6	16	28	41
Hot drinks	0	0	0	2	10
Pewter	23	20	21	11	8

Table 6.4 Continued

	1600–29	1630–59	1660–89	1690–1719	1720–49
Great chamber					
Cooking	0	0	4	0	1
Sleeping	77	94	93	96	98
Eating	9	12	12	14	26
Work	5	0	2	2	0
New chair	5	15	13	21	18
Clocks	0	3	3	2	3
Pictures	14	3	6	7	19
Mirrors	5	9	26	35	48
Hot drinks	0	0	1	3	9
Pewter	5	6	8	4	8
Service					
Cooking	23	24	37	64	77
Sleeping	7	9	14	14	12
Eating	25	20	29	35	37
Work	88	95	96	96	95
New chair	0	0	1	0	0
Clocks	0	0	0	0	1
Pictures	0	0	0	1	1
Mirrors	0	0	1	1	1
Hot drinks	0	0	0	1	7
Pewter	9	9	9	9	11

of room and shows for each 30-year period the proportions of inventories showing evidence of certain activities or objects. Thus for 1600–29, 64 per cent of halls have evidence of cooking, 4 per cent sleeping, and 32 per cent eating. These activities were identified by objects associated with them; for example, beds for sleeping, and a hearth and cooking utensils for cooking. It is more difficult to demonstrate that a room was used for eating. We have used such objects as salts, plates, trenchers and dishes and forks, but not tables unless they are explicitly referred to as dining tables.[14] The category 'working' is assigned if there is evidence of any kind of production activity (excluding cooking) ranging from weaving to brewing, and includes production for household use.

Table 6.5 presents room use in a different way, showing the frequencies with which each type of activity or object is mentioned in each of five room categories (hall, parlour, kitchen, chamber and great chamber). Thus in 1600–29 53 per cent of all cooking took place in halls, 2 per cent in parlours, and 32 per cent in kitchens. Activities in rooms other than the five categories are excluded so that the columns for each activity or object at each date sum to 100. For the activities of 'working' and 'spinning', service rooms are added as an additional category.

Since medieval times, the hall was the main living area of the house, where the inhabitants cooked, ate and slept. The proportion of houses

Table 6.5 Activities and objects in five room types in Kent houses (percentages)

	1600–29	1630–59	1660–89	1690–1719	1720–49
Cooking					
Hall	53	56	46	31	26
Parlour	2	3	2	3	4
Kitchen	32	35	45	63	65
Chamber	12	6	7	3	4
Great chamber	0	0	1	0	1
Sleeping					
Hall	3	2	2	2	1
Parlour	25	20	14	10	5
Kitchen	0	1	1	1	1
Chamber	70	71	70	62	61
Great chamber	2	5	14	26	32
Eating					
Hall	46	50	40	29	20
Parlour	3	6	5	5	6
Kitchen	23	24	32	44	39
Chamber	27	19	21	15	23
Great chamber	0	1	3	7	12
Working					
Hall	15	10	9	7	7
Parlour	1	2	3	3	4
Kitchen	22	24	22	17	18
Chamber	23	16	10	11	13
Great chamber	0	0	0	1	0
Service	40	48	56	61	58
Spinning					
Hall	36	27	17	16	12
Parlour	3	5	7	7	12
Kitchen	10	11	11	23	19
Chamber	34	41	40	36	47
Great chamber	0	0	1	2	0
Service	17	16	24	15	12
New chairs					
Hall	41	28	18	10	5
Parlour	19	25	37	29	21
Kitchen	3	0	4	3	4
Chamber	34	33	31	35	45
Great chamber	3	14	10	22	25
Clocks					
Hall	60	67	58	40	35
Parlour	0	0	13	7	11
Kitchen	40	0	10	41	41
Chamber	0	17	16	9	10
Great chamber	0	17	3	2	3

Table 6.5 Continued

	1600–29	1630–59	1660–89	1690–1719	1720–49
Pictures					
Hall	29	36	24	12	17
Parlour	22	36	26	19	21
Kitchen	0	0	0	5	10
Chamber	42	23	38	35	31
Great chamber	7	5	13	28	21
Mirrors					
Hall	11	33	11	9	10
Parlour	22	14	8	13	14
Kitchen	4	3	4	7	12
Chamber	59	45	58	47	40
Great chamber	4	5	19	24	25
Hot drinks					
Hall	0	0	0	4	12
Parlour	0	0	0	8	17
Kitchen	0	0	33	28	33
Chamber	0	0	33	36	26
Great chamber	0	0	33	24	12
Pewter					
Hall	47	50	40	32	25
Parlour	6	6	4	4	4
Kitchen	20	23	32	51	56
Chamber	27	21	22	12	10
Great chamber	0	0	2	2	5

with halls in Kent declined from over 94 per cent to 41 per cent between 1600–29 and 1720–49. Most of this decline took place between 1660–89 and 1690–1719, although halls continued to disappear slowly thereafter. The decline of the hall as the main living area was in fact even greater than these figures suggest, because in many houses at the end of our period it had become little more than a passage between rooms or an entrance lobby through which one passed to enter the living rooms. In the Middle Ages, halls were open to the roof and their decline in Kent houses is a reflection of the gradual process whereby a chimney stack was added and a ceiling inserted to create chambers above. Activities formerly undertaken in the hall were now located in more specialist rooms.[15] This process of change took place across the country, beginning in Kent during the late fifteenth century, although it continued into the seventeenth century.[16] However, from the early eighteenth century appraisers begin to describe rooms that had the characteristics of an early seventeenth-century hall as a 'fire room': these were rooms with fireplaces, cooking equipment, seating, and sometimes beds. Houses with such rooms did not have a hall or kitchen recorded.

There was a slight decline in the proportion of halls with cooking materials (Table 6.4), although more significantly cooking activity moved from the hall to the kitchen: Table 6.5 shows that in 1600–29, 53 per cent of cooking took place in the hall and 32 per cent in the kitchen, but by 1720–49 the proportions were 26 and 65 per cent respectively. Throughout the period, however, between 30 and 40 per cent of halls were not used for cooking. Eating continued to take place here; in larger houses where the master and his family ate in parlours or great chambers the servants may have eaten in the hall. In small houses the hall remained a general living area where cooking, eating, work and sitting took place. Beds were rarely found in halls throughout the seventeenth and eighteenth centuries, suggesting that halls were rarely used for sleeping from an early date. Similarly, production activities such as baking, brewing and spinning only took place in a small proportion of halls, since the majority of Kentish households in the inventory sample had at least one service room where the equipment for these types of work was kept. In larger houses, new functionally specialised rooms, notably the kitchen and parlour, were added, so the hall lost much of its former status. In small houses, however, the hall accumulated new furniture and furnishings in addition to the multitude of domestic functions it had before the seventeenth century. Although, as we have seen, the extent of spinning declined in Kent, the specialisation of household space saw spinning wheels move from the hall to the kitchen and to chambers. This might suggest something about the gendering of space, with women's work activities restricted to particular rooms, notably the kitchen and rooms upstairs.

The decline of the multi-functional hall is reflected in the rise of the kitchen. Kitchens were primarily used for cooking, although as many as 20 per cent did not have cooking equipment and the room was used as a multipurpose service area for processing foodstuffs.[17] The reason for having a kitchen lay not only in removing cooking from the hall but also in providing a room for the growing amount of equipment needed for baking, brewing and other types of food and drink processing. As Barley has suggested, with an expanding range of these processing activities, the hall was often retained as a cooking room, and the kitchen was a general store and workroom, sometimes referred to as a 'back kitchen'.[18] A higher proportion of kitchens had equipment associated with food and drink processing (such as brewing and baking) than any other room in the house. Just under 50 per cent in the first half of the seventeenth century had such equipment, although this figure declines as a result of an increase in specialised service rooms. Kitchens in Kent were also used for eating and sitting, possibly for servants in larger households. The development of a wider range of functions in the kitchen parallels the decline of the hall as the general living room. In large houses this change was associated with turning the parlour into a sitting room and using the hall as an entrance lobby; those who could not do this began using the kitchen as an eating and sitting room. Table 6.4 shows almost a doubling of the proportion of kitchens with goods indicating eating, but there might well be additional reasons for this. Servants are most likely to have eaten in the kitchen, and the increase in eating activity may reflect a growth in spatial segregation within the household. But eating is one of the more problematic categories and the presence of items such as plates and forks in a kitchen does not necessarily indicate they were being used there, merely that they were being stored.

In small houses the buttery, used for storing victuals and cooking pots, was the only service room. Just under 50 per cent of Kentish houses in our sample of inventories had at least one of these specialised rooms in the first three decades of the seventeenth century, increasing to 83 per cent by the turn of the eighteenth century.[19] As Table 6.3 shows, around 35 per cent of houses had a milk-house in the early seventeenth century, rising to over 50 per cent by the end of the century. The rise in the proportion of inventories recording brew-houses and wash-houses was more rapid. The increase in home brewing has already been discussed in Chapter 3 and the growth in specialist brew-houses is clear evidence of this. In many houses butteries also became more numerous and specialised, usually for storing drink, and in larger houses it was common to have a second or even third buttery. These are commonly described as the 'best drink buttery' and the 'small drink buttery', the latter for daily use, the former often next to a parlour and usually containing more special types of drink such as wine.[20] The incidence of wash-houses increased sixfold between the early seventeenth century and the early eighteenth, and, according to Barley, the idea of having, inside or near the house, a room with a water supply derived from a well or a pump was disseminated from London. Wash-houses are rarely found outside London and adjacent counties, and are particularly common in Kent. Brewing and dairying equipment were frequently found here, but a wash-house is distinguished from a kitchen, milk-house and brew-house by having a well.[21]

The presence of a parlour was clearly related to the size of house: the larger a house, the more likely that it would contain a parlour. Less than 10 per cent of the Kentish houses sampled with only two rooms had a parlour, while over 95 per cent of those with 15 rooms or more had one (see Table 6.6). However, the proportion of houses with parlours stayed roughly constant at about a half over the course of the whole period 1600–1749: many households added further service rooms and chambers to their houses before adding a parlour.

Parlours are known from the early Middle Ages as places to meet and converse with guests; from the fifteenth century they commonly had beds in them, when they came to be used as either guest bedchambers or, in smaller houses, as bed-sitting rooms. By the early sixteenth century beds had disappeared from parlours in the houses of the gentry, and they

Table 6.6 Great chambers in Kent inventories, 1600–1749

No. of rooms	No. of inventories	Great chambers		Parlours		Parlours and great chambers	
		No	%	No.	%	No.	%
1–3	359	7	2	58	16	0	0
4–6	975	123	13	328	34	35	4
7–9	867	216	25	492	57	107	12
10–14	569	171	30	440	77	127	22
15 or more	111	42	38	106	95	42	38

became eating and reception rooms only.[22] The function of the parlour in our sample of Kent inventories changed during the seventeenth century from a room for sleeping in, to one for sitting, eating and dining. In the first three decades of the seventeenth century just over 60 per cent of the Kentish households sampled had parlours which contained beds. Beds slowly disappeared from Kentish parlours over the seventeenth and eighteenth centuries, and were found in less than 17 per cent by the period 1720–49. Parlours contained tables and chairs, so their main function was for sitting and dining. New types of upholstered chairs were more commonly found here than in any other rooms. Their presence increased during the seventeenth century, after which they declined in number. In houses of the gentry, parlours were smaller, more intimate rooms than great chambers, which by the seventeenth century had developed into more formal reception rooms. Thus the parlour developed into a comfortable room (nearly all parlours had a fireplace), with increasingly specialised functions: sitting, entertaining and dining. Although parlours shared many functions with halls, they remained a more private space, with less evidence of everyday activity. This view is reinforced by the morphological analysis of the plans of seventeenth-century London houses which showed that most parlours had only one entrance and were well insulated from the kitchen and butteries, indicating they were rather private spaces, set apart from work within the home.[23]

By the mid-eighteenth century, sets of chairs, used around a table, appear in many cases to have replaced the upholstered types found in parlours during the seventeenth century, suggesting the parlour was increasingly used as a dining and gaming room.[24] Parlours also contained new china and other related equipment used for drinking tea and coffee: for example, Elizabeth Wells of Bridge had '5 china cups and saucers' in her parlour in 1743.[25] The parlour appears to have been a room where guests were entertained, and it was likely to contain decorative pictures and prints. Similarly, new items of furniture, notably small occasional tables for tea, were more commonly located here than in any other room. In the many households that did not have a parlour, the 'public' functions of the parlour were accommodated within other multi-functional rooms. It is notable, for example, that the equipment used for making and consuming tea was commonly found in kitchens in households without a parlour, reminding us that consumption practice had to be modified to fit individual circumstances.

The term 'chamber' was commonly applied as a general synonym for 'room' (hence 'wheat chamber' and 'dining chamber'), and therefore, covers a wide range of general-purpose living and service rooms. Chambers in Kent, however, were usually located above the ground floor, although at the start of the seventeenth century they were more general purpose, and more likely to be found on the ground floor than later on in the seventeenth and eighteenth centuries. This can sometimes be inferred from the description of a room; William Stroud of Elmham, for example, had 'a chamber joining the hall' and 'a chamber over the lower chamber', but a more helpful indicator is the presence of cooking equipment, which would normally be located in a ground-floor room. In the first three decades of the seventeenth century over 15 per cent of chambers contained cooking equipment; this figure steadily declined over the period, so that just over 4 per cent contained cooking equipment by the second quarter of the eighteenth century. As chambers became almost exclusively confined to the upper floors the term 'loft', referring to a room in the roof space, went out of use, as Table 6.3 shows. As Table 6.4 indicates, virtually all chambers contained beds and their primary purpose was as a room to sleep in, although they were also used quite extensively for storage.[26] The decline of beds in parlours is a sign of the growing specialisation in use of chambers, and of sleeping above the ground floor. This is also indicated by the decline in chambers used for domestic production, which fell from just under 30 per cent in the first three decades of the seventeenth century to 16 per cent in the period 1720–49.

One of the most interesting developments to have taken place during the seventeenth and eighteenth centuries in Kentish houses was the increasing popularity of a particular type of chamber, referred to as the 'great' or 'best' chamber. In the first three decades of the seventeenth century some 3 per cent of houses had such a room, but this increased to over 50 per cent during the 1720–49 period. This figure should probably be greater, since many bedchambers, such as the 'fore chamber', appear to have been principal bedrooms belonging to masters of houses, and are distinguished by their contents in the same way as great chambers from other bedchambers. In noble houses the great chamber was originally a room of state, increasingly used by the lord as he withdrew from dining in the hall with his entire household, preferring instead to eat with smaller, more exclusive groups of diners. During the fifteenth and sixteenth centuries the great chamber became a bed-sitting room, combining the functions of a private reception room and bedchamber, which could be used for sleeping, playing cards, receiving visitors and taking small meals.[27]

The functions of great chambers in Kent appear to echo those of the great houses: they almost certainly contained a bed, but also served as a dining and sitting room for the head of the household and his family. As in noble houses, the head of the household may have increasingly retired to the great chamber as a means of distancing himself from domestic servants. Great chambers often contained sets of chairs for sitting and possibly dining; upholstered furniture was also commonly located here, but not cooking equipment. They were more commonly used for sitting and dining than other chambers. Production activities were much less likely to be undertaken in great chambers than in any other room in the house.

Great chambers had many similarities with parlours. The high number of chairs, including upholstered chairs, suggests they were comfortable rooms in which guests could be received. However, great chambers usually had beds, and since they were above the ground floor they were not 'public' rooms in the same way as parlours. Moreover, whereas parlours became increasingly more specialised as dining rooms used for entertaining, great chambers appear to have remained essentially 'private' spaces with multiple uses. Large court cupboards, used to display plate and usually located in a room where meals were taken, were found in 50 per cent of great chambers in the early seventeenth century but had disappeared from them by 1725.

Great chambers were mostly confined to the larger households, as Table 6.6 demonstrates. Only 13 per cent of houses with six rooms or fewer had a great chamber, while 38 per cent of houses with fifteen or more rooms had such a room. However, it is not simply the case that houses with parlours added a great chamber to which the head of the household could retire, since 47 per cent of houses with a great chamber did not have a parlour. Larger households were more likely to have both a parlour and a great chamber, but there is no clear relationship between the size of the house and the presence of a great chamber without a parlour. It would appear that a significant proportion of households chose to have a great chamber instead of a parlour.

The development of houses illustrated in this chapter demonstrates how the spaces in which people lived changed considerably from the early seventeenth to the mid-eighteenth century. In general, houses had more rooms, and the increase in the number of rooms was associated with their greater functional specialisation. Thus the domestic environment became more complicated, with more possibilities for arranging the space of the household and the objects within it, and not only for segregating tasks but also the different members of the household. With the development of great chambers, for example, the master of the house could separate himself both from his children and his servants. When eating took place in more than one room, servants, and perhaps also children, need no longer eat with the household head.

This change came about from the sixteenth century onwards and usually involved flooring over the hall which had hitherto been open to the roof. There seem to be no obvious technological or economic reasons why such a change could not have taken place at an earlier date. The technology of chimney construction was available, and the costs of changing the layout of a house were not excessive. Cooper considers that 'the prestige attached to the open hall was waning, its social functions were increasingly obsolete and its symbolic functions corresponded less and less to the image that its owner sought to present'.[28] Johnson concludes that the open hall must be seen in terms of the social life within it, and that it reflected a 'medieval patriarchy'.[29] He characterises the ceiling over the hall and the creation of chambers above as a process of 'closure'. This involves

> a shift away from the idea of a house and household as *community* towards the house and household as *society*, in terms of its move towards segregation of social elements rather than unity and its stress on functional differentiation rather than social status.

Social segregation took place on the basis of age, gender, and master and servant. The move towards 'privacy' and 'comfort' are manifestations of this process of closure and should be seen in this wider context.[30] This 'desire for privacy' is commented upon by many historians, but there is no consensus regarding its explanation.[31]

Just as some spaces of the house were becoming more 'private', according to some historians others were becoming more self-consciously 'public' for receiving guests and acting as the locus of objects for display. Weatherill, for example, uses Goffman's concepts of 'frontstage' and 'backstage' to argue that new consumption goods were located in 'frontstage' rooms; that is, rooms where people present themselves to others.[32] There is some evidence of this in Kent inventories; pictures, mirrors, clocks and new types of chair do appear in parlours which can be regarded as 'frontstage' rooms in that this was where guests to the house were received. Conversely, pewter, which was gradually being usurped by earthenware and china, shifted from the hall to the 'backstage' kitchen and out of sight of visitors, along with the court cupboards used for its display.[33] Yet as Table 6.5 shows, by 1720–49 new consumption goods were more likely to be found in chambers, 'backstage' rooms that were for the use of particular individuals. Mirrors, for example, were much more likely to be located in chambers, and while some were found in halls and parlours where they might have been placed to be admired by others, those in chambers were strictly functional. Even pictures were more likely to be found in chambers than in parlours from the mid-seventeenth century. Clocks, which diffuse rapidly from the mid-seventeenth century, were also more likely to appear in the 'backstage' kitchen than the 'frontstage' hall from the 1690s, suggesting their main function was the utilitarian job of telling the time rather than serving as a decorative object to impress visitors. Materials associated with tea and coffee were most likely to be in the kitchen by the mid-eighteenth century; and while in some households they were probably just being stored here, in others tea and coffee were as likely to be drunk in a kitchen as in a parlour. Indeed, a third of those households with tea or coffee had no recorded parlour or great chamber.

Simple dichotomies like 'frontstage' and 'backstage' or 'public' and 'private' are too crude to capture the usages of rooms and their contents. Great chambers blur such distinctions because they were both a private place for sleeping and one in which other people could be entertained. They were 'public' to a limited extent: a social space restricted to a householder's family and close circle of intimate friends. Furthermore, an increasing number of houses contained servants, and the uses and meanings of social space within the house obviously differed between servants and their employers. Thus for many people the creation of a private, comfortable space was more important than having a public reception room in the form of a parlour. This is consistent with earlier discussion of the changes taking place in the domestic environment and the acquisition of new domestic goods that were primarily designed to enhance personal comfort and convenience rather than create a public arena in which to display one's wealth and good taste.

7 Wealth, occupation, status and location

Thus far we have looked at production and consumption separately: in this chapter we consider both together and explore some of the relationships between them. More specifically, we look at how wealth, status, occupation and location are related to consumption in terms of material culture and production for use within the household. Shammas, in her major study of material culture in early modern households, considered that 'wealth was the most important determinant of the value of the various categories of goods'.[1] But wealth is also related to status, inventoried wealth varies considerably between occupations, and the distribution of occupations in turn varies between town and countryside. More recent studies of consumption in early modern England are more cautious, suggesting that historians should not be 'too ready to accept that rising consumption follows automatically from rising wealth'.[2] We calculate a measure of wealth from inventories ('material wealth') and relate this to the ownership of various commodities. We then attempt to determine whether differences in wealth are responsible for the great differences in material culture between Cornwall and Kent identified in Chapter 5. Social status and occupation are also related to the ownership of goods and we look at some of the characteristics of the occupational groups identified in Chapter 3, together with the status groups of gentleman, yeoman, husbandman and widow, and how the ownership of a range of material goods varied between them. The third major factor we consider is location. It has long been assumed that towns were in the vanguard of the adoption of new material goods so we shall be comparing parishes in the countryside with those in the towns. But, as we shall see, a crude rural – urban dichotomy has been overplayed, and while there were differences between town and country, they varied between commodities, and there were also considerable differences between rural parishes. Finally, in an attempt to measure the relative importance of these three factors (wealth, occupation and status, and location), to both the ownership of material goods and the presence of production activities for use, we combine them in a multivariate analysis.

Wealth

The wealth of a household consists of anything that members of the household possess which can be sold for money or used to acquire other commodities: real property, durable goods, financial assets and human capital. Wealth must take into account both the value of property and financial assets owned by the household and its liabilities and or debts. It is an attribute of the household and family, and not simply of the husband or wife, even though some parts of this wealth may be divided between them.[3] In one respect at least inventories are an appropriate source with which to measure wealth because they record stocks at one point in time, and wealth is a stock concept, unlike income which is a flow. However, since they omit real estate and debts owed by the deceased to other people, there are serious difficulties in using inventories alone to measure wealth.[4] Real estate was not the concern of the ecclesiastical courts and while debts owing *to* the deceased were recorded in inventories, debts owed *by* the deceased were not because they were liabilities. Probate accounts can supply the missing information on these liabilities, and wills can reveal something of the holding of real estate, but the matching of these other probate documents to all the inventories used for Kent and Cornwall is beyond the scope of this study. Thus the measure of wealth used is material wealth – the total value of the items in the inventory less the value of leases and debts. Leases are real chattels: on the one hand as pieces of paper they are movable chattels and so are included in an inventory, but on the other they refer to the value of real estate. They are omitted to ensure consistency in the measurement of wealth between individuals. For example, the inventory of a farmer owning his own land contains no values that refer to his real estate, but a farmer renting land might have the value remaining on his lease included.

For the one parish of Milton, in Kent, inventories have been linked to both probate accounts and wills, and an alternative measure of wealth calculated.[5] This is net wealth, which is the value of the final estate from the probate account after debts have been collected and those owing by the deceased have been paid, excluding leases. The trend of net wealth over time is in line with the trend in material wealth, and the relationship between the two is remarkably uniform throughout the seventeenth century with mean net wealth being between 32 and 39 per cent of mean material wealth. For the sample as a whole the correlation between material wealth and net wealth is +0.65. There is also a clear relationship between the amount of real estate evident in a deceased's will and both their material and net wealth: those with little or no real estate were considerably poorer than those with several properties. This analysis of the relationships between holdings of real estate, and the levels of material wealth and net wealth, reveals a very significant finding: the material wealth recorded in the Milton inventories does, as a general rule, reflect other measures of wealth, and may not be such a misleading indicator of total wealth as historians have assumed it to be.

If these results for Milton are replicated in the rest of the county and in Cornwall then material wealth may be taken as a reasonable guide to the overall wealth of an individual. However, items included in an inventory (and therefore the sum of movable wealth) vary by occupation and social group. For example, in Kent during the 1650–99 period, consumption goods comprised 37 per cent of material wealth in the inventories of yeomen, whereas the corresponding proportion for widows was 78 per cent.[6] This is because yeomen's inventories contain a much higher proportion of capital goods than do widows': farm livestock are working capital, and the value of crops growing in the ground in the summer months represents their value as potential income to the farm (but not of course profit) for a year. It is clear therefore that comparisons of material wealth across occupations are an unreliable guide to differences in income, unless occupation is taken into account.

Furthermore, differences in the proportion of wealth held in household goods cannot be interpreted as differences in the propensity to consume. In the example given above, widows did not necessarily have a greater propensity to consume than yeomen, merely far fewer capital goods. Similarly the average urban inventory will have a higher proportion of its wealth in consumption goods than the average rural inventory because of occupational differences between town and country, so a straightforward comparison of the proportion of wealth in consumption goods between the two areas is highly misleading.[7]

Just as wealth is not the same as income, so the value of consumption goods is not the same as consumption. As we have already pointed out the stock of material goods in an inventory represents the accumulation of past consumption and may also include goods that have been inherited.[8] Thus relating material wealth to material culture must not be interpreted as a proxy for the propensity to consume. Shammas recognises this, yet goes on to correlate the value of consumer goods with the total inventory values, concluding that, 'from 60% to 67% of the variation in the value of consumer goods could be attributed to wealth', and then calculates 'elasticities' relating wealth to the value of consumer goods.[9] But as Table 7.1 shows, consumption goods make up over half the total value of an average inventory.[10] Clearly, the high correlations emerge because the two variables are not independent and it is difficult to argue a causal link between 'wealth' and 'consumption'. We shall therefore investigate the links between wealth and consumption using a different methodology.

Table 7.1 shows our preferred measure of wealth, material wealth, but also includes for comparative purposes the means and medians of total inventory values as recorded by the appraisers for samples of inventories in Hertfordshire, Lincolnshire and Worcestershire.[11] For Kent and Cornwall the totals are derived by adding up the values of individual items. The

Table 7.1 Measures of wealth derived from inventories

		1600–29	1630–59	1660–89	1690–1719	1720–49
Inventories used	Cornwall	837	517	1,122	964	635
	Kent	1,142	738	1,131	664	251
	Hertfordshire	842	397	497	298	135
	Lincolnshire	749	520	826	618	660
	Worcestershire	682	872	1,327	783	547
Appraisers' valuations (mean £)	Cornwall	59.10	71.13	93.60	73.44	99.89
	Kent	76.84	123.09	155.38	182.86	196.96
	Hertfordshire	48.77	93.28	124.14	154.45	163.26
	Lincolnshire	117.43	162.16	250.33	286.54	254.06
	Worcestershire	63.65	103.84	98.13	138.88	194.07
Appraisers' valuations (median £)	Cornwall	23.35	38.70	36.81	31.13	40.76
	Kent	35.08	51.92	75.27	104.71	99.28
	Hertfordshire	19.41	36.79	51.37	70.68	91.47
	Lincolnshire	74.02	105.00	140.32	193.82	156.71
	Worcestershire	35.81	60.40	40.51	74.51	118.80
Leases (mean £)	Cornwall	5.77	14.28	23.22	19.37	34.83
	Kent	2.04	3.54	3.42	0.46	0.54
Frequency of leases (%)	Cornwall	20	39	51	55	68
	Kent	10	9	4	1	2
Debts to (mean £)	Cornwall	6.37	12.04	23.97	15.92	17.76
	Kent	19.91	22.90	35.68	36.90	53.26
Frequency of debts to (%)	Cornwall	29	36	49	47	39
	Kent	46	47	50	57	47
Material wealth (mean £)	Cornwall	47.01	44.33	42.01	37.16	43.63
	Kent	53.47	89.23	111.05	134.99	144.53
Material wealth (median £)	Cornwall	17.56	23.10	18.49	15.91	17.50
	Kent	24.66	34.94	59.19	74.85	73.49
Consumption goods (mean £)	Cornwall	20.13	19.85	17.27	16.20	19.16
	Kent	21.97	33.35	45.75	48.23	53.75
Consumption goods (median £)	Cornwall	8.98	11.65	9.72	8.12	9.20
	Kent	12.37	17.46	25.83	34.11	38.78
Consumption goods as % of mean material wealth	Cornwall	59	58	64	62	62
	Kent	61	61	57	54	57

Lincolnshire and Worcestershire inventories are from Consistory courts; the remainder are from Archdeaconry courts, which might explain why the Lincolnshire sample has much higher average wealth, since Consistory courts probably dealt with richer individuals.[12] However, it is also the case that the Lincolnshire sample has a high proportion of farmers, which would bias the figures upwards. Over the period as a whole, mean wealth (at constant prices) grew by 0.82 per cent per annum in Kent, and 0.43 per cent in Cornwall.[13] The figure for Cornwall was the lowest for the five counties, that for Kent was slightly lower than that for Hertfordshire (1.01 per cent per annum) and Worcestershire (0.93 per cent per annum), but greater than Lincolnshire (0.64 per cent per annum).

Material wealth grew roughly threefold in Kent, almost at the same rate as total inventory values including debts and leases. As Table 7.1 shows, the mean value of leases in Kent fell over the course of the seventeenth century, although it was never very significant. Debts also remained a fairly constant proportion of inventory values. In Cornwall, however, the picture was very different and illustrates the importance of using material wealth as the indicator of wealth from inventories. While total inventory values almost doubled in Cornwall from 1600–29 to 1720–49, material wealth remained constant. The difference between the two is a result of a dramatic increase both in the proportion of Cornish inventories including chattel leases, and in the mean value of the term of the lease left to run, from £5.77 to £34.83. The contrast with Kent may be the result of different recording practices by appraisers since the status of leases as 'real chattels' could lead to confusion. It is also possible that the trend reflects an increase in the amount of land being leased, especially under pressure of population in the west. However, it is more likely to be a consequence of the conversion of customary land to leasehold, since the former would not appear in an inventory but the latter would.[14] The frequency of debts in Cornwall show a rise over the seventeenth century and then a fall towards the mid-eighteenth century. However, the proportion of the total inventory value taken up by debts changed little in both counties.

The final six rows of Table 7.1 look at the value of consumption goods and show that they reflect material wealth, since the median value tripled in Kent and stayed constant in Cornwall. Thus the mean proportion of material wealth taken up by consumer goods remained roughly constant. This trend has also been identified by Shammas, and apparently contradicts the evidence of the increased presence of material goods in Kent inventories.[15] The two most likely explanations are that the turnover of goods was increasing and that prices were falling. Increased turnover is implied by goods becoming less durable, as china and glass replaced pewter and wood for example, and we now have clear evidence of a downward movement in the prices of inventoried goods from the mid-seventeenth century.[16]

Rather than correlate inventoried wealth with the value of consumer goods we investigate the relationships between material wealth and the presence of particular items using simple point-biserial correlations.[17] These correlations must show a degree of positive bias since the presence of an item in an inventory will increase the total value of the inventory and therefore material wealth. Thus it is not surprising that most of the correlations in Table 7.2 are positive. However, there is no consistent

Table 7.2 Correlations between wealth and certain goods and activities

		1600–49	1650–99	1700–49
Mirrors	Cornwall	*0.06*	0.10	0.12
	Kent	0.14	0.23	0.22
Upholstered furniture	Cornwall	0.52	0.30	0.30
	Kent	0.51	0.43	0.24
Saucepans	Cornwall	–	*−0.01*	*0.07*
	Kent	*−0.01*	0.02	0.12
Linen quantities	Cornwall	0.47	0.17	0.24
	Kent	0.45	0.46	0.44
Hot drinks	Cornwall	–	–	0.09
	Kent	–	*−0.01*	0.13
Window curtains	Cornwall	*0.00*	*−0.01*	–
	Kent	0.16	0.21	0.16
Chests of drawers	Cornwall	*0.02*	0.14	0.17
	Kent	*0.11*	0.24	0.21
Plates	Cornwall	0.25	0.26	0.22
	Kent	0.34	0.38	0.19
Cauldrons	Cornwall	0.11	*0.01*	0.13
	Kent	0.05	*0.00*	*−0.03*
Milling for use	Cornwall	0.19	*0.04*	0.23
	Kent	0.21	0.22	0.17
Food preservation for use	Cornwall	0.26	0.15	0.22
	Kent	0.19	0.21	0.21
Baking for use	Cornwall	0.14	*−0.01*	0.10
	Kent	0.24	0.20	0.11
Dairying for use	Cornwall	*−0.04*	0.07	0.21
	Kent	*−0.02*	*−0.07*	*−0.15*
Alcohol for use	Cornwall	0.25	0.18	0.23
	Kent	0.33	0.30	0.23

Note
These are point-biserial correlations, except for those for linen which are Pearson product moment correlations. Italicised coefficients are not significant at the 99 per cent level.

relationship between the valuations of the items used to identify an object or activity and the value of material wealth in the inventory. For example, during the period 1600–49 the mean value of dairy equipment in Kent inventories is over £2 yet the correlation with wealth is not significant. On the other hand there is a stronger positive correlation between material wealth and upholstered furniture, yet the mean value of such items is less than two shillings. Thus for some goods, including upholstered furniture, chests of drawers and plates there are positive correlations with material wealth. On the other hand, for other commodities, including tea and coffee, window curtains and saucepans, the correlations are low and often statistically insignificant. There are positive and significant correlations between wealth and domestic production activities for use, with the exception of dairying in Kent and baking in Cornwall. Correlating the presence of individual items with material wealth shows a much weaker relationship than correlating wealth with the value of consumption goods, suggesting that Shammas's conclusions need some revision.[18]

We can shed further light on this by examining the dramatic difference in the level of material culture between Kent and Cornwall. We have already seen in Chapter 5 how levels of adoption of new material goods were much lower in Cornwall than in Kent, and from Table 7.1 that both the value of material wealth and consumption goods stayed constant in Cornwall while they tripled in Kent. If wealth were the major determinant of the adoption of new commodities we would expect the low levels of adoption in Cornwall to be the result of low levels of wealth. Table 7.3 investigates this by showing how certain material goods and activities are distributed by quartiles of material wealth for three time periods. The quartiles are calculated from the distribution of material wealth for the Kent and Cornwall inventories combined. Thus we are comparing rates of ownership between the two counties for individuals in the same wealth categories. For most material goods there is a clear relationship between wealth and ownership; for example, during the period 1650–99 inventories in the wealthiest quartile in Kent are over seven times more likely to contain a mirror than the poorest quartile. The richest had higher rates of adoption in the earlier periods when the gap between the poorest and the richest was also proportionally at its greatest. Thereafter the poorer groups begin to catch up as goods filter down the wealth hierarchy. This pattern is repeated for most other items shown in Tables 5.1–5.4. However, the difference between the adoption rates for the poorest and the richest does vary, reflecting the strength of the correlations in Table 7.2.

The take-up of new commodities was much slower in Cornwall, and although the richest were more likely to own particular material goods than the poorest, their rate of adoption was much lower than their equivalents in Kent. Because Table 7.3 uses quartiles based on the pooled distribution of wealth from Kent and Cornwall, the effect of the differences in wealth between the two counties is removed. Thus the 9.4 per cent of Cornish inventories in the top wealth quartile with a mirror in the period 1700–49 are in the same wealth category as the 53.1 per cent of Kent inventories that had one during the same period.[19] Cornwall's poor material culture therefore was not simply a function of its relative poverty.

The one exception to these trends is the ownership of plates. Although the Cornish were slower at adopting plates than their counterparts in Kent (see also Table 5.2), by the period 1700–49 they had higher adoption

Table 7.3 Ownership of certain items and production for use by quartiles of pooled material wealth (percentages)

	Cornwall			Kent		
	1600–49	*1650–99*	*1700–49*	*1600–49*	*1650–99*	*1700–49*
Mirrors						
Q1	0.4	1.5	1.5	1.8	4.1	22.2
Q2	0.7	3.2	4.7	1.4	8.8	18.3
Q3	1.6	6.6	8.9	3.8	16.0	41.7
Q4	2.2	10.4	9.4	11.2	31.0	53.1
Upholstered furniture						
Q1	0.6	0.4	0.5	0.0	3.6	50.0
Q2	0.0	2.7	3.6	1.4	37.1	42.9
Q3	0.9	9.5	10.5	21.7	59.6	66.7
Q4	4.7	23.9	17.9	61.7	92.3	84.2
Hot drinks						
Q1	0.0	0.0	0.0	0.0	0.0	5.6
Q2	0.0	0.0	2.7	0.0	0.0	8.5
Q3	0.0	0.0	3.3	0.0	0.3	11.4
Q4	0.0	0.0	5.1	0.0	0.6	16.8
Plates						
Q1	1.0	7.9	54.0	1.7	12.9	28.6
Q2	2.1	20.5	71.4	2.7	18.6	57.4
Q3	5.5	33.6	85.9	18.1	34.8	82.8
Q4	7.3	49.1	89.4	40.5	66.4	84.0
Baking for use						
Q1	1.2	0.0	0.2	11.6	14.6	3.1
Q2	4.2	1.4	0.0	24.1	26.9	46.5
Q3	4.1	1.3	1.7	38.2	40.1	39.8
Q4	11.3	0.0	2.6	54.6	52.8	49.5
Dairying for use						
Q1	19.1	14.0	12.4	12.9	20.2	6.3
Q2	54.9	43.1	46.3	45.3	46.6	38.4
Q3	63.8	58.0	64.9	55.6	53.8	51.5
Q4	44.1	48.3	59.7	35.9	43.4	42.8
Alcohol for use						
Q1	28.9	12.0	12.4	13.4	18.5	28.1
Q2	45.1	26.5	25.5	27.2	48.5	66.7
Q3	63.8	38.2	42.1	45.5	64.3	78.6
Q4	76.5	54.3	50.6	71.5	84.5	89.8

rates than Kent, with over half the poorest quarter of the Cornish sample possessing plates. The vast majority of these are pewter plates, and it seems therefore that those leaving inventories in Cornwall were keener to own pewter than those in Kent. We have already seen in Table 5.2 that the Cornish were relatively late in adopting pewter, but by the eighteenth century almost all inventories contained pewter. This was not because pewter was any cheaper in Cornwall, despite the production of tin in the county, but reflects the fact that pewter was a store of value and thus its ownership was a means of storing wealth rather than, strictly speaking, consuming it.

The remaining rows in Table 7.3 refer to the production of commodities for use in the household. As we have seen (in Table 3.7), the very little baking that took place in Cornish households declined to almost nothing by the eighteenth century, yet over 10 per cent of those in the richest quartile were baking in the early seventeenth century. In Kent there was little change in the proportion of households baking overall, but perhaps significantly the proportion in the lowest quartile dropped quite sharply in the first half of the eighteenth century. The proportion of households making their own alcohol in Cornwall declined over the course of the study period in a fairly uniform way with a 20 per cent fall in each wealth category. The growth in the production of alcohol in Kent moves down the wealth hierarchy so that two-thirds of those in the second wealth quartile made their own alcohol in the first half of the eighteenth century, compared with a quarter in Cornwall.

Table 7.2 shows that dairying for use is not significantly correlated with wealth, except in the final period when the relationship is positive in Cornwall and negative in Kent. However, Table 7.3 indicates that the relationship is not straightforward. In both counties the richest (those in the top quartile) are less likely to make their own dairy products than are those in the third quartile. Yet those in the poorest quartile are the least likely to have goods indicating dairying. Perhaps more so than the other domestic activities, dairying depends on access to land, since it is most unlikely that fresh milk would be bought from elsewhere to make dairy products, whereas the purchase of grain for brewing or baking was common. Dairying therefore is very highly correlated with agricultural activity, and the relationship of wealth with dairying is a reflection of the relationship of farming with material wealth.

Quite clearly, therefore, the relative poverty of the households in the Cornish sample of inventories does not alone explain why their level of material culture was so much lower. This 'county effect' can also be demonstrated through logistic regression equations that attempt to predict the presence of a particular item using wealth and county as the independent variables. Logistic regression is a technique designed for use when the dependent (or outcome) variable is categorical and the independent (or predictor) variables are categorical or continuous.[20] Each of the commodities or activities shown in Table 7.4 was used as the dependent variable with material wealth (divided by 50) and county (with Kent coded 1 and Cornwall 0) as the independent variables. As Table 7.4 shows, the county effect was almost always significant and high. The statistics given are the values of *exp(β)*, which gives the change in odds resulting from a unit change in the independent variable. A value greater than

1 indicates that as the value of the predictor variable increases the odds of the outcome occurring (for example the ownership of a mirror) also increases. A value of less than 1 indicates that as the predictor increases the odds of the outcome occurring decrease. All the *exp(β)* values for wealth in Table 7.4 are greater than 1, indicating that an increase in

Table 7.4 Exp(β) values from logistic regression equations predicting ownership of certain goods from material wealth and county of residence

	Mirrors			Clocks		
	1600–49	*1650–99*	*1700–49*	*1600–49*	*1650–99*	*1700–49*
WEALTH50	1.13	1.16	1.18	1.24	1.36	1.60
COUNTY	4.20	4.28	9.46	8.87	20.89	9.25

	Coal			Jacks		
	1600–49	*1650–99*	*1700–49*	*1600–49*	*1650–99*	*1700–49*
WEALTH50	1.01	1.07	1.06	1.25	1.37	1.33
COUNTY	5.41	5.96	11.20	17.16	24.15	13.59

	Upholstered furniture			Chests of drawers		
	1600–49	*1650–99*	*1700–49*	*1600–49*	*1650–99*	*1700–49*
WEALTH50	2.41	2.35	1.74	1.12	1.18	1.19
COUNTY	43.88	19.88	22.96	2.25	4.57	6.63

	New tables			Window curtains		
	1600–49	*1650–99*	*1700–49*	*1600–49*	*1650–99*	*1700–49*
WEALTH50	1.14	1.19	1.09	1.14	1.15	–
COUNTY	1.86	1.64	1.76	28.61	54.65	–

	Knives and forks	Hot drinks	Saucepans	Plates		
	1700–49	*1700–49*	*1700–49*	*1600–49*	*1650–99*	*1700–49*
WEALTH50	1.09	1.10	–	1.44	1.67	1.39
COUNTY	4.29	5.06	8.41	4.80	–	–

	Milling for use			Food preservation for use		
	1600–49	*1650–99*	*1700–49*	*1600–49*	*1650–99*	*1700–49*
WEALTH50	1.24	1.15	1.18	1.98	1.44	1.52
COUNTY	7.94	7.54	3.80	–	5.02	12.39

Table 7.4 Continued

	Baking for use			Dairying for use		
	1600–49	*1650–99*	*1700–49*	*1600–49*	*1650–99*	*1700–49*
WEALTH50	1.31	1.14	1.08	–	–	–
COUNTY	9.82	79.39	83.48	0.78	1.38	–

	Alcohol for use		
	1600–49	*1650–99*	*1700–49*
WEALTH50	2.02	1.56	1.53
COUNTY	0.52	3.11	6.36

wealth does increase the likelihood of ownership of particular goods – yet in most cases the values are quite close to 1 and thus a unit change in wealth will have little effect on the change in odds of a commodity or activity being present. Wealth is measured in units of £50, so in the period 1600–49, for example, an increase in the material wealth of the inventory by £50 will change the odds of a mirror being present by 1.13 times. On the other hand an inventory is 4.2 times more likely to include a mirror in this period if it is in Kent rather than Cornwall. Only *exp(β)* figures that are statistically significant at the 95 per cent level are shown: the dashes indicate values that are not significant. The magnitude of the *exp(β)* figures for the county effect are quite considerable, indicating quite dramatically that wealth is not the major explanation for the differences in material culture between Kent and Cornwall. Before exploring this further we shall broaden the analysis by looking at the differences between status and occupational groups.

Status and occupation

Appendix 3 gives the profiles of a mixture of status and occupational groups in the two counties for 50-year periods. These groups are based partly on occupation, or rather on commercial production activities as identified from inventories (waged, service, retail, maritime, commercial food processing, crafts, mining, commercial farming alone, and commercial farming in conjunction with other commercial activities), and partly on status (gentleman, yeoman, husbandman and widow).[21] The two groups overlap since some yeomen, for example, were both farmers and craftsmen, meaning that a given individual could appear in three categories. For Kent, Canterbury, Folkestone and Milton are defined as urban, as are Madron, Tregony and St Stephens by Saltash in Cornwall. Canterbury is clearly very different from the other towns since in 1676 it had over 7,000 inhabitants, whereas Milton had just over 800 in 1663/4 and Folkestone some 500 in 1671.[22] In Cornwall, it is doubtful whether our three 'urban' parishes can be considered urban at all since they did not consist of contiguous built-up areas as the Kent towns did, although like the Kent towns they had the lowest proportions of inventories indicating commercial agricultural production in our sample.[23] Appendix 3 also shows the proportion of each group with evidence of more than one commercial occupation, the mean number of production activities for each group, and the median values of material wealth and consumption goods (non-production goods in the household).[24] Finally, for Kent only the mean number of rooms for each group are also given.

The distributions of material wealth for each of the three status groups of gentleman, yeoman and husbandman are skewed and have high standard deviations, so while the means are different it is difficult to predict status from wealth. In both Kent and Cornwall for the period 1600–49, and in Kent for the period 1700–49, there is no significant difference between the mean wealth of gentlemen and yeomen. The wealth gap between yeomen and husbandmen was proportionately wider and the difference in mean wealth between yeomen and husbandmen is significant.[25] This confirms the contemporary view that Kentish yeoman were the wealthiest in the country.[26] For Kent, where appraisers record rooms reasonably consistently, the number of rooms in the house is a better indication of status. Although the differences between the mean number of rooms in the households of gentry, yeomen and husbandmen is not particularly large, the differences between the means are statistically significant with the exception of gentlemen and yeomen for the period 1700–49.[27]

The first part of Appendix 3, giving statistics for all inventories, summarises the trends already established in Chapters 3 and 4 for the two counties as a whole. In Cornwall, by-employment fell from 48 per cent to 30 per cent between the first half of the seventeenth and the first half of the eighteenth century, whereas in Kent it rose slightly from 48 per cent to 54 per cent. Hence, in Cornwall the mean number of commercial production activities per household fell from 1.79 to 1.27, whereas in Kent it rose from 1.58 to 1.74. While a move towards a more specialised household economy was evident in Cornwall the opposite was the case in Kent, and this trend is also evident with production for use: the mean number of activities per household fell in Cornwall from 1.78 to 1.09 whereas it rose in Kent from 1.58 to 1.74. We have already seen (in Table 7.1) how this was accompanied by no change in median material wealth in Cornwall and a near threefold increase in Kent. Reflecting this, the value of consumption goods in Cornwall also fell slightly, while it grew by over two and a half times in Kent. The proportion of consumption goods grew slightly in Cornwall, reflecting a reduction in goods indicating production activity, while it fell in Kent, reflecting an increase in goods used for production.

The reduction in by-employment in Cornwall was most significant in the crafts category (78 to 53 per cent), mining (67 to 27 per cent), and commercial agriculture (68 to 52 per cent). It was also reflected in the status groups, with major falls for yeomen and especially for husbandmen. Cornish farm households were therefore much less likely to have a dual occupation by the start of the eighteenth century than they had been a hundred years earlier. There was a slight overall rise in by-employment in Kent although it fell for service activities, crafts, and farming which were offset by rises in other categories (retail, maritime and especially widows). Changes in the extent of by-employment are reflected in the mean number of production activities for exchange. This fell for all groups in Cornwall, especially for crafts and mining, but one of the biggest falls of all was for husbandmen. By the first half of the eighteenth century the mean number of commercial production activities for husbandmen was 0.73, indicating a growing number with no evidence of any production activity who were presumably little more than labourers.[28] Increased production specialisation in Cornwall was also associated with a reduction in production activities for use by almost all the groups. The falls were sharpest in crafts and mining, but even commercial farmers appear to have been producing less for home consumption. Production for use rose slightly in Kent, most notably for the craft group and those exclusively involved in commercial agriculture.

These changes in production activity are reflected in changes in material wealth. As we have already seen median material wealth fell in Cornwall between the first half of the seventeenth century and the first half of the eighteenth, but there were distinct variations between occupational and status groups. Thus material wealth rose slightly for those who were engaged in retail, service, maritime activity and commercial agriculture alone, but fell significantly for those households involved with mining, commercial food processing and craft activity. Gentlemen became richer, but yeomen, husbandmen and widows saw major falls in median household wealth. The median wealth of commercial farmers as a whole stayed remarkably constant, at about £37, indicating that fewer yeomen, and especially husbandmen, were actually engaged in commercial farming. In Kent no group became poorer over the course of the seventeenth century and some became considerably richer, including those involved in agriculture and with maritime activities. The contrast in the fortunes of widows in the two counties is remarkable: in Cornwall their median material wealth fell by 37 per cent, while in Kent it rose by 157 per cent.

The potentially misleading relationships between total inventory values and the value of consumption goods has already been discussed.[29] We must be careful therefore in drawing conclusions about the overall consumption behaviour (as represented by material culture) of the various groups based on values alone. The proportion of material wealth accounted for by consumption goods reveals more about the stock of capital and production goods than it does about consumption. Thus the highest proportions are for widows and those in the service category, and the lowest for those groups concerned with farming, including the categories of commercial food and commercial agriculture, and the status groups of yeoman and husbandman. Differences in the proportions between Cornwall and Kent reflect the different levels of investment in capital goods between categories in the two counties. Thus the value of consumption goods as a proportion of material wealth is higher for those involved in maritime activities in Cornwall than it is in Kent, not because those in Cornwall had a higher propensity to consume but because those in Kent had more valuable equipment, and in the final period were more likely to be by-employed and thus have the capital goods of more than one occupation. The absolute value of consumption goods is a better guide to the relative level of material culture between the categories in Appendix 3. In both counties gentlemen head the list, followed by those involved with service and retailing.[30] Also in both counties the bottom four groups are the waged, husbandmen, widows and those involved in commercial agriculture as a single venture. In contrast, those farming in conjunction with another occupation have a richer material culture.

The data in Appendix 3 also show the proportion of the total inventory value represented by debts owing to the deceased. Some of the highest proportions are for those receiving wages: indeed, they are often identified as wage earners because the debts due to them are specifically recorded as wages. Also with a high proportion of debts owing are those in the professional services, and widows. It is possible that the latter were engaging in moneylending as an occupation as Holderness has suggested, although the proportion of inventory values accounted for by debts is much lower than his sample for Lincolnshire, and the pattern of debts is not one of small sums due from a variety of people but of a small number of large debts, often due on bond.[31] In any case, using inventories alone to discuss patterns of indebtedness is hazardous since debts owed by the deceased to other people are rarely recorded. Only when probate accounts are used in conjunction with inventories can a more balanced picture of indebtedness be revealed.[32]

While the value of consumption goods gives some indication of the variation in material culture between groups we can also show how the ownership of particular goods varied between the occupation and status groups just discussed. Appendix 4 takes a selection of objects and activities and breaks down their ownership by the occupation and status categories in Appendix 3. They have been chosen to illustrate a number of points about the relationships between wealth, status, occupation or production activity and material culture. Generally speaking those households involved in service, retail or maritime activities were much more likely to include new material goods. However, it was the gentry (especially in Kent) who were the pioneers with these items. The evidence for Cornwall is more difficult to interpret because the percentages are very low and the absolute numbers of people owning new objects are also very small, but in Kent the picture is quite clear. Even though other groups had a higher concentration of ownership in the first half of the eighteenth century, the gentry led the way with the highest adoption rates in the first half of the seventeenth century. This is evident with mirrors, jacks and upholstered furniture, but it is also the case with clocks, chests of drawers, new tables and window curtains. A century later the gentry were more likely to have these items than the average household, but in many cases the incidence of ownership was higher in the service, retail and maritime categories.

However, the gentry were not necessarily the pioneers of new forms of social behaviour associated with new ways of cooking and eating, and with the presence of tea or coffee. The service and maritime groups took to these rapidly and may have been leading the gentry: the speed of adoption and the coarseness of the time frame for the data in Appendix 4 make this difficult to disentangle. Nor were the gentry the most likely to have books recorded in their inventories. Although the trends appear rather erratic it was those in professional services that had the highest levels of ownership.[33] It is also worth pointing out that those households for which we have evidence of by-employment had more material goods than average, a greater variety of goods and higher than average material wealth. Far from being associated with poverty and subsistence, by-employment was associated with higher levels of consumption.

While the gentry, service, and maritime categories were consistently in the lead, those involved in farming generally lagged behind. In Kent, for example, those involved in commercial agriculture alone had the lowest ownership levels for mirrors, upholstered furniture, new tables, and window curtains during the first half of the eighteenth century, although they were quite likely to own a clock; indeed by the 1700–49 period yeomen had the highest proportion of clocks. The situation in Cornwall was very similar: farmers, and especially those who were involved only in farming as a commercial activity, were the least likely to own the new consumer goods of the seventeenth century. They were also much less likely to eat with forks, involve themselves with new forms of cooking, sit at new tables or drink tea. The most materially disadvantaged groups were husbandmen and those working for wages. We have already seen how the median material wealth of the Cornish husbandmen fell by some 46 per cent between the first half of the seventeenth century and the first half of the eighteenth. No Cornish husbandman in the sample possessed a mirror, clock, upholstered furniture, chest of drawers or jack; nor did they drink tea, eat with a fork or indulge in the new cooking. In Kent they were better off, but remained the most materially deprived group along with those working for wages. Only one husbandman in Kent was drinking tea, although he lived in Folkestone, had no evidence of agricultural activity, and was probably involved in fishing.[34]

Appendix 4 also shows the extent to which different occupational and status groups were involved in production for use. Milling was only undertaken by a very small proportion of Cornish households in the first half of the seventeenth century, but in Kent some 40 per cent of yeomen and by-employed commercial farmers were grinding their own flour. The proportion of yeomen milling grain fell to 9 per cent during the first half of the eighteenth century, and the proportion of commercial farmers doing so fell by a similar amount. As might be expected, the proportion of commercial millers in the Kent inventory sample doubles over the same period. Milling was thus one activity that moved out of the domestic realm and became more commercialised. This trend is repeated for most of the other production activities in Cornwall. The proportion of households preserving food more than halved, and the proportion making their own alcohol also nearly halved. In both cases the rate of decline was fairly uniform across the occupational and status categories, although the smallest fall was for gentlemen. We have already seen that domestic baking appears never to have been prevalent in Cornwall.[35]

Dairying is an exception to this general story of decline in production for use in Cornwall since the proportion of households with dairying activity for their own use fell only from 45 per cent to 40 per cent. However, there was some variation between the groups: generally speaking the prevalence of dairying increased in those households involved in agricultural production, while it decreased significantly for the service, retail and mining categories. Husbandmen and widows also showed a significant decline, reflecting their impoverishment already noted, and a decline in the proportion of them actually farming. With the exception of these last two groups, a decline in dairying suggests more specialisation in production, as those in the service and craft trades, for example, concentrated on their main activity and ceased to keep a dairy cow or cows. The increase in dairying for use by farmers reflects the move away from arable, and it might also suggest an increase in a form of subsistence agriculture as more households kept a house cow. Certainly, the proportion of households categorised in Group 2 in Table 3.3 (having no arable crops, one or two cattle, or under ten sheep) who had dairy equipment increased from 37 per cent to 53 per cent.

In Kent the proportion of households with dairy equipment rose slightly, although there were falls for the service and maritime categories. As in Cornwall the major increases were for those involved in farming. The other three categories of production for use also increased. Some 85 per cent of households had items indicating food preservation by the early eighteenth century, with major increases in the households of the gentry and those headed by widows. A higher proportion of widows were baking in the first half of the eighteenth century than in the first half of the seventeenth, as were husbandmen and those in the maritime and service categories. More spectacular growth took place in the proportion of households making their own alcohol, which almost doubled over the same period. This trend is evident for a variety of occupations and status groups in a variety of places. Those solely involved in agriculture, for example, saw a 119 per cent increase in the proportion making alcohol, while the proportion for retailers increased by 157 per cent.

Location

Material culture was also related to location in addition to wealth, status and occupation; indeed wealth, status and occupation also varied considerably between our sample parishes. In this section we show these variations, and also parish differences in levels of material culture and production for use. Not all parishes contain enough inventories to be included in the analysis, and the numbers for the remainder are sometimes quite small (see Appendix 1). Furthermore, to save space, the tables only include data for the period 1700–49. Thus the figures should only be taken as indicative, and must be subject to quite wide margins of error.

The median values of material wealth in Cornwall varied quite widely between parishes and, as might be expected, there is a correlation between the extent of commercial agriculture and wealth, reflecting the capital value of livestock in the wealth figures. Thus, as Table 7.5 indicates, the richest parish is Poughill in the extreme east of the county. Some of the poorest parishes are in mining areas, such as Kenwyn and Gwennap, and while there is a general tendency for the east of the county to be richer than the west, there are exceptions. St Stephens by Saltash, for example emerges, as the poorest parish, probably because of the low proportion of households involved in commercial agriculture and the relatively high proportion of those with craft activities.

The extent of commercial agriculture is also related to the incidence of by-employment, shown in Table 7.5 by the mean number of activities per inventory indicating production for exchange. The lowest levels of by-employment were in Madron and Tregony which had low proportions in commercial agriculture, whereas a high incidence of farming activity, in Boyton and Luxulyan for example, was associated with a higher mean number of commercial production activities. Another obvious influence was the presence of mining, since the western parishes of Gwennap, Illogan and Kenwyn in the stannary of Tywarnhayle had the next lowest mean number of production activities for exchange. Rapid expansion of mining activity in the west led to a decline in by-employment, a decline in agricultural activity, and impoverishment.[36] In Gwennap, for example, the incidence of by-employment fell from 64 per cent to 26 per cent between the periods 1600–49 and 1700–49, the proportion of households involved

Table 7.5 Wealth, status and occupational groups in Cornish parishes 1700–49 (percentages)

	Material wealth (median £)	Prod. exchange (mean)	Prod. use (mean)	Comm. food	Service	Retail	Maritime	Mining	Crafts	Comm. ag. only	Comm. ag. comb.	Gent.	Husb.	Widow
Altarnun	15.45	1.17	1.02	21	0	0	0	0	10	38	21	0	8	13
Boyton	28.74	1.33	1.88	8	4	0	0	0	17	50	21	0	13	0
Crantock	33.94	1.20	1.00	3	0	3	6	3	9	63	9	6	6	9
Gwennap	11.83	1.18	0.89	11	0	1	0	53	5	14	21	3	4	5
Illogan	16.50	1.12	1.05	3	1	3	0	26	4	34	20	3	1	11
Kenwyn	10.77	1.10	1.15	5	0	4	1	30	15	15	19	2	3	6
Launcells	26.34	1.51	2.00	24	0	0	0	0	14	41	32	5	8	16
Luxulyan	39.08	1.75	1.56	25	0	0	2	26	12	28	51	2	2	11
Madron	11.84	1.07	0.53	17	2	14	7	3	30	14	10	2	1	10
Poughill	47.67	1.38	1.53	22	0	9	3	0	6	34	28	9	16	13
Roche	19.21	1.58	0.88	12	2	0	0	47	7	21	42	2	4	9
St Clement	12.33	1.19	1.13	16	0	3	16	0	26	19	16	10	0	6
St Columb Major	23.89	1.50	1.24	16	2	13	2	5	23	26	24	8	1	7
St Erth	14.63	1.22	0.89	7	0	0	0	4	22	41	19	0	0	7
St Gennys	20.20	1.21	1.35	11	0	0	0	0	11	56	18	2	12	12
St Pinnock	21.09	1.31	1.25	6	0	0	0	0	13	56	13	0	3	6
St Stephens by Saltash	9.39	1.28	1.02	31	3	2	13	0	26	9	20	6	5	15
St Tudy	20.53	1.37	1.47	21	0	5	0	0	21	21	26	5	0	16
Talland	24.25	1.18	0.89	16	2	2	24	0	18	16	13	0	4	11
Tregony	13.55	1.06	0.92	13	0	15	0	4	31	8	15	13	0	15
Zennor	20.31	1.39	1.03	24	0	0	0	16	5	39	34	0	0	5
All parishes	16.75	1.27	1.09	15	1	5	4	13	16	27	22	4	4	10

Note
There is insufficient data for Cuby.

in commercial agriculture fell from 70 per cent to 35 per cent, and material wealth fell from a median of £21.67 to £11.83.

This contrasts with the agricultural parishes to the east. In Launcells, for example, the incidence of by-employment remained constant at 43 per cent, the proportion of households involved in commercial agriculture increased from 66 to 73 per cent, although material wealth did fall from a median of £33.35 to £26.34. But the east–west split of mining versus farming was not a simple one. In the stannary of Blackmoor, for example, the inventoried population of the parish of Roche became considerably poorer, as median wealth fell from £41.78 to £19.21. Yet during the period 1700–49 over 60 per cent of households had evidence of commercial farming and half had evidence of by-employment. The adjacent parish of Luxulyan, which had 26 per cent of its inventories indicating mining activity during 1700–49, saw an increase in median wealth from £21.29 to £39.08, and by 1700–49 had 79 per cent of its households involved in commercial agriculture and the highest incidence of by-employment in our sample of Cornish parishes. In part this is because the sample of inventories from Luxulyan includes a much higher proportion of tin adventurers than other mining parishes. These were men investing quite large sums of money in mining works. For example, William Roseveare, who died in 1745, was one of the richest men in our sample with an inventory valued at over £1,000, including part shares of tin bounds and tin adventures worth £38 7s, and white tin at Truro valued at £80.[37]

This explains why the negative correlation between material wealth and the proportion of inventories mentioning mining activity, shown in Table 7.7, is not stronger. The table does, however, indicate very clearly the strong positive relationship on a parish basis between material wealth and commercial farming and between by-employment and commercial farming. On the other hand there are strong negative associations between the median material wealth of a parish and the proportion of its inhabitants engaged in craft activity.

There are also wide variations in median material wealth between the Kent parishes, again partially due to the relatively small numbers of inventories on which the calculations in Table 7.6 are based. As with Cornwall there is some relationship between median wealth and the extent of commercial agriculture, although it is not as strong. The index of by-employment – that is, the mean number of activities involving production for exchange – shows a little fluctuation between parishes: generally speaking a higher incidence of by-employment is associated with relatively high levels of commercial farming (in Elmsted, Iwade and Sheldwich for example), and indeed the correlation between the two is quite high, as Table 7.7 indicates. As might be expected, maritime activities were confined to coastal parishes, and the lowest proportions in agriculture were in the towns. This is one reason why the degree of by-employment was lower (or production specialisation was higher) in Canterbury, although in the

Table 7.6 Wealth, status and occupational groups in Kent parishes 1700–49 (percentages)

	Material wealth (median £)	Number of rooms (mean)	Prod. exchange (mean)	Prod. use (mean)	Comm. food	Service	Retail	Maritime	Crafts	Comm. ag. only	Comm. ag. comb.	Gent.	Husb.	Widow
Benenden	48.24	8.7	2.08	2.64	47	0	3	0	31	19	44	6	11	6
Biddenden	102.26	9.2	1.85	2.74	31	0	8	0	28	26	36	0	8	13
Bridge	69.52	7.6	1.93	2.86	29	7	29	0	36	0	43	0	0	7
Canterbury	44.32	8.5	0.72	1.80	8	0	16	0	24	8	8	8	0	8
Chartham	78.02	7.5	1.71	2.57	43	0	0	0	29	14	38	0	0	5
Elham	74.27	7.9	1.86	2.69	49	3	9	0	23	9	46	3	3	6
Elmsted	101.98	7.1	2.00	2.87	47	0	0	0	13	40	60	0	0	7
Folkestone	57.17	6.6	1.94	2.15	46	3	10	57	12	4	7	0	4	12
Goudhurst	66.00	10.0	1.97	3.03	34	5	11	0	45	16	32	0	3	8
Headcorn	53.42	9.2	1.84	2.59	41	3	6	0	16	19	41	3	3	16
Iwade	129.19	6.4	2.07	3.00	43	0	7	36	0	36	57	0	36	7
Lenham	54.06	8.0	1.36	3.16	23	0	14	0	32	23	23	2	9	11
Milton	115.31	8.5	1.38	2.78	30	8	11	22	19	5	8	3	3	14
Minster in Thanet	38.76	9.6	1.56	2.56	28	0	6	6	11	11	44	0	0	17
Newington	156.47	9.3	1.56	2.44	50	0	11	0	11	22	44	6	8	11
Ruckinge	121.07	7.0	1.67	2.75	33	0	4	0	8	46	38	0	6	13
Sheldwich	85.04	9.5	2.12	3.12	35	0	0	0	35	24	53	6	6	6
Smarden	68.53	8.6	2.04	3.00	38	4	6	0	26	26	46	0	4	14
Ulcombe	219.11	8.9	1.81	2.94	50	0	6	0	6	25	44	0	0	13
Walmer	101.47	8.7	1.50	2.80	60	0	0	0	0	20	50	0	10	0
Waltham	85.98	7.1	2.09	3.00	27	0	9	0	45	36	27	0	0	0
Wye	69.77	7.3	1.24	2.63	37	3	5	0	21	21	24	8	3	8
All parishes	74.68	8.2	1.74	2.70	38	2	8	9	22	19	33	2	5	10

Note
There is insufficient data for Burmarsh, Ebony, Orlestone, River, Stelling and Westbere.

Table 7.7 Correlations between parish attributes 1700–49

		Material wealth	Commercial farming	By-employment	Crafts
Commercial farming	Cornwall	0.614**	–	–	–
	Kent	0.389	–	–	–
By-employment	Cornwall	0.320	0.366	–	–
	Kent	0.352	0.707**	–	–
Crafts	Cornwall	−0.395	−0.637**	−0.174	–
	Kent	−0.456*	−0.248	−0.084	–
Mining	Cornwall	−0.176	−0.027	0.241	−0.475*

Notes
* Significant at the 95 per cent level.
** Significant at the 99 per cent level.

towns of Milton and Folkestone maritime activities enabled the extent of by-employment to be greater. Canterbury also had the lowest incidence of production for use among the Kent parishes, but excluding Folkestone the range among the remaining parishes was fairly consistent at 2.44 to 3.16.

For most Kent parishes, the differences in median material wealth between the first half of the seventeenth century and the first half of the eighteenth were quite dramatic. In most cases this was associated with agricultural development and relatively high levels of by-employment, and the increase in median wealth was not as great in Canterbury where it rose from £30.50 to £44.32. In contrast the town of Milton (and Newington its neighbour) saw a fivefold growth in material wealth, reflecting the commercial opportunities of a port in such an important strategic position.

Tables 7.8 and 7.9 show the incidence of various consumption goods and activities in Cornwall and Kent by parish. We have already seen that those living in the more urban places in the two counties were more likely to adopt a particular item. In Cornwall (Table 7.8), Madron had the highest proportion of inventories indicating the consumption of hot drinks in the first half of the eighteenth century: at 11 per cent, this was considerably below the figure for the Kent towns, although higher than 12 rural Kent parishes. Madron and Tregony had the highest proportion of mirrors, while Madron and St Stephens had the most jacks. The general tendency for urban inventories to be more likely to contain new material goods than rural ones also applies to chests of drawers, new tables and, not surprisingly, to window curtains. Within the rural areas of the county there is no obvious pattern to the distribution of new consumption goods. Zennor had the lowest level of material culture in terms of the items in Table 7.8, and of all the 'new' goods being discussed only one inventory (out of 38 in the period 1700–49) had a chest of drawers – yet it was not a

Table 7.8 Selected commodities and production activities for use in Cornish parishes 1700–49 (percentages)

	Mirrors	Jacks	Clocks	Hot drinks	Saucepans	Coal	Milling	Food pres.	Baking	Dairying	Alcohol
Altarnun	0	0	6	0	0	0	0	27	0	35	25
Boyton	0	0	0	6	0	0	0	63	0	67	54
Crantock	4	0	0	0	0	0	3	20	0	43	29
Gwennap	7	2	5	5	4	2	0	7	0	39	17
Illogan	2	0	4	0	0	0	3	11	0	54	18
Kenwyn	4	4	2	2	2	1	1	19	1	38	29
Launcells	0	0	7	0	5	0	5	68	3	57	65
Luxulyan	6	0	8	4	0	0	2	39	4	54	53
Madron	18	12	7	11	9	11	2	5	1	23	8
Poughill	4	10	12	0	0	0	0	53	3	47	47
Roche	0	0	2	0	0	2	0	12	0	44	21
St Clement	10	11	5	5	12	5	0	16	6	35	39
St Columb Major	10	9	5	5	6	10	1	30	3	42	30
St Erth	0	0	6	0	0	0	0	11	0	52	15
St Gennys	0	0	7	0	0	0	0	44	0	44	39
St Pinnock	4	0	13	0	0	0	0	22	0	50	44
St Stephens by Saltash	7	12	11	4	5	5	0	23	1	25	35
St Tudy	7	0	0	7	0	0	5	42	0	47	42
Talland	10	3	10	0	3	2	2	20	0	27	27
Tregony	19	7	3	9	7	6	4	19	0	25	27
Zennor	0	0	0	0	0	0	0	11	0	61	11
All parishes	6	4	6	3	3	3	1	23	1	40	29

Note
There is insufficient data for Cuby.

particularly poor parish by Cornish standards and was adjacent to Madron with the highest rates of ownership. No place in Cornwall is very far from the sea, but evidence of coal burning in more than 10 per cent of inventories is only evident in Madron and St Columb Major, while many coastal parishes have no inventories indicating coal.

As we have seen, the fall in the proportion of households preserving their own food in Cornwall was quite dramatic.[38] The fall was uneven however, with the greatest falls in mining parishes: in Gwennap for example, the percentage fell from over 57 per cent in the first half of the seventeenth century to under 7 per cent in the first half of the eighteenth. In contrast, there was no change or a rise in the prevalence of food preservation in the eastern parishes of Boyton, Launcells and Poughill. Dairying was the one production for use activity that did not show a marked decline in Cornwall as a whole. However, once again there is an east–west split, with a significant increase in Poughill, Launcells and Boyton, and a fall in the western mining parishes, although Zennor and Illogan were exceptions to this trend. These patterns reflect the agricultural changes already discussed in Chapter 3. The lowest proportion of dairying for use was in Madron, the most urbanised Cornish parish in our sample. Overall, the proportion of inventoried Cornish households making their own alcoholic drink fell by almost a half. But there were increases in the three western parishes of Boyton, Launcells and Poughill. These were matched by steep reductions in the mining parishes, and also in Madron.

In Kent (Table 7.9) there is also a tendency for the urban parishes (Canterbury, Milton and Folkestone) to have higher rates of adoption of new material goods. These goods often appeared extensively in towns at an early date so that, for example, 25 per cent of inventories in the Canterbury sample had a jack in the first half of the seventeenth century, 14 per cent mirrors and 3.3 per cent a clock. The three towns were also conspicuously associated with the new practice of drinking tea and coffee: over 40 per cent of inventories in Milton had goods that were associated with hot drinks, compared with very small percentages in most remote rural areas. But the towns were not the only places to lead with the adoption of new items: for the same period 10 per cent of the inventories in Wye mention a mirror and 14 per cent a jack. Clocks in particular were a distinctly rural phenomenon: Milton ranked 15th in the adoption of clocks in the first half of the eighteenth century, while Folkestone was bottom.[39] The burning of coal in domestic grates was also an urban phenomenon, since in Kent over 80 per cent of Milton inventories indicate the burning of coal, with 70 per cent and 63 per cent in Canterbury and Folkestone respectively. The cost of transporting coal is also very evident in its location since coastal parishes, such as Iwade, Minster, Newington and Walmer have a much higher proportion of inventories indicating its presence than those without the benefit of navigable water.

The mean number of production for use activities rose between the

Table 7.9 Selected commodities and production activities for use in Kent parishes 1700–49 (percentages

	Mirrors	Jacks	Clocks	Hot drinks	Saucepans	Coal	Milling	Food pres.	Baking	Dairying	Alcohol
Benenden	29	39	35	6	10	10	11	81	33	42	83
Biddenden	27	52	42	6	15	12	15	85	44	46	82
Bridge	50	45	50	8	8	8	7	86	64	36	86
Canterbury	65	53	40	35	35	70	0	64	40	12	60
Chartham	47	71	53	18	12	12	0	76	57	33	76
Elham	45	45	39	19	42	6	9	86	51	31	80
Elmsted	27	20	60	7	0	7	0	100	53	60	73
Folkestone	68	33	34	27	50	63	4	76	38	12	76
Goudhurst	33	50	43	3	10	7	11	76	29	66	87
Headcorn	15	41	48	0	4	7	13	88	34	47	75
Iwade	77	38	54	8	15	31	0	100	50	57	86
Lenham	51	49	62	18	26	18	16	91	41	57	89
Milton	79	74	44	41	53	82	3	95	46	22	95
Minster in Thanet	50	69	50	29	43	57	11	78	44	33	72
Newington	53	73	73	13	13	47	11	78	28	39	78
Ruckinge	19	30	57	5	10	5	0	88	46	63	67
Sheldwich	64	43	71	29	7	14	0	82	82	59	82
Smarden	35	41	50	2	13	11	8	92	46	64	76
Ulcombe	44	63	75	6	13	19	0	94	38	63	88
Walmer	20	14	40	10	20	50	0	100	20	40	100
Waltham	56	22	56	11	0	22	0	91	73	64	64
Wye	23	40	43	3	9	11	5	87	42	39	74
All parishes	44	46	49	14	22	26	7	84	43	43	79

Note
There is insufficient data for Burmarsh, Ebony, Orlestone, River, Stelling and Westbere.

first half of the seventeenth century and the first half of the eighteenth in all Kent parishes, although home milling remained of some significance in only a few parishes. Food preservation became more common, and although it was fairly ubiquitous throughout the county it was at its lowest level in Canterbury where over 60 per cent of inventoried households were preserving their own food. In Kent as a whole the proportion of households baking their own bread rose slightly, but the pattern across parishes was rather uneven. There was no simple rural–urban dichotomy, some of the lowest proportions were in the rural parishes of Benenden, Goudhurst and Ulcombe, for example, and while 40 per cent of Canterbury inventories suggest bread making in the first half of the eighteenth century, the proportion a century earlier was only 24 per cent. As might be expected, dairying was a rural as opposed to an urban phenomenon, although there is evidence of dairying activity in 12 per cent of our Canterbury inventories and 22 per cent in Milton. In the rest of the county the distribution of dairying reflects the geography of pastoral production. The lowest proportion of inventories indicating the production of alcohol in Kent during the first half of the eighteenth century is for Canterbury, but even so some 60 per cent of households were brewing beer for themselves, triple the proportion doing so a century earlier. Once again there is no obvious urban–rural split, as the proportion in Milton was 95 per cent and there was considerable variation in rural parishes. These rural–urban differences will be explored further in the conclusion to this chapter.

The parish data in Tables 7.5, 7.6, 7.8 and 7.9 provide the opportunity to look at the interrelationships between the extent of ownership of material goods in a parish and other attributes of that parish, including, for example, how wealthy it is and its occupational structure. Table 7.10 shows the correlations for both Cornwall and Kent between four aspects of material culture (the presence of mirrors, jacks, clocks and equipment for hot drinks) and median material wealth, the proportions of the inventories in the parish indicating commercial farming, and the proportion of gentlemen in the parish. This is a restricted number of variables, but is sufficient to indicate some very clear associations which change over time. Because the incidence of adoption of these items was so low in Cornwall, the correlations are only shown for the final period.

The strongest relationship is the negative one between commercial farming and the presence or adoption of new items, reflecting the precocity of urban areas already discussed. Clocks are an exception to this, especially for Kent in the period 1700–49. In the early period, 1600–49, when the first three objects in the table are just starting to appear, they are associated with a high proportion of gentry in the parish. Thereafter, in our second period, the proportion of gentlemen remains a strong influence, but the median material wealth in the parish starts to play an equally important role and for clocks shows a stronger association than the proportion of gentlemen. By the eighteenth century, as these new goods

Table 7.10 Correlations between parish attributes and new consumer goods

		Mirror	*Jack*	*Clock*	*Hot drinks*
1600–49					
Material wealth	Kent	0.256	0.199	0.077	–
Commercial farming	Kent	−0.532**	−0.683**	−0.252	–
Gentleman	Kent	0.673**	0.671**	0.285	–
1650–99					
Material wealth	Kent	0.395*	0.451*	0.543**	–
Commercial farming	Kent	−0.394*	−0.233	0.315	–
Gentleman	Kent	0.364	0.451*	0.444*	–
1700–49					
Material wealth	Cornwall	−0.232	−0.165	0.161	−0.296
	Kent	0.076	0.171	0.624**	−0.188
Commercial farming	Cornwall	−0.761**	−0.653**	−0.104	−0.592**
	Kent	−0.398	−0.384	0.503*	−0.604**
Gentleman	Cornwall	0.519*	0.602**	0.009	0.378
	Kent	0.085	0.177	−0.041	0.264

Notes
* Significant at the 95 per cent level.
** Significant at the 99 per cent level.

become much more common in Kent, the proportion of gentry is not related to the degree of adoption. In Cornwall by contrast, where these items are still relatively new, they are strongly associated with the proportion of gentry (with the exception of clocks) and strongly negatively associated with the incidence of commercial farming. Wealth is now no longer so important an influence (with the exception of clocks for Kent). This suggests that new material goods are first associated with the gentry and with urban places, then with wealth, but by the time they are becoming commonplace they have diffused more widely within society, though still with an urban bias. But the figures also suggest that not all goods were the same: mirrors and jacks show similar trends, for example, but clocks are different. Drinking tea and coffee was again an urban phenomenon, or more strictly speaking a practice negatively associated with farming and not significantly associated with the proportion of gentry. These caveats make the obvious point that these new material goods need to be understood in the context of their use within the household.[40]

This analysis at parish level has its drawbacks. Sample sizes are small (21 for Cornwall and 22 for Kent), and within each parish the number of inventories contributing to the variables in the tables is also small. The number of those in the categories of waged, service and retail is too small to calculate a proportion for each parish and cannot be included in the analysis. More importantly, however, there is danger of the 'ecological fallacy'; that is, of inferring characteristics of individuals from aggregate data referring to a population of which they are members.[41] It is not parishes that make decisions about consumption and material culture, but individuals, and it is individual inventories, rather than the parish, that should be used as the basic unit in searching for relationships.

Once we move to the level of the individual it is no longer possible to seek relationships using correlation analysis or to predict outcomes with a conventional multiple regression. This is because most of the variables we are using are categorical, indicating the presence or absence of a particular object, or belonging or not belonging to a particular category. On the other hand some of the variables are continuous, including material wealth. As we have seen, the technique of logistic regression is particularly suitable in this situation since it predicts an outcome or dependent variable using a mixture of categorical and continuous variables.[42]

The results of logistic regression equations in which the outcome variable is the presence of a particular commodity or evidence of production for use in the household are reported in Appendix 5. The predictor variables are a variety of household attributes, although only those variables which are significant in the equations are included: thus mining as an occupational category is excluded because in no equation did mining have a statistically significant effect in predicting the ownership of particular goods or production for use. Logistic regressions generate a variety of statistics, but only two are shown. The first, labelled r^2, is the Nagelkerke R Square statistic which is analogous to the r^2 statistic in a conventional regression equation in that it measures the extent to which the predictor variables together account for change in the outcome variable. The second, the value of $exp(\beta)$, is an indicator of the change in odds resulting from a unit change in the independent variable. Only those values of $exp(\beta)$ that are statistically significant at the 95 per cent level or above are shown. Thus, to take mirrors in Cornwall as an example from Table A5.1 in Appendix 5 we can see that the equations account for a relatively small proportion of the variation in the ownership of mirrors, although by 1700–49 the predictor variables in the equation contribute 23 per cent of the variations.[43] During the period 1600–49 only three variables are statistically significant, location in an urban place, material wealth measured in £50 increments, and gentlemanly status.[44] The urban location was the more important of the three, in that an urban inventory was 4.25 times more likely to contain a mirror than a non-urban parish. On the other hand, an increase in the material wealth of the inventory of £50 made the appearance of a mirror only 1.18 times more likely.

Wealth has a positive influence in almost all the logistic regression equations, which is what we would expect given earlier findings in this chapter. For Kent, the number of rooms almost always has a positive influence. Clearly this is related to wealth, but the more rooms there are in a house the more likely that there will be more objects. Although the $exp(\beta)$

values for these two variables are usually significant and positive they do not have a great influence in predicting the presence of material objects in comparison with variables indicating location, status and occupation. Generally speaking the most important positive determinants are an urban location, service, retail and maritime occupations, and gentry status, while the major negative influence is farming as an occupation. The data confirm the earlier findings in this chapter that new items often appeared first in gentry households but then became more dominant in urban households and those of the professions and retailers, as is the case with mirrors, jacks, new tables, window curtains and chests of drawers. But the gentry were also laggards as well as leaders: although carpets disappeared during the seventeenth century they remained associated with gentry households in the first half of the eighteenth century.[45]

However, the gentry were not such conspicuous leaders in the possession of items which suggest new forms of behaviour in the household, again confirming our earlier results. The equations predicting the ownership of knives and forks, hot drinks and saucepans have low r^2 values, and in only two cases does the status significantly affect ownership. The strongest influence is the service occupational category which covers a diverse group of mainly professional people. Thus although the consumption of tea and coffee in Kent during the first half of the eighteenth century was an urban phenomenon, it was more strongly associated with service occupations. Only 38 per cent of these households were living in the urban parishes of Canterbury, Milton, Newington and Folkestone. This evidence contradicts Weatherill's generalisation that 'the indicators of new modes of eating and drinking were virtually unknown in the countryside and in the lesser towns'.[46] The very low r^2 values for knives and forks suggest that their ownership is not very strongly determined by any of the variables in the equation.

Appendix 5 also reports the *exp(β)* values for equations predicting the presence of production activities for use within the household. With the exception of dairying, the r^2 values for the equations are low, meaning that the equation is only accounting for a small proportion of the variation in production for use activity between households. As might be expected milling is associated with farming, but the extent of domestic milling was declining considerably. Food preservation was also associated with farming, since farmers produced the food to be preserved, and was negatively influenced by gentry households and households in urban parishes. The equations are particularly poor at predicting those households that were baking, and not much better at predicting those making their own beer or cider, indicating perhaps that these activities were found among all social groups. This is suggested by the data in Appendix 4, where there is relatively little variation among the occupation and status groups. As might be expected, the equations predicting dairying are rather different. The values of r^2 are higher, and the *exp(β)* values for farmers are extraordinarily high. But within the farming groups it is those who were apparently only engaged in commercial farming, with no by-employment, that were the most likely to be dairying.

Conclusion

Our analysis of the relationships between consumption, material culture, wealth, status, occupation and location is necessarily rather crude. In order to have enough inventories for each of our categories we had to employ a time-frame of only three 50-year periods, which is too coarse to trace the diffusion of new material goods with any precision. Furthermore, the precision of some of our quantitative analyses may in some cases be rather spurious. When sample sizes are low, as they are for example for our inventories referring to the professional service sector, or during the early stages of the adoption of new material goods, there is always the possibility that omissions or other errors in only one or two inventories may distort our results. Furthermore, the majority of the logistic regression equations account for only a small proportion of change in the dependent or outcome variable, suggesting that behaviour towards consumption goods reflecting lifestyle choices can only be partially captured by the variables that can be derived from inventories. Finally, as we have pointed out, we can only draw conclusions about consumption behaviour as it is represented by a limited range of material objects. Nevertheless, on many issues we are able to generalise from a large number of inventories drawn from a variety of places and referring to a wide range of households. Encouragingly, the variety of approaches to the data that have been adopted show a degree of consistency in their results, and the technique of logistic regression has enabled us to untangle the interconnections between the variables we are considering.

The significance of wealth as a predictor of the consumption of material goods has been overplayed. Shammas concluded that this was a major determinant of consumption patterns; yet this was rather inevitable given her methodology, which used inventory valuations to measure both wealth and consumption. We overcome this to some extent by using the presence of material goods and not their values as a measure of consumption, and by using material wealth, which excludes debts and leases, as opposed to the total value of the inventory as our indicator of wealth. Even so there is bound to be some relation between wealth and consumption if both are measured from inventories. In most cases the correlations between the presence of a consumption good and wealth are fairly low, in particular there is no significant correlation between the conspicuous innovations of the eighteenth century, hot drinks and saucepans, and an individual's material wealth.

As with many of our results the contrasts between Cornwall and Kent are striking. In Kent material wealth tripled between the early seventeenth century and the mid-eighteenth; in Cornwall it barely changed at all. However, the dramatic differences in material wealth between the two counties were not responsible for the great differences in material culture. We demonstrate this in two ways. First, by showing the incidence of ownership of certain commodities broken down by quartiles of pooled material wealth so that the differences in ownership between households in the two counties in equivalent wealth categories can be compared. Second, by using a logistic regression model that predicts ownership from wealth and county we show that in nearly all cases county of residence has a much greater influence on the probability of ownership than wealth. We return to the comparison between the two counties in the following chapter.

Social status and occupational category appear more strongly associated with the acquisition of new kinds of material goods than does wealth. The acquisition of new material goods is linked both to the status hierarchy of gentleman, yeoman, and husbandmen, and also to occupations associated with the service and retail trades, reinforcing Weatherill's findings.[47] But status and occupation is related both to wealth and to location, as we show by setting out some of the characteristics of our status and occupational groups. This is also borne out in our parish-based analysis of variations in the ownership of particular material goods and variations in wealth, status and occupation. The parish data enable us to reveal some relationships between wealth and occupation, and also between wealth, status and the ownership of material goods, demonstrating positive associations between the presence of new goods and both wealth and status.

A multivariate analysis based on individuals helps to unravel the relationships between wealth, occupation, status, location and material culture. Our results suggest at least two patterns in the adoption of new material goods over time. For most major new items, including mirrors, jacks, chests of drawers and upholstered furniture, the gentry are the group with the highest adoption rates in the first half of the seventeenth century. During the second half of the century these items become less exclusive and are associated with urban areas (and non-agricultural occupations) and with wealthier individuals. By our final period, in the first half of the eighteenth century the goods are more widespread and no longer have an association with towns or high-status groups. Weatherill's study, which starts in 1660, picked up the second phase of this process, as she found new consumer goods strongly associated with towns and ranks gentlemen below the dealing trades in her 'consumption hierarchy'.[48] However, there have been no major studies of the period before 1660 with which we can compare our results for the earlier period.

The second pattern is associated with material objects that suggest changes in behaviour and social rituals, such as utensils for hot drinks, saucepans and forks. These appear to originate with those involved in the professional services, often, but not exclusively, in an urban setting – although occupation was a more important predictor of these items than location. These trends are most clearly seen in Kent, and because of the later chronology of spread in Cornwall the category of 'gentleman' remains an important predictor of new material goods.

We can only speculate as to the reasons for these trends. The gentry were literate, well-connected, relatively mobile, and wealth was not a constraint on purchasing new commodities. Their culture of hospitality meant they were frequently in each other's houses and most had close links with London.[49] If a country gentleman did not own a house in London, then it was quite likely that one of his kin did so.[50] Thus they had the opportunities to see novel goods, to buy them, and to show them off to their peers. On the other hand, while a good proportion of the gentry embraced new social rituals such as tea drinking, the new cookery, and more intimate dining, as a group they were less likely to do so than the professional groups, perhaps indicating a reluctance among some gentry at least to change certain aspects of their behaviour.

The determinants of gentle status in early modern England were complicated and subtle: a mixture of lineage, landholding, wealth (and its sources) and office-holding, but it is most unlikely that the acquisition of the new material goods we are discussing would have made much difference to the acquisition of what we might call traditional or rural gentle status.[51] On the other hand, these goods might have been adopted by those urban families whose manner of life led them to be considered as gentlemen, even though they held no land. For these 'pseudo-gentry', 'material possessions became tokens of the manner of life through which their gentility was conferred'.[52]

Studies of the adoption of new material goods have emphasised the role of towns as the locus of new consumption patterns, and indeed, as we have seen, adoption rates were higher in our urban inventories than rural ones. In his pioneering study, de Vries considered curtains, clocks and books as 'obviously urban cultural artifacts', and in his study of Bristol and neighbouring parishes, Estabrook concluded that 'the strongest factors guiding the ownership of possessions and the uses of dwelling space were the urbane and rustic attitudes associated with topographical settings', although these concepts are never adequately explained.[53] Without addressing the multivariate nature of the influences on the ownership of material goods, or making rural comparisons, the argument that towns in themselves are associated with the early adoption of new material goods becomes tautological.[54] Weatherill noted the higher incidence of adoption of new material goods in urban places and speculated that the close proximity of people in urban areas encouraged them to turn inwards and make their living spaces as pleasant as possible as a compensation for the inconveniences of town life.[55] Above all, Borsay emphasises the central role that towns played in the consumer revolution of Georgian England as part of his 'urban renaissance'.[56] Given these findings it is not surprising that a recent summary considered that 'consumption changes were earliest and most rapid in towns, over and above the differences expected in virtue of urban populations' wealth and status'.[57]

However, our results show that this was not generally the case for Kent and Cornwall. Tables 7.8 and 7.9 show differences in the adoption of new commodities between rural and urban parishes, but also considerable differences between the rural parishes, reflecting differences in wealth, and especially occupation and status. Thus although individuals in towns were more likely to own the new commodities we have been discussing, in only a few cases was an urban location in itself the most important predictor of the presence of a particular commodity in the logistic regressions shown in Appendix 5. Status and occupation were usually of much more significance, and service occupations were not exclusively urban. If we take the pattern of adoption of new tables in Kent as an example (Table A5.2 in Appendix 5), in all three periods the presence of an individual in a town increased the likelihood that they would own a new style of table. But the increase in odds was greater for both the gentry and those in professional service occupations in the first two periods, and greater for professional services alone in the third.[58]

These findings are consistent with Weatherill's recent reworking of her data. Although she uses a different methodology she investigates the statistical relationship between ownership of five categories of goods and location, wealth, and status. As with our study she finds variations in these influences for particular goods, but her conclusion is that 'status and wealth acting together were more influential in determining ownership than whether someone lived in town or country'.[59] Nevertheless, as Appendix 5 shows, there was still an 'urban factor' at work since in many equations the urban variable was significant, although not as high as those for status and occupation.

We can only speculate as to what this 'urban factor' might be. A possibility is the supply or availability of goods, and while it is true that certain esoteric imports would only be found in London, the items we are considering were obtainable almost anywhere. Adoption rates in Cornwall were low, but all the items we have been considering were available to those who wanted them and could afford them. Perhaps of more significance was the relative anonymity of an urban environment. Anonymity provided more opportunity to fashion an identity, whereas in rural areas anonymity was impossible, people were known to each other and identities were well established and difficult to change.[60] As Fawconer put it in 1765:

> In so large and populous a City, the generality of the inhabitants must be entire Strangers to each other. And, where the exteriors form our Judgement of the Man, and appearance in the Vulgar Eye passes for the only Criterion of true worth: every one is ready to assume the marks of a superior Condition, in order to be esteemed more than what he really is...[61]

In the countryside such deceit was impossible, but as with the towns it was not 'rurality' that was the most important influence on the absence of new material goods, but status and occupation. In particular, being a commercial farmer reduced the odds of owning new material goods. We can only speculate as to why this was the case. Campbell uses contemporary accounts to paint a picture of the stereotypical yeomen as industrious, thrifty and frugal, with a dislike of ostentation and display, and our findings lend credence to this view.[62]

The major exception to this trend is the ownership of clocks, which were more of a rural phenomenon than an urban one, so that the highest ownership rates (in Kent) were for yeomen, and by the first half of the eighteenth century commercial farmers with no other production activities were twice as likely to have a clock as other groups. There were more public clocks in urban places than there were in rural ones, but the presence of clocks in rural farming households (often in the kitchen) suggests that both household and farming tasks were being timed.[63] Household production activities of baking, brewing and food preparation would be more efficient if they were timed, and relatively accurate timing would enable labour to be paid by the hour rather than by the day, which was of inconsistent length. Moreover, a clock would enable the co-ordination of the increasing variety of activities taking place within the household, and facilitate its smoother running. The chronology of the introduction of clocks to rural households tends to undermine Thompson's argument that time discipline dates from the end of the eighteenth century in the context of the industrial factory.[64] To the yeoman, clocks were an indication not of thrift but of industry.

8   Conclusions

In our introduction we outlined some simple models of the pre-industrial economy that have been applied to England in the early modern period. All fail to accommodate satisfactorily the changes we have observed in the economies of Cornwall and Kent from 1600 to 1750. There is very little evidence of 'peasant' behaviour; many of the generalisations about proto-industry fail to apply; and far from household production becoming more specialised in line with the model of an industrious revolution, in Kent at least increased consumption is associated with increased diversification of household production. A longer-term perspective on changes in consumption and the comparison between Cornwall and Kent also casts the 'consumer revolution' in a new light. This is not surprising since these models of historical change ultimately have their origins in particular empirical studies, and, as is so often the case, the development of ideas from this original work has outpaced further archival work, resulting in a mismatch between what is supposed to have taken place and what we can identify empirically as having taken place.

Inventories

Our perspective of economic and social change in Cornwall and Kent is entirely dependent on the evidence from probate inventories and thus before discussing our conclusions we must emphasise their limitations. We can say nothing about the poor, the 40 per cent or so of the population that were exempt from most taxes and who were most unlikely to have an inventory made for them, but nor is our sample confined to the middling sort; at the other end of the scale perhaps only the wealthiest 10 per cent of the population are missing. Inventories only measure a minority of consumption activities, and production activities can only be inferred from goods that might be used for production together with appraisers' descriptions. There are many reasons why an individual inventory may not itemise all the goods in a household, which means inventories can only be used in a positive sense; if something is not mentioned we cannot assume it was not present. In general, Kent inventories become more detailed over time and Cornish inventories less so. However, this is a consequence of economic changes in the two counties rather than a change in the appraisal process. As the material environment became richer in Kent so appraisers needed to record goods in more detail. The opposite was the case in Cornwall: as the material environment became poorer there was less need for detailed description. Rooms were not recorded because houses were small. The few affluent households were recorded in as much detail as their equivalents in Kent, and even in poorer households some commodities, such as plates, are carefully recorded. It is unlikely that the contrasts between Kent and Cornwall, and in particular the relative impoverishment in Cornwall, are a function of changes in the way inventories were made.

Cornwall and Kent

The trajectories of the household production profiles in Cornwall and Kent between 1600 and 1750 were very different, and each county shows a different path of development towards capitalism. In Cornwall there is evidence of specialisation of production, although it is not associated with material enrichment but with increasing poverty. This is partly a result of proletarianisation within the mining industry, but poverty was not confined to miners or those in mining parishes. Farm incomes failed to grow (and those of yeomen and husbandmen fell considerably) as farms became more specialised in livestock production, meaning that more grain was imported into the county as it became more integrated with the wider English economy. Household production activities declined, particularly spinning, which all but disappeared from rural households. In Kent the picture is one of prosperity based on the diversification of household production for exchange. Despite 'de-industrialisation' and decline in the textile industry, material wealth grew threefold. Production did not become specialised but by-employment continued to be the norm, increasingly indicative of entrepreneurial drive rather than a retreat into self-sufficiency. Continued diversification of production was not associated with a withdrawal from the market – quite the reverse, it indicated increased engagement with the market. Similarly, the extension of household production for use in Kent is not indicative of a survivalist self-sufficiency but of a strategy aimed at controlling the quality of the food and drink consumed in the household by producing it in the household.

Proto-industry and by-employment

The concept of proto-industrialisation is ceasing to have much meaning as it expands to accommodate more and more empirical departures from the original model.[1] Mendels' model of pro-industrialisation as defined in the early 1980s does not seem to fit our findings.[2] Regions of proto-industry do not sit alongside regions of commercial farming: industry and agriculture are closely intertwined in the same households. Nor is there a consistent relationship between the type of farming and industrial activity. Only in mining, which had originally been excluded from the proto-industrial model, can we find evidence of the combination of industrial and agricultural activity on a small scale in a distinctive region producing a commodity for export.[3] But it is not long before this was replaced by more fully fledged capitalist production relations. Furthermore, although the concept of proto-industry is applied to those industries producing commodities for sale outside their region of production, the vast majority of production activity within the household was not directed towards such products but towards goods for local consumption, or, indeed, for consumption within the household. Nor were many of the new consumer goods the products of proto-industrial production. Clocks, mirrors and upholstered furniture, for example, were made in towns, and only some linen and metal goods were likely to have been produced in a proto-industrial context.

We have not been able to address a number of issues in proto-industrialisation theory because of our reliance on inventories. We cannot contribute to the demographic themes in the debate, and cannot say very much about industrial organisation, although we have been able to do this to some extent for the Cornish mining industry. Our main emphasis has been on production, and as far as proto-industry is concerned with more than one household production activity or by-employment. While there was a decline in by-employment in Cornwall, the general prosperity in Kent was associated with no such decline, indeed a slight rise occurred. As we show in Chapter 4, there were some instances of by-employment that accord with the traditional model of combining craft activity with agriculture as a form of risk-aversion. It is this kind of by-employment that is assumed to have disappeared as households became less self-sufficient and more specialised as they engaged more with the market. More prevalent, at least in Kent, was another kind of by-employment, associated with more market engagement, which we can describe as entrepreneurial by-employment.

Given the economy of the early eighteenth century there was more likelihood of maintaining or raising income by engaging in more than one production activity than by specialising in one. As in colonial North America, capital would be invested in complementary activities if it could yield a higher return than the activity from which it came.[4] This kind of economic behaviour echoes that of Thomas Griggs, an Essex clothier and grocery retailer of the mid-eighteenth century, who was 'prepared to invest in any sort of potential profit'.[5] It has also been noted in other areas of the country in both rural and urban contexts. Moore considered that 'with the exception of most labourers, by-employments remained the rule even for heads of households well into the 18th century', and in his study of Lincoln inventories Johnston remarked that 'diversification of occupation was a characteristic of urban life'.[6] In colonial North America Carr and Walsh argue for a process of production diversification associated with increasing consumption.[7] From the late seventeenth century households engaged in more production activities, which resulted in an increase in local exchange. Diversification in production led to a more stable economy, which encouraged expenditure on more than bare necessities.

Industrious revolution

This continuing by-employment does not accord with de Vries's notion of an industrious revolution in that he argued that more market engagement (driven by the desire for consumption goods) was accompanied by specialisation in production for exchange and a decline in production for use.[8] Moreover, there is no sign that

> Goods previously produced at home are now purchased; services provided for oneself are provided by specialists; certain consumption habits inevitably change altogether, since the market offers goods made by different methods, new goods, and new relative prices to replace those implicit in home production.[9]

In Kent the production of goods for use within the household increased rather than declined.

An empirical contribution to many of de Vries's ideas about his industrious revolution are derived from inventories made for Friesland farmers between 1550 and 1750.[10] When broken down this is not a particularly large sample of inventories from an area of specialist livestock production. While his study looks at a range of household goods, such as mirrors and clocks, it does not explicitly consider production for use within the household, so one of the main planks of the argument does not have a body of evidence to hold it up. Even so, there is no reason to doubt that in this area of the Netherlands unspecialised peasant households of the early sixteenth century became specialised commercial farm enterprises surrounded by non-agricultural specialists in crafts, transportation, marketing and fuel supply.[11] But this was not the case in Cornwall or Kent.

According to de Vries, a desire for consumer goods was an important stimulus for changes in production and household organisation. Entrepreneurial by-employment in Kent was accompanied by an enrichment of material culture and the acquisition of new consumption goods. Whether this desire for new goods was driving production changes is hard to say. We see very little change in the nature of production in Kent despite major changes to the material culture of households, suggesting that a major change in production was not a pre-requisite for changes in consumption. Nor was the demand for new goods insatiable: they were not taken up indiscriminately by all, and some were never taken up even though they were available to households that could afford them.

Consumption and emulation

Fashion, emulation and social competition have been the most frequently invoked as explanations for the development of modern consumerism, which many historians have argued emerged in England during the eighteenth century.[12] The theoretical model of society and taste formation that these explanations assume has been criticised by anthropologists and sociologists for presenting a narrow view of society which is incapable of fully appreciating the complexity of social relations and the motives involved in individual consumption choices.[13] It may be argued that new 'conspicuous' goods, such as clocks and mirrors, can be taken to illustrate a desire to be fashionable and as copying social superiors, but seen in context (where they were situated within the household), more complex meanings are suggested. Clocks, for example, were more commonly placed in halls and kitchens than in any other room, which reminds us of their functional role as timepieces in addition to how they may have been used to reflect their owner's status. On the other hand, mirrors were most commonly found in bedchambers, indicating their use as primarily private objects. Only in the eighteenth century did mirrors come to be used as decorative objects, found elsewhere in the house.

We identify two broad categories of new material goods. First are those such as upholstered chairs, chests of drawers, and jacks, which improved comfort and convenience in the home but did not imply changes in behaviour. We use comfort in the modern sense, and while we agree with Crowley that this modern meaning emerges in the early eighteenth century, on the basis of our inventory evidence we disagree with his contention that the 'Anglo-American' population at the beginning of the eighteenth century 'made gentility much more explicit than comfort as an imperative in material culture'.[14] Second, utensils for hot drinks, forks, saucepans and non-rectangular tables imply new social rituals associated with new styles of cooking and ways of eating or entertaining in the home. In this context it is possible that other items, such as clocks or decorative mirrors, could be used for purposes of display, whereas in other contexts (for example a yeoman farming household) they were not. The adoption or take-up of these two types was different, with the established gentry pioneering the first and the service professions the second. While gentry preceded yeomen in adopting new goods, who in turn preceded husbandmen, there was no simple process of 'trickle down' since the social hierarchy itself was not as simple as this, and it is uncertain as to who was emulating whom. These new goods, and the social practices associated with them, were a means to establish social differences rather than simply express them.[15]

The date at which goods were acquired and their combinations provide further insight into the consumption of early modern households. The adoption of plates and knives and forks, and the decline of platters, follows the development of new styles of dining identified by Jean-Louis Flandrin, but significantly they were not all acquired at the same time in Kent or Cornwall.[16] Fashions in dining, therefore, as with other types of consumption, can be said to have 'filtered down' the social hierarchy, but they were not adopted wholesale by each social group. Rather, new fashions were integrated into existing practices when it became feasible to do so. This usually depended on the item becoming available, or cheap enough to be afforded by those below the aristocracy. Tea, for example, became popular very quickly in the second quarter of the eighteenth century as imports of this commodity increased, prices fell, and it provided a cheap and satisfying alternative drink. Goods such as knives and forks required a much greater cultural change for most social groups. Some 'fashions', therefore, took longer to be integrated by non-elite groups, and some were entirely ignored. It would have been possible for most of the households sampled in Kent to have purchased knives and forks much earlier had they wanted to. The use of knives and forks, and a new style of eating which this entailed, required a modification of existing practices. Simply copying a fashion would have made little sense to most non-elite social groups. The types of goods, and the date at which these were acquired, suggest that the majority of consumers in Kent and Cornwall did not slavishly copy new fashions, or passively adopt new cultural practices, but were active in renegotiating their cultural meanings to suit their own particular needs. This process is more accurately described as appropriation rather than emulation.

Does the consumption activity manifest in changing material cultures amount to a consumer revolution? McKendrick considered a consumer boom became revolutionary in the third quarter of the eighteenth century and our evidence ends in mid-century.[17] While the acquisition of consumer goods accelerated towards the mid-eighteenth century there was no decisive turning point during the period covered by our study; there was no 'unmistakable breakthrough' indicating a transition to a new order of consumption activity. Instead we see a cyclical pattern, with goods disappearing from households as well as new ones appearing. The richer and more varied material culture we identify (in Kent) was not revolutionary.

Cultures of consumption

For Cornwall, we could almost argue for the reverse of a consumer revolution. The material culture of many households became poorer, partly because people were getting poorer. But poverty was not the main reason why the material culture of Cornwall was so much more impoverished than that in Kent. In Chapter 7 we identified a 'county factor' that was much more important in explaining the difference than wealth or status. This had nothing to do with the availability of goods. Many Cornish gentlemen enjoyed a material culture that would have been quite familiar in Kent: indeed they 'shared in a national gentry culture'.[18] Thomas Stephens of St Columb Major, for example, had cane chairs, elbow chairs, round mahogany tea tables, japanned square tables, a backgammon table, china punch bowls, delft punch bowls, flint decanters, a copper tea kettle, coffee pots, five different sorts of teapots, copper saucepans and six black-handled knives and forks.[19] These goods, and others, could be found in the warehouses of Cornish merchants from at least the first decade of the seventeenth century.[20] Furthermore, in the early seventeenth century about two-thirds of Cornish inventories mention brassware. This is significant in that it reveals that networks of trade were sufficiently established from the start of the seventeenth century to supply Cornish households with imported goods, since no English brass was produced in this period.[21] Clearly, Cornish households could acquire goods from any part of the country and from abroad, if there was a demand for them.

While the remoteness of Cornwall may not have affected the availability or supply of material goods it may well have contributed to a difference in the interest in and information about material objects and therefore had some influence on demand. Celia Fiennes commented on the lack of knowledge Cornish people showed of places outside of their immediate vicinity:

> The people here are very ill guides and know very little from home, only to some market town they frequent, but will be very solicitous to know where you go and how far, and from whence you came and where is your abode.[22]

Thus a relative lack of knowledge of, and participation in, an urban commercial culture where consumerism was at its greatest may have been one reason why most Cornish households shunned the material goods their counterparts were acquiring in Kent. As Crowley argues, 'comfort', which we consider to be an important influence on the acquisition of new goods in Kent, is historically constructed.[23] It is tempting to see this rejection of material goods as a rejection of English cultural values as the Cornish became more self-conscious of their 'otherness', or as one historian has recently suggested, a more positive (or political) reaction against what was perceived as an encroaching metropolitan culture.[24] The only goods that they did acquire in large numbers were pewter plates, a more traditional and durable commodity whose value lay primarily in the intrinsic value of the metal. Moreover, this cultural rejection may well have economic origins in that the poverty of the county was a consequence of its integration into the English economy.

The analyses conducted in this study have demonstrated the statistical significance of wealth, location, and material context in affecting patterns of ownership of household goods. They have also indicated the possible economic and social consequences of these patterns. In doing so, they provide a picture of the early modern English economy that is both familiar and perplexing. It is familiar because it reinforces the well-known hierarchy of material possession from gentleman, to yeoman and then to husbandman; and the contrast in consumption patterns between town and countryside and centre and periphery. It is perplexing because some of these familiar distinctions do not appear in the ways we expect them to, or with the consequences we might have anticipated. By-employment does not necessarily imply risk-aversion, or precede a slide into poverty. Household economies were diverse and complicated, but this study has demonstrated that men did not labour exclusively for the market, and that women's production activities were not consumed entirely within the household. There were differences in the patterns of ownership of goods between urban and rural residents, but the importance of the 'urban factor' appears muted when compared to the effects of status or wealth.

In early modern England, therefore, this study suggests that 'capitalism' did not develop in a uniform linear manner. While Kent appears to have become fully integrated into a metropolitan economy, Cornwall experienced relative deprivation and exploitation more reminiscent of the Irish than the English experience in this period. This is not to deny that other models of development are not helpful. The concept of proto-industrialisation is undoubtedly useful in understanding change in certain areas (for example, in the West Riding of Yorkshire), and the process of the 'industrious revolution' has been identified in the Netherlands and may have been at work in other areas of England. It is rather an obvious point perhaps, but capitalist development was not a single process but several different processes, although they led to a common outcome.

Appendix 1

The distribution of the inventory
samples by parish

Table A1.1 The distribution of the Cornwall inventory sample

Parish	1600s	1610s	1620s	1630s	1640s	1650s	1660s	1670s	1680s	1690s	1700s	1710s	1720s	1730s	1740s	Total
Altarnun	5	20	10	16	24	1	28	11	10	25	15	14	8	6	10	203
Boyton	5	8	13	8	12	0	24	9	11	9	8	6	3	6	1	123
Crantock	11	11	12	6	5	4	10	11	7	9	5	10	7	4	10	122
Cuby	2	6	3	6	6	0	1	1	4	5	4	1	2	0	2	43
Gwennap	2	19	10	12	8	1	20	25	36	38	9	19	17	14	17	247
Illogan	7	10	8	9	6	0	9	17	17	32	17	11	19	16	11	189
Kenwyn	10	23	13	14	9	1	14	24	23	17	24	18	24	18	22	254
Launcells	13	23	21	15	15	0	19	19	23	18	8	12	9	7	2	204
Luxulyan	5	11	13	11	11	3	9	13	8	22	12	13	9	15	8	163
Madron	13	15	24	22	29	2	35	37	41	41	34	25	24	28	16	386
Poughill	7	19	15	8	5	0	10	15	14	10	10	12	4	4	2	135
Roche	7	11	10	8	5	0	8	16	16	11	14	16	8	15	4	149
St Clement	9	6	11	5	2	0	10	10	13	10	2	11	5	7	6	107
St Columb Major	33	35	28	26	19	1	29	40	45	30	37	21	24	11	14	393
St Erth	7	6	5	6	4	2	12	12	8	13	4	4	6	9	6	104
St Gennys	14	17	10	12	22	2	11	19	18	17	19	14	12	6	6	199
St Pinnock	3	8	9	8	12	0	4	6	9	9	7	7	8	5	6	101
St Stephens by Saltash	23	16	35	8	14	1	41	48	53	39	32	32	21	11	10	384
St Tudy	8	11	14	9	4	1	9	19	15	7	9	0	5	2	3	116
Talland	22	16	25	18	18	5	20	19	9	12	12	14	10	10	9	219
Temple	1	0	0	0	0	0	0	5	2	0	1	1	0	2	0	12
Tregony	7	10	21	14	16	1	13	8	15	12	11	6	11	7	13	165
Zennor	8	8	4	5	12	0	1	7	8	10	9	7	8	6	8	101
Total	222	309	314	246	258	25	337	391	405	396	303	274	244	209	186	4,119

Table A1.2 The distribution of the Kent inventory sample

Place	1600s	1610s	1620s	1630s	1640s	1650s	1660s	1670s	1680s	1690s	1700s	1710s	1720s	1730s	1740s	Total
Benenden	15	20	24	20	12	0	24	27	25	15	12	8	11	3	2	218
Biddenden	16	42	28	26	19	1	20	23	18	19	15	14	6	4	0	251
Bridge	9	6	4	3	1	1	5	5	4	4	3	3	4	3	1	56
Burmarsh	1	4	6	4	3	0	2	8	6	7	1	5	1	2	0	50
Canterbury	20	27	30	31	15	5	20	31	31	9	6	7	7	3	2	244
Chartham	14	24	13	19	11	1	17	19	21	14	6	4	5	5	1	174
Ebony	8	11	5	4	5	1	3	2	2	3	1	5	0	1	0	51
Elham	7	16	27	19	20	1	22	25	27	17	9	4	11	7	4	216
Elmsted	10	8	6	12	8	2	9	5	9	5	7	3	3	1	1	89
Folkestone	13	19	27	25	13	1	6	10	12	18	14	15	16	15	8	212
Goudhurst	19	21	22	31	24	1	29	32	21	14	15	17	3	3	0	252
Headcorn	3	19	13	10	11	1	14	14	16	15	10	5	14	2	1	148
Iwade	9	6	6	11	2	0	4	1	3	2	4	5	4	1	0	58
Lenham	7	20	22	18	20	1	22	20	14	12	7	13	9	12	5	202
Milton	8	22	35	20	10	0	25	30	19	14	15	12	10	0	0	220
Minster in Thanet	14	35	16	21	18	1	18	11	12	10	4	7	6	2	0	175
Newington	11	16	17	16	6	0	15	18	15	13	5	9	3	0	1	145
Orlestone	4	5	4	7	4	0	3	5	6	2	4	4	1	0	0	49
River	5	6	2	5	7	0	2	6	3	4	3	0	1	0	0	44
Ruckinge	17	16	10	16	6	2	5	10	20	4	12	8	0	3	1	130
Sheldwich	7	13	10	9	3	0	13	13	11	4	2	7	5	3	0	100
Smarden	14	43	29	29	16	1	14	30	25	13	21	19	8	2	0	264
Stelling	5	10	8	7	9	0	8	6	5	3	5	3	0	2	0	71
Ulcombe	9	16	5	11	8	0	13	12	14	8	8	2	3	3	0	112
Walmer	5	4	5	13	8	0	3	7	9	6	–	5	3	2	0	70
Waltham	4	7	3	5	4	4	9	8	5	3	4	5	1	1	0	63
Westbere	2	3	6	8	11	3	4	1	5	0	2	1	0	0	0	46
Wye	22	32	28	25	25	2	24	31	28	14	13	15	6	4	0	269
Total	278	471	411	425	299	29	353	410	386	252	208	205	141	84	27	3,979

Appendix 2
Production categories

Inventories are assigned to the production categories used in Chapter 3 by the presence of goods that indicate the activity was taking place or, rather, could take place. In some cases a particular activity is suggested but cannot be picked up mechanistically by the inventory software. In these cases the likely occupation was explicitly added to the inventory.

Farming
The four categories of farming are defined in Table 3.3 on p. 40. Groups 1 and 2 are non-commercial farmers and groups 3 and 4 commercial farmers. Group 4 includes all inventories with crops whether in the ground or in storage except where grain has clearly been purchased – for example, where there is a very small quantity. Significant tools and equipment such as ploughs and harrows are taken as indicating farming activity, but not small hand tools.

Textiles
'Spinning and preparation' is identified by spinning wheels or turns and wool cards or combs, plus other relevant equipment. Inventories listing wool and yarn together without a wheel are also taken to indicate spinning.
'Finishing and dyeing' is identified from the inventory header, specific tools, dyestuffs and dye vats.
'Weaving' is mainly identified by looms and loom tackle, but the presence of 'new cloth' with wool is also taken to indicate weaving.

Leather working
This is identified by tan keeves, large stocks of leather and bark.

Metalworking
Many items indicate metalworking, such as anvils, sledges, bellows, bicirons and horseshoes. The category includes those making metal goods in addition to blacksmiths.

Woodworking
The various wood crafts are identified from the header to the inventory or from a large collection of tools. A few basic tools (for example a saw, chisel, or hammer) are not sufficient for an inventory to be placed in this category.

Building
In Cornwall builders are identified by stocks of stones or tiles. In Kent the category includes bricklayers, and brick makers with large kilns and stocks of bricks. More specialist activities such as thatching are also identified from inventory headers or by specialist tools.

Clothing
Tailors are mostly identified through the header. Shoemakers and glovers can also be identified by specialist equipment such as lasts, and by stocks of leather, shoes, or gloves.

Miscellaneous crafts
These are a diverse group of activities not fitting into other categories. They include potter, tallow chandler, mason, salt maker, pipemaker, rope-maker, and saddler, and were mostly identified by designation in the inventory header.

Luxury crafts
These include goldsmith, silversmith, cutler and clockmaker, and were identified from the header and descriptions of material in the inventory.

Butchering
This was usually identified by the occupational designation in the header. Sometimes it was revealed by such specialised equipment as a gambrel.

Maritime
This includes all those with shares of boats, and fishing equipment. It does not include wage-earning navy seamen who appear in the waged category or merchants who appear with retailers.

Tin mining
This category includes all those involved in tin (and copper) mining, evidenced by bounds, leases, stocks of ore, and mining equipment, in addition to the designation in the header.

Retailing
This category includes shop retailers, merchants, victuallers and innholders. They are mostly identified by the header designation or a large amount of stock.

Services
This is a diverse group, including barbers, apothecaries, surgeons, lawyers, clerics, scriveners and schoolmasters. They are usually identified by the inventory header.

Waged
A diverse group including both labourers, servants and other waged workers such as soldiers and seamen. They are identified by header information or presence of wages.

Dairying
The general dairying category includes inventories with dairy houses or cows since these indicate the potential for dairy production. Butter and cheese making is identified by the presence of specific items used in their production.

Milling
This is corn milling, identified by mill equipment and leases in addition to the header.

Baking
This is identified by references such as bakehouses, kneading troughs, moulding boards, and dough keeves.

Malting
This is usually identified by large quantity of malt listed with barley, or by equipment such as oast cloths or malting rooms. It excludes those inventories with a small quantity of malt which may have been purchased.

Brewing
This includes all households with beer or ale, specific brewing equipment or brew-houses. For Cornwall potential category includes those with 'tubs and keeves'.

Distilling
This is identified by presence of a still or limbeck.

Cider making
This includes those with specific equipment or stocks of cider.

Food preservation
This is identified mainly through goods associated with salting of meat and fish. It also includes those with stocks of salt meat or smoked meat hanging from the roof. In Cornwall potential food processors include all those with 'tubs and keeves'.

Composite categories are as follows:

Crafts
This category consists of woodworking, metalworking, leather working, tailoring, weaving, miscellaneous crafts, building, finishing, dyeing and luxury crafts.

Commercial food processing
This brings together a number of categories and part-categories. It includes all those inventories identified as being involved in butchering, plus part of cider making, malting, brewing, dairying, milling and brewing. Whether or not the activity is commercial is decided by the nature and scale of production in each case. For instance, all those with more than four cows are considered commercial dairy producers.

Domestic food processing
This consists of those in the above category who are not considered to be commercial producers.

Appendix 3

Some characteristics of occupation and status groups

The following table shows some characteristics of certain occupational and status groups. The status labels (gentleman, yeoman, husbandman and widow) are taken from the inventory headers. The occupational categories are defined in Appendix 2. The categories are not mutually exclusive: many of the yeomen, for example, were also in the commercial farming categories discussed in Chapter 7. By-employment is discussed in Chapter 4.

Table A3.1 Some characteristics of occupation and status groups

	Cornwall			Kent		
	1600– 49	*1650– 99*	*1700– 49*	*1600– 49*	*1650– 99*	*1700– 49*
All inventories	1,330	1,538	1,207	1,852	1,411	663
Urban (%)	20	25	23	21	21	26
By-employed (%)	48	27	30	48	50	54
Prod. for use (mean no.)	1.78	1.12	1.09	2.21	2.43	2.70
Prod. for exchange (mean no.)	1.79	1.24	1.27	1.58	1.60	1.74
Material wealth (median £)	19.16	17.88	16.75	26.88	61.78	74.68
Consumption goods (median £)	9.78	9.31	8.89	14.07	26.25	36.61
Consump. as % of material (mean)	59	63	62	61	57	55
Debts to as % of all wealth (mean)	12	19	14	17	15	16
No. of rooms (mean)	–	–	–	6.6	7.8	8.2
Waged	18	21	18	42	26	9
Urban (%)	11	48	17	12	15	11
By-employed (%)	61	19	44	64	58	56
Prod. for use (mean no.)	1.17	0.57	0.33	2.05	2.46	2.11
Prod. for exchange (mean no.)	2.22	1.33	1.50	2.00	2.15	1.56
Material wealth (median £)	8.00	3.31	10.26	11.57	15.32	12.90
Consumption goods (median £)	3.92	3.05	3.76	6.13	10.11	12.00
Consump. as % of material (mean)	65	90	69	57	63	62
Debts to as % of all wealth (mean)	21	49	36	22	15	34
No. of rooms (mean)	–	–	–	4.2	5.7	5.0

continued

Table A3.1 Continued

	Cornwall			Kent		
	1600– 49	*1650– 99*	*1700– 49*	*1600– 49*	*1650– 99*	*1700– 49*
Service	7	8	12	30	29	13
Urban (%)	43	38	50	53	31	38
By-employed (%)	71	13	67	71	45	31
Prod. for use (mean no.)	2.00	0.75	1.00	2.50	2.21	2.54
Prod. for exchange (mean no.)	3.00	1.38	1.92	2.50	2.28	1.46
Material wealth (median £)	36.99	17.39	44.88	70.20	92.40	79.79
Consumption goods (median £)	19.08	16.26	24.70	41.32	61.73	69.87
Consump. as % of material (mean)	58	85	83	68	77	89
Debts to as % of all wealth (mean)	16	9	29	22	26	14
No. of rooms (mean)	–	–	–	7.7	10.0	9.8
Retail	24	53	56	42	83	52
Urban (%)	83	57	48	36	41	40
By-employed (%)	75	64	70	71	73	79
Prod. for use (mean no.)	2.21	1.09	1.38	2.43	2.41	2.69
Prod. for exchange (mean no.)	2.50	2.30	2.23	2.43	2.43	2.50
Material wealth (median £)	49.17	47.45	55.82	60.74	108.39	96.47
Consumption goods (median £)	24.68	24.36	29.63	35.01	49.05	40.22
Consump. as % of material (mean)	66	57	59	68	53	50
Debts to as % of all wealth (mean)	8	15	17	14	12	14
No. of rooms (mean)	–	–	–	10.0	9.6	9.4
Maritime	50	50	48	60	51	58
Urban (%)	38	70	48	52	67	81
By-employed (%)	58	58	56	68	47	72
Prod. for use (mean no.)	2.08	1.20	1.25	2.07	2.24	2.33
Prod. for exchange (mean no.)	2.80	2.18	2.08	2.40	1.98	2.45
Material wealth (median £)	18.25	28.61	22.83	34.00	65.92	92.35
Consumption goods (median £)	12.13	15.67	13.41	11.84	36.17	41.32
Consump. as % of material (mean)	68	60	68	49	54	54
Debts to as % of all wealth (mean)	12	14	16	12	9	7
No. of rooms (mean)	–	–	–	5.9	6.7	6.5
Commercial food processing	256	188	181	545	442	249
Urban (%)	19	37	34	17	14	22
By-employed (%)	96	81	83	96	94	88
Prod. for use (mean no.)	2.02	1.27	1.41	2.90	2.77	2.76
Prod. for exchange (mean no.)	3.25	2.47	2.52	2.93	2.74	2.62
Material wealth (median £)	89.05	67.44	47.43	91.34	143.94	176.03
Consumption goods (median £)	28.08	23.16	19.15	26.95	47.88	55.07
Consump. as % of material (mean)	40	49	52	38	40	41
Debts to as % of all wealth (mean)	6	13	10	11	12	11
No. of rooms (mean)	–	–	–	8.3	9.6	9.6

Table A3.1 Continued

	Cornwall			Kent		
	1600–49	*1650–99*	*1700–49*	*1600–49*	*1650–99*	*1700–49*
Crafts	236	198	198	326	265	144
Urban (%)	31	40	40	28	20	24
By-employed (%)	78	54	53	79	72	67
Prod. for use (mean no.)	2.14	1.20	1.18	2.52	2.68	2.94
Prod. for exchange (mean no.)	2.87	2.06	2.02	2.58	2.35	2.35
Material wealth (median £)	24.04	19.90	16.06	35.01	59.08	53.01
Consumption goods (median £)	15.09	11.75	9.62	16.84	27.18	31.38
Consump. as % of material (mean)	67	69	70	55	56	60
Debts to as % of all wealth (mean)	8	13	11	16	17	20
No. of rooms (mean)	–	–	–	7.1	8.0	8.4
Tin Mining	97	172	113	–	–	–
Urban (%)	12	5	4	–	–	–
By-employed (%)	88	69	61	–	–	–
Prod. for use (mean no.)	1.89	1.15	1.16	–	–	–
Prod. for exchange (mean no.)	3.38	2.15	1.99	–	–	–
Material wealth (median £)	35.31	25.37	16.57	–	–	–
Consumption goods (median £)	10.00	9.78	9.07	–	–	–
Consump. as % of material (mean)	38	47	52	–	–	–
Debts to as % of all wealth (mean)	6	12	10	–	–	–
Commercial agriculture only	478	470	321	323	306	129
Urban (%)	10	14	10	10	10	13
By-employed (%)	43	15	13	51	42	35
Prod. for use (mean no.)	1.98	1.50	1.39	2.54	2.93	3.12
Prod. for exchange (mean no.)	1.63	1.33	1.22	1.53	1.43	1.35
Material wealth (median £)	23.27	29.33	34.05	33.15	64.62	92.10
Consumption goods (median £)	8.64	11.03	9.62	11.00	20.08	29.55
Consump. as % of material (mean)	42	40	35	39	39	38
Debts to as % of all wealth (mean)	7	11	6	10	9	13
No. of rooms (mean)	–	–	–	5.3	6.8	7.3
Commercial agriculture (comb.)	366	295	260	544	465	221
Urban (%)	17	20	16	14	11	9
By-employed (%)	100	100	100	100	100	100
Prod. for use (mean no.)	2.12	1.35	1.47	2.94	2.86	2.88
Prod. for exchange (mean no.)	3.17	2.59	2.58	3.04	2.83	2.81
Material wealth (median £)	69.00	56.20	49.73	94.43	147.22	178.89
Consumption goods (median £)	23.03	17.95	17.54	25.88	45.72	51.20
Consump. as % of material (mean)	41	38	40	34	35	36
Debts to as % of all wealth (mean)	5	10	8	10	12	12
No. of rooms (mean)	–	–	–	8.2	9.4	9.7

continued

Table A3.1 Continued

	Cornwall			Kent		
	1600– 49	*1650– 99*	*1700– 49*	*1600– 49*	*1650– 99*	*1700– 49*
Gentleman	59	86	45	45	75	15
Urban (%)	31	47	31	51	23	27
By-employed (%)	49	40	31	31	53	40
Prod. for use (mean no.)	1.85	1.36	1.44	2.29	2.52	2.67
Prod. for exchange (mean no.)	2.02	1.49	1.31	1.09	1.63	0.93
Material wealth (median £)	44.41	48.62	64.30	94.62	151.57	229.29
Consumption goods (median £)	20.52	24.92	32.73	69.34	79.95	81.15
Consump. as % of material (mean)	53	62	57	78	58	51
Debts to as % of all wealth (mean)	16	17	19	17	17	21
No. of rooms (mean)	–	–	–	10.5	12.3	10.5
Husbandman	140	91	45	104	85	35
Urban (%)	11	8	13	20	9	23
By-employed (%)	47	14	11	54	51	46
Prod. for use (mean no.)	1.87	1.44	1.02	2.43	2.80	2.91
Prod. for exchange (mean no.)	1.76	0.97	0.73	1.70	1.49	1.34
Material wealth (median £)	25.49	12.43	13.82	24.45	36.08	43.88
Consumption goods (median £)	7.97	5.56	5.00	10.75	15.03	19.54
Consump. as % of material (mean)	47	59	57	45	47	46
Debts to as % of all wealth (mean)	12	25	20	15	11	14
No. of rooms (mean)	–	–	–	4.9	6.2	6.1
Yeoman	172	318	271	206	232	110
Urban (%)	9	12	10	12	7	10
By-employed (%)	66	32	35	73	71	74
Prod. for use (mean no.)	2.16	1.38	1.39	2.86	2.81	2.95
Prod. for exchange (mean no.)	2.13	1.35	1.44	2.24	2.08	2.16
Material wealth (median £)	60.66	38.42	38.44	99.85	135.91	181.38
Consumption goods (median £)	23.06	15.12	13.00	27.97	39.68	53.54
Consump. as % of material (mean)	45	47	45	43	37	37
Debts to as % of all wealth (mean)	9	15	10	16	12	14
No. of rooms (mean)	–	–	–	8.3	8.8	9.3
Widow	139	208	118	200	157	68
Urban (%)	20	25	31	20	27	29
By-employed (%)	25	11	10	16	22	28
Prod. for use (mean no.)	1.42	0.99	0.77	1.66	2.01	2.25
Prod. for exchange (mean no.)	1.07	0.72	0.62	0.79	0.84	1.10
Material wealth (median £)	12.64	10.50	7.96	15.84	30.59	40.63
Consumption goods (median £)	8.32	7.89	5.90	13.27	23.93	28.54
Consump. as % of material (mean)	71	75	84	85	78	75
Debts to as % of all wealth (mean)	18	28	22	21	20	19
No. of rooms (mean)	–	–	–	5.4	6.6	7.5

Table A3.1 Continued

	Cornwall			Kent		
	1600–49	*1650–99*	*1700–49*	*1600–49*	*1650–99*	*1700–49*
By-employed	635	1124	846	893	712	308
Urban (%)	15	23	20	18	13	21
By-employed (%)	100	100	100	100	100	100
Prod. for use (mean no.)	2.80	2.50	2.51	2.68	2.59	2.61
Prod. for exchange (mean no.)	2.13	1.49	1.49	2.86	2.94	2.95
Material wealth (median £)	42.67	49.66	45.21	61.68	118.54	137.29
Consumption goods (median £)	16.27	16.62	17.05	21.83	40.27	44.75
Consump. as % of material (mean)	46	42	45	42	42	43
Debts to as % of all wealth (mean)	6	11	9	11	11	13
No. of rooms (mean)	–	–	–	7.4	8.8	9.0
Urban	261	384	279	392	294	174
Urban (%)	100	100	100	100	100	100
By-employed (%)	38	24	24	40	31	43
Prod. for use (mean no.)	1.49	0.95	0.78	1.63	1.90	2.49
Prod. for exchange (mean no.)	1.56	1.18	1.15	1.39	1.18	1.50
Material wealth (median £)	15.08	15.18	11.83	28.28	49.35	61.41
Consumption goods (median £)	11.90	11.55	8.25	16.70	28.10	38.06
Consump. as % of material (mean)	73	75	76	70	67	64
Debts to as % of all wealth (mean)	11	22	18	16	14	11
No. of rooms (mean)	–	–	–	6.6	7.2	7.6

Appendix 4

The ownership of material goods by status and occupation

The following table shows how the ownership of various objects, and the presence of production activities for use, varied between the status and occupational groups described in Appendix 3.

Table A4.1 Ownership of material goods by status and occupation (percentages)

	Cornwall			Kent		
	1600–49	1650–99	1700–49	1600–49	1650–99	1700–49
Mirrors						
Waged	0.0	0.0	0.0	0.0	9.5	0.0
Service	0.0	0.0	37.5	18.8	56.5	80.0
Retail	0.0	11.8	34.5	9.1	29.8	61.3
Maritime	2.1	15.9	20.0	5.7	53.2	76.4
Commercial food	2.0	9.3	9.2	7.5	22.2	52.3
Crafts	1.7	6.5	11.6	6.8	19.9	47.7
Tin mining	0.0	2.5	4.8	–	–	–
Comm. farming only	1.0	2.3	1.6	2.8	12.5	31.9
Comm. farming comb.	1.1	5.2	6.7	7.6	20.3	49.1
Gentleman	2.2	23.3	23.3	26.8	43.1	76.9
Yeoman	1.3	1.5	3.6	6.5	19.2	43.4
Husbandman	0.0	0.0	0.0	5.4	6.4	34.4
Widow	2.5	5.2	10.0	5.9	18.9	33.3
By-employed	1.3	7.0	8.1	7.2	21.1	50.6
Urban	2.6	10.4	12.6	11.1	36.0	65.8
All	1.2	4.4	5.9	5.7	20.2	44.1
Jacks						
Waged	0.0	0.0	0.0	3.3	20.0	28.6
Service	0.0	0.0	33.3	26.7	82.6	60.0
Retail	0.0	15.4	39.1	19.4	70.2	74.2
Maritime	0.0	10.0	21.9	12.2	53.5	34.0
Commercial food	0.5	2.9	7.1	9.6	48.7	59.9
Crafts	0.0	2.1	6.8	7.0	38.8	46.5
Tin mining	1.8	0.0	2.7	–	–	–
Comm. farming only	0.3	0.3	0.9	3.5	20.1	38.6
Comm. farming comb.	0.8	2.8	4.8	9.4	45.2	59.0

Table A4.1 Continued

	Cornwall			Kent		
	1600–49	*1650–99*	*1700–49*	*1600–49*	*1650–99*	*1700–49*
Gentleman	0.0	6.1	28.6	51.3	76.2	61.5
Yeoman	0.8	0.9	2.5	10.0	36.9	56.7
Husbandman	0.0	0.0	0.0	1.1	10.5	18.8
Widow	1.0	1.3	5.3	4.2	22.0	29.8
By-employed	0.6	2.0	6.1	8.5	41.1	51.7
Urban	0.0	5.7	10.9	13.8	56.1	48.7
All	0.3	1.6	4.2	7.3	35.5	45.9
Upholstered furniture						
Waged	0.0	0.0	0.0	0.0	20.0	0.0
Service	0.0	25.0	33.3	66.7	91.7	100.0
Retail	33.3	45.5	66.7	83.3	87.5	100.0
Maritime	5.0	33.3	23.8	28.6	77.8	90.0
Commercial food	5.5	18.3	13.9	42.0	89.0	85.2
Crafts	4.9	8.9	12.6	16.7	88.9	88.9
Tin mining	3.3	2.9	8.3	–	–	–
Comm. farming only	0.0	2.0	2.3	13.3	56.3	47.6
Comm. farming comb.	2.4	10.4	8.1	37.3	88.5	85.7
Gentleman	7.7	52.2	52.9	100.0	97.0	100.0
Yeoman	0.0	1.4	3.7	43.8	75.0	80.0
Husbandman	0.0	0.0	0.0	0.0	20.0	0.0
Widow	0.0	6.6	5.7	21.1	47.2	70.0
By-employed	1.6	12.4	9.5	32.6	86.4	83.8
Urban	3.0	10.1	19.6	51.6	83.5	88.7
All	0.8	5.2	6.2	20.9	70.7	77.0
Clocks						
Waged	0.0	0.0	0.0	0.0	9.5	28.6
Service	0.0	0.0	37.5	6.3	34.8	30.0
Retail	0.0	2.9	13.8	0.0	25.5	41.9
Maritime	0.0	4.5	10.0	1.9	23.4	30.9
Commercial food	0.0	3.7	14.5	1.5	33.5	61.7
Crafts	0.4	0.6	6.5	1.0	19.9	44.6
Tin mining	0.0	1.7	6.4	–	–	–
Comm. farming only	0.0	0.0	3.6	0.3	13.6	54.3
Comm. farming comb.	0.3	2.4	9.8	1.5	32.1	67.0
Gentleman	0.0	6.7	33.3	7.3	60.0	69.2
Yeoman	0.0	0.4	7.2	1.6	28.5	73.6
Husbandman	0.0	0.0	0.0	0.0	2.6	40.6
Widow	0.0	0.0	0.0	0.0	12.1	23.3
By-employed	0.2	2.0	9.1	1.2	28.1	58.7
Urban	0.0	2.1	8.0	1.9	18.0	43.9
All	0.1	0.8	5.6	0.9	20.4	48.7
Hot drinks						
Waged	0.0	0.0	0.0	0.0	0.0	0.0
Service	0.0	0.0	37.5	0.0	4.3	60.0

continued

Table A4.1 Continued

	Cornwall			Kent		
	1600–49	*1650–99*	*1700–49*	*1600–49*	*1650–99*	*1700–49*
Retail	0.0	0.0	17.2	0.0	0.0	32.3
Maritime	0.0	0.0	10.0	0.0	2.1	30.9
Commercial food	0.0	0.0	5.9	0.0	0.2	14.5
Crafts	0.0	0.0	7.7	0.0	0.0	13.1
Tin mining	0.0	0.0	3.2	–	–	–
Comm. farming only	0.0	0.0	0.4	0.0	0.0	5.2
Comm. farming comb.	0.0	0.0	4.0	0.0	0.2	11.8
Gentleman	0.0	0.0	20.0	0.0	1.5	23.1
Yeoman	0.0	0.0	1.3	0.0	0.0	11.3
Husbandman	0.0	0.0	0.0	0.0	0.0	3.1
Widow	0.0	0.0	2.5	0.0	0.0	6.7
By-employed	0.0	0.0	5.2	0.0	0.3	14.8
Urban	0.0	0.0	6.9	0.0	0.8	29.0
All	0.0	0.0	2.9	0.0	0.3	13.8
Plates						
Waged	0.0	14.3	57.1	0.0	27.3	40.0
Service	0.0	0.0	100.0	33.3	66.7	100.0
Retail	0.0	44.4	94.4	33.3	70.6	96.0
Maritime	2.7	37.5	82.8	17.4	63.0	97.7
Commercial food	9.8	38.4	86.2	27.2	60.6	85.1
Crafts	9.4	29.5	82.0	12.1	47.4	73.7
Tin mining	4.9	27.9	81.1	–	–	–
Comm. farming only	3.0	18.2	69.5	8.7	23.3	75.3
Comm. farming comb.	5.7	34.3	85.2	25.3	55.3	82.9
Gentleman	13.8	63.9	100.0	84.2	90.7	90.0
Yeoman	3.0	17.0	78.7	33.3	45.7	83.8
Husbandman	0.0	2.4	25.0	5.9	9.7	63.6
Widow	1.2	20.9	62.0	14.3	35.0	80.0
By-employed	4.8	34.7	83.2	19.9	48.9	83.9
Urban	3.4	27.8	78.6	24.1	52.7	85.8
All	3.7	20.8	73.0	17.4	41.9	79.3
Books						
Waged	0.0	20.0	0.0	10.0	4.8	0.0
Service	66.7	50.0	62.5	71.9	65.2	30.0
Retail	43.8	20.6	3.4	33.3	14.9	25.8
Maritime	12.8	18.2	7.5	30.2	29.8	36.4
Commercial food	16.1	11.7	7.9	29.6	29.7	27.7
Crafts	20.1	8.9	7.7	33.9	27.4	28.5
Tin mining	16.4	7.5	7.2	–	–	–
Comm. farming only	5.0	6.1	2.8	14.5	20.4	12.9
Comm. farming comb.	15.3	9.5	6.7	30.1	31.3	23.1
Gentleman	33.3	33.3	26.7	75.6	53.8	46.2
Yeoman	11.5	7.7	4.5	32.3	26.6	23.6
Husbandman	1.6	1.3	0.0	14.0	24.4	3.1
Widow	5.0	2.3	5.0	18.3	20.5	16.7
By-employed	12.5	12.6	7.1	27.6	29.9	25.6

Table A4.1 Continued

	Cornwall			Kent		
	1600–49	*1650–99*	*1700–49*	*1600–49*	*1650–99*	*1700–49*
Urban	12.3	12.8	6.9	37.0	29.3	28.4
All	9.0	7.9	5.7	24.1	25.1	23.1
Milling for use						
Waged	0.0	0.0	0.0	9.5	3.8	0.0
Service	0.0	0.0	0.0	28.9	20.7	0.0
Retail	4.2	0.0	3.6	33.3	14.5	15.4
Maritime	4.0	0.0	0.0	21.7	5.9	3.4
Commercial food	9.0	1.1	2.2	40.4	18.1	12.4
Crafts	5.5	1.5	1.0	20.6	6.4	6.3
Tin mining	2.7	1.9	2.0	–	–	–
Comm. farming only	3.1	1.9	1.6	27.2	5.6	3.1
Comm. farming comb.	7.9	1.7	2.3	40.4	17.8	12.7
Gentleman	11.9	7.0	6.7	15.6	8.0	20.0
Yeoman	7.6	1.3	1.5	40.8	17.2	9.1
Husbandman	0.7	1.1	0.0	18.3	9.4	2.9
Widow	2.9	0.5	0.0	14.0	3.2	5.9
By-employed	6.1	1.9	1.9	34.8	14.0	10.1
Urban	0.0	0.3	1.8	14.8	3.1	6.3
All	3.5	1.0	1.2	23.4	8.2	6.6
Food preservation						
Waged	33.3	14.3	5.6	59.5	76.9	66.7
Service	71.4	12.5	33.3	68.4	72.4	84.6
Retail	79.2	32.1	39.3	83.3	84.3	84.6
Maritime	66.0	32.0	31.3	68.3	76.5	81.0
Commercial food	86.3	50.5	40.3	90.1	92.8	93.2
Crafts	72.0	31.3	25.8	77.9	85.3	89.6
Tin mining	67.6	28.2	14.5	–	–	–
Comm. farming only	65.7	42.8	29.9	75.5	83.3	89.1
Comm. farming comb.	84.7	45.1	38.5	90.6	93.5	96.4
Gentleman	49.2	40.7	28.9	66.7	74.7	86.7
Yeoman	76.2	43.1	35.8	80.1	84.1	96.4
Husbandman	65.7	42.9	31.1	78.8	85.9	82.9
Widow	43.9	26.9	19.5	52.0	67.5	76.5
By-employed	78.6	48.6	37.4	88.4	92.3	94.9
Urban	49.8	25.4	14.0	54.1	66.0	82.2
All	60.6	32.1	22.9	67.1	76.7	84.5
Baking						
Waged	0.0	0.0	0.0	28.6	42.3	33.3
Service	14.3	0.0	0.0	34.2	41.4	46.2
Retail	0.0	0.0	1.8	45.2	45.8	36.5
Maritime	12.0	2.0	6.3	28.3	39.2	44.8
Commercial food	10.9	1.6	3.9	52.8	54.3	47.8
Crafts	9.7	1.5	2.5	43.3	45.7	50.0
Tin mining	5.4	0.6	1.3	–	–	–

continued

Table A4.1 Continued

	Cornwall			Kent		
	1600–49	*1650–99*	*1700–49*	*1600–49*	*1650–99*	*1700–49*
Comm. farming only	2.3	0.4	0.3	31.9	40.2	45.7
Comm. farming comb.	9.0	1.0	2.7	53.9	53.8	51.1
Gentleman	6.8	3.5	2.2	37.8	46.7	26.7
Yeoman	5.8	0.0	1.8	49.0	48.7	47.3
Husbandman	5.0	0.0	0.0	32.7	41.2	42.9
Widow	5.0	0.5	1.7	22.0	28.0	36.8
By-employed	6.8	0.7	2.8	49.3	52.9	51.3
Urban	4.6	1.2	0.7	25.0	33.3	40.8
All	4.4	0.7	1.0	33.7	39.3	43.3
Dairying						
Waged	44.4	19.0	11.1	47.6	50.0	44.4
Service	42.9	25.0	25.0	34.2	13.8	15.4
Retail	45.8	22.6	33.9	23.8	27.7	42.3
Maritime	34.0	28.0	31.3	20.0	21.6	15.5
Commercial food	16.4	18.6	34.8	30.5	24.2	27.7
Crafts	45.3	34.8	34.8	41.1	46.0	46.5
Tin mining	47.3	42.3	53.3	–	–	–
Comm. farming only	78.2	69.6	71.7	80.2	91.5	89.1
Comm. farming comb.	39.3	46.1	57.7	39.5	35.9	38.9
Gentleman	47.5	38.4	53.3	33.3	37.3	46.7
Yeoman	51.7	50.0	54.2	41.7	46.1	46.4
Husbandman	56.4	44.0	37.8	58.7	58.8	68.6
Widow	41.0	26.0	17.8	30.0	40.8	30.9
By-employed	50.7	49.8	56.0	45.7	47.2	44.5
Urban	31.4	24.5	24.0	20.7	26.5	25.3
All	45.0	36.0	39.9	37.9	43.2	43.3
Alcohol						
Waged	16.7	14.3	11.1	28.6	46.2	44.4
Service	71.4	12.5	33.3	65.8	55.2	84.6
Retail	66.7	30.2	39.3	26.2	49.4	67.3
Maritime	72.0	38.0	37.5	58.3	66.7	82.8
Commercial food	73.0	39.9	40.9	67.5	79.6	83.1
Crafts	62.7	31.8	33.8	52.8	71.3	84.7
Tin mining	60.8	28.2	26.3	–	–	–
Comm. farming only	49.0	35.7	35.2	39.0	72.9	85.3
Comm. farming comb.	71.0	41.0	45.4	69.3	84.7	89.1
Gentleman	57.6	40.7	44.4	60.0	76.0	80.0
Yeoman	66.9	36.2	38.0	68.9	81.0	93.6
Husbandman	52.9	38.5	24.4	41.3	74.1	74.3
Widow	32.4	23.6	23.7	28.0	47.8	61.8
By-employed	65.7	43.2	44.3	59.8	80.1	87.3
Urban	45.6	27.6	21.5	37.0	51.4	81.0
All	49.6	27.4	28.6	42.2	63.2	79.2

Appendix 5
Logistic regression statistics

The following tables report the r^2 and $exp(\beta)$ statistics for the logistic regressions discussed in Chapter 7. Only $exp(\beta)$ statistics that are significant at the 95 per cent level are included: the dashes indicate non-significant values.

Table A5.1 Exp(β) statistics from logistic regression equations predicting the ownership of goods in Cornwall

Variable	Mirrors		Clocks		Books	
	1600–49	*1650–99*	*1700–49*	*1650–99*	*1700–49*	*1600–49*
r^2	0.10	0.19	0.23	0.26	0.16	0.20
URBAN	4.25	3.00	–	–	–	–
SERVICE	–	–	8.14	–	10.98	15.00
RETAIL	–	–	8.07	–	–	8.44
MARITIME	–	–	–	–	–	–
AG34ONLY	–	–	0.21	–	–	–
AG34COMB	–	–	0.41	–	–	–
WEALTH50	1.18	–	1.58	–	1.58	1.36
GENT	2.34	7.63	4.22	11.50	4.64	3.91
HUSB	–	–	–	–	–	–

	Books		Jacks		Upholstered furniture	
	1650–99	*1700–49*	*1650–99*	*1700–49*	*1650–99*	*1700–49*
r^2	0.13	0.15	0.31	0.42	0.42	0.48
URBAN	–	–	14.01	3.52	–	6.12
SERVICE	14.99	28.43	–	19.26	11.61	–
RETAIL	3.58	–	7.58	18.90	16.11	32.45
MARITIME	–	–	–	5.02	4.95	–
AG34ONLY	–	0.26	–	0.09	0.17	0.10
AG34COMB	–	0.39	–	0.20	–	0.21
WEALTH50	–	1.45	–	2.40	1.94	3.53
GENT	5.92	5.00	–	15.69	33.82	18.49
HUSB	–	–	–	–	–	–

continued

Table A5.1 Continued

Variable	Chests of drawers		New tables		Carpets	
	1650–99	*1700–49*	*1600–49*	*1650–99*	*1700–49*	*1600–49*
r^2	0.10	0.28	0.16	0.15	0.11	0.23
URBAN	–	2.86	–	–	–	–
SERVICE	–	28.50	–	–	–	–
RETAIL	–	7.29	26.38	–	3.79	–
MARITIME	–	–	–	–	–	–
AG34ONLY	–	0.24	–	–	–	–
AG34COMB	–	–	–	–	–	1.76
WEALTH50	1.16	1.72	1.23	1.17	–	1.86
GENT	4.65	2.78	–	9.10	5.88	–
HUSB	–	–	–	–	–	–

	Carpets	Plates	Knives and forks		Hot drinks	
	1650–99	*1600–49*	*1650–99*	*1700–49*	*1650–99*	*1700–49*
r^2	0.16	0.15	0.20	0.19	0.17	0.29
URBAN	–	–	1.66	–	–	–
SERVICE	–	–	–	–	12.97	27.42
RETAIL	8.71	–	–	–	–	7.93
MARITIME	–	–	–	–	–	–
AG34ONLY	–	–	–	–	–	0.09
AG34COMB	–	–	–	–	–	0.15
WEALTH50	–	1.56	1.98	2.27	–	1.87
GENT	–	–	3.99	–	–	–
HUSB	–	–	–	0.15	–	–

	Saucepans
	1700–49
r^2	0.26
URBAN	3.85
SERVICE	–
RETAIL	6.32
MARITIME	4.42
AG34ONLY	–
AG34COMB	–
WEALTH50	–
GENT	8.88
HUSB	–

Table A5.2 Exp(β) statistics from logistic regression equations predicting the ownership of goods in Kent

Variable	Mirrors			Clocks		
	1600–49	1650–99	1700–49	1600–49	1650–99	1700–49
r^2	0.16	0.26	0.30	0.41	0.37	0.32
URBAN	2.73	2.34	3.79	–	–	–
SERVICE	2.91	3.00	–	15.39	–	–
RETAIL	–	–	–	–	–	–
MARITIME	–	4.74	5.27	–	–	–
AG34ONLY	–	0.55	–	–	–	1.98
AG34COMB	–	0.40	–	–	–	–
WEALTH50	–	1.08	–	1.13	1.16	1.40
GENT	–	–	12.21	8.56	–	–
HUSB	–	–	–	–	0.21	–
NROOMS	1.20	1.23	1.25	1.23	1.34	1.13

	Books			Jacks		
	1600–49	1650–99	1700–49	1600–49	1650–99	1700–49
r^2	0.21	0.15	0.10	0.30	0.45	0.30
URBAN	1.79	1.53	–	1.99	5.08	–
SERVICE	5.49	4.84	–	3.42	–	–
RETAIL	–	3.43	–	–	–	3.34
MARITIME	–	–	2.61	–	–	0.45
AG34ONLY	–	–	–	–	0.39	–
AG34COMB	–	–	–	0.40	0.42	–
WEALTH50	1.07	–	–	1.10	1.21	1.17
GENT	8.90	1.91	–	4.20	–	–
HUSB	–	–	–	–	–	–
NROOMS	1.17	1.18	1.16	1.30	1.39	1.28

	Upholstered furniture			Chest of drawers		
	1600–49	1650–99	1700–49	1600–49	1650–99	1700–49
r^2	0.86	0.66	0.63	0.22	0.25	0.20
URBAN	23.13	5.82	–	5.8	2.01	1.69
SERVICE	–	–	–	–	–	–
RETAIL	–	–	–	11.86	–	–
MARITIME	–	–	14.89	–	3.37	4.72
AG34ONLY	–	–	–	–	0.32	–
AG34COMB	0.02	–	–	–	0.39	0.57
WEALTH50	–	1.74	–	–	1.12	1.16
GENT	–	–	–	–	2.22	–
HUSB	–	–	–	–	–	–
NROOMS	2.24	1.87	2.53	–	1.15	1.11

continued

Table A5.2 Continued

Variable	New tables			Carpets		
	1600–49	*1650–99*	*1700–49*	*1600–49*	*1650–99*	*1700–49*
r^2	0.26	0.34	0.22	0.31	0.28	0.16
URBAN	1.82	3.75	3.58	1.80	1.59	–
SERVICE	3.80	6.58	7.33	–	–	–
RETAIL	–	–	–	–	–	–
MARITIME	–	–	–	–	–	4.36
AG34ONLY	–	0.26	–	0.54	0.57	–
AG34COMB	0.39	0.39	–	–	–	–
WEALTH50	–	1.11	–	–	1.10	–
GENT	4.31	4.20	–	5.77	3.81	10.29
HUSB	–	–	–	–	–	–
NROOMS	1.27	1.21	1.11	1.34	1.25	1.30

	Window curtains			Plates		
	1600–49	*1650–99*	*1700–49*	*1600–49*	*1650–99*	*1700–49*
r^2	0.24	0.32	0.25	0.44	0.50	0.30
URBAN	2.93	2.69	3.12	–	1.75	–
SERVICE	–	3.81	–	–	–	–
RETAIL	–	–	–	–	–	–
MARITIME	–	–	–	–	–	13.36
AG34ONLY	–	0.28	0.36	–	0.25	–
AG34COMB	–	0.37	0.36	0.40	0.34	–
WEALTH50	–	–	1.09	–	1.32	–
GENT	4.43	2.31	–	4.94	4.29	–
HUSB	–	–	–	–	–	–
NROOMS	1.25	1.30	1.21	1.51	1.41	1.53

	Knives and forks		Hot drinks	Saucepans	
	1650–99	*1700–49*	*1700–49*	*1650–99*	*1700–49*
r^2	0.28	0.11	0.26	0.18	0.24
URBAN	–	–	4.30	–	3.83
SERVICE	12.62	–	5.82	4.15	–
RETAIL	–	–	2.66	–	–
MARITIME	–	–	–	4.79	2.20
AG34ONLY	–	–	–	–	–
AG34COMB	–	–	–	–	0.37
WEALTH50	–	–	1.10	–	1.09
GENT	4.45	–	–	–	–
HUSB	–	–	–	–	–
NROOMS	1.22	1.16	1.13	1.19	1.14

Table A5.3 Exp(β) statistics from logistic regression equations predicting the presence of production for use in Cornwall

Variable	Milling			Food preservation		
	1600–49	*1650–99*	*1700–49*	*1600–49*	*1650–99*	*1700–49*
r^2	0.19	0.14	0.17	0.28	0.12	0.17
URBAN	–	–	–	0.68	–	0.49
SERVICE	–	–	–	–	–	–
RETAIL	–	–	–	4.62	–	3.01
MARITIME	–	–	–	–	–	2.67
AG34ONLY	–	–	–	4.67	3.25	3.67
AG34COMB	8.76	–	–	6.95	3.45	4.53
AG12	–	–	–	3.35	2.56	2.29
WEALTH50	–	–	1.35	2.00	1.15	1.21
GENT	3.56	6.82	–	0.30	–	–
HUSB	–	–	–	–	1.80	2.04

	Baking			Dairying		
	1600–49	*1650–99*	*1700–49*	*1600–49*	*1650–99*	*1700–49*
r^2	0.12	0.07	0.12	0.46	0.46	0.52
URBAN	–	–	–	–	–	–
SERVICE	–	–	–	–	–	–
RETAIL	–	–	–	7.03	–	–
MARITIME	–	–	–	–	–	–
AG34ONLY	–	–	–	177.46	140.68	223.14
AG34COMB	7.02	–	–	34.74	53.34	99.86
AG12	6.32	–	–	20.76	32.78	103.61
WEALTH50	1.14	–	–	0.77	–	–
GENT	–	–	–	–	–	–
HUSB	–	–	–	–	–	–

	Alcohol		
	1600–49	*1650–99*	*1700–49*
r^2	0.20	0.11	0.13
URBAN	–	–	0.64
SERVICE	–	–	–
RETAIL	–	–	–
MARITIME	3.28	–	–
AG34ONLY	2.72	2.70	2.59
AG34COMB	3.86	2.89	3.27
AG12	2.80	1.72	1.86
WEALTH50	1.63	1.26	1.27
GENT	–	–	–
HUSB	–	2.36	–

Table A5.4 Exp(β) statistics from logistic regression equations predicting the presence of production for use in Kent

Variable	Milling			Food preservation		
	1600–49	1650–99	1700–49	1600–49	1650–99	1700–49
r^2	0.12	0.21	0.14	0.13	0.25	0.20
URBAN	0.66	–	–	0.44	0.39	–
SERVICE	–	3.73	–	–	–	–
RETAIL	–	2.22	3.27	–	–	–
MARITIME	–	–	–	–	–	–
AG34ONLY	1.99	–	–	–	–	–
AG34COMB	2.22	6.74	–	2.56	4.30	–
AG12	–	–	–	–	3.02	–
WEALTH50	–	–	–	–	–	–
GENT	–	–	–	–	0.25	–
HUSB	–	–	–	–	–	–
NROOMS	1.12	1.13	–	1.20	1.38	1.33

	Baking			Dairying		
	1600–49	1650–99	1700–49	1600–49	1650–99	1700–49
r^2	0.14	0.09	0.04	0.30	0.47	0.52
URBAN	–	–	–	0.57	–	0.54
SERVICE	–	–	–	–	–	–
RETAIL	–	–	–	–	–	–
MARITIME	–	–	–	–	–	–
AG34ONLY	–	–	–	28.56	157.19	131.70
AG34COMB	–	–	–	3.30	2.71	6.00
AG12	–	–	–	3.72	5.76	10.38
WEALTH50	–	–	–	0.86	0.89	0.72
GENT	0.45	–	–	–	–	–
HUSB	–	–	–	–	–	–
NROOMS	1.19	1.17	1.12	–	–	–

	Alcohol		
	1600–49	1650–99	1700–49
r^2	0.26	0.27	0.14
URBAN	–	–	–
SERVICE	–	–	–
RETAIL	0.09	0.14	0.20
MARITIME	–	2.30	–
AG34ONLY	–	2.62	–
AG34COMB	–	2.28	–
AG12	–	–	–
WEALTH50	1.29	1.19	1.25
GENT	–	–	–
HUSB	–	–	–
NROOMS	1.24	1.24	–

Notes

1 Household economies and economic development in early modern England

1 M. Overton, *Agricultural revolution in England: the transformation of the agrarian economy 1500–1850*, Cambridge: Cambridge University Press, 1996, p. 22; more generally see R. Britnell, *The commercialisation of English society 1000–1500*, Cambridge: Cambridge University Press, 1993.

2 The historiography of the family is usefully reviewed in K. Wrightson, 'The family in early modern England: continuity and change', in S. Taylor, R. Connors and C. Jones (eds) *Hanoverian Britain and empire: essays in memory of Philip Lawson*, Woodbridge: Boydell Press, 1998, pp. 1–22; N. Tadmor, *Family and friends in eighteenth-century England: household, kinship and patronage*, Cambridge: Cambridge University Press, 2001, pp. 1–9; P. Collinson, *The birthpangs of Protestant England: religious and cultural change in the sixteenth and seventeenth centuries*, Basingstoke: Macmillan, 1988, pp. 60–93; and A. Knotter, 'Problems of the "family economy", peasant economy, domestic production and labour markets in pre-industrial Europe', in M. Prak (ed.) *Early modern capitalism: economic and social change in Europe, 1400–1800*, London: Routledge, 2001, pp. 135–60.

3 Tadmor, *Family and friends*, p. 272; J. Schlumbohm, 'Labour in proto-industrialization: big questions and micro-answers', in M. Prak (ed.) *Early modern capitalism: economic and social change in Europe, 1400–1800*, London: Routledge, 2001, pp. 125–34.

4 The household economy is touched on by C. Muldrew, *The economy of obligation: the culture of credit and social relations in early modern England*, Basingstoke: Palgrave, 1998, pp. 157–8; in discussions of 'proto-industrialization', for example, P. Hudson, 'Proto-industrialization in England', in S. Ogilvie and M. Cerman (eds) *European proto-industrialization*, Cambridge: Cambridge University Press, 1996, pp. 57–8; and more thoroughly in K. Wrightson, *Earthly necessities: economic lives in early modern Britain*, New Haven, Conn.: Yale University Press, 2000, pp. 30–68.

5 A. Smith, *The wealth of nations*, ed. E. Cannan, Chicago, Ill.: University of Chicago Press, 1976.

6 K. Marx, *Capital*, Moscow: Progress Publishers, 3 vols, 1954–9; and K. Marx, *Pre-Capitalist economic formations*, London: Lawrence and Wishart, 1964.

7 M. Weber, *The protestant ethic and the spirit of capitalism*, ed. S. Kalberg, Los Angeles, Calif.: Roxbury Publishing, 2002.

8 The best introduction is still E.R. Wolf, *Peasants*, Englewood Cliffs, N.J.: Prentice-Hall, 1966.

9 A.V. Chayanov, *On the theory of peasant economy*, eds D. Thorner, B. Kerblay and R.E.F. Smith, Madison: University of Wisconsin Press, 1986.

10 J.C. Scott, *The moral economy of the peasant*, New Haven, Conn.: Yale University Press, 1976, pp. 4–5.

11 A. Macfarlane, *The origins of English individualism: the family, property and social transition*, Oxford: Basil Blackwell, 1978. See, for instance, F. Cancian, 'Economic behaviour in peasant communities', in S. Plattner (ed.) *Economic anthropology*, Stanford, Calif.: Stanford University Press, 1989, pp. 127–70; P.C.C. Huang, *The peasant family and rural development in the Yangzi Delta, 1350–1988*, Stanford, Calif.: Stanford University Press, 1990; T. Scott (ed.) *The peasantries of Europe from the fourteenth to the eighteenth centuries*, London: Longman, 1998.

12 E.A. Wrigley, 'Urban growth and agricultural change: England and the continent in the early modern period', *Journal of Interdisciplinary History* 15, 1985, p. 700.

13 S.C. Ogilvie and M. Cerman, 'The theories of proto-industrialization', in Ogilvie and Cerman (eds) *European proto-industrialization*, p. 1. The theory is clearly set out in F.F. Mendels, 'Proto-industrialization: theory and reality. General report', *Eighth International Economic History Congress. 'A' Themes*, Budapest: Akadémiai Kiadó, 1982, pp. 69–107, and critically reviewed by L.A. Clarkson, *Proto-industrialization: the first phase of industrialization?* Basingstoke: Macmillan, 1985. Debate and modification of the concept continues, for example, Schlumbohm, 'Labour in proto-industrialization'.

14 For a pioneering exploration of these issues, unencumbered by the concept of proto-industrialisation, see J. Thirsk, 'Industries in the countryside', in F.J. Fisher (ed.) *Essays in the economic and social history of Tudor and Stuart England, in honour of R.H. Tawney*, Cambridge: Cambridge University Press, 1961, pp. 70–88.

15 For instance see F. Ellis, *Peasant economics: farm households and agrarian development*, Cambridge: Cambridge University Press, 1988, pp. 165–85.

16 A. Clark, *Working life of women in the seventeenth century* (3rd edn), ed. A.L. Erickson, London: Routledge, 1992.

17 L. Tilly and J. Scott, *Women, work, and family*, London: Holt, Rinehart and Winston, 1978.

18 These tasks are often labelled 'social reproduction'. This term has been avoided here due to the definitional confusion it brings.

19 J. Whittle, 'The gender division of labour: the skills and work of women in rural households, England 1450–1650', unpublished MSS.

20 J. de Vries, 'Between purchasing power and the world of goods: understanding the household economy in early modern Europe', in J. Brewer and R. Porter (eds) *Consumption and the world of goods*, London: Routledge, 1993, p. 119.

21 Ibid., n. 65, p. 126; see also J. de Vries, 'The industrial revolution and the industrious revolution', *Journal of Economic History* 54, 1994, 249–70.

22 De Vries, 'Between purchasing power and the world of goods', p. 108.

23 Ibid., pp. 112–13; J. Thirsk, *Economic policy and projects: the development of a consumer society in early modern England*, Oxford: Clarendon Press, 1978.

24 De Vries, 'Between purchasing power and the world of goods', p. 108.

25 Ibid., p. 114.

26 See particularly J. de Vries 'Peasant demand patterns and economic development: Friesland 1550–1750' in W.N. Parker and E.L. Jones (eds) *European peasants and their markets: essays in agrarian economic history*, Princeton, N.J.: Princeton University Press, 1975, pp. 205–66.

27 For changes in production see Thirsk, *Economic policy and projects*, and

J. Thirsk, *England's agricultural regions and agrarian history, 1500–1750*, London: Macmillan, 1987; for changes in consumption see L. Weatherill, *Consumer behaviour and material culture in Britain 1660–1760*, London: Routledge, 1988, and C. Shammas, *The pre-industrial consumer in England and America*, Oxford: Clarendon Press, 1990.

28 Shammas, like Everitt, found a noticeable decline in livestock ownership by poorer households in this period: Shammas, *Pre-industrial consumer*, p. 292; A.M. Everitt, 'Farm labourers', in J. Thirsk (ed.) *The agrarian history of England and Wales vol. IV, 1500–1640*, Cambridge: Cambridge University Press, 1967, pp. 396–465.

29 S. Pennell, 'Consumption and consumerism in early modern England', *The Historical Journal* 42, 1999, 549–64; P. Glennie, 'Consumption within historical studies', in D. Miller (ed.) *Acknowledging consumption: a review of new studies*, London: Routledge, 1995, pp. 164–203.

30 D. Miller, 'Consumption as the vanguard of history: a polemic by way of introduction', in Miller (ed.) *Acknowledging consumption*, pp. 30–4; B. Fine and E. Leopold, *The world of consumption*, London: Routledge, 1993.

31 R. Bocock, *Consumption*, London: Routledge, 1993, p. 3.

32 N. McKendrick, 'The consumer revolution of eighteenth-century England', in N. McKendrick, J. Brewer and J.H. Plumb, *The birth of a consumer society: the commercialization of eighteenth-century England*, London: Hutchinson, 1983, p. 11.

33 Glennie, 'Consumption within historical studies', p. 164.

34 Shammas *Pre-industrial consumer*, pp. 291, 294; de Vries, 'Between purchasing power and the world of goods', p. 107.

35 In particular see Weatherill, *Consumer behaviour and material culture* and Shammas, *Pre-industrial consumer*.

36 M. Overton, 'Prices from probate inventories', in T. Arkell, N. Evans and N. Goose (eds) *When death do us part: understanding and interpreting the probate records of early modern England*, Oxford: Leopard's Head Press, 2000, pp. 120–43; C. Shammas, 'The decline of textile prices in England and British America prior to industrialisation', *Economic History Review*, 2nd series 47, 1994, 483–507.

37 P. Langford, *A polite and commercial people: England 1727–1783*, Oxford: Oxford University Press, 1989, p. 67; McKendrick, 'The consumer revolution of eighteenth-century England'.

38 See, for example, H.R. French, '"Ingenious & learned gentlemen" – social perceptions and self-fashioning among parish elites in Essex, 1680–1740', *Social History* 25, 2000, 44–66.

39 P. Bourdieu, *La distinction: critique sociale du jugement*, Paris: Les Editions de Minuit, 1979; see the discussion by A. Vickery, 'Women and the world of goods: a Lancashire consumer and her possessions, 1751–81', in Brewer and Porter (eds) *Consumption and the world of goods*, p. 278.

40 D. Roche, *A history of everyday things: the birth of consumption in France*, Cambridge: Cambridge University Press, 2000, pp. 1–8.

41 M. Douglas and B. Isherwood, *The world of goods: towards an anthropology of consumption*, London: Routledge, 1996, pp. 48–9; a striking definition is that material culture should study, 'the imaginative act by which people fuse their surroundings into a meaningful whole', D. Upton, 'Form and user: style, mode, fashion, and the artifact', in G.L. Pocius (ed.) *Living in a material world: Canadian and American approaches to material culture*, St John's, Newfoundland: Institute of Social and Economic Research, 1991, pp. 158–9. For a good example of an historical study that ascribes meanings to contemporary objects see, H.C. Dibbits, 'Between society and family values: the linen cupboard in

early-modern households', in A. Schuurman and P. Spierenburg (eds) *Private domain, public inquiry: families and life-styles in the Netherlands and Europe, 1550 to the present*, Hilversum: Verloren, 1996, pp. 125–45.

42 M. Quennell and C. Quennell, *A history of everyday things in England*, vol. 1, London: Batsford, 1918, p. v. This is the first of a series of books by the Quennells which cover the period 1066–1968.

43 For example, G. Jekyll, *Old English household life: some account of cottage objects and country folk*, London: Batsford, 1925; C. Hole, *English home life 1500 to 1800*, London: Batsford, 1947; L. Wright, *Warm and snug: the history of the bed*, London: Routledge & Kegan Paul, 1962; D. Hartley, *Made in England*, London: Methuen, 1939; J. Seymour, *Forgotten household crafts*, London: Dorling Kindersley, 1987.

44 F. Braudel, *Civilisation matérielle et capitalisme (15–18 siècle)*, vol. 1, Paris: Librairie Armand Colin, 1967.

45 Weatherill, *Consumer behaviour and material culture*. The other study, Shammas, *Pre-industrial consumer*, takes an economic approach.

46 Our usage of these terms follows A. Sayer, *Method in social science: a realist approach* (2nd edn), London: Routledge, 1992, pp. 241–51.

47 Thirsk, *Economic policy and projects*.

48 Pennell, 'Consumption and consumerism in early modern England'.

49 C. Campbell, *The romantic ethic and the spirit of modern consumerism*, Oxford: Blackwell, 1987.

50 C. Campbell, 'The sociology of consumption', in Miller (ed.) *Acknowledging consumption*, pp. 96–126.

51 Strictly speaking, of course, inventories refer to individuals not households; see pp. 27–8.

52 Though there are some important studies, for example, D.G. Hey, 'A dual economy in south Yorkshire', *Agricultural History Review* 17, 1969, 108–19; P. Frost, 'Yeomen and metalsmiths: livestock in the dual economy in south Staffordshire, 1560–1720', *Agricultural History Review* 29, 1981, 29–41; G.F.R. Spenceley, 'The origins of the English pillow lace industry', *Agricultural History Review* 21, 1973, 81–93.

53 For a similar plea for a wider understanding of work, see R.E. Pahl, *Divisions of labour*, Oxford: Basil Blackwell, 1984.

54 J. Boulton, 'London 1540–1700', in P. Clark (ed.) *The Cambridge urban history of Britain, vol. II 1540–1840*, Cambridge: Cambridge University Press, 2000, p. 316; L. Schwarz, 'London 1700–1840', in Clark (ed.) *Cambridge urban history*, p. 650; P. Brandon and B. Short, *The South East from AD 1000*, London: Longman, 1990, pp. 153–237; B.M. Short, 'The de-industrialisation process: a case study of the Weald, 1600–1850', in P. Hudson (ed.) *Regions and industries. A perspective on the Industrial Revolution in Britain*, Cambridge: Cambridge University Press, 1989, pp. 156–74.

55 T.S. Willan, *The English coasting trade, 1600–1750*, Manchester: Manchester University Press, 1938, pp. 203–5; C.W. Chalkin, *Seventeenth-century Kent: a social and economic history*, London: Longman, 1965, pp. 160–88; A.J.F. Dulley, 'People and homes in the Medway towns: 1687–1783', *Archæologia Cantiana* 77, 1963, 160–76.

56 D. Ormrod, 'Industry, 1640–1800', in A. Armstrong (ed.) *The economy of Kent 1640–1914*, Woodbridge: Boydell Press, 1995, p. 105.

57 J. Barry, 'Population distribution and growth in the early modern period', in R. Kain and W. Ravenhill (eds) *Historical atlas of south-west England*, Exeter: University of Exeter Press, 1999, p. 117.

58 D.H. Cullum, 'Society and economy in west Cornwall, c.1588–1750', Unpublished Ph.D. thesis, University of Exeter, 1993, pp. 32, 146.

59 C.W. Chalklin, 'South-east', in Clark (ed.) *Cambridge urban history*, p. 58; J. Barry, 'South-west', in Clark (ed.) *Cambridge urban history*, pp. 71, 76.

60 P. Glennie and I. Whyte, 'Towns in an agrarian economy 1540–1700', in Clark (ed.) *Cambridge urban history*, pp. 188–9.

61 M. Stoyle, *West Britons: Cornish identities and the early modern British state*, Exeter: University of Exeter Press, 2002, p. 1.

2 Probate inventories

1 There is an extensive literature on probate inventories. One of the best introductions is J. Cox and N. Cox, 'Probate 1500–1800: a system in transition', in T. Arkell, N. Evans and N. Goose (eds) *When death do us part: understanding and interpreting the probate records of early modern England*, Oxford: Leopard's Head Press, 2000, pp. 14–37; see also J.S. Moore, 'Probate inventories: problems and prospects', in P. Riden (ed.) *Probate records and the local community*, Gloucester: Sutton, 1985, pp. 11–28; a rather dated bibliography is M. Overton, *Bibliography of British probate inventories*, Newcastle upon Tyne: University of Newcastle Department of Geography, 1983. There are many printed collections of inventories: one of the most useful, because it contains transcriptions of wills and probate accounts as well as inventories, is P. Wyatt (ed.), *The Uffculme wills and inventories*, Devon and Cornwall Record Society, new series 40, 1997; while the introduction to F.W. Steer (ed.), *Farm and cottage inventories of mid-Essex 1635–1749*, Essex Record Office Publications, No. 8, 1950, pp. 8–51, provides the best description of the likely contents of a collection of inventories.

2 T. Arkell, 'Interpreting probate inventories', in Arkell, Evans and Goose (eds) *When death do us part*, pp. 72–102, reviews a large number of studies using probate inventories. He does not mention some of the studies of North American inventories, for example, L.G. Carr and L.S. Walsh, 'Changing lifestyles and consumer behavior in the Colonial Chesapeake', in C. Carson, R. Hoffman and P.J. Albert (eds) *Of consuming interests: the style of life in the eighteenth century*, Charlottesville: University Press of Virginia, 1994, pp. 59–166, and M.C. Beaudry, 'Words for things: linguistic analysis of probate inventories', in M.C. Beaudry (ed.) *Documentary archaeology in the New World*, Cambridge: Cambridge University Press, 1988, pp. 43–50.

3 Moore, 'Probate inventories', pp. 16–17. Arkell, 'Interpreting probate inventories', p. 72, thinks 'one million or so' survive.

4 M. Johnson, *Housing culture: traditional architecture in an English landscape*, London: UCL Press, 1993, pp. 84–6, 95–6, attempts to trace the path of the appraisers through the house.

5 For probate courts, see A. Tarver, *Church court records: an introduction for family and local historians*, Chichester: Phillimore, 1995, 56–81; R.A. Marchant, *The church under the law*, Cambridge: Cambridge University Press, 1969.

6 21 Hen. VIII, c.5.

7 One of the best known texts is R. Burn, *Ecclesiastical law*, 2 vols, London, 1763, II, pp. 644–54.

8 See pp. 138–41. However, using wills and probate accounts in conjunction with inventories can overcome these problems to a certain extent: M. Overton and D. Dean, 'Wealth, indebtedness, consumption and the life-cycle in early modern England', forthcoming. Some North American inventories include real estate.

9 Burn, *Ecclesiastical law*, I, pp. 647–8.

10 M. Spufford, 'The limitations of the probate inventory', in J. Chartres and D. Hey (eds) *English rural society, 1500–1800: essays in honour of Joan Thirsk*,

Cambridge: Cambridge University Press, 1990, pp. 139–74; Cox and Cox, 'Probate 1500–1800'.

11 L.C. Orlin, 'Fictions of the early modern English probate inventory', in H.S. Turner (ed.) *The culture of capital: property, cities, and knowledge in early modern England*, London: Routledge, 2002, pp. 51–83, lists 12 ways in which the goods in an inventory might differ from the goods owned by an individual just before death. This is undoubtedly correct, or at least logically possible, but is not much help if we do not know how common they were.

12 See pp. 121–2.

13 A.L. Erickson, *Women and property in early modern England*, London: Routledge, 1993, pp. 33–4.

14 The inventories Richard Turner of Smarden and Ann Carley of Biddenden in Kent name the individuals to whom items were sold (Centre for Kentish Studies (CKS) 11.50.87 1686 and 11.61.29 1698), as is the case in Cornwall with the inventory of John Pascoe of Luxulyan, administered by Stephen Hoskyn in 1703 (Cornwall Record Office (CRO) P2128 1703).

15 Examples are given in D.G. Vaisey (ed.), *Probate inventories of Lichfield and district 1568–1680*, Collections for a history of Staffordshire, fourth series, vol. V, Staffordshire Record Society, 1969, pp. 3–4.

16 M.W. Farr (ed.), 'Nicholas Eyffeler of Warwick, Glazier: executors' accounts and other documents concerning the foundation of his almshouse charity, 1592–1621', in R. Brearman (ed.) *Miscellany I*, Publications of the Dugdale Society, vol. XXXI, 1977, pp. 29–110.

17 CRO H1032 1640.

18 CKS 11.21.65 1663.

19 CKS 11.36.16 1674; See also U. Priestley and P.J. Corfield, 'Rooms and room use in Norwich housing, 1580–1730', *Post-Medieval Archaeology* 16, 1982, p. 95.

20 CKS 11.28.124 1666 and 11.28.123 1667.

21 Erickson, *Women and property*, pp. 26, 145–6; Burn, *Ecclesiastical law*, II, pp. 649–52.

22 CRO C1255 1662.

23 Cox and Cox, 'Probate 1500–1800', p. 25.

24 Logistic regression is considered on pp. 145–7.

25 CKS 11.80.239 1735.

26 M. Overton, 'Prices from probate inventories' in Arkell, Evans and Goose (eds) *When death do us part*, pp. 120–43.

27 M. Overton, 'Computer analysis of an inconsistent data source: the case of probate inventories', *Journal of Historical Geography* 3, 1977, 317–26.

28 For an agricultural example, see M. Overton, 'English probate inventories and the measurement of agricultural change', *A.A.G. Bijdgragen* 23, 1980, p. 211.

29 The software has been under development since 1972. It started as a series of FORTRAN programs, but the most recent version, written by Mark Allen, is in C++ and runs on a PC under a Windows environment. For a more technical description see M. Overton, 'Computer analysis of probate inventories: from portable micro to mainframe', in D. Hopkin and P. Denley (eds) *History and computing*, Manchester: Manchester University Press, 1987, pp. 96–104; M. Overton, 'Computer standardization of probate inventories', in J.-P. Genet (ed.) *Standardisation et échange des bases de données historiques*, Paris: CNRS, 1988, pp. 145–51; and M. Overton, 'A computer management system for probate inventories', *History and Computing* 8, 1995, 10–17.

30 The programs do set limits to the number of items that can be assigned, and to other aspects of the program, but they have yet to be exceeded in practice.

31 M. Overton, 'Probate inventories and the reconstruction of agrarian land-scapes', in M. Reed (ed.) *Discovering past landscapes*, London: Croom Helm, 1984, pp. 167–94; Overton, 'English probate inventories and the measurement of agricultural change'.

32 Overton, 'Probate inventories and the reconstruction of agrarian landscapes', pp. 173–4.

33 In Cornwall the occupation or status was also taken from the will since wills and inventories are filed together.

34 C.W. Chalklin, *Seventeenth-century Kent: a social and economic history*, London: Longman, 1965, p. 191; A. Duffin, *Faction and faith: politics and religion of the Cornish gentry before the Civil War*, Exeter: University of Exeter Press, 1996, p. 15.

35 The Consistory Court of Canterbury in Kent, and in Cornwall the Consistory Court and the Principal Registry of the Bishop of Exeter.

36 See p. 36.

37 For example CKS 11.40.99 1678.

38 T.L. Stoate (ed.), *Cornwall hearth and poll taxes 1660–1664: direct taxation in Cornwall in the reign of Charles II*, Almondsbury: T.L. Stoate, 1981, p. xv; D. Harrington (ed.), *Kent Hearth Tax assessment Lady Day 1664*, British Record Society Hearth Tax Series vol. II, Kent Archaeological Society Kent Records vol. XXIX, London: British Record Society, 2000.

39 C. Husbands, 'Hearths, wealth and occupations: an exploration of the hearth tax in the later seventeenth century', in K. Schurer and T. Arkell (eds) *Surveying the people*, Oxford: Leopard's Head Press, 1992, pp. 70–1.

40 See pp. 29–31, and Appendix 1.

41 H.R. French, 'Social status, localism and the "middle sort of people" in England 1620–1750', *Past & Present* no. 166, 2000, pp. 90–3.

42 Those exempt from the tax on grounds of poverty were supposed to be those who did not contribute to church or poor rates because they were poor, and tenants living in houses worth less than 20 shillings a year, unless they owned land, tenements or goods valued at £10 or more. S. Pearson, 'Kent Hearth Tax records: context and analysis', in Harrington, *Kent Hearth Tax*, pp. xlix–liii.

43 χ^2 tests for both Cornwall and Kent indicate a probability of greater than 99 per cent that the observed distribution of inventories does not match the expected distribution given the distribution of hearths.

44 For Kent as a whole 32 per cent of households were exempt from the 1664 Hearth Tax on grounds of poverty; T. Arkell, 'The incidence of poverty in England in the later seventeenth century', *Social History* 12, 1987, 23–47.

45 If Consistory court inventories and those from the Prerogative court were included the richest 10 per cent would be included.

46 J. Kent, 'The rural "middling sort" in early modern England, circa 1640–1740: some economic, political and socio-cultural characteristics', *Rural History* 10, 1999, p. 24.

47 H.R. French, 'Social status, localism and the "middle sort of people"', pp. 66–99.

48 K. Wrightson, *Earthly necessities: economic lives in early modern Britain*, New Haven, Conn.: Yale University Press, 2000, p. 290. See also J. Barry and C. Brooks (eds), *The middling sort of people: culture, society and politics in England, 1500–1800*, Basingstoke: Macmillan, 1994.

49 These are discussed by R. Wall, 'Regional and temporal variations in English household structure from 1650', in J. Hobcraft and P. Rees (eds) *Regional demographic development*, London: Croom Helm, 1977, pp. 89–113, and K. Schurer, 'Variations in household structure in the late seventeenth century:

towards a regional analysis', in Schurer and Arkell (eds) *Surveying the people*, pp. 253–78.

50 See p. 81. The majority of the Cornish inventories cannot be used to analyse room use, see below pp. 122–3.

51 Dean and Overton, 'Wealth, indebtedness, consumption and the lifecycle in early modern England', this was achieved by matching inventories to accounts, wills, and parish registers to reveal the ages of the deceased and his or her offspring.

52 CKS 11.45.268 1681 and 11.49.175 1685/6.

53 Harrington, *Kent Hearth Tax*, p. 343.

54 CKS 11.43.131 1680.

55 See pp. 84–6 for further discussion of similar inventories.

56 R.M. Glencross (ed.), *Calendar of wills, administrations and accounts relating to the counties of Cornwall and Devon in the Connotorial Archidiaconal Court of Cornwall*, British Record Society Index Library, *Part I 1569–1699*, London, 1929, and *Part II 1700–1799*, London, 1932. The Cornwall Record Office has indexes to its probate records by surname, parish and occupation.

57 E.A. Fry (ed.), *Calendars of wills and administrations relating to the counties of Devon and Cornwall, proved in the Court of the Principal Registry of the Bishop of Exeter, 1559–1799; and of Devon only, proved in the Court of the Archdeaconry of Exeter, 1540–1799: all now preserved in the Probate Registry at Exeter*, London: British Record Society, 1908; E.A. Fry (ed.), *Calendar of the wills and administrations relating to the counties of Devon and Cornwall proved in the Consistory Court of the Bishop of Exeter 1532–1800*, London: British Record Society, 1914. The geography of the courts can be found in, C.R. Humphery-Smith (ed.), *The Phillimore atlas and index of parish registers*, 2nd edn, Chichester: Phillimore, 1995.

58 PRO PROB 4/5710 St Erth 1676, PROB 4/20554 Boyton 1681 and PROB 4/9529 Poughill 1699.

59 CKS PRC 10 and PRC 11. The Papers have been indexed by name, place, date and occupation. The Registers are indexed only up to 1587.

60 PRO PROB3, PROB4 and PROB5.

61 These sampling concepts are discussed in W.G. Cochran, *Sampling techniques*, London: Wiley, 1963, pp. 1–6.

62 Overton, 'Prices from probate inventories', pp. 125–6.

3 Household production

1 P. Glennie, *'Distinguishing men's trades': occupation sources and debates from pre-census England*, Historical Geography Research Series No. 25, 1990.

2 D. Cressy, *Literacy and the social order: reading and writing in Tudor and Stuart England*, Cambridge: Cambridge University Press, 1980, pp. 124–7.

3 C.G.A. Clay, *Economic expansion and social change: England 1500–1700, vol. II, industry, trade and government*, Cambridge: Cambridge University Press, 1984, pp. 100–2; R.E. Pahl, *Divisions of labour*, Oxford: Basil Blackwell, 1984, pp. 46–8.

4 J. Patten, 'Changing occupational structures in the East Anglian countryside, 1500–1700', in H.S.A. Fox and R.A. Butlin (eds) *Change in the countryside: essays on rural England, 1500–1900*, London: Institute of British Geographers, 1979, pp. 103–21.

5 CRO G471 1640.

6 J.H. Andrews, 'The Thanet seaports, 1650–1750', in M. Roake and J. Whyman (eds) *Essays in Kentish history*, London: Cass, 1973, pp. 119–26.

7 T. Gray (ed.), *Early-Stuart mariners and shipping: the maritime surveys of Devon and*

Cornwall, 1619–35, Exeter: Devon and Cornwall Record Society 33, 1990, pp. xviii–xxiii; J. Whetter, *Cornwall in the 17th century: an economic history of Kernow*, Padstow: Lodenek Press, 1974, pp. 99–100.

8 See pp. 116–17.

9 A.M. Everitt, 'The making of the agrarian landscape of Kent', *Archæologia Cantiana* 92, 1976, p. 27.

10 For consistency and to enable comparison, most of the tables in the book show data grouped into 30-year periods, reflecting a trade-off between short periods necessary to show change over short periods of time, and the need for a sufficient number of inventories within each period. When the number of available inventories is small 50-year periods are used.

11 G. Mingay, 'Agriculture', in A. Armstrong (ed.) *The economy of Kent 1640–1914*, Woodbridge: Boydell Press, 1995, p. 53.

12 As defined by J. Thirsk, 'Agriculture in Kent, 1540–1640', in M. Zell (ed.) *Early modern Kent, 1540–1640*, Woodbridge: Boydell Press, 2000, pp. 75–103.

13 R. Blome, *Britannia: or a geographical description of the kingdoms of England, Scotland and Ireland*, London, 1673, p. 59; G.V. Harrison, 'The south-west: Dorset, Somerset, Devon and Cornwall', in J. Thirsk (ed.) *The agrarian history of England and Wales vol. V, 1640–1750. I. Regional farming systems*, Cambridge: Cambridge University Press, 1984, p. 360.

14 M. Overton, 'English probate inventories and the measurement of agricultural change', *A.A.G. Bijdgragen* 23, 1980, 205–15; M. Overton, 'Probate inventories and the reconstruction of agrarian landscapes', in M. Reed (ed.) *Discovering past landscapes*, London: Croom Helm, 1984, pp. 167–94; M. Overton, *Agricultural revolution in England: the transformation of the agrarian economy 1500–1850*, Cambridge: Cambridge University Press, 1996, pp. 94–5.

15 Whetter, *Cornwall in the 17th century*, p. 25.

16 D.H. Cullum, 'Society and economy in west Cornwall, *c.*1588–1750', Unpublished Ph.D. thesis, University of Exeter, 1993, pp. 278–9.

17 N.J.G. Pounds, 'The population of Cornwall before the first census', in W.E. Minchinton (ed.) *Population and marketing: two studies in the history of the south-west*, Exeter: University of Exeter, 1976, pp. 11–30; J. Barry, 'Population distribution and growth in the early modern period', in R. Kain and W. Ravenhill (eds) *Historical atlas of south-west England*, Exeter: University of Exeter Press, 1999, pp. 110–18.

18 J. Whetter, 'Cornish trade in the seventeenth century: an analysis of the port books', *Journal of the Royal Institution of Cornwall*, new series 4, 1964, p. 403.

19 W. Marshall, *The review and abstract of the county reports to the Board of Agriculture*, 5 vols, York, 1818, vol. 5, p. 413; Everitt, 'Making of the agrarian landscape of Kent', pp. 5–6; P. Brandon and B. Short, *The South East from AD 1000*, London: Longman, 1990, p. 6; B.M. Short, 'The south-east: Kent, Surrey and Sussex', in Thirsk (ed.) *The agrarian history of England and Wales vol. V*, pp. 270–313.

20 C.W. Chalklin, *Seventeenth-century Kent: a social and economic history*, London: Longman, 1965, pp. 64–5.

21 S. Hipkin, 'Tenant farming and short-term leasing on Romney Marsh, 1587–1705', *Economic History Review*, 2nd series 53, 2000, 646–76.

22 J. Thirsk, 'The farming regions of England', in J. Thirsk (ed.) *The agrarian history of England and Wales vol. IV, 1500–1640*, Cambridge: Cambridge University Press, 1967, pp. 55–64, 71–80; Harrison, 'The south-west', pp. 358–89; Whetter, *Cornwall in the 17th century*, pp. 21–58; Chalklin, *Seventeenth-century Kent*, pp. 73–109; Thirsk, 'Agriculture in Kent, 1540–1640'; Mingay, 'Agriculture'; D. Baker, 'Agricultural prices, production and marketing with special reference to the hop industry: north-east Kent, 1680–1760', Ph.D. thesis, University of Kent, 1976; subsequently published in facsimile, New York: Garland,

1985; see also D. Baker, 'The marketing of corn in the first half of the eighteenth century: north-east Kent', *Agricultural History Review* 18, 1970, 126–50.

23 M. Overton and B.M.S. Campbell, 'Norfolk livestock farming 1250–1740: a comparative study of manorial accounts and probate inventories', *Journal of Historical Geography* 18, 1992, p. 380.

24 These are statute acres. On the assumption that customary acres were used in the inventories, Cornish acreage figures have been multiplied by 1.19 and those for Kent by 0.94. R.E. Zupko, *A dictionary of weights and measures for the British Isles: the Middle Ages to the twentieth century*, Philadelphia, Pa.: American Philosophical Society, 1985, pp. 6–7.

25 Chalklin, *Seventeenth-century Kent*, p. 82.

26 Overton, *Agricultural revolution*, pp. 103–5.

27 Chalklin, *Seventeenth-century Kent*, pp. 86–7.

28 J. Lewis, *The History and antiquities, ecclesiastical and civil, of the Isle of Tenet in Kent*, London, 1723, pp. 8–12.

29 This is roughly the same as the proportion so doing in Norfolk and Suffolk in the early eighteenth century: M. Overton, 'The diffusion of agricultural innovations in early modern England: turnips and clover in Norfolk and Suffolk, 1580–1740', *Transactions of the Institute of British Geographers*, new series 10, 1985, pp. 205–21.

30 Whetter, *Cornwall in the 17th century*, pp. 29–30.

31 M. Overton, 'The 1801 crop returns for Cornwall', in M. Havinden (ed.) *Husbandry and marketing in the south-west*, Exeter Papers in Economic History, no. 8, 1973, p. 44.

32 Harrison, 'The south-west', pp. 375–8.

33 Chalklin, *Seventeenth-century Kent*, pp. 99–101.

34 Whetter, *Cornwall in the 17th century*, pp. 33–4; Cullum, 'Society and economy in West Cornwall', p. 279.

35 Everitt, 'Making of the agrarian landscape of Kent', pp. 17–18.

36 These figures are for all inventories, not just those of farmers.

37 By the late 1720s, reports to the Treasury Board suggested that about one-third of the English hop acreage lay in Kent, producing an average annual output of just over 2,500 tons. Chalklin, *Seventeenth-century Kent*, pp. 108–9; Mingay, 'Agriculture', p. 63; Baker, 'Agricultural prices, production and marketing', pp. 704–9.

38 Baker, 'Agricultural prices, production and marketing', p. 571.

39 E. Melling, *Kentish sources III: aspects of agriculture and industry*, Maidstone: Kent County Council, 1961, pp. 85–90; D.W. Harvey, 'Locational change in the Kentish hop industry and the analysis of land use patterns', *Transactions and Papers of the Institute of British Geographers* 33, 1963, 91–103.

40 CKS 10.69.18 1635; J. Thirsk, *Alternative agriculture, a history from the Black Death to the present day*, Oxford: Oxford University Press, 1997, p. 64.

41 Cullum, 'Society and economy in West Cornwall', p. 278.

42 The methods for calculating crop yields is outlined in M. Overton, 'Re-estimating crop yields from probate inventories', *Journal of Economic History* 50, 1990, 931–5; M. Overton, 'The determinants of land productivity in early modern England', in B.M.S. Campbell and M. Overton (eds) *Land, labour and livestock: historical studies in European agricultural productivity*, Manchester: Manchester University Press, 1991, pp. 284–322. Too few Cornish inventories give a post-harvest price of harvested grain, so yields were calculated using a national price index. Contemporary estimates of yields in Cornwall are given in R.G.F. Stanes, 'A georgicall account of Devonshire and Cornwalle', *Report and Transactions of the Devonshire Association* 96, 1964, pp. 290–2.

43 Whetter, *Cornwall in the 17th century*, pp. 112–16; J. Smedley, 'A history of the

Cornish wool industry and its people', *Journal of the Royal Institution of Cornwall*, new series II 1994, pp. 87–9.

44 Smedley, 'A history of the Cornish wool industry', pp. 90–1.

45 Ibid., p. 89.

46 J. Andrewes, 'Industries in Kent, *c.* 1500–1640', in M. Zell (ed.) *Early modern Kent, 1540–1640*, Woodbridge: Boydell Press, 2000, p. 108.

47 The large numbers of people involved in clothmaking (clothiers, weavers, fullers and shearmen) between 1565 and 1599 in a few parishes is striking: Biddenden 30 per cent, Cranbrook 25 per cent, Benenden 23 per cent, Smarden 20 per cent, Hawkhurst 17 per cent, Goudhurst 15 per cent, Staplehurst 13 per cent, Bethersden 11 per cent, Marden 9 per cent and Rolvenden 8 per cent. M. Zell, *Industry in the countryside: Wealden society in the sixteenth century*, Cambridge: Cambridge University Press, 1994, p. 118.

48 B. Short, 'The de-industrialisation process: a case study of the Weald, 1600–1850', in P. Hudson, (ed.) *Regions and industries: a perspective on the Industrial Revolution in Britain*, Cambridge: Cambridge University Press, 1989, pp. 156–74.

49 E. Kerridge, *Textile manufactures in early modern England*, Manchester: Manchester University Press, 1985, pp. 27–9.

50 The figures for Kent are broadly in line with those found by Zell for the whole of the Weald during the sixteenth century. He found 42 out of 106 broadweavers with two looms or more. Zell, *Industry in the countryside*, p. 171.

51 Smedley, 'A history of the Cornish wool industry', pp. 89–91.

52 Zell, *Industry in the countryside*, pp. 155–6.

53 K.G. Ponting, *The woollen industry of south-west England*, Bath: Adams & Dart, 1971, pp. 60–1.

54 D. Ormrod, 'Industry 1640–1800', in A. Armstrong (ed.) *The economy of Kent, 1640–1914*, Woodbridge: Boydell Press, pp. 94–5.

55 Ibid., p. 93.

56 B.R. Mitchell and P. Deane, *Abstract of British historical statistics*, Cambridge: Cambridge University Press, 1962, pp. 150–4.

57 D.B. Barton, *A history of tin mining and smelting in Cornwall*, Truro: D. Bradford Barton, 1967, p. 18; Whetter, *Cornwall in the 17th century*, pp. 59–60. Penzance also became a coinage town in 1663.

58 Barton, *A history of tin mining*, p. 17; Whetter, *Cornwall in the 17th century*, pp. 116–18; A.K. Hamilton Jenkin, *The Cornish miner* (3rd edn), Newton Abbot: David & Charles, 1972, pp. 48–82.

59 CRO L985 1696, Veale 1708, P2551 1722, R2133 1735, L1482 1741, Q69 1743.

60 S. Gerrard, 'The tin industry in sixteenth- and seventeenth-century Cornwall', in R. Kain and W. Ravenhill (eds) *Historical atlas of south-west England*, Exeter: University of Exeter Press, 1999, pp. 330–7.

61 Whetter, *Cornwall in the 17th century*, pp. 59–83.

62 J. Dodridge, *The history of the ancient and moderne estate of the principality of Wales, Duchy of Cornewall, and Earldome of Chester*, London, 1630, pp. 94–5.

63 Whetter, *Cornwall in the 17th century*, pp. 60–1, 75.

64 This corroborates R. Burt, 'The international diffusion of technology in the early modern period: the case of the British non-ferrous mining industry', *Economic History Review*, 2nd series 44, 1991, 247–91.

65 Quoted in A.R. Wilson, *Forgotten harvest: the story of cheesemaking in Wiltshire*, Calne: A.R. Wilson, 1995, pp. 57–8, 93.

66 In Cornwall five cows were used as the criterion, rather than four, as pastures were generally poorer and livestock smaller in stature.

67 This contradicts Chalklin, *Seventeenth-century Kent*, p. 98, who states: 'there was rarely more than an occasional sale of butter and cheese in the local market'.

68 See pp. 57–8.
69 Whetter, *Cornwall in the 17th century*, p. 92.
70 CKS 11.30.214 1666/7; CRO H1744 1672, Agnes Hunking, widow of St Stephens.
71 P. Mathias, *The brewing industry in England, 1700–1830*, Cambridge: Cambridge University Press, 1959, pp. 542–3.
72 Baker, 'Agricultural prices, production and marketing', p. 321.
73 Chalklin, *Seventeenth-century Kent*, p. 173.
74 CRO H1744 1672.
75 CKS 10.33.228 1606.
76 CKS 11.64.77 1703.
77 D. Defoe, *A tour through the whole island of Great Britain*, London: Dent, 1962, pp. 122–3.
78 R. Craig and J. Whyman, 'Kent and the sea', in A. Armstrong (ed.) *The economy of Kent, 1640–1914*, Woodbridge: Boydell and Brewer, 1995, pp. 164–9.
79 Whetter, *Cornwall in the 17th century*, pp. 147–8.
80 For the development of retailing, see N. Cox, *The complete tradesman: a study of retailing, 1550–1820*, Aldershot: Ashgate, 2000; D. Collins, 'Primitive or not? Fixed-shop retailing before the Industrial Revolution', *Journal of Regional and Local Studies* 13, 1993, 23–38; H.-C. Mui and L.H. Mui, *Shops and shopkeeping in eighteenth-century England*, London: Routledge, 1989. Expansion of the service sector is masked by the inclusion of clerics since they decline in number over time in both counties, probably as a result of having their probate increasingly administered in the Consistory Court. See also, C. North, 'Fustians, figs and frankincense: Jacobean shop inventories for Cornwall', *Journal of the Royal Institution of Cornwall*, new series, 2, 1995, pp. 32–77, and C. North, 'Merchants and retailers in seventeenth-century Cornwall', in T. Arkell, N. Evans and N. Goose (eds) *When death do us part: understanding and interpreting the probate records of early modern England*, Oxford: Leopard's Head Press, 2000, pp. 285–305; B.A. Holderness, 'Rural tradesmen, 1660–1850: a regional study in Lindsey, *Lincolnshire History and Archaeology* 7, 1972, 77–83.
81 CKS 11.82.18.
82 Mui and Mui, *Shops and shopkeeping*, pp. 135–47.
83 This is particularly the case with the maritime category where the absence of the requisite number of coastal parishes in both counties has probably led to significant under-representation.
84 Chalklin, *Seventeenth-century Kent*, pp. 146–7.
85 Whetter, 'Cornish trade', p. 394.
86 Chalklin, *Seventeenth-century Kent*, pp. 140–4. The naval dockyards lay outside our study area, but most of the Kentish ports had small shipyards which benefited from the proximity of naval facilities.
87 S. Paston-Williams, *The art of dining: a history of cooking & eating*, London: National Trust, 1993, p. 203.
88 Ibid., p. 171.
89 G. Worgan, *General view of the agriculture of the county of Cornwall*, London: B. McMillan, 1811, p. 65.
90 Arthur Young's words, quoted in C.A. Wilson, *Food and drink in Britain: from the Stone Age to recent times*, London: Constable, 1973, pp. 255–7; G. Goodwin, *Manchet and trencher*, London: Gelofer, *c.* 1983, pp. 6–7.
91 J.J. Cartwright (ed.) *The travels through England of Dr. Richard Pococke . . . during 1750, 1751 and later years*, vol. 1, London: Camden Society, new series 42, 1888, p. 131.

92 Mathias, *The brewing industry in England*, pp. xvii–xxviii; P. Clark, *The English alehouse, 1200–1830*, London: Longman, 1983, p. 213.
93 C. Shammas, *The pre-industrial consumer in England and America*, Oxford: Clarendon Press, 1990, pp. 20–5.
94 J.M. Bennett, *Ale, beer and brewsters in England*, Oxford: Oxford University Press, 1996, pp. 77–97; M. Mate, *Daughters, wives and widows after the Black Death*, Woodbridge: Boydell Press, 1998, pp. 64–75.
95 Mathias, *The brewing industry in England*, pp. 3–12; M. Lawrence, *The encircling hop: a history of hops and brewing*, Sittingbourne: SAWD, *c.* 1990, pp. 6–7.
96 Bennett, *Ale, beer and brewsters in England*, p. 81; Mate, *Daughters, wives and widows after the Black Death*, pp. 64–75.
97 Clark, *The English alehouse*, p. 101; P. Sambrook, *Country house brewing in England, 1500–1900*, London: Hambledon Press, 1996, pp. 17–18, 108–11.
98 Described in Sambrook, *Country house brewing in England*, pp. 21–88.
99 Clark, *The English alehouse*, p. 96.
100 Ibid., p. 178.
101 Ewes' and goats' milk was also used in dairying during the seventeenth century, but appears to have been of limited importance in both countries.
102 Wilson, *Food and drink in Britain*, pp. 164–76.
103 Chalklin, *Seventeenth-century Kent*, pp. 98, 176.
104 Wilson, *Food and drink in Britain*, p. 175.
105 R. Fraser, *General view of the County of Devon with observations on the means of its improvement*, London, 1794, pp. 30–1.
106 Risdon, quoted in P. Sainsbury, *The transition from tradition to technology: a history of the dairy industry in Devon*, Tiverton: P.T. Sainsbury, 1991, pp. 7–8.
107 Shammas, *Pre-industrial consumer*, p. 27.
108 Wilson, *Food and drink in Britain*, p. 199; Whetter, *Cornwall in the 17th century*, pp. 127–8.
109 Mingay, 'Agriculture', p. 65.
110 Wilson, *Food and drink in Britain*, p. 199.
111 D. Hartley, *Food in England*, London: Little Brown, 1996, pp. 331–3.
112 S. Peachey, *Civil War and salt fish: military and civilian diet in the C17th*, Leigh-on-Sea: Partizan, 1988, p. 31.
113 Quoted in S. Ferguson, *Food*, London: Batsford, 1971, p. 22.
114 Sambrook, *Country house brewing in England*, pp. 23–4.
115 D. Simonton, *A history of European women's work: 1700 to the present*, London: Routledge, 1998, p. 97.
116 Sambrook, *Country house brewing in England*, pp. 109–14.
117 See pp. 5–6.

4 By-employment, women's work and 'unproductive' households

1 J. Thirsk, 'Industries in the countryside', in F.J. Fisher (ed.) *Essays in the economic and social history of Tudor and Stuart England, in honour of R.H. Tawney*, Cambridge: Cambridge University Press, 1961, pp. 70–88; J. Thirsk, 'The farming regions of England', in J. Thirsk (ed.) *The agrarian history of England and Wales vol. IV, 1500–1640*, Cambridge: Cambridge University Press, 1967, pp. 1–112; J. Thirsk (ed.), *The agrarian history of England and Wales, vol. V, 1640–1750. I. Regional farming systems*, Cambridge: Cambridge University Press, 1984; D.G. Hey, 'A dual economy in south Yorkshire', *Agricultural History Review* 17, 1969, 108–19; M.B. Rowlands, *Masters and men in the West Midland metalware trades before the Industrial Revolution*, Manchester: Manchester University Press, 1975, pp. 41–3; P. Frost, 'Yeomen and metalsmiths: livestock in the dual economy in south Staffordshire, 1560–1720', *Agricultural History Review*

29, 1981, 29–41; P. Hudson, *The genesis of industrial capital: a study of the west Riding wool textile industry c. 1750–1850*, Cambridge: Cambridge University Press, 1986, pp. 61–7; J.T. Swain, *Industry before the Industrial Revolution: north-east Lancashire, c. 1500–1640*, Manchester: Chetham Society, 1986, pp. 118–22; D. Woodward, *Men at work: labourers and building craftsmen in the towns of Northern England, 1450–1750*, Cambridge: Cambridge University Press, 1995, pp. 236–41. See also M. Overton, *Agricultural revolution in England: the transformation of the agrarian economy 1500–1850*, Cambridge: Cambridge University Press, 1996, pp. 46–62.

2 See Chapter 1, n.13.

3 E.P. Thompson, 'Time, work discipline and industrial capitalism', *Past & Present* no. 38, 1967, pp. 71–3.

4 Overton, *Agricultural revolution*, p. 60; D. Gregory, 'Proto-industrialization', in R.J. Johnston *et al.* (eds) *The dictionary of human geography* (4th edn), Oxford: Blackwell, 2000, pp. 651–3.

5 See pp. 35–6.

6 CKS 11.9.39 1642. 10.63.39 1629.

7 CKS 11.77.25 1723.

8 CKS 10.29.175 1600.

9 CRO K107 1625.

10 CLS 11.74.201 1710.

11 J. Whetter, *Cornwall in the 17th century: an economic history of Kernow*, Padstow: Lodenek Press, 1974, pp. 84–103.

12 CRO M1790 1713, Paynter 1743.

13 Whetter, *Cornwall in the 17th century*, pp. 85–7.

14 C.W. Chalklin, *Seventeenth-century Kent: a social and economic history*, London: Longman, 1965, pp. 150–1.

15 See pp. 55–6.

16 CKS 11.63.34 1702, 11.76.244 1722.

17 CKS 10.41.297 1612–14.

18 CLS 11.75.182 1719.

19 CKS 11.5.37 1638, 11.71.187 1712.

20 CKS 11.19.113 1662.

21 CRO G958 1686.

22 M. Overton, 'English probate inventories and the measurement of agricultural change', *A.A.G. Bijdgragen* 23, 1980, 205–15; M. Overton, 'Probate inventories and the reconstruction of agrarian landscapes', in M. Reed (ed.) *Discovering past landscapes*, London: Croom Helm, 1984, pp. 167–94.

23 The monthly ratio of the value of cereals to livestock does not vary very much over the course of the year.

24 See pp. 41–2, 51–2.

25 Overton, *Agricultural revolution*, pp. 16–22.

26 R. Grassby, *The business community of seventeenth-century England*, Cambridge: Cambridge University Press, 1995, pp. 91–8.

27 Overton, *Agricultural revolution*, pp. 20–2.

28 F.B., *The office of the good housewife*, London, 1672, pp. 19–20.

29 A. Fitzherbert, *The Book of Husbandry*, ed. W.W. Skeat, London: English Dialect Society, 1882; T. Tusser, *Five hundred points of good husbandry*, Oxford: Oxford University Press, 1984; G. Markham, *The English housewife*, ed. M.R. Best, Montreal: McGill-Queen's University Press, 1986; A. Clark, *Working life of women in the seventeenth century* (3rd edn), ed. A.L. Erickson, London: Routledge, 1992; G.E. Fussell and K. Fussell, *The English countrywoman*, London: Andrew Melrose, 1953, p. 91; N. Verdon, '"...subjects deserving of the highest praise": farmers' wives and the farm economy in England *c.* 1700–1850', *Agri-*

cultural History Review 51, 2003, 23–39; K. Wrightson, *Earthly necessities: economic lives in early modern Britain*, New Haven, Conn.: Yale University Press, 2000, pp. 44–8. S. Mendelson and P. Crawford, *Women in early modern England*, Oxford: Clarendon Press, 1998, pp. 256–344. Male children may have undertaken such 'female' tasks as spinning. Swain, *Industry before the Industrial Revolution*, p. 112.

30 D. Valenze, 'The art of women and the business of men: women's work and the dairy industry *c.* 1740–1840', *Past & Present* no. 130, 1991, pp. 144–50.

31 See pp. 193–4.

32 Clark, *Working life of women*, pp. 6–8.

33 P. Earle, *The making of the English middle class: business, society and family life in London, 1660–1730*, London: Methuen, 1989, pp. 163–6.

34 R.B. Shoemaker, *Gender in English society, 1650–1850: the emergence of separate spheres?*, London: Longman, 1998, pp. 113–22.

35 See pp. 140–1.

36 See Table 6.3 on p. 125.

37 See pp. 122–4.

38 E.A. Wrigley, R. Davies, J. Oeppen and R. Schofield, *English population history from family reconstitution 1580–1837*, Cambridge: Cambridge University Press, 1997, p. 355.

39 See pp. 140–1.

40 B. Hill, *Women, work, and sexual politics in eighteenth-century England*, Oxford: Basil Blackwell, 1989, pp. 39–42.

41 Ibid., pp. 48–9.

42 I. Pinchbeck, *Women workers and the Industrial Revolution, 1750–1850*, London: Cass, 1969 (reprint of the 1930 edition); Clark, *Working life of women*; Hill, *Women, work and sexual politics*.

43 J.M. Bennett, 'Medieval women, modern women: across the great divide', in D. Aers (ed.) *Culture and history 1350–1600: essays on English communities, identities and writing*, London: Harvester Wheatsheaf, 1992, p. 152.

44 K.D.M. Snell, *Annals of the labouring poor: social change and agrarian England, 1660–1900*, Cambridge: Cambridge University Press, 1985, p. 63.

45 Bennett, 'Medieval women, modern women', pp. 158–9.

46 P. Mathias, *The brewing industry in England, 1700–1830*, Cambridge: Cambridge University Press, 1959, pp. 3–12.

47 G.E. Fussell (ed.), *Robert Loder's farm accounts 1610–1620*, Camden Society, 3rd series 53, 1936, p. 71; Markham, *English housewife*, pp. 207–36.

48 H.-C. Mui and L.-H. Mui, *Shops and shopkeeping in eighteenth-century England*, London: Routledge, 1989, pp. 29–45.

49 Bennett, 'Medieval women, modern women', p. 159.

50 CRO E317 1673. Since wills and accounts are filed with inventories in Cornwall they were used to obtain occupational information to supplement the inventory.

51 See pp. 18–19.

52 CKS 11.78.57 1726; CRO D713 1676; CKS 11.44.122 1680.

53 N.W. Alcock, *People at home: living in a Warwickshire village, 1500–1800*, Chichester: Phillimore, 1993, pp. 164–7.

54 CKS 10.62.252 1629; 11.7.208 1640.

55 That evidence is readily available in wills which we have not used in this study.

56 CKS 11.48.84 1683; 11.39.141 1677; 11.56.181 1691.

5 The material culture of consumption

1 J. de Vries, 'Between purchasing power and the world of goods: understanding the household economy in early modern Europe', in J. Brewer and R. Porter (eds) *Consumption and the world of goods*, London: Routledge, 1993, pp. 102–4.

2 C. Shammas, *The pre-industrial consumer in England and America*, Oxford: Clarendon Press, 1990, p. 100.

3 See pp. 14–18.

4 H. Phelps Brown and S.V. Hopkins, 'Seven centuries of the prices of consumables, compared with builders' wage-rates', *Economica* 23, 1956, 296–314; reprinted in *A perspective on wages and prices*, London: Methuen, 1981, pp. 13–59; L. Weatherill, *Consumer behaviour and material culture in England, 1660–1760*, London: Routledge, 1988, pp. 112–36.

5 De Vries, 'Between purchasing power and the world of goods', pp. 102–4.

6 This is explored further on p. 139.

7 De Vries, 'Between purchasing power and the world of goods', p. 102; M. Douglas and B. Isherwood, *The world of goods: towards an anthropology of consumption*, London: Routledge, 1996, pp. 48–9.

8 J. de Vries, 'Peasant demand patterns and economic development: Friesland 1500–1750', in W.N. Parker and E.L. Jones (eds) *European peasants and their markets: essays in agrarian economic history*, Princeton, N.J.: Princeton University Press, 1975, pp. 205–66; Weatherill, *Consumer behaviour and material culture*. Other studies include: L.G. Carr and L.S. Walsh, 'Changing lifestyles and consumer behavior in the Colonial Chesapeake', in C. Carson, R. Hoffman, and P.J. Albert (eds) *Of consuming interests: the style of life in the eighteenth century*, Charlottesville: University Press of Virginia, 1994, pp. 59–166; A.J. Schuurman, 'Materiële cultuur en levensstijl', *A.A.G. Bijdragen* 30, 1989; T. Wijsenbeek-Olthuis, *Achter de gevels van Delft. Bezit en bestaan van rijk en arm in een periode van achteruitgang, 1700–1800*, Hilversum: Verloren, 1987; C. Dessureault, J.A. Dickinson and T. Wien, 'Living standards of Norman and Canadian peasants 1690–1835', in A.J. Schuurman and L.S. Walsh (eds) *Material culture: consumption, life-style, standard of living, 1500–1900*, Proceedings B4 of the Eleventh International Economic History Congress, Milan, 1994, pp. 95–112; J.A. Kamermans, 'Materiële cultuur in de Krimpenerwaard in de Zeventiende en achttiende eeuw', *A.A.G. Bijdragen* 39, 1999.

9 Shammas, *Pre-industrial consumer*.

10 C. Muldrew, *The economy of obligation: the culture of credit and social relations in early modern England*, Basingstoke: Palgrave, 1998, pp. 24–32.

11 The phrase 'material culture' appears to have no consistent meaning in its usage by historians, anthropologists, archaeologists and sociologists. It is increasingly used as a synonym for material goods.

12 A. Vickery, 'Women and the world of goods: a Lancashire consumer and her possessions, 1751–81', in Brewer and Porter (eds) *Consumption and the world of goods*, p. 276; T.H. Breen, 'The meaning of things: interpreting the consumer economy in the eighteenth century', in Brewer and Porter, *Consumption and the world of goods*, p. 251.

13 G. Wills, *English Furniture 1550–1760*, Middlesex: Guinness Superlatives, 1971, p. 78.

14 See p. 94 for a discussion of gateleg tables.

15 R.W. Symonds, 'The "Dyning Parlour" and its Furniture', *The Connoisseur*, CXIII, 1944, p. 15.

16 R. Holme, *Academy of armory; or, a storehouse of armory & blazon*, ed. I.H. Jeayes, London: Roxburghe Club, 1905, p. 4. This is the first printing of Book III

of Holme's work, produced in the 1670s and 1680s and not published with his original *Academy of armory*, Chester, 1688. Holme's work, including many of his original drawings, is available in N.W. Alcock and N. Cox (eds), *Living and working in seventeenth century England: descriptions and drawings from Randle Holme's Academy of Armory*, Compact Disc, London: British Library, 2000.

17 These figures are likely to be underestimates because they were probably not always described as such in inventories, the appraisers instead describing items such as 'large carved cupboards' that could be either a press, dresser or court cupboard.

18 CRO A98 1616.

19 D. Knell, *English country furniture: the vernacular tradition*, Princes Risborough: Shire Publications, 1993, p. 45.

20 'Joined' and 'panelled' furniture was constructed using wooden joints, made by a skilled craftsman such as a joiner or cabinet-maker; 'boarded' furniture was nailed and generally of a poorer quality.

21 The median for all items of furniture is also six: this is because fewer inventories could be used for counting all items of furniture and the inventories that are excluded are often for larger households, giving a downward bias. This is not such a problem for analysing the Kent inventories because their level of detail is better and more consistent. See pp. 115–17.

22 The term 'gateleg' describes the folding mechanism of this type of table. One, or more commonly two, legs were hinged to the body of the table. These can be opened out to support the folded table-top when in use. S. Pennell, 'Great house layouts', in M. Snodin and J. Styles (eds) *Design & the decorative arts: Britain, 1500–1900*, London: V&A Publications, 2001, p. 106.

23 E. Kowaleski-Wallace, *Consuming subjects: women, shopping, and business in the eighteenth century*, New York: Columbia University Press, 1997, pp. 19–69.

24 Wills, *English furniture*, p. 91.

25 Knell, *English country furniture*, p. 53.

26 F. Montgomery, *Textiles in America 1650–1870*, New York: W.W. Norton, 1984, pp. 99, 368.

27 A well-documented example of a local furniture maker in Kent is Ambrose Haywood of Selling. C. Gilbert, *English vernacular furniture 1750–1900*, New Haven, Conn.: Yale University Press, 1991, pp. 15–17.

28 D. Defoe, *The complete English tradesman in familiar letters: directing him in all the several parts and progressions of trade* (2nd edn), London, 1727, reprinted New York: Kelley, 1969, vol. 1, pp. 332–3.

29 C.D. Edwards, *Eighteenth-century furniture*, Manchester: Manchester University Press, 1996, p. 44.

30 P. Kirkham, *The London furniture trade, 1700–1870*, London: Furniture History Society, 1988, pp. 34–6.

31 Defoe, *Complete English tradesman*, vol.1, p. 333.

32 Wills, *English furniture*, p. 91; Edwards, *Eighteenth-century furniture*, p. 118.

33 A. Bowett, 'The commercial introduction of mahogany and the Naval Stores Act of 1721', *Furniture History* 30, 1994, pp. 43–56; Edwards, *Eighteenth-century furniture*, p. 77.

34 It is possible that a proportion of upholstered furniture was made of mahogany, which would increase these figures.

35 Edwards, *Eighteenth-century furniture*, p. 118.

36 See pp. 123–5.

37 L. Wright, *Home fires burning: the history of domestic heating and cooking*, London: Routledge & Kegan Paul, 1964; L.A. Shuffrey, *The English fireplace: a history of the development of the chimney, chimney-piece and firegrate with their accessories*,

London: Batsford, 1912; D. Eveleigh, *Firegrates and kitchen ranges*, Princess Risborough: Shire Publications, 1983, pp. 3, 15; D. Hartley, *Food in England*, London: Little Brown, 1996, pp. 48–50; B. Trinder and N. Cox (eds), *Miners & mariners of the Severn Gorge*, Chichester: Phillimore, 2000, pp. 56–7.

38 J. Hatcher, *The history of the British coal industry, vol. 1 before 1700: towards the age of coal*, Oxford: Oxford University Press, 1993, pp. 51–3. Valuations of coal in Kentish inventories are similar to Houghton's prices: there are no entries in the Cornish sample for coal valued by the chaldron.

39 J. Whetter, 'Cornish trade in the seventeenth century: an analysis of the port books', *Journal of the Royal Institution of Cornwall*, new series 4, 1964, p. 399.

40 Hatcher, *British coal industry*, pp. 409–18.

41 See n. 48, this chapter.

42 Hartley, *Food in England*, pp. 36–9.

43 S. Pennell, 'The material culture of food in early modern England *c.*1650–1750', in S. Tarlow and S. West (eds) *The familiar past? Archaeologies of later historical Britain*, London: Routledge, 1999, pp. 40–1; S. Pennell, ' "Pots and pans history": the material culture of the kitchen in early modern England', *Journal of Design History* 11, 1998, 201–16.

44 They were supported either on a brigg, a horizontal framework bridging the topmost firebars, or on a trivet, a tall three-legged iron stand (shorter versions are known as 'brandreths') which stood in front of the fire to take advantage of the radiant heat. P. Brears, *Food and cooking in 17th century Britain: history and recipes*, London: Historic Buildings & Monuments Commission for England, 1985; reprinted in P. Brears *et al.*, *A taste of history: 10,000 years of food in Britain*, London: English Heritage in association with British Museum Press, 1993, p. 191; Holme, *Academy of armory*, 1905, pp. 7–8; see the stock of pots and pans held by the brazier, Robert Cragge of Canterbury, CKS 11.45.68 1681.

45 H.D. Roberts, *Downhearth to bar-grate: an illustrated account of the evolution of cooking due to the use of coal instead of wood*, Avebury, Marlborough, Wilts.: Wiltshire Folk Life Society, *c.*1981, p. 7; J. Stead, 'Georgian Britain', in Brears *et al.*, *A taste of history*, pp. 220–1.

46 H. Glasse, *The art of cookery, made plain and easy: which far exceeds any thing of the kind ever yet published*, London, 1747.

47 Brears, *Food and cooking in 17th century Britain*, 1993, p. 190.

48 D. Eveleigh, *Old cooking utensils*, Princess Risborough: Shire Publications, 1986, p. 24.

49 C. Morris (ed.), *The journey of Celia Fiennes*, London: Crescent Press, 1947, p. 262.

50 W. Harrison, *The description of England: the classic contemporary account of Tudor social life*, ed. G. Edelen, Ithaca, N.Y.: Cornell University Press for the Folger Shakespeare Library, 1994, p. 201. The other two things were the erection of chimneys and the use of beds. 'Treen' means wooden.

51 Holme, *Academy of armory*, 1905, p. 4; M. Visser, *The rituals of dinner: the origins, evolution, eccentricities, and meaning of table manners*, Harmondsworth: Penguin Books, 1991, p. 191.

52 P.R.G. Hornsby, R. Weinstein and R.F. Homer, *Pewter: a celebration of the craft 1200–1700*, London: Museum of London, 1989, pp. 21–2. Douch has identified 87 pewterers working in Cornwall between 1600–1750, with the vast majority operating in the late seventeenth century and the eighteenth. J. Whetter, *Cornwall in the 17th century: an economic history of Kernow*, Padstow: Lodenek Press, 1974, pp. 75–8; H.L. Douch, 'Cornish pewterers', *Journal of the Royal Institution of Cornwall*, new series 6, 1969, 69–80.

53 J. Hatcher and T.C. Barker, *A history of British pewter*, London: Longman, 1974,

pp. 279–301; S. Richards, *Eighteenth-century ceramics: products for a civilised society*, Manchester: Manchester University Press, 1999.

54 J. Allen, 'Some post-medieval documentary evidence for the trade in ceramics', in P. Davey and R. Hodges (eds) *Ceramics and trade: the production and distribution of later medieval pottery in north-west Europe*, Sheffield: Department of Prehistory and Archaeology, University of Sheffield, 1983, pp. 37–48; J.G. Hurst, D.S. Neal and H.J.E. van Beuningen, *Pottery produced and traded in north-west Europe 1350–1650*, Rotterdam: Museum Boymans-van Beuningen, 1986.

55 L. Weatherill, 'The growth of the pottery industry in England, 1660–1815', *Post-Medieval Archaeology* 17, 1983, p. 27.

56 Tin-glazed potteries were also set up in Bristol and Liverpool in the late seventeenth century: G.B. Hughes, *English and Scottish earthenware, 1660–1860*, London: Abbey Fine Arts, 1961, pp. 17–28; Weatherill, 'Growth of the pottery industry', p. 34.

57 D. Dean, 'The design, production and consumption of English lead-glazed earthenware in the seventeenth century', Unpublished Ph.D. thesis, Royal College of Art, London 1997, pp. 44–53.

58 CRO B99 1605.

59 Hughes, *English and Scottish earthenware*, pp. 29–57.

60 E. Gooder, 'The finds from the cellar of the Old Hall, Temple Balsall, Warwickshire', *Post-Medieval Archaeology* 18, 1984, 149–249.

61 Most earthenware is not recorded in inventories because of its low value. Pottery plates, as distinct from dishes, however, were not commonly made as tableware until the early eighteenth century. Pottery plates are more consistently recorded because they were usually of higher quality and were therefore more valuable than most earlier forms of lead-glazed pottery. Dean, 'English lead-glazed earthenware', pp. 259–62, 382–4. The sample of inventories for the 1740s is small, although the growth in the ownership of earthenware plates found is consistent with the growth in production during the second quarter of the eighteenth century when potteries in Staffordshire and London greatly expanded. The earthenware plates found before the 1680s are most likely to have been decorative pieces, rather than used for eating: Weatherill, 'Growth of the pottery industry', pp. 15–29.

62 On 22 March 1776 a hundred tinners assembled at Redruth where they destroyed all the Staffordshire pottery ware in the market and shops. They then proceeded to Falmouth. The tinners and pewterers were protesting about the damage done to their business by the great quantities of Staffordshire pottery being taken into Cornwall. Douch, 'Cornish pewterers', p. 72.

63 Shammas, *Pre-industrial consumer*, pp. 76–7. Pewter was, of course, more durable than pottery, but it should not be assumed that once pewter was purchased it would not have to be replaced. Pewter scratched fairly easily, and could also be bent and broken. It therefore required polishing regularly, and refashioning occasionally. 'Most people would only need to buy [pewter] once or twice in a decade, but institutions, where pewter received heavy use, needed more frequent purchases. Winchester College, for example, bought pewter in eight out of ten years towards the end of the 17th century ... It seems likely that, if well cared for, most domestic pewter would last ten years or so.' Hornsby *et al.*, *Pewter*, pp. 21–2, although Hatcher and Barker consider the life cycle of a piece of a pewter to be 20 or 30 years: *A history of British pewter*, p. 132.

64 A lead-glazed dish was typically valued at around 2d or less, some four or five times cheaper than a pewter dish. A number of archaeological excavations suggest that amongst those who could afford to do so, pottery tableware was

replaced by new sets of wares. At the Old Hall, Temple Balsall, for example, a large stock of pottery appears to have been thrown away when the owners moved up the social scale. Dean, 'English lead-glazed earthenware', pp. 382–4; Gooder, 'Finds from the cellar of the Old Hall', pp. 149–249.

65 E.L. Jones, 'The fashion manipulators: consumer tastes and British industries, 1660–1800', in L.P. Cain and P.J. Uselding (eds) *Business enterprise and economic change: essays in honor of Harold F. Williamson*, Kent, O: Kent State University Press, 1973, pp. 216–22; N. McKendrick, 'Josiah Wedgwood and the commercialisation of the Potteries', in McKendrick, Brewer and Plumb, *The birth of a consumer society*, pp. 100–45.

66 Holme, *Academy of armory*, 1905, p. 4.

67 J.A. Anderson, 'Solid sufficiency: an ethnography of yeoman foodways in Stuart England', Unpublished Ph.D. Thesis, University of Pennsylvania, 1971, pp. 243–4.

68 CRO B155, 1606.

69 G. Wills, *English looking-glasses: a study of the glass, frames and makers (1670–1820)*, London: Country Life, 1965, pp. 41–51; E.M. Hewitt, 'Industries', in W. Page (ed.) *The Victoria History of the County of Kent*, vol. 3, London: The St Catherine Press, 1932, pp. 400–2; see also W.A. Thorpe, *English glass* (3rd rev. edn), London: A. & C. Black, 1961, pp. 135–63; C. Macleod, 'Accident or design? George Ravenscroft and the invention of lead crystal glass', *Technology and Culture* 28, 1987, 776–803.

70 R. Davis, 'English foreign trade, 1660–1700', *Economic History Review*, 2nd series 7, 1954, p. 164; B.R. Mitchell and P. Deane, *Abstract of British historical statistics*, Cambridge: Cambridge University Press, 1962, p. 285.

71 G. Brett, *Dinner is served: a history of dining in England, 1400–1900*, London: Hart-Davis, 1968, p. 61.

72 J.-L. Flandrin, 'Distinction through taste', in R. Chartier (ed.) *Passions of the Renaissance*, trans. A. Goldhammer, Cambridge, Mass.: Belknap Press of Harvard University, 1989, pp. 265–6. Originally published as *Histoire de la vie privée*, T.3, Paris: Seuil, 1986, under the direction of P. Ariès and G. Duby.

73 Visser, *The rituals of dinner*, pp. 189–92.

74 Brett, *Dinner is served*, p. 62; T. Coryate, *Coryats crudities*, London, 1611, p. 90; A. Bryson, *From courtesy to civility: changing codes of conduct in early modern England*, Oxford: Clarendon Press, 1998, p. 81.

75 Shammas, *Pre-industrial consumer*, p. 84.

76 S. Smith, 'Accounting for taste: British coffee consumption in historical perspective', *Journal of Interdisciplinary History* 27, 1996, 183–214.

77 Only 26 inventories are available for the 1740s, so the Kent sample is rather small, but similar conclusions regarding the growth of tea and coffee consumption have been found by a number of historians. Shammas, *Pre-industrial consumer*, pp. 83–4; Kowaleski-Wallace, *Consuming subjects*, p. 22.

78 Before about 1680 the figures for plates in Cornwall are not reliable because the number of inventories used is very small.

79 Hartley, *Food in England*, p. 559.

80 The maximum variety in Cornwall is 60, while in Kent it is 94.

81 R. Carew, *The survey of Cornwall*, London, 1602, p. 67.

82 Harrison, *Description of England*, p. 201.

83 These figures for Cornwall are not as reliable as those for Kent because linen is often lumped together in Cornish inventories. This lack of detail, however, suggests linen was not held in great quantities or was not as valuable a part of the household's goods as it was in Kent.

84 CRO C1126 1644.

85 Brett, *Dinner is served*, p. 122.

86 Shammas, *Pre-industrial consumer*, p. 98; C. Shammas, 'The decline of textile prices in England and British America prior to industrialisation', *Economic History Review*, 2nd series 47, 1994, pp. 483–507; M. Overton, 'Prices from probate inventories', in T. Arkell, N. Evans and N. Goose (eds) *When death do us part: understanding and interpreting the probate records of early modern England*, Oxford: Leopard's Head Press, 2000, pp. 120–43.

87 H. Dibbits, 'Between society and family values: the linen cupboard in early modern households, in A. Schuurman and P. Spierenburg (eds) *Private domain, public enquiry: families and life-styles in the Netherlands and Europe, 1550 to the present*, Hilversum: Verloren, 1996, pp. 125–45; M. Campbell, *The English yeoman under Elizabeth and the early Stuarts*, New Haven, Conn.: Yale University Press, 1942, pp. 240–1.

88 Richard Chamond Esq. of Launcells, CRO C200 1609.

89 G.J. Whitrow, *Time in history: the evolution of our general awareness of time and temporal perspective*, Oxford: Oxford University Press, 1988, pp. 112, 123–7.

90 For example, by John Pye of St. Columb Major: CRO P2989 1740.

91 This is considerably higher than in the country as a whole, and slightly lower than Weatherill's sample of London Orphan Court inventories between 1675–1725. Weatherill, *Consumer behaviour and material culture*, pp. 26–7.

92 Valuations range from the two looking-glasses owned by Susanna Basacke of Walmer at sixpence in 1695 (CKS 11.59.253) to the looking-glass worth £10 in Sir Arnold Braems's chamber in 1681 (CKS 11.46.27). It is possible that some mirrors were made of polished steel rather than glass, but 'looking glass' is the most common phrase used in inventories. S. Melchoir-Bonnet, *The mirror: a history*, trans. K.H. Jewett, New York: Routledge, 2001. (Originally published as *Histoire du Miroir*, 1994), p. 13; Wills, *English-looking glasses*, pp. 41–6.

93 Edwards, *Eighteenth-century furniture*, p. 113; Holme, *Academy of armory*, 1905, p. 12. See also J.E. Crowley, *The invention of comfort: sensibilities and design in early modern Britain and early America*, Baltimore, Md.: The Johns Hopkins University Press, 2000, pp. 122–30.

94 These are likely to have been more expensive than products of native manufacture. Jones, 'The fashion manipulators', p. 204; Thorpe, *English glass*, pp. 152–3.

95 Melchoir-Bonnet, *The mirror*, pp. 28–9, 91.

96 A. Globe, *Peter Stent, London printseller, circa 1642–1665: being a catalogue raisonné of his engraved prints and books with an historical and bibliographical introduction*, Vancouver: University of British Columbia Press, 1985, pp. 1–12. See also, I. Pears, *The discovery of painting: the growth of interest in the Arts in England, 1680–1768*, New Haven, Conn.: Yale University Press, 1988.

97 See pp. 152, 198.

98 See pp. 122–4.

99 V.M. Chesher and F.J. Chesher, *The Cornishman's house. An introduction to the history of traditional domestic architecture in Cornwall*, Truro: D. Bradford Barton, 1968, pp. 39–92; Carew, *Survey of Cornwall*, p. 53.

100 Weatherill, *Consumer behaviour and material culture*, p. 44; P. Clark, 'The ownership of books in England, 1560–1640: the example of some Kentish townsfolk', in L. Stone (ed.) *Schooling and society: studies in the history of education*, Baltimore, Md.: The Johns Hopkins University Press, 1976, p. 99.

101 D. Cressy, *Literacy and the social order: reading and writing in Tudor and Stuart England*, Cambridge: Cambridge University Press, 1980, pp. 142–74.

102 M. Stoyle, *West Britons: Cornish identities and the early modern British state*, Exeter: University of Exeter Press, 2002, p. 157.

103 M.C. Beaudry, 'Words for things: the linguistic analysis of probate inventories', in M.C. Beaudry (ed.) *Documentary archaeology in the New World*, Cambridge: Cambridge University Press, 1988, pp. 43–50.

104 See pp. 104, 107, 109–11.

105 Variety has been calculated by counting all the unique items within the house. The analysis includes all domestic goods, some of which were for domestic production, but excludes commercial production goods where they could be identified; goods used for domestic production, such as baking, have been included since this domestic activity can be understood as a type of consumption.

106 Weatherill, *Consumer behaviour and material culture*, pp. 80, 52–3, 58–9; she does not analyse the adoption of new types of furniture.

107 C. North, 'Fustians, figs and frankincense: Jacobean shop inventories for Cornwall', *Journal of the Royal Institution of Cornwall*, new series 2, 1995, 32–77. The most extraordinary merchant's inventory is that of Robert Bennett of Tregony, CRO B155 1606. He had a wide variety of textiles from Manchester, Norwich and Coventry, lace from France and silks from Italy; sugar, marmalade, herbs and spices, and 22 'Venice glasses'. He sold his wares at a number of markets and fairs in Cornwall, including those at Madron, Probus and Helston.

108 North, 'Fustians, figs and frankincense', p. 44.

109 J. Smedley, 'A history of the Cornish wool industry and its people', *Journal of the Royal Institution of Cornwall*, new series II 1994, p. 90.

110 North, 'Fustians, figs and frankincense', p. 44.

111 There is no reason to believe that the lifetime of any type of domestic good was radically extended during the seventeenth and eighteenth centuries, which would be necessary if inheritance is to account for the accumulation of greater variety and quantities of goods. Shammas has argued for a reduced life-span for many goods, what she has termed 'semi-durables'; the increasing use of these types of goods would have had the opposite effect – namely, that greater levels of consumption would have been needed to maintain the same stock of goods. Shammas, *Pre-industrial consumer*, pp. 76–7.

112 T.S. Willan, *The inland trade: studies in English internal trade in the sixteenth and seventeenth centuries*, Manchester: Manchester University Press, 1976, pp. 1–105; H.-C. Mui and L.-H. Mui, *Shops and shopkeeping in eighteenth-century England*, London: Routledge, 1989, pp. 8–72; Overton, 'Prices from probate inventories'.

113 Overton, 'Prices from probate inventories'; Shammas, 'The decline of textile prices. See also pp. 140–1.

114 W. Rybczynski, *Home: a short history of an idea*, London: Pocket Books, 2001, p. 218.

115 Visser, *The rituals of dinner*, pp. 122–4.

6 Rooms and room use

1 Those that have include M.W. Barley, *The English farmhouse and cottage*, London: Routledge & Kegan Paul, 1961; U. Priestley and P.J. Corfield, 'Rooms and room use in Norwich housing, 1580–1730', *Post-Medieval Archaeology* 16, 1982, 93–123; C. Husbands, 'Standards of living in north Warwickshire in the seventeenth century', *Warwickshire History* 4, 1980/1, 203–15; L. Hall, 'Yeoman or gentleman? Problems in defining social status in seventeenth- and eighteenth-century Gloucestershire', *Vernacular Architecture* 22, 1991, 2–19; N.W. Alcock, *People at home: living in a Warwickshire village, 1500–1800*, Chichester: Phillimore, 1993; P. Earle, *The making of the English*

middle class: business, society and family life in London, 1660–1730, London: Methuen, 1989, pp. 290–301; M. Johnson, *Housing culture: traditional architecture in an English landscape*, London: UCL Press, 1993, pp. 122–8; S. Cottman, 'A Hook Norton family, the Calcotts', *Cake and Cockhorse* 9, 1982, 7–13.

2 L.C. Orlin, 'Fictions of the early modern English probate inventory', in H.S. Turner (ed.) *The culture of capital: property, cities, and knowledge in early modern England*, London: Routledge, 2002, pp. 57–63.

3 A rarity is the inventory of Richard Verrier of Folkestone which records items in 'the space between chambers': CKS 11.79.250 1731 (and also a 'prison chamber').

4 A. Dyer, 'Urban housing: a documentary study of four Midland towns 1530–1700', *Post-Medieval Archaeology* 15, 1981, p. 208, excludes the inventories of widows from his analysis because their houses are 'under-occupied'.

5 B. Hillier and J. Hanson, *The social logic of space*, Cambridge: Cambridge University Press, 1984. Their methods are employed in a historical context by F. Brown, 'Continuity and change in the urban house: developments in domestic space organisation in seventeenth-century London', *Comparative Studies in Society and History* 28, 1986, 558–90.

6 E.M. Jope, 'Cornish houses, 1400–1700', in E.M. Jope (ed.) *Studies in building history: essays in recognition of the work of B.H. St. J. O'Neil*, London: Odhams, 1961, pp. 192–222; V.M. Chesher and F.J. Chesher, *The Cornishman's house. An introduction to the history of traditional domestic architecture in Cornwall*, Truro: D. Bradford Barton, 1968.

7 R. Carew, *The survey of Cornwall*, London, 1602, pp. 67, 66.

8 CRO H477 1620.

9 Carew, *Survey of Cornwall*, p. 64.

10 This table uses the same room categories as Priestley and Corfield, 'Rooms and room use', p. 100; see also, D. Portman, 'Vernacular building in the Oxford region in the sixteenth and seventeenth centuries', in C.W. Chalklin and M.A. Havinden (eds) *Rural change and urban growth 1500–1800*, London: Longman, p. 151.

11 W.G. Hoskins, 'The rebuilding of rural England, 1570–1640', *Past & Present* no. 4, 1953, 44–59; R. Machin, 'The great rebuilding: a reassessment', *Past & Present* no. 77, 1977, 33–56; M.W. Barley, 'Rural housing in England', in J. Thirsk (ed.) *The agrarian history of England and Wales, vol. IV, 1500–1640*, Cambridge: Cambridge University Press, 1967, pp. 734–60; M.W. Barley, 'Rural building in England', in J. Thirsk (ed.) *The agrarian history of England and Wales, vol. V, 1640–1750. II. agrarian change*, Cambridge: Cambridge University Press, 1985, pp. 590–685; C. Platt, *The great rebuildings of Tudor and Stuart England*, London: UCL Press, 1994, pp. 1–2, refers to the period 1570 to 1640 as the 'first great rebuilding'.

12 Barley, *The English farmhouse and cottage*, pp. 134–85; C.W. Chalklin, *Seventeenth-century Kent: a social and economic history*, London: Longman, 1965, p. 239.

13 CKS 11.46.27 1681. Part of the house still stands: A. Quiney, *Kent houses: English domestic architecture*, Woodbridge: Antique Collectors' Club, 1993, pp. 99, 232; on billiards see J.T. Cliffe, *The world of the country house in seventeenth-century England*, New Haven, Conn.: Yale University Press, 1999, p. 160; for a general discussion of room use in gentry households see N. Cooper, *Houses of the gentry 1480–1680*, New Haven, Conn.: Yale University Press, 1999, pp. 273–322, and N. Cooper, 'Rank, manners and display: the gentlemanly house, 1500–1750', *Transactions of the Royal Historical Society*, sixth series 12, 2002, 291–310.

14 This may explain why our results for eating in parlours are lower than those found by Priestley and Corfield for Norwich, 'Rooms and room use', p. 109.

15 J.E. Crowley, *The invention of comfort: sensibilities and design in early modern Britain and early America*, Baltimore, Md.: The Johns Hopkins University Press, 2000, pp. 54–5.

16 S. Pearson, *The medieval houses of Kent: an historical analysis*, London: HMSO, 1994, pp. 108–15.

17 Crowley, *The invention of comfort*, p. 55.

18 M.W. Barley, 'A glossary of names for rooms in houses of the sixteenth and seventeenth centuries', in I.L. Foster and L. Alcock (eds) *Culture and environment: essays in honour of Sir Cyril Fox*, London: Routledge & Kegan Paul, 1963, p. 493; Priestley and Corfield, 'Rooms and room use', p. 106.

19 In the final period, 1720–49, the proportion falls to 73 per cent, although the sample size for this period is small.

20 Barley, *English farmhouse and cottage*, pp. 185–6.

21 Barley, 'Glossary of names', p. 500; Barley, *English farmhouse and cottage*, pp. 134–5.

22 M. Girouard, *Life in the English country house: a social and architectural history*, New Haven, Conn.: Yale University Press, 1978, pp. 58–9.

23 Brown, 'Continuity and change in the urban house', pp. 583–4.

24 'Cooking' in parlours is indicated by the presence of 'stoves', but these were probably used for keeping food warm rather than for cooking a complete meal.

25 CKS 11.82.116 1743.

26 M.W. Barley, 'The use of upper floors in rural houses', *Vernacular Architecture* 22, 1991, pp. 20–2; Barley, 'Rural building in England', pp. 664–5.

27 Girouard, *Life in the English country house*, p. 88; Cooper, *Houses of the gentry*, p. 293.

28 Cooper, *Houses of the gentry*, p. 277.

29 Johnson, *Housing culture*, p. 55.

30 Ibid., pp. 120, 108.

31 P. Ariès, 'Introduction', in R. Chartier (ed.) *Passions of the Renaissance*, trans. A. Goldhammer, Cambridge, Mass.: Belknap Press of Harvard University, 1989, pp. 1–9 (originally published as *Histoire de la vie privée*, T.3, Paris: Seuil, 1986, under the direction of P. Ariès and G. Duby), introduces some major themes in the history of privacy; L. Stone and J.C. Stone, *An open elite? England 1540–1880*, Oxford: Clarendon Press, 1984, p. 343.

32 L. Weatherill, *Consumer behaviour and material culture in Britain 1660–1760*, London: Routledge, 1988, p. 9; E. Goffman, *The presentation of self in everyday life*, London: Penguin Books, 1990.

33 S. Richards, *Eighteenth-century ceramics: products for a civilised society*, Manchester: Manchester University Press, 1999, p. 109.

7 Wealth, occupation, status and location

1 C. Shammas, *The pre-industrial consumer in England and America*, Oxford: Clarendon Press, 1990, p. 173.

2 J.M. Ellis, 'Consumption and wealth', in L.K.J. Glassey (ed.) *The reigns of Charles II and James VII & II*, Basingstoke: Macmillan, 1997, p. 204.

3 F.M. Magrabi, *The economics of household consumption*, London: Praeger, 1991, pp. 83, 158; A.H. Jones, *Wealth of a nation to be: the American Colonies on the eve of the Revolution*, New York: Columbia University Press, 1980, pp. 14–25.

4 J.P.P. Horn, 'The distribution of wealth in the Vale of Berkeley, Gloucestershire, 1660–1700', *Southern History* 3, 1981, 81–109; C. Shammas, 'The

determinants of personal wealth in seventeenth-century England and America', *Journal of Economic History* 37, 1977, 677–89; C. Shammas, 'Constructing a wealth distribution from probate records', *Journal of Interdisciplinary History* 9, 1978, 297–307; J.D. Marshall, 'Social structure and wealth in pre-industrial England', *Economic History Review*, 2nd series 33, 1980, 503–21.

5 M. Overton and D. Dean, 'Wealth, indebtedness, consumption and the life-cycle in early modern England', forthcoming.

6 See Appendix 3. Consumption goods are all those not involved in production, both for use and exchange.

7 C.B. Estabrook, *Urbane and rustic England: cultural ties and social spheres in the provinces 1660–1780*, Manchester: Manchester University Press, 1998, pp. 140–1, overlooks this point when he compares the 'wealth' of rural and urban households.

8 See pp. 87–8.

9 Shammas, *Pre-industrial consumer*, pp. 102–4.

10 Shammas finds much lower proportions in her samples, which may be because we relate consumer goods to material wealth rather than total inventoried wealth: ibid, pp. 86–8.

11 These were collected as part of the study 'Prices from probate inventories in England, 1550–1750' (B00232211), funded by the ESRC: see M. Overton, 'Prices from probate inventories', in T. Arkell, N. Evans and N. Goose (eds) *When death do us part: understanding and interpreting the probate records of early modern England*, Oxford: Leopard's Head Press, 2000, pp. 120–41. This project did not record complete inventories, so material wealth cannot be calculated.

12 M. Overton, 'Probate inventories and the reconstruction of agrarian landscapes', in M. Reed (ed.) *Discovering past landscapes*, London: Croom Helm, 1984, pp. 174–6.

13 Price weights are from Overton, 'Prices from probate inventories', p. 140.

14 C.G.A. Clay, 'Lifeleasehold in the western counties of England, 1650–1750', *Agricultural History Review* 29, 1981, 83–96. The median figures for the value of leases and debts are not shown because in some cases more than 50 per cent of the values are zero.

15 Shammas, *Pre-industrial consumer*, pp. 86–100.

16 Overton, 'Prices from probate inventories'.

17 With point-biserial correlations one variable is continuous (in this case material wealth) and the other is dichotomous.

18 The product moment correlations between the value of consumer goods and material wealth are 0.68, 0.64 and 0.67 for the three periods in Kent, and 0.87, 0.59 and 0.71 in Cornwall.

19 The distributions of wealth within each quartile are roughly the same for the two counties for the first three quartiles. In the fourth quartile the Kent inventories are slightly richer than the Cornish ones for the first two periods and quite significantly so for the period 1700–49.

20 C.H. Feinstein and M. Thomas, *Making history count: a primer in quantitative methods for historians*, Cambridge: Cambridge University Press, 2002, pp. 384–432; A. Field, *Discovering statistics using SPSS for Windows: advanced techniques for the beginner*, London: Sage Publications, 2000, pp. 163–204. The Nagelkerke R Square values were used.

21 See Appendix 2 below for definitions of these production groups.

22 C. Chalklin, 'The towns', in A. Armstrong (ed.) *The economy of Kent, 1640–1914*, Woodbridge: Boydell Press, 1995, pp. 205–13, and Appendix IIIA, p. 280; towns are taken as places over 400 people with evidence of a market and non-agrarian occupations.

23 See Tables 7.5 and 7.6 on pp. 154 and 156.

24 The 'commercial agriculture only' category might be expected to have zero by-employment. The category excludes farmers with any other commercial production activity except spinning, so the decline in by-employment reflects the decline in spinning.

25 The significance of the difference between the means was carried out using a one-tailed t test: the same results hold true when comparing the medians with a Mann–Whitney U test.

26 E. Chamberlayne, *Angliæ Notitia; or, the present state of England* (5th edn), London, 1671, p. 312. See also J. Bower, 'The Kent yeoman in the seventeenth century', *Archæologia Cantiana* 114, 1995, p. 156.

27 This contradicts L. Hall, 'Yeoman or gentleman? Problems in defining social status in seventeenth- and eighteenth-century Gloucestershire', *Vernacular Architecture* 22, 1991, 2–19.

28 See also Table 4.8 on p. 85.

29 See p. 139.

30 Shop goods have been ignored in calculating the values of consumer goods.

31 B.A. Holderness, 'Credit in a rural community, 1660–1800: some neglected aspects of probate inventories', *Midland History* 3, 1975, 94–114; B.A. Holderness, 'Widows in preindustrial society: an essay upon their economic functions', in R.M. Smith (ed.) *Land, kinship and life-cycle*, Cambridge: Cambridge University Press, 1985, pp. 435–42.

32 Overton and Dean, 'Wealth, indebtedness, consumption and the life-cycle'; A. Poole, 'Debt in the Cranbrook region in the late seventeenth century', *Archæologia Cantiana* 123, 2003, 81–93.

33 In recording book ownership we attempted to make the distinction between printed books and books in which to record financial transactions.

34 CKS 11.80.108 1733.

35 See p. 58.

36 S. Gerrard, 'The tin industry in sixteenth- and seventeenth-century Cornwall', in R. Kain and W. Ravenhill (eds) *Historical atlas of south-west England*, Exeter: University of Exeter Press, 1999, pp. 330–2.

37 CRO Roseveare, Luxulyan, 1645. See pp. 50–2.

38 See Table 3.7 on p. 57.

39 Estabrook, *Urbane and rustic England*, pp. 140–1, also finds this for Bristol and surrounding parishes, as does L. Weatherill, *Consumer behaviour and material culture in Britain 1660–1760*, London: Routledge, 1988, pp. 76–80, for her Cambridgeshire sample, though not for other areas except Kent.

40 The associations for chests of drawers and new tables are similar to jacks; those for saucepans and forks are similar to those for hot drinks.

41 R.J. Johnston, 'Ecological fallacy', in R.J. Johnston *et al.* (eds) *The dictionary of human geography* (4th edn), Oxford: Blackwell, 2000, pp. 190–1.

42 See pp. 145–7.

43 There are other measures of r^2 which give slightly lower values.

44 'Urban parishes' are defined on pp. 147–8.

45 They could be regarded as laggards if the carpets were still covering furniture, but as leaders if the carpets were on the floor. Unfortunately we cannot tell this from inventories.

46 Weatherill, *Consumer behaviour and material culture*, p. 77.

47 Ibid., pp. 184–5.

48 Ibid., pp. 70–90, 184–5.

49 F. Heal and C. Holmes, *The gentry in England and Wales, 1500–1700*, Basingstoke: Macmillan, 1994, pp. 288, 312–18. For the life of the 'upper gentry' in London see S.E. Whyman, *Sociability and power in late-Stuart England: the cul-*

tural worlds of the Verneys 1660–1720, Oxford: Oxford University Press, 1999, pp. 55–180.

50 J. Grant, 'The gentry of London in the reign of Charles I', *University of Birmingham Historical Journal* 8, 1962, 197–202.

51 Heal and Holmes, *The gentry*, pp. 6–19.

52 H.R. French, ' "Ingenious & learned gentlemen" – social perceptions and self-fashioning among parish elites in Essex, 1680–1740', *Social History* 25, 2000, p. 46; the phrase 'pseudo-gentry' comes from A.M. Everitt, 'Social mobility in early modern England', *Past & Present* no. 33, 1966, 56–73.

53 J. de Vries, 'Peasant demand patterns and economic development: Friesland 1500–1750', in W.N. Parker and E.L. Jones (eds) *European peasants and their markets: essays in agrarian economic history*, Princeton, N.J.: Princeton University Press, 1975, p. 219; Estabrook, *Urbane and rustic England*, p. 129.

54 This criticism can also be levied against J. Beckett and C. Smith, 'Urban renaissance and consumer revolution in Nottingham, 1688–1750', *Urban History* 27, 2000, 31–50.

55 Weatherill, *Consumer behaviour and material culture*, pp. 81–3.

56 P. Borsay, *The English urban renaissance: culture and society in the provincial town 1660–1770*, Oxford: Clarendon Press, 1989, pp. 34, 222–3.

57 P. Glennie and I. Whyte, 'Towns in an agrarian economy 1540–1700', in P. Clark (ed.) *The Cambridge urban history of Britain, vol. II 1540–1840*, Cambridge: Cambridge University Press, 2000, p. 188.

58 The results for the period 1700–49 must remain tentative since the sample size for the professional service category is very small, and Canterbury is not represented.

59 L. Scammell, 'Town versus country: the property of everyday consumption in the late seventeenth and early eighteenth centuries', in J. Stobart and A. Owens (eds) *Urban fortunes: property and inheritance in the town, 1700–1900*, Aldershot: Ashgate, 2000, p. 35.

60 C.D. Edwards, *Eighteenth-century furniture*, Manchester: Manchester University Press, 1996, p. 166.

61 S. Fawconer, *A discourse on modern luxury*, London, 1765, pp. 7–8, quoted in I. Pears, *The discovery of painting: the growth of interest in the Arts in England, 1680–1768*, New Haven, Conn.: Yale University Press, p. 5.

62 M. Campbell, *The English yeoman under Elizabeth and the early Stuarts*, New Haven, Conn.: Yale University Press, 1942, pp. 374–80.

63 The author of a pamphlet published in 1703 thought London well supplied with public clocks: 'Two things could never be wanted in London, a wife and a watch; because one may have a whore, and see what it is a clock, at the end of every street': Anon., 'The Levellers: a dialogue between two young ladies, concerning matrimony', *The Harleian Miscellany* 12, London, 1811, p. 197.

64 E.P. Thompson, 'Time, work discipline and industrial capitalism', *Past & Present* no. 38, 1967, 56–97; see also the review and critique by P. Glennie and N. Thrift, 'Reworking E.P. Thompson's "Time, work discipline and industrial capitalism" ', *Time and Society* 5, 1996, 275–99.

8 Conclusions

1 For example, J. Schlumbohm, 'Labour in proto-industrialization: big questions and micro-answers', in M. Prak (ed.) *Early modern capitalism: economic and social change in Europe, 1400–1800*, London: Routledge, 2001, pp. 125–34.

2 F.F. Mendels, 'Proto-industrialization: theory and reality. General report',

Eighth International Economic History Congress. 'A' Themes, Budapest: Akadémiai Kiadó, 1982, pp. 69–107.

3   This reinforces the argument of R. Burt, 'Proto-industrialization and "stages of growth" in the metal mining industries', *Journal of European History* 27, 1998, pp. 85–104.

4   A.C. Land, 'Economic base and social structure: the Northern Chesapeake in the eighteenth century', *Journal of Economic History* 25, 1965, 639–54.

5   K.H. Burley, 'An Essex clothier of the eighteenth century', *Economic History Review*, 2nd series 11, 1958, p. 291.

6   J.S. Moore, *The goods and chattels of our forefathers: Frampton Cotterell and district probate inventories 1539–1804*, Chichester: Phillimore, 1976, pp. 26–7; J.A. Johnston (ed.), *Probate inventories of Lincoln citizens 1661–1714*, Lincoln Record Society vol. 80, Woodbridge: Boydell Press, 1991, p. lix.

7   L.G. Carr and L.S. Walsh, 'Changing lifestyles and consumer behavior in the Colonial Chesapeake', in C. Carson, R. Hoffman and P.J. Albert (eds) *Of consuming interests: the style of life in the eighteenth century*, Charlottesville: University of Virginia Press, 1994, pp. 120–3.

8   J. de Vries, 'Peasant demand patterns and economic development: Friesland 1550–1750', in W.N. Parker and E.L. Jones (eds) *European peasants and their markets: essays in agrarian economic history*, Princeton, N.J.: Princeton University Press, 1975, pp. 207–8.

9   Ibid., p. 208.

10 Ibid.

11 J. de Vries, *The Dutch rural economy in the Golden Age*, New Haven, Conn.: Yale University Press, 1974, pp. 119–73.

12 N. McKendrick, 'The consumer revolution of eighteenth-century England', in N. McKendrick, J. Brewer and J.H. Plumb, *The birth of a consumer society: the commercialization of eighteenth-century England*, London: Hutchinson, 1983, pp. 9–33, and idem, 'The commercialisation of fashion', pp. 34–99.

13 M. Douglas, 'Bad taste in furnishing,' in M. Douglas, *Thought styles*, London: Sage, 1996, pp. 56–9; B. Fine and E. Leopold, *The world of consumption*, London: Routledge, 1993, pp. 120–47; C. Campbell, *The romantic ethic and the spirit of modern consumerism*, Oxford: Blackwell, 1987, pp. 49–57.

14 J.E. Crowley, 'The sensibility of comfort', *American Historical Review* 104, 1999, p. 759.

15 R. Bocock, *Consumption*, London: Routledge, 1993, p. 64.

16 J.-L. Flandrin, 'Distinction through taste', in R. Chartier (ed.) *Passions of the Renaissance*, trans. A. Goldhammer, Cambridge, Mass.: Belknap Press of Harvard University, 1989; originally published as *Histoire de la vie privée*, T.3, Paris: Seuil, 1986, under the direction of P. Ariès and G. Duby, pp. 265–307.

17 McKendrick, 'The consumer revolution of eighteenth-century England', p. 9.

18 A. Duffin, 'The political allegiance of the Cornish gentry *c.*1600–*c.*1642', Unpublished Ph.D. thesis, University of Exeter, 1989, p. 93.

19 CRO inventory of Thomas Stephens, St Columb Major, 29/5/1746.

20 C. North, 'Fustians, figs and frankincense: Jacobean shop inventories for Cornwall', *Journal of the Royal Institution of Cornwall*, new series II, 1995, 32–77; CRO B155 1606. See also J. Whetter, 'Cornish trade in the seventeenth century: an analysis of the port books', *Journal of the Royal Institution of Cornwall*, new series 4, 1964, pp. 402–3.

21 H. Hamilton, *The English brass and copper industries to 1800* (2nd edn), London: Frank Cass & Co. Ltd, 1967, pp. 57–68.

22 C. Morris (ed.), *The journey of Celia Fiennes*, London: Crescent Press, 1947, p. 128.

23 Crowley, 'The sensibility of comfort'.

24 P. Payton, *The making of modern Cornwall: historical experience and the persistence of 'difference'*, Redruth: Dyllansow Truran, 1992, pp. 40–68; M. Stoyle, 'Rediscovering the difference: the recent historiography of early modern Cornwall', *Cornish Studies* 10, 2002, 104–15.

Bibliography

Alcock, N.W., *People at home: living in a Warwickshire village, 1500–1800*, Chichester: Phillimore, 1993.

Alcock, N.W. and Cox, N. (eds), *Living and working in seventeenth century England: descriptions and drawings from Randle Holme's Academy of Armory*, Compact Disc, London: British Library, 2000.

Allen, J., 'Some post-medieval documentary evidence for the trade in ceramics', in P. Davey and R. Hodges (eds) *Ceramics and trade: the production and distribution of later medieval pottery in north-west Europe*, Sheffield: Department of Prehistory and Archaeology, University of Sheffield, 1983, 37–48.

Anderson, J.A., 'Solid sufficiency: an ethnography of yeoman foodways in Stuart England', Unpublished Ph.D. thesis, University of Pennsylvania, 1971.

Andrewes, J., 'Industries in Kent, *c.*1500–1640', in M. Zell (ed.) *Early modern Kent, 1540–1640*, Woodbridge: Boydell Press, 2000, pp. 105–39.

Andrews, J.H., 'The Thanet seaports, 1650–1750', in M. Roake and J. Whyman (eds) *Essays in Kentish history*, London: Cass, 1973, pp. 119–26.

Anon., 'The Levellers: a dialogue between two young ladies, concerning matrimony', *The Harleian Miscellany* 12, London, 1811.

Ariès, P., 'Introduction', in R. Chartier (ed.) *Passions of the Renaissance*, trans. A. Goldhammer, Cambridge, Mass.: Belknap Press of Harvard University, 1989, pp. 1–9; originally published as *Histoire de la vie privée*, T.3, Paris: Seuil, 1986, under the direction of P. Ariès and G. Duby.

Arkell, T., 'The incidence of poverty in England in the later seventeenth century', *Social History* 12, 1987, 23–47.

—— 'Interpreting probate inventories', in Arkell, T., Evans N. and Goose N. (eds) *When death do us part: understanding and interpreting the probate records of early modern England*, Oxford: Leopard's Head Press, 2000, pp. 72–102.

Baker, D., 'The marketing of corn in the first half of the eighteenth century: north-east Kent', *Agricultural History Review* 18, 1970, 126–50.

—— 'Agricultural prices, production and marketing with special reference to the hop industry: north-east Kent, 1680–1760', Ph.D. thesis, University of Kent, 1976; subsequently published in facsimile, New York: Garland, 1985.

Barley, M.W., *The English farmhouse and cottage*, London: Routledge & Kegan Paul, 1961.

—— 'A glossary of names for rooms in houses of the sixteenth and seventeenth centuries', in I.L. Foster and L. Alcock, (eds) *Culture and environment: essays in honour of Sir Cyril Fox*, London: Routledge & Kegan Paul, 1963, pp. 479–501.

—— 'Rural housing in England', in Thirsk, J. (ed.) *The agrarian history of England and Wales, vol. IV, 1500–1640*, Cambridge: Cambridge University Press, 1967, pp. 734–60.

—— 'Rural building in England', in J. Thirsk (ed.) *The agrarian history of England and Wales, vol. V, 1640–1750. II. agrarian change*, Cambridge: Cambridge University Press, 1985, pp. 590–685.

—— 'The use of upper floors in rural houses', *Vernacular Architecture* 22, 1991, 20–2.

Barry, J., 'Population distribution and growth in the early modern period', in R. Kain and W. Ravenhill (eds) *Historical atlas of south-west England*, Exeter: University of Exeter Press, 1999, pp. 110–18.

—— 'South-west', in P. Clark (ed.) *The Cambridge urban history of Britain, vol. II 1540–1840*, Cambridge: Cambridge University Press, 2000, pp. 67–92.

Barry, J. and Brooks, C. (eds) *The middling sort of people: culture, society and politics in England, 1500–1800*, Basingstoke: Macmillan, 1994.

Barton, D.B., *A history of tin mining and smelting in Cornwall*, Truro: D. Bradford Barton, 1967.

Beaudry, M.C., 'Words for things: linguistic analysis of probate inventories', in M.C. Beaudry (ed.) *Documentary archaeology in the New World*, Cambridge: Cambridge University Press, 1988, 43–50.

Beckett, J. and Smith, C., 'Urban renaissance and consumer revolution in Nottingham, 1688–1750', *Urban History* 27, 2000, 31–50.

Bennett, J.M., 'Medieval women, modern women: across the great divide', in D. Aers (ed.) *Culture and history 1350–1600: essays on English communities, identities and writing*, London: Harvester Wheatsheaf, 1992, pp. 147–75.

—— *Ale, beer and brewsters in England*, Oxford: Oxford University Press, 1996.

Blome, R., *Britannia: or a geographical description of the kingdoms of England, Scotland and Ireland*, London, 1673.

Bocock, R., *Consumption*, London: Routledge, 1993.

Borsay, P., *The English urban renaissance: culture and society in the provincial town 1660–1770*, Oxford: Clarendon Press, 1989.

Boulton, J., 'London 1540–1700', in P. Clark (ed.) *The Cambridge urban history of Britain, vol. II 1540–1840*, Cambridge: Cambridge University Press, 2000, pp. 315–46.

Bourdieu, P., *La distinction: critique sociale du jugement*, Paris: Les Editions de Minuit, 1979.

Bower, J., 'The Kent yeoman in the seventeenth century', *Archæologia Cantiana* 114, 1995, 149–63.

Bowett, A., 'The commercial introduction of mahogany and the Naval Stores Act of 1721', *Furniture History* 30, 1994, 43–56.

Brandon, P. and Short, B., *The South East from AD 1000*, London: Longman, 1990.

Braudel, F., *Civilisation matérielle et capitalisme (15–18 siècle)*, vol. 1, Paris: Librairie Armand Colin, 1967.

Brears, P., *Food and cooking in 17th century Britain: history and recipes*, London: Historic Buildings & Monuments Commission for England, 1985; reprinted in P. Brears *et al.*, *A taste of history: 10,000 years of food in Britain*, London: English Heritage in association with British Museum Press, 1993, pp. 179–216.

Breen, T.H., 'The meaning of things: interpreting the consumer economy in the eighteenth century', in J. Brewer, and R. Porter (eds) *Consumption and the world of goods*, London: Routledge, 1993, pp. 249–60.

Brett, G., *Dinner is served: a history of dining in England, 1400–1900*, London: Hart-Davis, 1968.

Britnell, R., *The commercialisation of English society 1000–1500*, Cambridge: Cambridge University Press, 1993.

Brown, F., 'Continuity and change in the urban house: developments in domestic space organisation in seventeenth-century London', *Comparative Studies in Society and History* 28, 1986, 558–90.

Bryson, A., *From courtesy to civility: changing codes of conduct in early modern England*, Oxford: Clarendon Press, 1998.

Burley, K.H., 'An Essex clothier of the eighteenth century', *Economic History Review*, 2nd series 11, 1958, 289–301.

Burn, R., *Ecclesiastical law*, 2 vols, London, 1763.

Burt, R., 'The international diffusion of technology in the early modern period: the case of the British non-ferrous mining industry', *Economic History Review*, 2nd series 44, 1991, 247–91.

—— 'Proto-industrialization and "stages of growth" in the metal mining industries', *Journal of European History* 27, 1998, 85–104.

Campbell, C., *The romantic ethic and the spirit of modern consumerism*, Oxford: Blackwell, 1987.

—— 'The sociology of consumption', in D. Miller (ed.) *Acknowledging consumption: a review of new studies*, London: Routledge, 1995, pp. 96–126.

Campbell, M., *The English yeoman under Elizabeth and the early Stuarts*, New Haven, Conn.: Yale University Press, 1942.

Cancian, F., 'Economic behaviour in peasant communities', in S. Plattner (ed.) *Economic anthropology*, Stanford, Calif.: Stanford University Press, 1989, pp. 127–70.

Carew, R., *The survey of Cornwall*, London, 1602.

Carr, L.G. and Walsh, L.S., 'Changing lifestyles and consumer behavior in the Colonial Chesapeake', in C. Carson, R. Hoffman and P.J. Albert (eds) *Of consuming interests: the style of life in the eighteenth century*, Charlottesville: University Press of Virginia, 1994, pp. 59–166.

Cartwright, J.J. (ed.) *The travels through England of Dr. Richard Pococke . . . during 1750, 1751 and later years*, vol. 1, London: Camden Society, new series 42, 1888.

Chalklin, C.W., *Seventeenth-century Kent: a social and economic history*, London: Longman, 1965.

—— 'The towns', in A. Armstrong (ed.) *The economy of Kent, 1640–1914*, Woodbridge: Boydell Press, 1995, pp. 205–34.

—— 'South-east', in P. Clark (ed.) *The Cambridge urban history of Britain, vol. II 1540–1840*, Cambridge: Cambridge University Press, 2000, pp. 49–66.

Chamberlayne, E., *Angliæ Notitia; or, the present state of England* (5th edn), London, 1671.

Chayanov, A.V., *On the theory of peasant economy*, eds D. Thorner, B. Kerblay and R.E.F. Smith, Madison: University of Wisconsin Press, 1986.

Chesher, V.M. and Chesher, F.J., *The Cornishman's house. An introduction to the history of traditional domestic architecture in Cornwall*, Truro: D. Bradford Barton, 1968.

Clark, A., *Working life of women in the seventeenth century* (3rd edn), ed. A.L. Erickson, London: Routledge, 1992.

Clark, P., 'The ownership of books in England, 1560–1640: the example of some Kentish townsfolk', in L. Stone (ed.) *Schooling and society: studies in the history of education*, Baltimore, Md.: The Johns Hopkins University Press, 1976, pp. 95–111.

—— *The English alehouse, 1200–1830*, London: Longman, 1983.

Clarkson, L.A., *Proto-industrialization: the first phase of industrialization?* Basingstoke: Macmillan, 1985.

Clay, C.G.A., 'Lifeleasehold in the western counties of England, 1650–1750', *Agricultural History Review* 29, 1981, 83–96.

—— *Economic expansion and social change: England 1500–1700, vol. II, industry, trade and government*, Cambridge: Cambridge University Press, 1984.

Cliffe, J.T., *The world of the country house in seventeenth-century England*, New Haven, Conn.: Yale University Press, 1999.

Cochran, W.G., *Sampling techniques*, London: Wiley, 1963.

Coleman, D., 'The economy of Kent under the later Stuarts', Unpublished Ph.D. thesis, University of London, 1951.

Collins, D., 'Primitive or not? Fixed-shop retailing before the Industrial Revolution', *Journal of Regional and Local Studies* 13, 1993, 23–38.

Collinson, P., *The birthpangs of Protestant England: religious and cultural change in the sixteenth and seventeenth centuries*, Basingstoke: Macmillan, 1988.

Cooper, N., *Houses of the gentry 1480–1680*, New Haven, Conn.: Yale University Press, 1999.

—— 'Rank, manners and display: the gentlemanly house, 1500–1750', *Transactions of the Royal Historical Society*, 6th series 12, 2002, 291–310.

Coryate, T., *Coryats crudities*, London, 1611.

Cottman, S., 'A Hook Norton family, the Calcotts', *Cake and Cockhorse* 9, 1982, 7–13.

Cox, J. and Cox, N., 'Probate 1500–1800: a system in transition', in T. Arkell, N. Evans and N. Goose (eds) *When death do us part: understanding and interpreting the probate records of early modern England*, Oxford: Leopard's Head Press, 2000, pp. 14–37.

Cox, N., *The complete tradesman: a study of retailing, 1550–1820*, Aldershot: Ashgate, 2000.

Craig, R. and Whyman, J., 'Kent and the sea', in A. Armstrong (ed.) *The economy of Kent, 1640–1914*, Woodbridge: Boydell and Brewer, 1995, pp. 161–204.

Cressy, D., *Literacy and the social order: reading and writing in Tudor and Stuart England*, Cambridge: Cambridge University Press, 1980.

Crowley, J.E., 'The sensibility of comfort', *American Historical Review* 104, 1999, 749–82.

—— *The invention of comfort: sensibilities and design in early modern Britain and early America*, Baltimore, Md.: The Johns Hopkins University Press, 2000.

Cullum, D.H., 'Society and economy in west Cornwall, *c.* 1588–1750', Unpublished Ph.D. thesis, University of Exeter, 1993.

Davis, R., 'English foreign trade, 1660–1700', *Economic History Review*, 2nd series 7, 1954, 150–66.

Dean, D., 'The design, production and consumption of English lead-glazed earthenware in the seventeenth century', Unpublished Ph.D. thesis, Royal College of Art, London 1997.

Defoe, D., *A tour through the whole island of Great Britain*, London: Dent, 1962.

—— *The complete English tradesman in familiar letters: directing him in all the several parts and progressions of trade* (2nd edn), London, 1727, reprinted New York: Kelley, 1969.

Dessureault, C., Dickinson, J.A. and Wien, T., 'Living standards of Norman and Canadian peasants 1690–1835', in A.J. Schuurman and L.S. Walsh (eds) *Material culture: consumption, life-style, standard of living, 1500–1900*, Proceedings B4 of the Eleventh International Economic History Congress, Milan, 1994, pp. 95–112.

Dibbits, H.C., 'Between society and family values: the linen cupboard in early-modern households', in A. Schuurman and P. Spierenburg (eds) *Private domain, public enquiry: families and life-styles in the Netherlands and Europe, 1550 to the present*, Hilversum: Verloren, 1996, pp. 125–45.

Dodridge, J., *The history of the ancient and moderne estate of the principality of Wales, Duchy of Cornewall, and Earldome of Chester*, London, 1630.

Douch, H.L., 'Cornish pewterers', *Journal of the Royal Institution of Cornwall*, new series 6, 1969, 69–80.

Douglas, M., 'Bad taste in furnishing,' in M. Douglas, *Thought styles*, London: Sage, 1996, pp. 50–76.

Douglas, M. and Isherwood, B., *The world of goods: towards an anthropology of consumption*, London: Routledge, 1996.

Duffin, A., 'The political allegiance of the Cornish gentry *c.*1600–*c.*1642', unpublished Ph.D. thesis, University of Exeter, 1989.

—— *Faction and faith: politics and religion of the Cornish gentry before the Civil War*, Exeter: University of Exeter Press, 1996.

Dulley, A.J.F., 'People and homes in the Medway towns: 1687–1783', *Archæologia Cantiana* 77, 1963, 160–76.

Dyer, A., 'Urban housing: a documentary study of four Midland towns 1530–1700', *Post-Medieval Archaeology* 15, 1981, 207–18.

Earle, P., *The making of the English middle class: business, society and family life in London, 1660–1730*, London: Methuen, 1989.

Edwards, C.D., *Eighteenth-century furniture*, Manchester: Manchester University Press, 1996.

Ellis, F., *Peasant economics: farm households and agrarian development*, Cambridge: Cambridge University Press, 1988.

Ellis, J.M., 'Consumption and wealth', in L.K.J. Glassey (ed.) *The reigns of Charles II and James VII & II*, Basingstoke: Macmillan, 1997, pp. 191–210.

Erickson, A.L., *Women and property in early modern England*, London: Routledge, 1993.

Estabrook, C.B., *Urbane and rustic England: cultural ties and social spheres in the provinces 1660–1780*, Manchester: Manchester University Press, 1998.

Eveleigh, D., *Firegrates and kitchen ranges*, Princess Risborough: Shire Publications, 1983.

—— *Old cooking utensils*, Princess Risborough: Shire Publications, 1986.

Everitt, A.M., 'Social mobility in early modern England', *Past & Present* no. 33, 1966, 56–73.

—— 'Farm labourers', in J. Thirsk (ed.) *The agrarian history of England and Wales vol. IV, 1500–1640*, Cambridge: Cambridge University Press, 1967, pp. 396–465.

—— 'The making of the agrarian landscape of Kent', *Archæologia Cantiana* 92, 1976, 1–31.

Farr, M.W. (ed.), 'Nicholas Eyffeler of Warwick, Glazier: executors' accounts and other documents concerning the foundation of his almshouse charity, 1592–1621', in R. Brearman (ed.) *Miscellany I*, Publications of the Dugdale Society, vol. XXXI, 1977, pp. 29–110.

F.B., *The office of the good housewife*, London, 1672.

Feinstein, C.H. and Thomas, M., *Making history count: a primer in quantitative methods for historians*, Cambridge: Cambridge University Press, 2002.

Ferguson, S., *Food*, London: Batsford, 1971.

Field, A., *Discovering statistics using SPSS for Windows: advanced techniques for the beginner*, London: Sage Publications, 2000.

Fine, B. and Leopold, E., *The world of consumption*, London: Routledge, 1993.

Fitzherbert, A., *The Book of Husbandry*, ed. W.W. Skeat, London: English Dialect Society, 1882.

Flandrin, J.-L., 'Distinction through taste', in R. Chartier (ed.) *Passions of the Renaissance*, trans. A. Goldhammer, Cambridge, Mass.: Belknap Press of Harvard University, 1989; originally published as *Histoire de la vie privée*, T.3, Paris: Seuil, 1986, under the direction of P. Ariès and G. Duby.

Fraser, R., *General view of the County of Devon with observations on the means of its improvement*, London, 1794.

French, H.R., ' "Ingenious & learned gentlemen" – social perceptions and self-fashioning among parish elites in Essex, 1680–1740', *Social History* 25, 2000, 44–66.

—— 'Social status, localism and the "middle sort of people" in England 1620–1750', *Past & Present* no. 166, 2000, 66–99.

Frost, P., 'Yeomen and metalsmiths: livestock in the dual economy in south Staffordshire, 1560–1720', *Agricultural History Review* 29, 1981, 29–41.

Fry, E.A. (ed.), *Calendars of wills and administrations relating to the counties of Devon and Cornwall, proved in the Court of the Principal Registry of the Bishop of Exeter, 1559–1799; and of Devon only, proved in the Court of the Archdeaconry of Exeter, 1540–1799: all now preserved in the Probate Registry at Exeter*, London: British Record Society, 1908.

—— (ed.), *Calendar of the wills and administrations relating to the counties of Devon and Cornwall proved in the Consistory Court of the Bishop of Exeter 1532–1800*, London: British Record Society, 1914.

Fussell, G.E. (ed.) *Robert Loder's farm accounts 1610–1620*, Camden Society, 3rd series 53, 1936.

Fussell, G.E. and Fussell, K., *The English countrywoman*, London: Andrew Melrose, 1953.

Gerrard, S., 'The tin industry in sixteenth- and seventeenth-century Cornwall', in R. Kain and W. Ravenhill (eds) *Historical atlas of south-west England*, Exeter: University of Exeter Press, 1999, pp. 330–7.

Gilbert, C., *English vernacular furniture 1750–1900*, New Haven, Conn.: Yale University Press, 1991.

Girouard, M., *Life in the English country house: a social and architectural history*, New Haven, Conn.: Yale University Press, 1978.

Glasse, H., *The art of cookery, made plain and easy: which far exceeds any thing of the kind ever yet published*, London, 1747.

Glencross, R.M. (ed.), *Calendar of wills, administrations and accounts relating to the counties of Cornwall and Devon in the Connotorial Archidiaconal Court of Cornwall, Part I 1569–1699*, London: British Record Society Index Library, 1929.

—— (ed.), *Calendar of wills, administrations and accounts relating to the counties of Cornwall and Devon in the Connotorial Archidiaconal Court of Cornwall, Part II 1700–1799*, London: British Record Society Index Library, 1932.

Glennie, P., *'Distinguishing men's trades': occupation sources and debates from pre-census England*, Historical Geography Research Series No. 25, 1990.

—— 'Consumption within historical studies', in D. Miller (ed.) *Acknowledging consumption: a review of new studies*, London: Routledge, 1995, pp. 164–203.

Glennie, P. and Thrift, N., 'Reworking E.P. Thompson's "Time, work discipline and industrial capitalism"', *Time and Society* 5, 1996, 275–99.

Glennie, P. and Whyte, I., 'Towns in an agrarian economy 1540–1700', in P. Clark (ed.) *The Cambridge urban history of Britain, vol. II 1540–1840*, Cambridge: Cambridge University Press, 2000, pp. 167–93.

Globe, A., *Peter Stent, London printseller, circa 1642–1665: being a catalogue raisonné of his engraved prints and books with an historical and bibliographical introduction*, Vancouver: University of British Columbia Press, 1985.

Goffman, E., *The presentation of self in everyday life*, London: Penguin Books, 1990.

Gooder, E., 'The finds from the cellar of the Old Hall, Temple Balsall, Warwickshire', *Post-Medieval Archaeology* 18, 1984, 149–249.

Goodwin, G., *Manchet and trencher*, London: Gelofer, *c.*1983.

Grant, J., 'The gentry of London in the reign of Charles I', *University of Birmingham Historical Journal* 8, 1962, 197–202.

Grassby, R., *The business community of seventeenth-century England*, Cambridge: Cambridge University Press, 1995.

Gray, T. (ed.), *Early-Stuart mariners and shipping: the maritime surveys at Devon and Cornwall, 1619–35*, Exeter: Devon and Cornwall Record Society 33, 1990.

Gregory, D., 'Proto-industrialization', in R.J. Johnston *et al.* (eds) *The dictionary of human geography* (4th edn), Oxford: Blackwell, 2000, pp. 651–3.

Hall, L., 'Yeoman or gentleman? Problems in defining social status in seventeenth- and eighteenth-century Gloucestershire', *Vernacular Architecture* 22, 1991, 2–19.

Hamilton, H., *The English brass and copper industries to 1800* (2nd edn), London: Frank Cass & Co. Ltd, 1967.

Hamilton Jenkin, A.K., *The Cornish miner* (3rd edn), Newton Abbot: David & Charles, 1972.

Harrington, D. (ed.), *Kent Hearth Tax assessment Lady Day 1664*, British Record Society Hearth Tax Series vol. II, Kent Archaeological Society Kent Records vol. XXIX, London: British Record Society, 2000.

Harrison, G.V., 'The south-west: Dorset, Somerset, Devon and Cornwall', in J. Thirsk (ed.) *The agrarian history of England and Wales vol. V, 1640–1750. I. Regional farming systems*, Cambridge: Cambridge University Press, 1984, pp. 358–89.

Harrison, W., *The description of England: the classic contemporary account of Tudor social life*, ed. G. Edelen, Ithaca, N.Y.: Cornell University Press for the Folger Shakespeare Library, 1994.

Hartley, D., *Made in England*, London: Methuen, 1939.

—— *Food in England*, London: Little Brown, 1996.

Harvey, D.W., 'Locational change in the Kentish hop industry and the analysis of land use patterns', *Transactions and Papers of the Institute of British Geographers* 33, 1963, 91–103.

Hatcher, J., *The history of the British coal industry, vol. 1 before 1700: towards the age of coal*, Oxford: Oxford University Press, 1993.

Hatcher, J. and Barker, T.C., *A history of British pewter*, London: Longman, 1974.

Heal, F. and Holmes, C., *The gentry in England and Wales, 1500–1700*, Basingstoke: Macmillan, 1994.

Hewitt, E.M., 'Industries', in W. Page (ed.) *The Victoria History of the County of Kent*, vol. 3, London: The St Catherine Press, 1932, pp. 371–435.

Hey, D.G., 'A dual economy in south Yorkshire', *Agricultural History Review* 17, 1969, 108–19.

Hill, B., *Women, work, and sexual politics in eighteenth-century England*, Oxford: Basil Blackwell, 1989.

Hillier, B. and Hanson, J., *The social logic of space*, Cambridge: Cambridge University Press, 1984.

Hipkin, S., 'Tenant farming and short-term leasing on Romney Marsh, 1587–1705', *Economic History Review*, 2nd series 53, 2000, 646–76.

Holderness, B.A., 'Rural tradesmen, 1660–1850: a regional study in Lindsey, *Lincolnshire History and Archaeology* 7, 1972, 77–83.

—— 'Credit in a rural community, 1660–1800: some neglected aspects of probate inventories', *Midland History* 3, 1975, 94–114.

—— 'Widows in preindustrial society: an essay upon their economic functions', in R.M. Smith (ed.) *Land, kinship and life-cycle*, Cambridge: Cambridge University Press, 1985, pp. 423–42.

Hole, C., *English home life 1500 to 1800*, London: Batsford, 1947.

Holme, R., *Academy of armory*, Chester, 1688.

—— *Academy of armory; or, a storehouse of armory & blazon*, ed. I.H. Jeayes, London: Roxburghe Club, 1905.

Horn, J.P.P., 'The distribution of wealth in the Vale of Berkeley, Gloucestershire, 1660–1700', *Southern History* 3, 1981, 81–109.

Hornsby, P.R.G., Weinstein, R. and Homer, R.F., *Pewter: a celebration of the craft 1200–1700*, London: Museum of London, 1989.

Hoskins, W.G., 'The rebuilding of rural England, 1570–1640', *Past & Present* no. 4, 1953, 44–59.

Huang, P.C.C., *The peasant family and rural development in the Yangzi Delta, 1350–1988*, Stanford, Calif.: Stanford University Press, 1990.

Hudson, P., *The genesis of industrial capital: a study of the west Riding wool textile industry c.1750–1850*, Cambridge: Cambridge University Press, 1986.

—— 'Proto-industrialization in England', in S. Ogilvie and M. Cerman (eds) *European proto-industrialization*, Cambridge: Cambridge University Press, 1996, pp. 49–66.

Hughes, G.B., *English and Scottish earthenware, 1660–1860*, London: Abbey Fine Arts, 1961.

Humphery-Smith, C.R. (ed.), *The Phillimore atlas and index of parish registers* (2nd edn), Chichester: Phillimore, 1995.

Hurst, J.G., Neal, D.S. and van Beuningen, H.J.E., *Pottery produced and traded in north-west Europe 1350–1650*, Rotterdam: Museum Boymans-van Beuningen, 1986.

Husbands, C., 'Standards of living in north Warwickshire in the seventeenth century', *Warwickshire History* 4, 1980/1, 203–15.

—— 'Hearths, wealth and occupations: an exploration of the hearth tax in the later seventeenth century', in K. Schurer and T. Arkell (eds) *Surveying the people*, Oxford: Leopard's Head Press, 1992, pp. 65–77.

Jekyll, G., *Old English household life: some account of cottage objects and country folk*, London: Batsford, 1925.

Johnson, M., *Housing culture: traditional architecture in an English landscape*, London: UCL Press, 1993.

Johnston, J.A. (ed.), *Probate inventories of Lincoln citizens 1661–1714*, Lincoln Record Society vol. 80, Woodbridge: Boydell Press, 1991.

Johnston, R.J., 'Ecological fallacy', in R.J. Johnston *et al.* (eds) *The dictionary of human geography* (4th edn), Oxford: Blackwell, 2000, pp. 190–1.

Jones, A.H., *Wealth of a nation to be: the American Colonies on the eve of the Revolution*, New York: Columbia University Press, 1980.

Jones, E.L., 'The fashion manipulators: consumer tastes and British industries, 1660–1800', in L.P. Cain and P.J. Uselding (eds) *Business enterprise and economic change: essays in honor of Harold F. Williamson*, Kent, O.: Kent State University Press, 1973, pp. 198–226.

Jope, E.M., 'Cornish houses, 1400–1700', in E.M. Jope (ed.) *Studies in building history: essays in recognition of the work of B.H. St. J. O'Neil*, London: Odhams, 1961, pp. 192–222.

Kamermans, J.A., 'Materiële cultuur in de Krimpenerwaard in de Zeventiende en achttiende eeuw', *A.A.G. Bijdragen* 39, 1999.

Kent, J., 'The rural "middling sort" in early modern England, circa 1640–1740: some economic, political and socio-cultural cultural characteristics', *Rural History* 10, 1999, pp. 19–54.

Kerridge, E., *Textile manufactures in early modern England*, Manchester: Manchester University Press, 1985.

Kirkham, P., *The London furniture trade, 1700–1870*, London: Furniture History Society, 1988.

Knell, D., *English country furniture: the vernacular tradition*, Princes Risborough: Shire Publications, 1993.

Knotter, A., 'Problems of the "family economy", peasant economy, domestic production and labour markets in pre-industrial Europe', in M. Prak (ed.) *Early modern capitalism: economic and social change in Europe, 1400–1800*, London: Routledge, 2001, pp. 135–60.

Kowaleski-Wallace, E., *Consuming subjects: women, shopping, and business in the eighteenth century*, New York: Columbia University Press, 1997.

Land, A.C., 'Economic base and social structure: the Northern Chesapeake in the eighteenth century', *Journal of Economic History* 25, 1965, 639–54.

Langford, P., *A polite and commercial people: England 1727–1783*, Oxford: Oxford University Press, 1989.

Lawrence, M., *The encircling hop: a history of hops and brewing*, Sittingbourne: SAWD, c.1990.

Lewis, J., *The History and antiquities, ecclesiastical and civil, of the Isle of Tenet in Kent*, London, 1723.

Macfarlane, A., *The origins of English individualism: the family, property and social transition*, Oxford: Basil Blackwell, 1978.

McKendrick, N., 'Josiah Wedgwood and the commercialisation of the Potteries', in N. McKendrick, J. Brewer and J.H. Plumb, *The birth of a consumer society: the commercialization of eighteenth-century England*, London: Hutchinson, 1983, pp. 100–45.

—— 'The consumer revolution of eighteenth-century England', in N. McKendrick,

J. Brewer and J.H. Plumb, *The birth of a consumer society: the commercialization of eighteenth-century England*, London: Hutchinson, 1983, pp. 9–33.

—— 'The commercialisation of fashion', in N. McKendrick, J. Brewer and J.H. Plumb, *The birth of a consumer society: the commercialization of eighteenth-century England*, London: Hutchinson, 1983, pp. 34–99.

Macleod, C., 'Accident or design? George Ravenscroft and invention of lead crystal glass', *Technology and Culture* 28, 1987, 776–803.

Machin, R., 'The great rebuilding: a reassessment', *Past & Present* no. 77, 1977, 33–56.

Magrabi, F.M., *The economics of household consumption*, London: Praeger, 1991.

Marchant, R.A., *The church under the law*, Cambridge: Cambridge University Press, 1969.

Markham, G., *The English housewife*, ed. M.R. Best, Montreal: McGill-Queen's University Press, 1986.

Marshall, J.D., 'Social structure and wealth in pre-industrial England', *Economic History Review*, 2nd series 33, 1980, 503–21.

Marshall, W., *The review and abstract of the county reports to the Board of Agriculture*, 5 vols, York, 1818.

Marx, K., *Capital*, Moscow: Progress Publishers, 3 vols, 1954–9.

—— *Pre-Capitalist economic formations*, London: Lawrence and Wishart, 1964.

Mate, M., *Daughters, wives and widows after the Black Death*, Woodbridge: Boydell Press, 1998.

Mathias, P., *The brewing industry in England, 1700–1830*, Cambridge: Cambridge University Press, 1959.

Melchoir-Bonnet, S., *The mirror: a history*, trans. K.H. Jewett, New York: Routledge, 2001. (Originally published as *Histoire du Miroir*, 1994).

Melling, E., *Kentish sources III: aspects of agriculture and industry*, Maidstone: Kent County Council, 1961.

Mendels, F.F., 'Proto-industrialization: theory and reality. General report', *Eighth International Economic History Congress. 'A' Themes*, Budapest: Akadémiai Kiadó, 1982, pp. 69–107.

Mendelson, S. and Crawford, P., *Women in early modern England*, Oxford: Clarendon Press, 1998.

Miller, D., 'Consumption as the vanguard of history: a polemic by way of introduction', in D. Miller (ed.) *Acknowledging consumption: a review of new studies*, London: Routledge, 1995, pp. 1–57.

Mingay, G., 'Agriculture', in A. Armstrong (ed.) *The economy of Kent 1640–1914*, Woodbridge: Boydell Press, 1995, pp. 51–83.

Mitchell, B.R. and Deane, P., *Abstract of British historical statistics*, Cambridge: Cambridge University Press, 1962.

Montgomery, F., *Textiles in America 1650–1870*, New York: W.W. Norton, 1984.

Moore, J.S., *The goods and chattels of our forefathers: Frampton Cotterell and district probate inventories 1539–1804*, Chichester: Phillimore, 1976.

—— 'Probate inventories: problems and prospects', in P. Riden (ed.) *Probate records and the local community*, Gloucester: Sutton, 1985, pp. 11–28.

Morris, C. (ed.), *The journey of Celia Fiennes*, London: Crescent Press, 1947.

Mui, H.-C. and Mui, L.H., *Shops and shopkeeping in eighteenth-century England*, London: Routledge, 1989.

Muldrew, C., *The economy of obligation: the culture of credit and social relations in early modern England*, Basingstoke: Palgrave, 1998.

North, C., 'Fustians, figs and frankincense: Jacobean shop inventories for Cornwall', *Journal of the Royal Institution of Cornwall*, new series II, 1995, 32–77.

—— 'Merchants and retailers in seventeenth-century Cornwall', in T. Arkell, N. Evans and N. Goose (eds) *When death do us part: understanding and interpreting the probate records of early modern England*, Oxford: Leopard's Head Press, 2000, pp. 285–305.

Ogilvie, S.C. and Cerman, M., 'The theories of proto-industrialization', in S.C. Ogilvie and M. Cerman (eds) *European proto-industrialization*, Cambridge: Cambridge University Press, 1996, pp. 1–37.

Orlin, L.C., 'Fictions of the early modern English probate inventory', in H.S. Turner (ed.) *The culture of capital: property, cities, and knowledge in early modern England*, London: Routledge, 2002, pp. 51–83.

Ormrod, D., 'Industry, 1640–1800', in A. Armstrong (ed.) *The economy of Kent 1640–1914*, Woodbridge: Boydell Press, 1995, pp. 85–109.

Overton, M., 'The 1801 crop returns for Cornwall', in M. Havinden (ed.) *Husbandry and marketing in the south-west*, Exeter Papers in Economic History, no. 8, 1973, pp. 39–62.

—— 'Computer analysis of an inconsistent data source: the case of probate inventories', *Journal of Historical Geography* 3, 1977, 317–26.

—— 'English probate inventories and the measurement of agricultural change', *A.A.G. Bijdgragen* 23, 1980, 205–15.

—— *Bibliography of British probate inventories*, Newcastle upon Tyne: University of Newcastle Department of Geography, 1983.

—— 'Probate inventories and the reconstruction of agrarian landscapes', in M. Reed (ed.) *Discovering past landscapes*, London: Croom Helm, 1984, pp. 167–94.

—— 'The diffusion of agricultural innovations in early modern England: turnips and clover in Norfolk and Suffolk, 1580–1740', *Transactions of the Institute of British Geographers*, new series 10, 1985, pp. 205–21.

—— 'Computer analysis of probate inventories: from portable micro to mainframe', in D. Hopkin and P. Denley (eds) *History and computing*, Manchester: Manchester University Press, 1987, pp. 96–104.

—— 'Computer standardization of probate inventories', in J.-P. Genet (ed.) *Standardisation et échange des bases de données historiques*, Paris: CNRS, 1988, pp. 145–51.

—— 'Re-estimating crop yields from probate inventories', *Journal of Economic History* 50, 1990, 931–5.

—— 'The determinants of land productivity in early modern England', in B.M.S. Campbell and M. Overton (eds) *Land, labour and livestock: historical studies in European agricultural productivity*, Manchester: Manchester University Press, 1991, pp. 284–322.

—— 'A computer management system for probate inventories', *History and Computing* 8, 1995, pp. 10–17.

—— *Agricultural revolution in England: the transformation of the agrarian economy 1500–1850*, Cambridge: Cambridge University Press, 1996.

—— 'Prices from probate inventories', in T. Arkell, N. Evans and N. Goose (eds) *When death do us part: understanding and interpreting the probate records of early modern England*, Oxford: Leopard's Head Press, 2000, pp. 120–43.

Overton, M. and Campbell, B.M.S., 'Norfolk livestock farming 1250–1740: a comparative study of manorial accounts and probate inventories', *Journal of Historical Geography* 18, 1992, 377–96.

Overton, M. and Dean, D., 'Wealth, indebtedness, consumption and the life-cycle in early modern England', forthcoming.

Pahl, R.E., *Divisions of labour*, Oxford: Basil Blackwell, 1984.

Paston-Williams, S., *The art of dining: a history of cooking & eating*, London: National Trust, 1993.

Patten, J., 'Changing occupational structures in the East Anglian countryside, 1500–1700', in H.S.A. Fox and R.A. Butlin (eds) *Change in the countryside: essays on rural England, 1500–1900*, London: Institute of British Geographers, 1979, pp. 103–21.

Payton, P., *The making of modern Cornwall: historical experience and the persistence of 'difference'*, Redruth: Dyllansow Truran, 1992.

Peachey, S., *Civil War and salt fish: military and civilian diet in the C17th*, Leigh-on-Sea: Partizan, 1988.

Pears, I., *The discovery of painting: the growth of interest in the Arts in England, 1680–1768*, New Haven, Conn.: Yale University Press, 1988.

Pearson, S., *The medieval houses of Kent: an historical analysis*, London: HMSO, 1994.

—— 'Kent Hearth Tax records: context and analysis', in D. Harrington (ed.) *Kent Hearth Tax assessment Lady Day 1664*, British Record Society Hearth Tax Series vol. II, Kent Archaeological Society Kent Records vol. XXIX, London: British Record Society, 2000, pp. xxiii–cxii.

Pennell, S. '"Pots and pans history": the material culture of the kitchen in early modern England', *Journal of Design History* 11, 1998, 201–16.

—— 'The material culture of food in early modern England c.1650–1750', in S. Tarlow and S. West (eds) *The familiar past? Archaeologies of later historical Britain*, London: Routledge, 1999, pp. 35–50.

—— 'Consumption and consumerism in early modern England', *The Historical Journal* 42, 1999, 549–64.

—— 'Great house layouts', in M. Snodin and J. Styles (eds) *Design & the decorative arts: Britain, 1500–1900*, London: V&A Publications, 2001.

Phelps Brown, H. and Hopkins, S.V., 'Seven centuries of the prices of consumables, compared with builders' wage-rates', *Economica* 23, 1956, 296–314; reprinted in *A perspective on wages and prices*, London: Methuen, 1981, pp. 13–59.

Pinchbeck, I., *Women workers and the Industrial Revolution, 1750–1850*, London: Cass, 1969 (reprint of the 1930 edition).

Platt, C., *The great rebuildings of Tudor and Stuart England*, London: UCL Press, 1994.

Ponting, K.G., *The woollen industry of south-west England*, Bath: Adams & Dart, 1971.

Poole, A., 'Debt in the Cranbrook region in the late seventeenth century', *Archæologia Cantiana* 123, 2003, 81–93.

Portman, D., 'Vernacular building in the Oxford region in the sixteenth and seventeenth centuries', in C.W. Chalklin and M.A. Havinden (eds) *Rural change and urban growth 1500–1800*, London: Longman, pp. 133–68.

Pounds, N.J.G., 'The population of Cornwall before the first census', in W.E. Minchinton (ed.) *Population and marketing: two studies in the history of the south-west*, Exeter: University of Exeter, 1976, pp. 11–30.

Priestley, U. and Corfield, P.J., 'Rooms and room use in Norwich housing, 1580–1730', *Post-Medieval Archaeology* 16, 1982, 93–123.

Quennell, M. and Quennell, C., *A history of everyday things in England*, London: Batsford, 4 pts, 1918–31.

Quiney, A., *Kent houses: English domestic architecture*, Woodbridge: Antique Collectors' Club, 1993.

Richards, S., *Eighteenth-century ceramics: products for a civilised society*, Manchester: Manchester University Press, 1999.

Roberts, H.D., *Downhearth to bar-grate: an illustrated account of the evolution of cooking due to the use of coal instead of wood*, Avebury, Marlborough, Wilts.: Wiltshire Folk Life Society, *c.*1981.

Roche, D., *A history of everyday things: the birth of consumption in France*, Cambridge: Cambridge University Press, 2000.

Rowlands, M.B., *Masters and men in the West Midland metalware trades before the Industrial Revolution*, Manchester: Manchester University Press, 1975.

Rybczynski, W., *Home: a short history of an idea*, London: Pocket Books, 2001.

Sainsbury, P., *The transition from tradition to technology: a history of the dairy industry in Devon*, Tiverton: P.T. Sainsbury, 1991.

Sambrook, P., *Country house brewing in England, 1500–1900*, London: Hambledon Press, 1996.

Sayer, A., *Method in social science: a realist approach* (2nd edn), London: Routledge, 1992.

Scammell, L., 'Town versus country: the property of everyday consumption in the late seventeenth and early eighteenth centuries', in J. Stobart and A. Owens (eds) *Urban fortunes: property and inheritance in the town, 1700–1900*, Aldershot: Ashgate, 2000, pp. 26–49.

Schlumbohm, J., 'Labour in proto-industrialization: big questions and micro-answers', in M. Prak (ed.) *Early modern capitalism: economic and social change in Europe, 1400–1800*, London: Routledge, 2001, pp. 125–34.

Schurer, K., 'Variations in household structure in the late seventeenth century: towards a regional analysis', in K. Schurer and T. Arkell (eds) *Surveying the people*, Oxford: Leopard's Head Press, 1992, pp. 253–78.

Schuurman, A.J., 'Materiële cultuur en levensstijl', *A.A.G. Bijdragen* 30, 1989.

Schwarz, L., 'London 1700–1840', in P. Clark (ed.) *The Cambridge urban history of Britain, vol. II 1540–1840*, Cambridge: Cambridge University Press, 2000, pp. 641–71.

Scott, J.C., *The moral economy of the peasant*, New Haven, Conn.: Yale University Press, 1976.

Scott, T. (ed.), *The peasantries of Europe from the fourteenth to the eighteenth centuries*, London: Longman, 1998.

Seymour, J., *Forgotten household crafts*, London: Dorling Kindersley, 1987.

Shammas, C., 'The determinants of personal wealth in seventeenth-century England and America', *Journal of Economic History* 37, 1977, 677–89.

—— 'Constructing a wealth distribution from probate records', *Journal of Interdisciplinary History* 9, 1978, 297–307.

—— *The pre-industrial consumer in England and America*, Oxford: Clarendon Press, 1990.

—— 'The decline of textile prices in England and British America prior to industrialisation', *Economic History Review*, 2nd series 47, 1994, 483–507.

Shoemaker, R.B., *Gender in English society, 1650–1850: the emergence of separate spheres?*, London: Longman, 1998.

Short, B.M., 'The south-east: Kent, Surrey and Sussex', in J. Thirsk (ed.) *The agrarian history of England and Wales vol. V, 1640–1750. I. Regional farming systems*, Cambridge: Cambridge University Press, 1984, pp. 270–313.

—— 'The de-industrialisation process: a case study of the Weald, 1600–1850', in P. Hudson (ed.) *Regions and industries. A perspective on the Industrial Revolution in Britain*, Cambridge: Cambridge University Press, 1989, pp. 156–74.

Shuffrey, L.A., *The English fireplace: a history of the development of the chimney, chimneypiece and firegrate with their accessories*, London: Batsford, 1912.

Simonton, D., *A history of European women's work: 1700 to the present*, London: Routledge, 1998.

Smedley, J., 'A history of the Cornish wool industry and its people', *Journal of the Royal Institution of Cornwall*, new series II, 1994, 85–109.

Smith, A., *The wealth of nations*, ed. E. Cannan, Chicago, Ill.: University of Chicago Press, 1976.

Smith, S., 'Accounting for taste: British coffee consumption in historical perspective', *Journal of Interdisciplinary History* 27, 1996, 183–214.

Snell, K.D.M., *Annals of the labouring poor: social change and agrarian England, 1660–1900*, Cambridge: Cambridge University Press, 1985.

Spenceley, G.F.R., 'The origins of the English pillow lace industry', *Agricultural History Review* 21, 1973, 81–93.

Spufford, M., 'The limitations of the probate inventory', in J. Chartres and D. Hey (eds) *English rural society, 1500–1800: essays in honour of Joan Thirsk*, Cambridge: Cambridge University Press, 1990, pp. 139–74.

Stanes, R.G.F., 'A georgicall account of Devonshire and Cornwalle', *Report and Transactions of the Devonshire Association* 96, 1964, 269–302.

Stead, J., 'Georgian Britain', in P. Brears *et al.*, *A taste of history: 10,000 years of food in Britain*, London: English Heritage in association with British Museum Press, 1993, pp. 217–61.

Steer, F.W. (ed.), *Farm and cottage inventories of mid-Essex 1635–1749*, Essex Record Office Publications, No. 8, 1950.

Stoate, T.L. (ed.), *Cornwall hearth and poll taxes 1660–1664: direct taxation in Cornwall in the reign of Charles II*, Almondsbury: T.L. Stoate, 1981.

Stone, L. and Stone, J.C., *An open elite? England 1540–1880*, Oxford: Clarendon Press, 1984.

Stoyle, M., 'Re-discovering the difference: the recent historiography of early modern Cornwall', *Cornish Studies* 10, 2002, 104–15.

—— *West Britons: Cornish identities and the early modern British state*, Exeter: University of Exeter Press, 2002.

Swain, J.T., *Industry before the Industrial Revolution: north-east Lancashire, c.1500–1640*, Manchester: Chetham Society, 1986.

Symonds, R.W., 'The "Dyning Parlour" and its furniture', *The Connoisseur* CXIII, 1944, 11–17.

Tadmor, N., *Family and friends in eighteenth-century England: household, kinship and patronage*, Cambridge: Cambridge University Press, 2001.

Tarver, A., *Church court records: an introduction for family and local historians*, Chichester: Phillimore, 1995.

Thirsk, J., 'Industries in the countryside', in F.J. Fisher (ed.) *Essays in the economic and social history of Tudor and Stuart England, in honour of R.H. Tawney*, Cambridge: Cambridge University Press, 1961, pp. 70–88.

—— 'The farming regions of England', in J. Thirsk (ed.) *The agrarian history of England and Wales vol. IV, 1500–1640*, Cambridge: Cambridge University Press, 1967, pp. 1–112.

—— *Economic policy and projects: the development of a consumer society in early modern England*, Oxford: Clarendon Press, 1978.

—— (ed.), *The agrarian history of England and Wales, vol. V, 1640–1750. I. Regional farming systems*, Cambridge: Cambridge University Press, 1984.

—— *England's agricultural regions and agrarian history, 1500–1750*, London: Macmillan, 1987.

—— *Alternative agriculture, a history from the Black Death to the present day*, Oxford: Oxford University Press, 1997.

—— 'Agriculture in Kent, 1540–1640', in M. Zell (ed.) *Early modern Kent, 1540–1640*, Woodbridge: Boydell Press, 2000, pp. 75–103.

Thompson, E.P., 'Time, work discipline and industrial capitalism', *Past & Present* no. 38, 1967, 56–97.

Thorpe, W.A., *English glass* (3rd rev. edn), London: A. & C. Black, 1961.

Tilly L. and Scott, J., *Women, work, and family*, London: Holt, Rinehart and Winston, 1978.

Trinder, B. and Cox, N. (eds), *Miners & mariners of the Severn Gorge*, Chichester: Phillimore, 2000.

Tusser, T., *Five hundred points of good husbandry*, Oxford: Oxford University Press, 1984.

Upton, D., 'Form and user: style, mode, fashion, and the artifact', in G.L. Pocius (ed.) *Living in the material world: Canadian and American approaches to material culture*, St John's, Newfoundland: Institute of Social and Economic Research Books, 1991, pp. 156–69.

Vaisey, D.G. (ed.), *Probate inventories of Lichfield and district 1568–1680*, Collections for a history of Staffordshire, fourth series, vol. V, Staffordshire Record Society, 1969.

Valenze, D., 'The art of women and the business of men: women's work and the dairy industry *c.* 1740–1840', *Past & Present* no. 130, 1991, 142–69.

Verdon, N., '". . . subjects deserving of the highest praise": farmers' wives and the farm economy in England *c.* 1700–1850', *Agricultural History Review* 51, 2003, 23–39.

Vickery, A., 'Women and the world of goods: a Lancashire consumer and her possessions, 1751–81', in J. Brewer and R. Porter (eds) *Consumption and the world of goods*, London: Routledge, 1993, pp. 274–301.

Visser, M., *The rituals of dinner: the origins, evolution, eccentricities, and meaning of table manners*, Harmondsworth: Penguin Books, 1991.

Vries, J. de, *The Dutch rural economy in the Golden Age*, New Haven, Conn.: Yale University Press, 1974.

—— 'Peasant demand patterns and economic development: Friesland 1550–1750', in W.N. Parker and E.L. Jones (eds) *European peasants and their markets: essays in agrarian economic history*, Princeton, N.J.: Princeton University Press, 1975, pp. 205–66.

—— 'Between purchasing power and the world of goods: understanding the household economy in early modern Europe', in J. Brewer and R. Porter (eds) *Consumption and the world of goods*, London: Routledge, 1993.

—— 'The industrial revolution and the industrious revolution', *Journal of Economic History* 54, 1994, 249–70.

Wall, R., 'Regional and temporal variations in English household structure from 1650', in J. Hobcraft and P. Rees (eds) *Regional demographic development*, London: Croom Helm, 1977, pp. 89–113.

Weatherill, L., 'The growth of the pottery industry in England, 1660–1815', *Post-Medieval Archaeology* 17, 1983, 15–46.

—— *Consumer behaviour and material culture in Britain 1660–1760*, London: Routledge, 1988.

Weber, M., *The protestant ethic and the spirit of capitalism*, ed. S. Kalberg, Los Angeles, Calif.: Roxbury Publishing, 2002.

Whetter, J., 'Cornish trade in the seventeenth century: an analysis of the port books', *Journal of the Royal Institution of Cornwall*, new series 4, 1964, 388–412.

—— *Cornwall in the 17th century: an economic history of Kernow*, Padstow: Lodenek Press, 1974.

Whitrow, G.J., *Time in history: the evolution of our general awareness of time and temporal perspective*, Oxford: Oxford University Press, 1988.

Whyman, S.E., *Sociability and power in late-Stuart England: the cultural worlds of the Verneys 1660–1720*, Oxford: Oxford University Press, 1999.

Wijsenbeek-Olthuis, T., *Achter de gevels van Delft. Bezit en bestaan van rijk en arm in een periode van achteruitgang, 1700–1800*, Hilversum: Verloren, 1987.

Willan, T.S., *The English coasting trade, 1600–1750*, Manchester: Manchester University Press, 1938.

—— *The inland trade: studies in English internal trade in the sixteenth and seventeenth centuries*, Manchester: Manchester University Press, 1976.

Wills, G., *English looking-glasses: a study of the glass, frames and makers (1670–1820)*, London: Country Life, 1965.

—— *English furniture 1550–1760*, Middlesex: Guinness Superlatives, 1971.

Wilson, A.R., *Forgotten harvest: the story of cheesemaking in Wiltshire*, Calne: A.R. Wilson, 1995.

Wilson, C.A., *Food and drink in Britain: from the Stone Age to recent times*, London: Constable, 1973.

Wolf, E.R., *Peasants*, Englewood Cliffs, N.J.: Prentice-Hall, 1966.

Woodward, D., *Men at work: labourers and building craftsmen in the towns of Northern England, 1450–1750*, Cambridge: Cambridge University Press, 1995.

Worgan, G., *General view of the agriculture of the county of Cornwall*, London: B. McMillan, 1811.

Wright, L., *Warm and snug: the history of the bed*, London: Routledge & Kegan Paul, 1962.

—— *Home fires burning: the history of domestic heating and cooking*, London: Routledge & Kegan Paul, 1964.

Wrightson, K., 'The family in early modern England: continuity and change', in S. Taylor, R. Connors, and C. Jones (eds) *Hanoverian Britain and empire: essays in memory of Philip Lawson*, Woodbridge: Boydell Press, 1998, pp. 1–22.

—— *Earthly necessities: economic lives in early modern Britain*, New Haven, Conn.: Yale University Press, 2000.

Wrigley, E.A., 'Urban growth and agricultural change: England and the continent in the early modern period', *Journal of Interdisciplinary History* 15, 1985, 683–728.

Wrigley, E.A., Davies, R., Oeppen, J. and Schofield, R., *English population history from family reconstitution 1580–1837*, Cambridge: Cambridge University Press, 1997.

Wyatt, P. (ed.), *The Uffculme wills and inventories*, Devon and Cornwall Record Society, new series 40, 1997.

Zell, M., *Industry in the countryside: Wealden society in the sixteenth century*, Cambridge: Cambridge University Press, 1994.

Zupko, R.E., *A dictionary of weights and measures for the British Isles: the Middle Ages to the twentieth century*, Philadelphia, Pa.: American Philosophical Society, 1985.

Index

agriculture 39–47, 181; arable farming 43–4, 73–5; cattle 44; cereal yields 47; clover 43–4; commercial 40–3, 154–7, 162, 187, 190–200; flax 46; hemp 46; hops 45–6; pasture farming 73–5; pigs 45; potatoes 44; sainfoin 44; sheep 45; subsistence 40–3, 154, 156, 199–200
alcohol production 53–4, 57–60, 142, 144–5, 147, 153, 158–60, 164, 194, 199–200
Altarnun 23, 30, 154, 158, 179

bachelors 79, 85
Baker, D. 46
baking 37, 183; commercial 53, 74; for use 58, 79, 142, 144–5, 147, 158, 160, 193–4, 199–200
Barley, M.W. 130–1
Baxter, R. 63
beds 81, 91, 110, 132
benches 91, 93–4
Benenden 46, 48, 156, 160, 180
Bennett, J.M. 59
Biddenden 16, 46, 48, 59, 71, 156, 160, 180
blacksmiths 72
books 111, 113, 192–3, 195, 197
Borlase, W. 47
Borsay, P. 167
bottles 105
Boyton 30, 153, 154, 158, 159, 179
Braudel, F. 8
Breen, T.H. 89
brewing 37, 74, 183; commercial 53–54; for use 58–60, 67–8, 79; see also alcohol production
Bridge 44, 46, 70, 125, 132, 156, 160, 180

brine tubs 62
building 37–8, 56, 74, 182
Burmarsh 42–3, 48, 180
butchering 37, 74, 182
butter making 37, 183; see also dairying
by-employment 10–11, 34, 65–78, 148–9, 151, 153–5, 157, 185–9, 189, 190–4; and arable farming 67–8; and craft activities 73–5; entrepreneurial 70–3, 77–8, 172; and farming 69–73; and farming type 73–5; and food processing 67–8; and maritime 67–8; and mining 67–8, 70–1; and pasture farming 67–8; and retailing 67–8, 71; and spinning 67–8; and textiles 65, 70; and woodworking 69

cabinets 93
Campbell, C. 10
Campbell, M. 169
candles 117
cane furniture 97, 118
Canterbury 17, 31, 84, 86, 113, 147–8, 155–7, 159–60, 180
Carew, Richard 109, 123
carpentry 37, 74, 182; see also woodworking
carpets 91, 94–5, 196, 198
Carr, L.G. 173
cauldrons 98–100, 142
chairs 91, 93–4, 126–8
Chartham 84, 106, 456, 160, 180
Chayanov, A.V. 3–4
cheese 37, 183; see also dairying
chests 90–1
chests of drawers 90–2, 118, 142, 146, 196, 197
children 86
chimneys 124, 135

china 103, 132
chocolate *see* hot drinks
cider making 37, 54, 58, 183
Clark, A. 4–5
Clark, P. 59, 113
clergy 22
clocks 111–12, 126–8, 135–6, 146, 151, 158–62, 169, 174, 191, 195, 197
cloth finishing 37
clothiers 47–9, 72
clothing 182
coal 11, 98, 118, 146, 158–60
coffee *see* hot drinks
Colepress 44
comfort 174
consumer behaviour 118–19
consumer revolution 7–8, 118, 175
consumption 7, 87, 161–5
consumption goods 140–1, 185–9
cooking 98–102, 126–8, 130
Cooper, N. 135
cooper's work 37, 182
Cornish 'otherness' 176
Cornwall and Kent compared 143–7, 165–6, 171
court cupboards 91–2
Cox, J. 16
Cox, N. 16, 55
crafts 37, 39, 56, 67–9, 73–5, 79, 154, 156–7, 182, 184, 187, 190–4
Crantock 30, 70, 92, 154, 158, 179
crocks 100
Crowley, J.E. 174, 176
Cuby 30, 48, 179
cultures of consumption 175–7
curtains *see* window curtains
cushions 91, 95
customary land 141

dairying: commercial 53, 79, 82; for use 37, 60–1, 67–8, 70, 142, 144–5, 147, 152, 158–60, 183, 194, 199–200
de Vries, J. 5–6, 87–8, 167, 173
debts 140–1, 150, 185–9
Defoe, D. 96
distilling 37, 58, 183
Dodridge, J. 51
domestic space 94
drinking vessels 105–6, 108
dual occupations *see* by-employment
dyeing 37, 181

earthenware 117

eating 119, 126–8, 130–2
Ebony 31, 180
ecological fallacy 163
Elmham 28, 31, 133, 156, 160, 180
Elmsted 31, 46, 155–6, 160, 180
emulation 118–20, 174–5
Erondell, Peter 106
esquires 22, 29, 85
Estabrook, C.B. 167

family 1–2
farming *see* agriculture
fashion 118–20, 174–5
Fawconer, S. 168
Fiennes, Celia 101, 176
fish preservation 37, 53, 55, 183
fishing 37, 71, 182; *see also* maritime
Flandrin, J.L. 175
Folkestone 55, 148, 156–7, 159, 160, 180
food preservation 37, 53, 62–3, 79, 142, 146, 152–4, 158–60, 164, 183, 199–200
food processing 52–4, 67–8, 184, 186, 190–4
forks *see* knives and forks
Friesland 173
Furniture and furnishings 90–8

gaming 132
gender division of labour 38–9, 59, 66, 78–83
gendering of space 130
gentlemen 22, 34, 79–80, 84, 148, 151, 154, 161–2, 164, 166–7, 188, 190–200
gingerbread 117
glass bottles 99
Glasse, Hannah 100
glasses *see* drinking glasses
glazing 37, 71, 182
Glennie, P. 7
glove making 37, 182
Goffman, E. 135
Goudhurst 31, 44, 46, 48, 70, 72, 156, 160, 180
'great rebuilding' 124
grocery 74
Gwennap 24–5, 30, 41–2, 50–1, 153–4, 158–9, 179

haberdashery 117
Hanson, J. 122

hardware 117
Harrison, William 102, 109
Headcorn 31, 48, 156, 160, 180
Hearth Tax 23–6
hearths 98–102
heirlooms 16
Hertfordshire 140
Hillier, B. 122
Holderness, B.A. 150
Holme, R. 92, 112
hops 72
hot drinks 94, 99, 106–7, 117, 119,
    126–7, 129, 132, 136, 142, 144, 146,
    158–62, 166, 191–2, 196, 198
Houghton, J. 98
households 1–2, 26–8, 33; division of
    labour in 78–83; 'unproductive'
    84–6
husbandmen 22, 79, 80, 85, 148–9,
    151–2, 154, 156, 188, 190–200

Illogan 30, 50–2, 153–4, 158–9, 179
industrious revolution 5, 173–4
innholders 54, 71
inventories 13–32, 170–1; appraisers'
    descriptions 114–16; categorisation
    of items 20; and computer analysis *see*
    ITEM; and consumption 87; contents
    and omissions 14–18; in Cornwall
    28–9; and debts 138; foodstuffs in 15;
    and Hearth Tax 23–6; inconsistencies
    in 18–19; in Kent 29; legal framework
    14; levels of detail 17, 35–6, 58–9, 62,
    70, 115–17; linguistic analysis 114–16;
    and married women 16; and material
    culture 88–90; representativeness
    22–6; and room use 121–2; rooms in
    15; sampling 29–31; survival 13;
    urban 185–9, 190–200; and wealth
    138–9; and wills 15–16; and women
    22–3, 27
ITEM 19–21
Iwade 31, 71, 155–6, 159–60, 180

jacks 99, 101, 118, 146, 158–9, 160–2,
    190–1, 195, 197
Johnson, M. 135
Johnston, J.A. 173

Kent and Cornwall compared 143,
    165–6, 171
Kenwyn 30, 42, 51, 84, 153–4, 158, 179
kitchen 133

knives and forks 99, 106, 119, 146, 164,
    166, 196, 198

labourers 22, 37, 183
Launcells 30, 48, 154–5, 158–9, 179
leases 138, 140–1
leather production 37, 74, 181
Lenham 31, 46, 48, 156, 160, 180
life cycle 27
Lincolnshire 140
linen 108–11, 118–19, 142
linguistic analysis 114–16
logistic regression 17, 145, 163
looking glasses *see* mirrors
Luxulyan 25, 30, 51, 123, 153–5, 158,
    179
luxury crafts 37, 182

Macfarlane, A. 3
McKendrick, N. 7–8, 175
Madron 16, 30, 42, 51, 53, 153, 154,
    157–9, 179
mahogany 96–7
maiden *see* virgin
malting 37, 54, 183
maritime 37–8, 55, 79, 154, 164, 182,
    186, 190–200
Markham, G. 53
masons 56
Mate, M. 59
material culture 8, 88–9
material wealth 138, 140–1, 185–9
Mathias, P. 59
Mendels, F. 171
metalworking 37, 74, 181
middling sort 26
milling 37, 54, 61, 74, 142, 146, 152,
    158, 160, 164, 183, 193, 199–200
Milton 27–8, 31, 53–4, 72, 106, 138,
    148, 156–7, 159–60, 180
mining 50–2, 79, 155, 157, 182, 187,
    190–4
Minster in Thanet 31, 86, 156, 159, 160,
    180, 190–4
mirrors 111–12, 126–7, 129, 135, 144,
    146, 158–62, 174, 190, 195, 197
Moore, J.S. 172
Muldrew, C. 89
mustard milling 62

napkins 109, 119
Naval and military 37, 183
Newington 31, 46, 156–7, 159–60, 180

occupation 147–54; and material culture 150–3
Orlestone 31, 180
Orlin, L.C. 121

paper 117
parishes *see* sample parishes
part households 84–6
Patten, J. 34
peasant studies 3
pewter 99, 102–4, 120, 126–7, 129, 135, 144–5
pictures 111–13, 126–7, 129, 135
pilchards 53, 71
pillowcases 110
pipes 117
plates 99, 102, 104, 107–8, 142–4, 146, 192, 196, 198
platters 99, 105
Poll Tax 24–5
porringers 107
pottery 99, 103–4
Poughill 30, 48, 153–4, 158–9, 179
press cupboards 91–2
prices 141
prints *see* pictures
privacy 119, 121, 132–6
probate accounts 138, 150
probate inventories *see* inventories
production activities per household 76
production: categories of 181–4; as consumption 88; definitions 181–4; for exchange 39–57, 154, 156, 185–9; identifying 34–6, 86; potential 36, 38, 58; scale 35, 53; for use 154, 156, 159–61, 164–5, 185–9
propensity to consume 139
proto-industrialisation 4, 65, 171–2
pseudo-gentry 167

Quennell, M. and Quennell, C. 8

raisins 117
ranges 98, 100
Ravenscroft, George 105
real chattels 138
retailing 37–8, 55, 75, 79, 83, 116–17, 154, 156, 164, 182, 186, 190–200
retired people 84–6
rice 117
River 31, 180
Roche 25, 30, 51, 154–5, 158, 179

Romney Marsh 43
room use 125–36
rooms: bakehouse 125; billiard 125; boulting house 125; brew-house 63, 124–5, 131; buttery 131; chambers 124–6, 133–4; drink buttery 125; fire room 125, 129; great chambers 125, 127, 133, 136; hall 125, 126–30; kitchen 125–6, 130–1; loft 125, 133; milk-house 125; number 122–4, 156, 185–9, 197–8; parlour 125–6, 130; servants' 125; service 124–5, 127, 130–1; shop 124; types 124–5; wash-house 124–5, 131
Ruckinge 31, 156, 160, 180

St Clement 30, 154, 158, 179
St Columb Major 30, 48, 84, 154, 158–9, 176, 179
St Erth 30, 154, 158, 179
St Gennys 23, 30, 103, 154, 158, 179
St Pinnock 30, 48, 154, 158, 179
St Stephens 30, 48, 54, 73, 153–4, 157–8, 179
St Tudy 30, 154, 158, 179
salting trough 62
sample parishes: in Cornwall 30, 179; in Kent 31, 180
saucepans 99–101, 142, 146, 158, 160, 166, 196, 198
Scott, J. 5
Scott, J.C. 3
scythesmith 72
servants 22, 37, 80–1, 131, 183
service sector 55, 79, 154, 156, 164, 183, 186, 190–200
services 37, 183
Shammas, C. 59, 61, 137, 139, 141, 143–7, 165
sheets 109–10
Sheldwich 31, 55–6, 160, 180
shoemaking 37, 74, 182
single people 85–6
singlewomen 85
skillets 99–101
sleeping 126–8
Smarden 31, 46, 48–9, 54, 70–1, 156, 160, 180
soap 117
spices 117
spinning 37, 47–8, 79, 128, 130, 181
spinster 79, 85
spit 101

status 22–3, 147–54
Stelling 31, 46, 48, 180
stools 91, 94
sugar 117

tableboards 95
tablecloths 109–10
tables 91, 94, 146, 196, 198
tableware 99, 102–8
tailoring 37, 74, 182
tailors 35
Talland 30, 53, 71, 154, 158, 179
tea *see* hot drinks
Temple 179
textiles 47–50, 181; *see also* spinning
thatching 37, 182
Thirsk, J. 5–6, 9, 65
Thompson, E.P. 169
tile and brick making 37, 182
Tilly, L. 5
tin mining *see* mining
tobacco 117
towels 109
Tregony 30, 105, 117, 153–4, 157–8, 179

Ulcombe 48, 70, 156, 160, 180
unproductive households *see* households, unproductive
upholstered furniture 91, 93–6, 132, 134, 142, 144, 146, 191, 195, 197
urban parishes 147–8, 163–4, 167–9

Venice glasses 105
Vickery, A. 89

victuallers 54, 71
virgins 86

waged work 79, 183, 185, 190–4
Walmer 31, 156, 159–160, 180
Walsh, L.S. 173
Waltham 31, 46, 48, 156, 160, 180
wealth and income 88–9, 138–47, 149–50, 153–5, 195–200
weapons 111, 114
Weatherill, L. 88, 111, 114, 135, 164, 166–8
weaving 37, 74, 181; *see also* textiles
Westbere 31, 180
Wheelwright's work 37, 182
Whetter, J. 41
widows 22–3, 27, 79–80, 86, 139, 149–50, 154, 156, 188, 190–4
window curtains 111, 113, 142, 146, 198
wine 105
women's work *see* gender division of labour
wood, decorative 91, 96–7
woodworking 37, 56–7, 74, 182
wool preparation 37, 181
Worcestershire 140
work 126–8
Wrigley, E.A. 4
Wye 31, 86, 156, 159, 160, 180

yeoman 22, 34, 79, 80, 84–5, 139, 148, 151, 188, 190–4

Zennor 30, 51, 154, 157–9, 179